watchOS 2 by Tutorials

By the raywenderlich.com Tutorial Team

Ryan Nystrom, Scott Atkinson, Soheil Azarpour,
Matthew Morey, Ben Morrow, Audrey Tam, & Jack Wu

watchOS 2 by Tutorials

Ryan Nystrom, Scott Atkinson, Soheil Azarpour, Matthew Morey, Ben Morrow, Audrey Tam, & Jack Wu

Notice of Rights

Notice of Liability

Trademarks

ISBN: 978-1-942878-12-4

Dedications

"To my amazing wife and family, who encourage me to never stop."

— *Ryan Nystrom*

"To my loving parents and supportive wife, Scarlett."

— *Jack Wu*

"To Kerri, my beautiful and supportive wife, who gave me my Mac and encouraged me to do something different."

— *Scott Atkinson*

"To my lovely, always supportive wife Elnaz, our son Kian and my parents."

— *Soheil Azarpour*

"To my amazing wife Tricia, and my parents - thank you for always supporting me."

— *Matthew Morey*

"To Patrick Maruthmmotil, who listened relentlessly and inspired joy each and every day."

— *Ben Morrow*

"To my parents and teachers, who set me on the path that led me to the here and now."

— *Audrey Tam*

About the authors

Ryan Nystrom is an iOS Engineer at Instagram and passionate open source contributor for both Facebook and his personal work. In his free time, Ryan enjoys flying planes as a private pilot. You can reach Ryan on Twitter at @_ryannystrom.

Jack Wu is the lead iOS developer at ModiFace. He has built dozens of iOS apps and enjoys it very much. Outside of work, Jack enjoys coding on the beach, coding by the pool, and sometimes just having a quick code in the park.

Scott Atkinson is a software developer in Alexandria, Virginia. USA. For a day job, Scott is the iOS developer for Homesnap, a really great real estate discovery app. When he's not developing, Scott rows on the Potomac River, explores new restaurants and cooks great food.

Soheil Azarpour is an engineer, developer, author, creator, husband and father. He enjoys bicycling, boating and playing the piano. He lives in Manchester, NH. Soheil creates iOS apps both professionally and independently.

Matthew Morey is an engineer, author, hacker, creator and tinkerer. As an active member of the iOS community and Director of Mobile Engineering at MJD Interactive he has led numerous successful mobile projects worldwide. When not developing apps he enjoys traveling, snowboarding, and surfing. He blogs about technology and business at MatthewMorey.com.

Ben Morrow is a developer, author and hackathon organizer. Within the Apple Watch community, he's been teaching the tools and techniques for the past few months to help others launch their apps now the device is finally available.

Audrey Tam retired in 2012 from a 25yr career as a computer science academic. Her teaching included many programming languages, as well as UI design and evaluation. Before moving to Australia, she worked on Fortran and PL/1 simulation software at IBM. Audrey now teaches iOS app development to non-programmers.

About the editors

Eric Cerney is a tech editor of this book. He is an iOS Software Engineer in San Francisco. After being acquired by Capital One, he likes to spend his days at work hanging out with Samuel L. Jackson and asking everyone "What's in your wallet?" Lately his main focus has been with Swift and gaining a deeper knowledge of programming languages at the core.

Mike Oliver is a tech editor of this book. has been a mobile junkie every since his first "Hello World" on a spinach-screened Blackberry. Lately, he works primarily with iOS, but he's always looking for new ways to push the envelope from your pocket. Mike is currently the Director of Engineering at RunKeeper, where he tries to make the world a healthier place, one app at a time.

Bradley C. Phillips is the editor of this book. He splits his time between the full volume of New York City and the enchanting, dark and quiet Catskill Mountains. He was the first editor to come aboard raywenderlich.com, and he makes sure you've got the clearest, most engaging programming material available, whether you're reading the site's books or tutorials.

Scott Atkinson is a final pass editor of this book. He's a software developer in Alexandria, Virginia. USA. For a day job, Scott is the iOS developer for Homesnap, a really great real estate discovery app. When he's not developing, Scott rows on the Potomac River, explores new restaurants and cooks great food.

Sam Davies is a final pass editor of this book. Sam is a strange mashup of developer, writer and trainer. By day you'll find him recording videos for Razeware, writing tutorials, attending conferences and generally being a good guy. By night he's likely to be out entertaining people, armed with his trombone and killer dance moves. He'd like it very much if you were to say "hi" to him on twitter at @iwantmyrealname.

Brian Moakley is a final pass editor of this book. He's not only an iOS developer and fiction writer, he also holds the honor being Razeware's first full-time employee. Brian joined Razeware with experience from companies such as ESPN's online fantasy team and Disney's Internet Group. When not writing or coding, Brian enjoys story driven first person shooters, reading some great books, and he runs his own "Let's Play" channel on YouTube.

Mic Pringle is a final pass editor of this book. He is a developer, editor, podcaster and video tutorial maker. He's also Razeware's third full-time employee. When not knee-deep in Swift or standing in front of his green screen, he enjoys spending time with his wife Lucy and their daughter Evie, as well as attending the football matches of his beloved Fulham FC.

About the artist

William Szilveszter is the artist for this book, working primarily on interface and icon design. He has a Bachelor of Arts in Applied Psychology, with special focus on human factors and cognitive ergonomics. He has been interested and working in visual design since he got his trusty 300 MHz Celeron powered PC and a copy of Photoshop. Since that time, he has branched out from PCs to design almost exclusively for iOS, watchOS and OS X. Racing motorcycles, hiking and then gym pre-occupy his leisure time.

Table of Contents:

Introduction

Apple released the inaugural watchOS SDK to eager developers on November 18, 2014. But, at that time the hardware was still under heavy development, and didn't see a public release until April 24, 2015. As this was so close to WWDC '15, many developers, myself included, weren't expecting to see a brand new version of watchOS during the keynote; it would have been perfectly understandable were Apple to stick to an annual release cycle, with each new version coming in November.

How wrong we were! Apple suprised us all by announcing watchOS 2, just six weeks after the release of the Watch itself, and to our amazement this wasn't simply a maintenance release, oh no. Instead, it was jam packed full of fantastic new features.

First up are native apps. *Out* is the hybrid architecture where the interface resided on the Watch, but the code executed as an extension on the paired iPhone. *In* is a much more familiar, although still quite unique, flavor of architecture where the code is still executed as an extension, but within the Watch app running on the device itself.

Next, complications. A brand new framework that allows third party developers to build custom complications, which can take up permanent residence on a wearers chosen watch face. It's great to see Apple opening up other areas of the platform, and this is easily the feature I'm personally most excited about.

Apple also announced Watch Connectivity, a framework that facilitates communication between the Apple Watch and the paired iPhone. This was much needed after the move to native apps, since many Watch apps depend on data from the their companion iOS apps to function, but Apple certainly outdid themselves with these new APIs.

Finally, Apple has brought several of the more popular frameworks from iOS over to the Watch, including Core Data, Core Location, Core Motion, and many, many others. If you're yet to begin your journey of Apple Watch development, you couldn't have picked a better time!

Prepare yourself for your own private tour through the amazing new features of watchOS 2. By the time you're done, your watchOS knowledge will be completely up to date and you'll be able to benefit from the amazing new opportunities presented by Apple's smart watch platform.

Sit back, relax and prepare for some high-quality tutorials!

What you need

To follow along with the tutorials in this book, you'll need the following:

- **A Mac running OS X Yosemite or later.** You'll need this to be able to install the latest version of Xcode.
- **Xcode 7.0 or later.** Xcode is the main development tool for iOS. You'll need Xcode 7.0 or later for all tasks in this book as Xcode 7.0 is the first version of Xcode to supports iOS 9 and Swift 2.0. You can download the latest version of Xcode for free on the Mac app store here: apple.co/1FLn51R
- **To run the samples on physical hardware, you'll need an iPhone running iOS 9.0 or later and an Apple Watch running watchOS 2.0 or later**. Almost all of the chapters in the book let you run your code on the iOS and Apple Watch simulators that come bundled with Xcode. However, a couple of chapters later in the book do require one or more physical devices for testing.

Once you have these items in place, you'll be able to follow along with every chapter in this book.

Who this book is for

This book is for intermediate or advanced iOS developers who already know the basics of iOS and Swift development and want to broaden their horizons by exploring Apple's smart watch platform.

- **If you are a complete beginner to iOS development**, we recommend you read through *The iOS Apprentice, 4th Edition* first. Otherwise this book may be a bit too advanced for you.
- **If you are a beginner to Swift**, we recommend you read through either *The iOS Apprentice, 4th Edition* (if you are a complete beginner to programming), or *The Swift Apprentice* (if you already have some programming experience) first.

If you need one of these prerequisite books, you can find them on our store here:

- raywenderlich.com/store

As with raywenderlich.com, all the tutorials in this book are in Swift.

How to use this book

This book can be read from cover to cover, but we don't recommend using it this way unless you have a lot of time and are the type of person who just "needs to know everything". (It's okay; a lot of our tutorial team is like that, too!)

Instead, we suggest a more pragmatic approach — pick and choose the chapters that interest you the most, or the chapters you need immediately for your current projects. The chapters are self-contained, so you can go through the book in any order you wish.

Looking for some recommendations of important chapters to start with? Here's our suggested Core Reading List:

- Chapter 1, "Hello, Apple Watch!"
- Chapter 2, "Architecture"
- Chapter 5, "Layout"
- Chapter 7, "Tables"
- Chapter 13, "Watch Connectivity"

That covers the "Big 5" topics of watchOS 2; from there you can dig into other topics of particular interest to you.

Book overview

The Apple Watch is still a relatively new platform, and watchOS 2 is the latest iteration of the OS powering the amazing hardware, built on a unique architecture, with lots of new and unusual concepts and paradigms.

Here's what you'll be learning about in this book:

1. **Chapter 1, Hello, Apple Watch!**: Dive straight in and build your first watchOS 2 app–a very modern twist on the age-old "Hello, world!" app.
2. **Chapter 2, Architecture**: watchOS 2 might support native apps, but they still have an unusual architecture. This chapter will teach you everything you need to know about this unique aspect of watch apps.
3. **Chapter 3, UI Controls**: There's not a `UIView` to be found! In this chapter you'll dig into the suite of interface objects that ship with WatchKit–watchOS' user interface framework.
4. **Chapter 4, Pickers**: `WKInterfacePicker` is the only programmatic way to work with the Digital Crown. You'll learn how to set one up, what the different visual modes are, and how to respond to the user interacting with the Digital Crown via the picker.
5. **Chapter 5, Layout**: Auto Layout? Nope. Springs and Struts then? Nope. Guess again. Get an overview of the layout system you'll use to build the interfaces for your watchOS apps.
6. **Chapter 6, Navigation**: You'll learn about the different modes of navigation available on watchOS, as well as how to combine them.
7. **Chapter 7, Tables**: Tables are the staple ingredient of almost any watchOS app. Learn how to set them up, how to populate them with data, and just how much they differ from `UITableView`.

8. **Chapter 8, Menus**: Context menus are the watchOS equivalent of action sheets on iOS. You'll get your hands dirty and learn everything you need to know about creating them and responding to user interaction.
9. **Chapter 9, Animation**: The way you animate your interfaces has changed with watchOS 2, with the introduction of a single, `UIView`-like animation method. You'll learn everything you need to know about both animated image sequences and the new API in this chapter.
10. **Chapter 10, Glances**: Think of a glance as a read-only, quick and lightweight view of your app, providing your users with timely information. You'll learn about the interface of a glance, as well as how to provide the underlying data.
11. **Chapter 11, Notifications**: watchOS offers support for several different types of notifications, and allows you to customize them to the individual needs of your watch app. In this chapter, you'll get the complete overview.
12. **Chapter 12, Complications**: Complications are small elements that appear on the user's selected watch face and provide quick access to frequently used data from within your app. This chapter will walk you through the process of setting up your first complication, along with introducing each of the complication families and their corresponding layout templates.
13. **Chapter 13, Watch Connectivity**: With the introduction of native apps, the way the watch app and companion iOS app share data has fundamentally changed. Out are App Groups, and in is the Watch Connectivity framework. In this chapter you'll learn the basics of setting up device-to-device communication between the Apple Watch and the paired iPhone.
14. **Chapter 14, Audio and Video**: As a developer, you can now play audio and video on the Apple Watch with watchOS 2. In this chapter, you'll gain a solid understanding of how to implement this, as well as learn about some of the idiosyncrasies of the APIs, which are related to the unique architecture of a watch app.
15. **Chapter 15, Advanced Layout**: Take your watch app interfaces to the next level by leveraging the new, and extremely powerful, layout engine in watchOS. Chapter 5 may have set the scene, but in this chapter you'll take a deep-dive into this new system and learn how to take full advantage of it.
16. **Chapter 16, Advanced Tables**: Building on what you learned in Chapter 7, it's time to supercharge your tables. You'll learn how to use different row controllers, customize table row appearance, and even implement sections, which aren't natively supported in the APIs provided by Apple.
17. **Chapter 17, Advanced Animation**: The proper use of animation in an interface is often the difference between a good watch app and a *great* watch app! In this chapter

you'll learn how to add subtle and engaging animations to you watch app, as well as how to leverage Grand Central Dispatch to work around some of the limitations of the API.

18. **Chapter 18, Advanced Watch Connectivity**: In Chapter 13, you learned how to set up a Watch Connectivity session and update the application context. In this chapter, you'll take a look at some of the other features of the framework, such as background transfers and real-time messaging.
19. **Chapter 19, Advanced Complications**: Now that you know how to create a basic complication, this chapter will walk you through adding Time Travel support, as well giving you the lowdown on how to efficiently update the data presented by your complication.
20. **Chapter 20, Handoff**: Want to allow your watch app users to begin a task on their watch and then continue it on their iPhone? Sure you do, and this chapter will show exactly how to do that through the use of Handoff.
21. **Chapter 21, Core Motion**: The Apple Watch doesn't have every sensor the iPhone does, but you can access what is available via the Core Motion framework. In this chapter, you'll learn how to set up Core Motion, how to request authorization, and how to use the framework to track the user's steps.
22. **Chapter 22, HealthKit**: The HealthKit framework allows you to access much of the data stored in user's health store, including their heart rate! This chapter will walk you through incorporating HealthKit into your watch app, from managing authorization to recording a workout session.
23. **Chapter 23, Core Location**: A lot of apps are now location aware, but in order to provide this functionality you need access to the user's location. With watchOS 2, developers now have exactly that via the Core Location framework. Learn everything you need to know about using the framework on the watch in this chapter.
24. **Chapter 24, Networking**: `NSURLSession`, meet Apple Watch. That's right, you can now make network calls directly from the watch, and this chapter will show you the in's and out's of doing just that.
25. **Chapter 25, Haptic Feedback**: The Taptic Engine in the Apple Watch allows apps to send taps to the wearers wrist, as a subtle and discreet way to communicate information or provide feedback. In this chapter, you'll learn how to take advantage of the Taptic Engine to provide Haptic feedback to your users.
26. **Chapter 26, Localization**: Learn how to expand your reach and grow a truly international audience by localizing your watch app using the tools and APIs provided by Apple.
27. **Chapter 27, Accessibility**: You want as many people as possible to enjoy your watch

app, right? Learn all about the assistive technologies available in watchOS, such as VoiceOver and Dynamic Type, so you can make your app just as enjoyable for those with disabilities as it is for those without.

Book source code and forums

You can get the source code for the book here:

raywenderlich.com/store/watchos-2-by-tutorials/source-code

Almost all of the chapters have starter projects or other required resources, so you'll definitely want them close at hand as you go through the book.

We've also set up an official forum for the book at raywenderlich.com/forums. This is a great place to ask questions about the book, discuss making apps with watchOS 2, or to submit any errors you may find.

PDF Version

We also have a PDF version of this book available, which can be handy if you ever want to copy and paste code, or search for a specific term within the book as you're developing.

And speaking of the PDF version, we have some good news!

Since you purchased the print version of this book, you're eligible to buy the PDF version at a significant discount. For more details, please visit the upgrade page on our site: raywenderlich.com/store/watchos-2-by-tutorials/upgrade.

License

By purchasing *watchOS 2 by Tutorials*, you have the following license:

- You are allowed to use and/or modify the source code in *watchOS 2 by Tutorials* in as many apps as you want, with no attribution required.
- You are allowed to use and/or modify all art, images, or designs that are included in *watchOS 2 by Tutorials* in as many apps as you want, but must include this attribution line somewhere inside your app: "Artwork/images/designs: from the *watchOS 2 by Tutorials* book, available at raywenderlich.com".
- The source code included in *watchOS 2 by Tutorials* is for your own personal use only.

Acknowledgments

We would like to thank many people for their assistance in making this possible:

- **Our families:** For bearing with us in this crazy time as we worked all hours of the night to get this book ready for publication!
- **Everyone at Apple:** For developing several amazing operating systems and sets of APIs, for constantly inspiring us to improve our apps and skills, and for making it possible for many developers to have their dream jobs!
- **And most importantly, the readers of raywenderlich.com — especially you!** Thank you so much for reading our site and purchasing this book. Your continued readership and support is what makes all of this possible!

Chapter 1: Hello, Apple Watch!

Audrey Tam

The Apple Watch: coolest device ever to come out of Cupertino? I'm sure I'm not alone in answering with an unreserved, "Yes!" I got my Watch as soon as possible and seized the opportunity to upgrade my faithful old 4S to a 6. :]

If you are reading this book, then you're likely just as excited as I am about developing Watch apps. This chapter will get you comfortable with the basics of creating a Watch app and running it in the simulator. This is where it all begins!

You'll start by running the empty Watch app template. Next, you'll add a label to display the traditional "Hello, World!" text. Then, to put a fun spin on an old hat, you'll change the label to this:

Finally, you'll take your app a step further by making it display randomized emoji fortunes like this one:

This fortune suggests you're in for a chapter that is fun, successful, rewarding, thrilling and cool, so let's get started!

Getting started

Open the **HelloAppleWatch** starter project, and build and run:

This simple iPhone app displays **Hello, Apple Watch!** in emoji and then shows an emoji fortune. Tap the button add the bottom of the view to see a new fortune. You're about to create an Apple Watch app that does the same thing.

> **Note**: If you're not in Apple's paid developer program and you want to run this app on your iPhone and watch, follow Apple's instructions on **Launching Your App on Devices Using Free Provisioning**, available here: apple.co/1LONZGW.

In the same way that an iPhone app uses a storyboard and a view controller to display and control its UI, an Apple Watch app uses a storyboard and an interface controller. To create these, you'll add a Watch app target to your project.

> **Note**: In the future, if you're starting without an existing iPhone app, use the **New Project** template **watchOS\Application\iOS App with WatchKit App**. It already has the Watch app target added for you.

Select **File\New\Target...** from the Xcode menu.

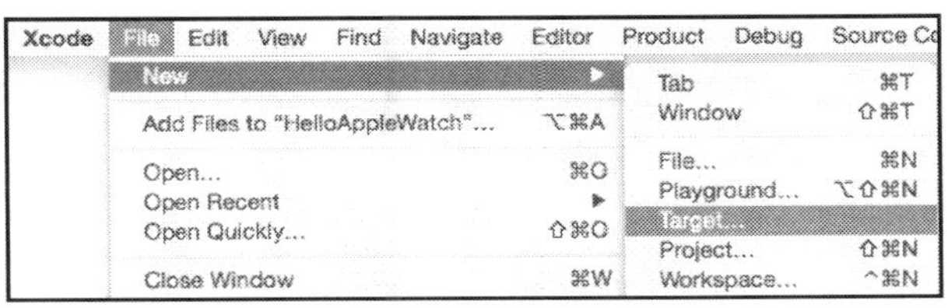

Select **watchOS\Application\WatchKit App** in the target template window—*not* iOS \Apple Watch\WatchKit App, which creates a **watchOS 1** app.

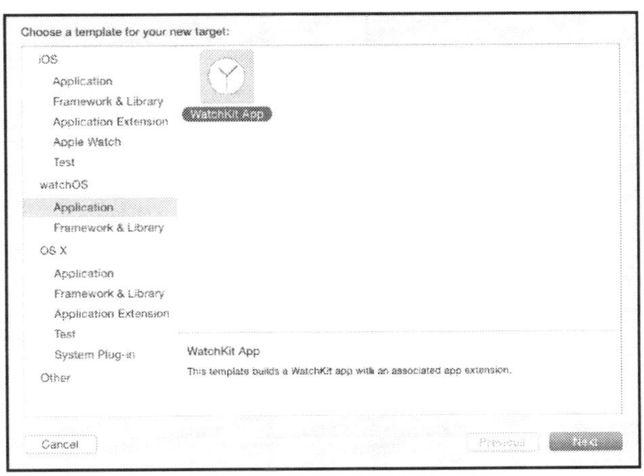

Click **Next**. In the target options window, type **HelloAppleWatch WatchKit App** in the **Product Name** field, personalize the **Organization Name**, **uncheck** the **Include Notification Scene** option and click **Finish**.

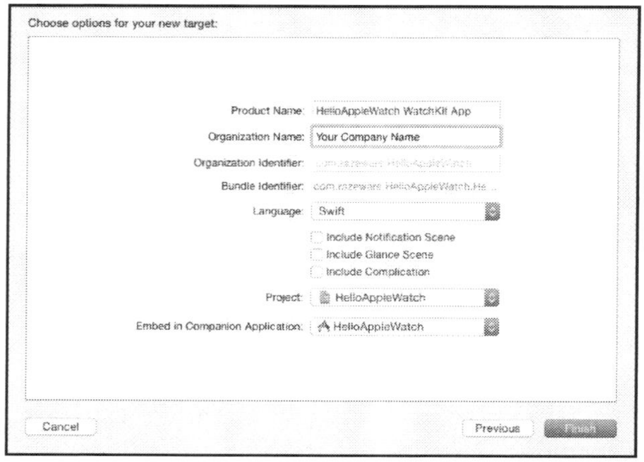

Click the **Activate** button in the pop-up window that appears; this creates an option on the Scheme menu to run the Watch app. Try this now: From the **Scheme** menu, select **HelloAppleWatch WatchKit App\iPhone 6 Plus + Apple Watch - 42mm**.

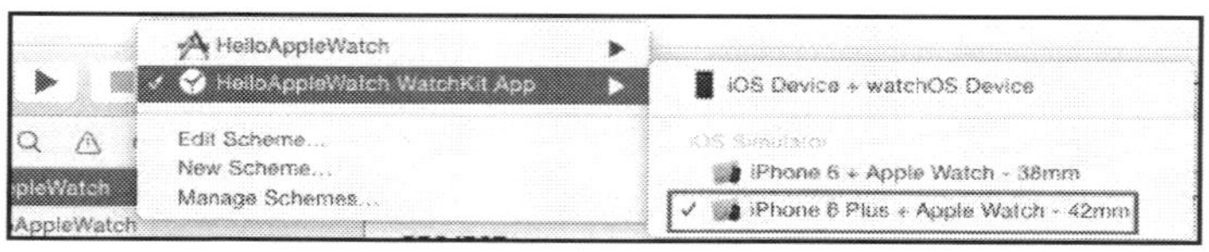

Build and run. You'll see **two** simulators: one for iPhone 6 Plus and another for the 42mm Apple Watch! The first time you run your Watch app, it might take a while for the simulation to appear, as Apple has gone to great lengths to make the simulator reflect the performance of the real device as closely as possible.

Eventually, the Watch simulator will show a watch face, then the app's default launch screen, and then a black screen with the time in the upper-right corner.

> **Note**: If the Watch simulator shows the watch face after flashing the app's launch screen, just run the app again.

The Watch simulator is a separate app from the iPhone simulator and has its own menus. For example, the **Hardware** menu lets you simulate shallow and deep presses. You can also run the iPhone app at the same time as the Watch app.

Two new groups now appear in the project navigator:

1. **HelloAppleWatch WatchKit App** contains **Interface.storyboard**, which you'll use to lay out your app.
2. **HelloAppleWatch WatchKit App Extension** contains **InterfaceController.swift**, which is similar to `UIViewController` on iOS.

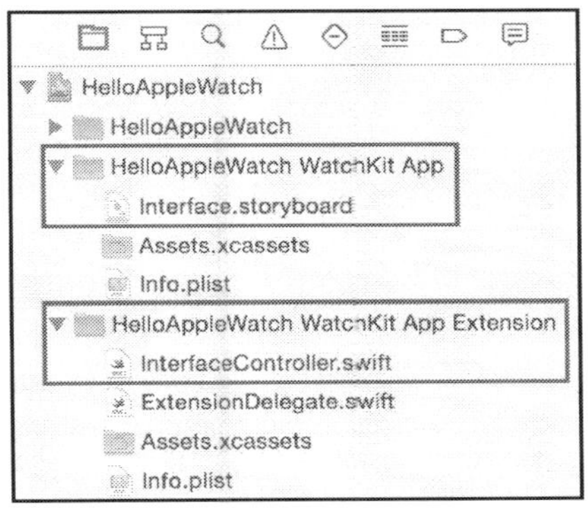

The workflow for creating a Watch app is similar to that of an iPhone app: You set up the UI in the storyboard and then connect the UI objects to outlets and actions in the controller.

Hello, World!

This is the traditional "Hello, World!" inaugural app. :]

It's simply a label, the text of which you set in the Attributes Inspector, but it will give you a taste of the capabilities and limitations of the Apple Watch interface. You'll learn more about creating interfaces for Apple Watch in Chapter 3, "UI Controls".

Open **Interface.storyboard**. In this chapter, you don't need the document outline, which covers the left side of the canvas. Click the square button in the lower-left corner of the canvas to close it. Then show the **Utilities** and the **Object Library**.

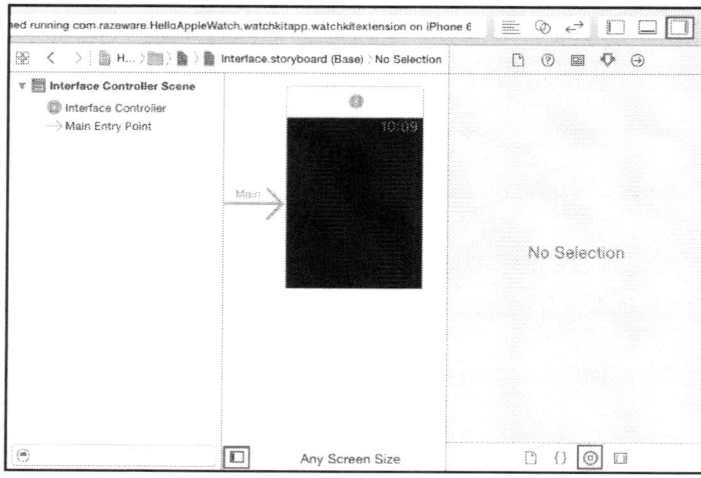

Enter **label** in the search field, and then drag a label from the Object Library onto the single interface controller. Show the Attributes Inspector to see options for customizing the label.

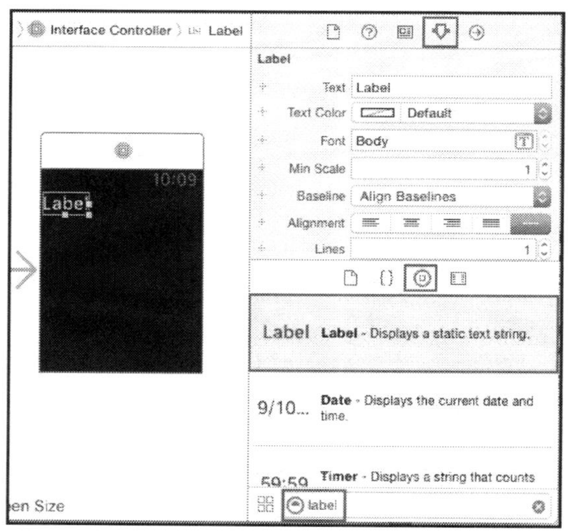

By default, the label sits at the top-left of the interface. Unlike when designing for iOS, you can't move the label by simply dragging it around in the interface—if you try, it just reverts back to the top-left position. But the Attributes Inspector gives you some control over it—make these changes, to set its text and center it on the screen:

1. Set **Text** to **Hello, World!**
2. Set **Alignment\Horizontal** to **Center**
3. Set **Alignment\Vertical** to **Center**

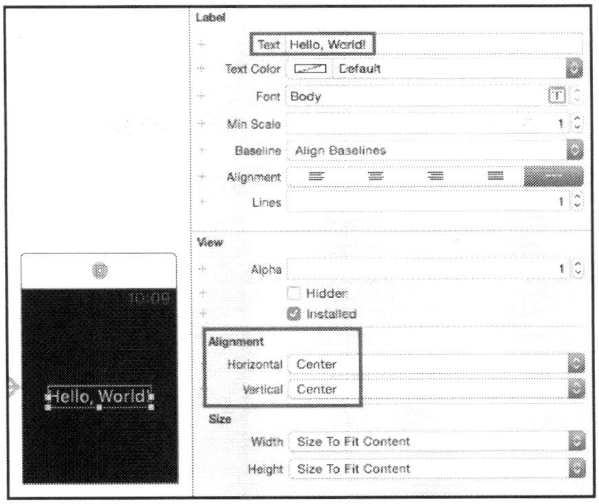

> **Note**: When you edit the text field in the Attributes Inspector, the change doesn't take effect until you press the Return key. You can also double-click on the label itself to select the text and then change it there.

Notice that **Size\Width** and **Size\Height** are both **Size to Fit Content**, so the label resizes itself to fit its text.

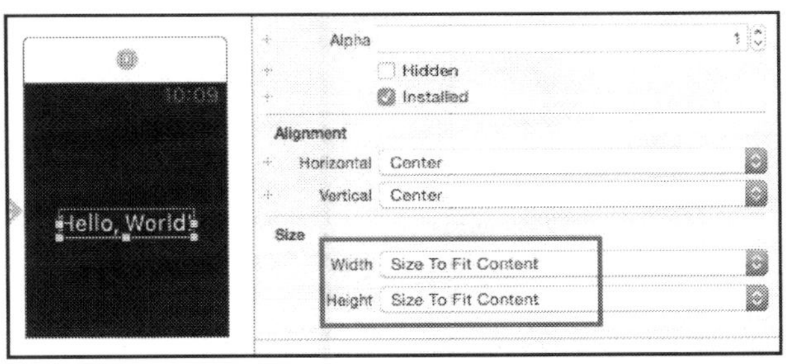

Build and run the Watch app. You should see the following:

Congratulations on creating your very first Watch app!

Setting label text in code

You'd probably like your Watch app to be a little more dynamic—at the very least, you'd want to set the label's text in the controller code. To do that, you need to create an outlet for the label in **InterfaceController.swift**.

Open the **assistant editor** and check that it's set to **Automatic**, so that it displays **InterfaceController.swift**.

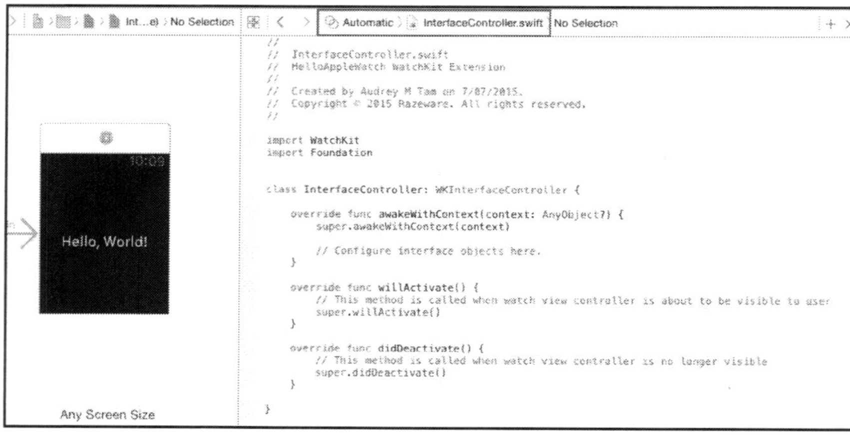

Select the **label** and, holding down the **Control** key, drag from the **label** into **InterfaceController.swift**, to the space just below the class title. Xcode will prompt you to **Insert Outlet**. Release your mouse button and a pop-up window will appear, as shown in the following screenshot. Check that **Type** is set to `WKInterfaceLabel`, then set **Name** to `label` and click **Connect**.

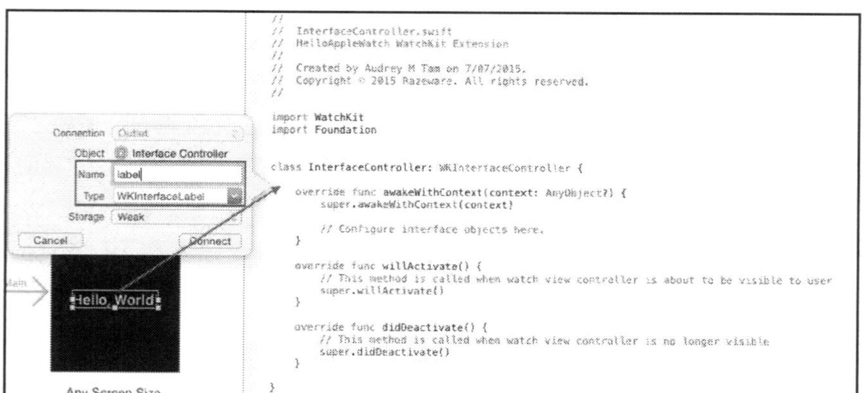

The following `@IBOutlet` declaration will appear in **InterfaceController.swift**:

```
@IBOutlet var label: WKInterfaceLabel!
```

Your code now has a reference to the label in your Watch app interface, so you can use this to set its text.

Add the following line to `willActivate()`, below `super.willActivate()`:

```
label.setText("Hello, Apple Watch!")
```

Build and run your app:

Fantastic! You've added a label to the Watch interface and set its text from code. This is impressive stuff—the code you wrote is actually *running on the Watch!*

Apple's color emoji font

This text is a tight squeeze on the smaller Watch face. If you want to make the font bigger or the text longer, you could change the label's **Lines** attribute from **1** to **0**, which informs WatchKit to give the text as many lines as it needs.

However, you don't need to do that for *this* app, because you're going to use **Apple's color emoji** font instead, which use much less space and are way more fun!

First, select the label in the storyboard. Next, click on the **T** icon in the **Font** attribute in the Attributes Inspector to invoke the font pop-up. Change **Font** to **System** and increase **Size** to **24**, then click **Done**.

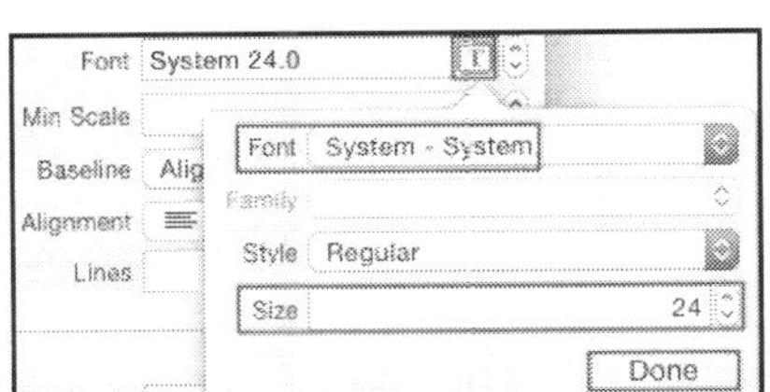

Next, edit the `Hello, Apple Watch!` string in **InterfaceController.swift**:

1. Select `Hello` and press **Control-Command-Space** to pop up the **emoji character viewer** beneath the selected text.

2. Click in the **Search** field and type **waving**, and the **waving hand** emoji will appear. Click it and it will replace `Hello`.

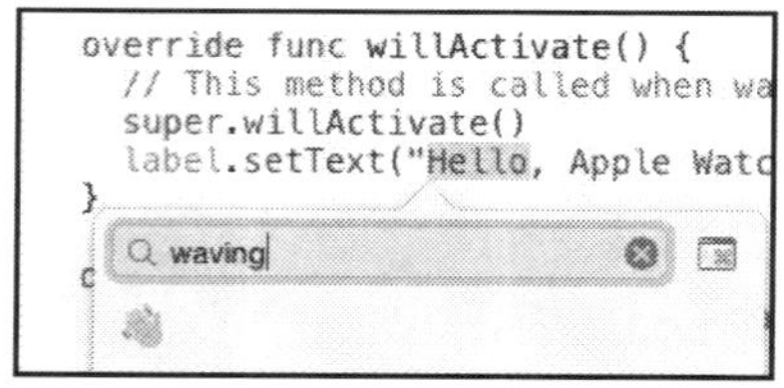

Repeat these steps to replace `Apple`, `Watch`, and the exclamation mark with suitable emoji.

Delete the comma and spaces so your string looks like this:

Build and run your app:

An ultra-cool greeting to an über-cool gadget! Now you're going to take this font and run with it.

Casting emoji fortunes

On April 9th, 2014, @nrrrdcore tweeted "Free idea: Emoji Fortune Cookies", and on May 14th, Luke Karrys launched emojifortun.es:

Wouldn't that look cool on an Apple Watch? Just the emoji, not the words, and more is better:

Sharing EmojiData.swift between iPhone and Watch apps

Open **EmojiData.swift**: it contains an `Int` extension with a simple `random()` function and five arrays of emoji: `people`, `nature`, `objects`, `places` and `symbols`. You can use the emojis I've picked or have fun selecting your own. Feel free to add as many emojis as you want to each array:

```
let people = ["😁", "😚", "😔", "😠", "😕", "👯", "👵"]
let nature = ["🐣", "🍀", "🌺", "🌴", "⛅", "🐳", "🐴"]
let objects = ["🎁", "⌛", "🍎", "🎵", "💰", "⌚"]
let places = ["✈", "♨", "🎭", "🚲", "🏧"]
let symbols = ["🔁", "🔀", "⏩", "⏪", "🆒"]
```

It's easy to share this file between the iPhone app and the Watch app. **Right-click EmojiData.swift** in the project navigator and select **New Group from Selection**. Name this group **Shared** and *move it out of the HelloAppleWatch folder*, so it sits between the HelloAppleWatch and HelloAppleWatch WatchKit App folders.

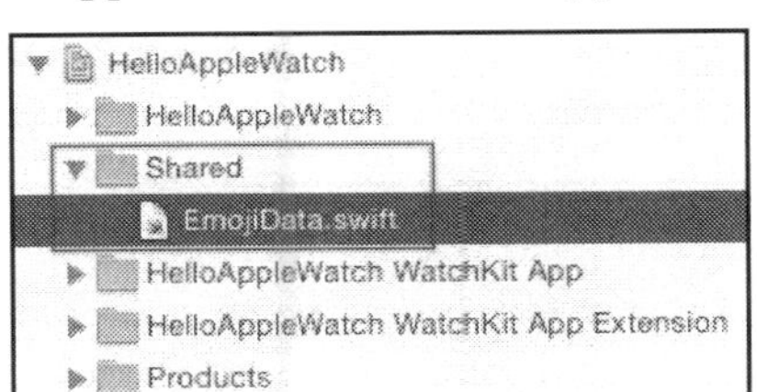

Open the **Shared** folder, select **EmojiData.swift** and show the File Inspector. In the **Target Membership** section, check **HelloAppleWatch WatchKit App Extension**. That's it! Now **InterfaceController.swift** can use **EmojiData.swift**.

Creating a random emoji fortune

In **InterfaceController.swift**, do the following:

1. Below the `@IBOutlet` statement, just above `awakeWithContext(_:)`, create an `EmojiData` object:

```
let emoji = EmojiData()
```

2. In `willActivate()`, replace `label.setText()` with the following lines. The last line, beginning with `label.setText`, must be a single line that wraps—don't press the Return key while typing it:

```
// 1
let peopleIndex = emoji.people.count.random()
let natureIndex = emoji.nature.count.random()
let objectsIndex = emoji.objects.count.random()
let placesIndex = emoji.places.count.random()
let symbolsIndex = emoji.symbols.count.random()
// 2
label.setText("\(emoji.people[peopleIndex])
  \(emoji.nature[natureIndex])\(emoji.objects[objectsIndex])
    \(emoji.places[placesIndex])\(emoji.symbols[symbolsIndex])")
```

`random()` calls a pseudo-random number generator `arc4random_uniform()`. The code above:

1. Generates a random number between `0` and the array's `count` property, for each array;
2. Uses the five random numbers to pick emoji from the arrays to create the label text.

Build and run your Watch app. Have fun trying to figure out whether your fortune is good, bad, indifferent or just unfathomable.

Tell me another one...

If you're running your app on the simulator, it's easy to run it again to get a new fortune. But to run it again on your Watch, you must return to the Home screen. You need a button you can press to get a new fortune! This isn't hard to implement, and the task will give you a chance to *refactor* your code.

Replacing the label with a button

Open **Interface.storyboard** and delete the label—yes, you heard that right! Drag a **button** onto the interface controller: it will snap to the top, but you'll make it cover most of the screen. Then, tapping almost anywhere will get you a new fortune.

In the Attributes Inspector, set the button's **Font** to **System 22.0**, **Alignment \Horizontal** to **Center** and **Alignment\Vertical** to **Bottom**. Set the button's **Size \Height** to **Relative to Container** with value **0.9**—this makes the button 90% of the screen height.

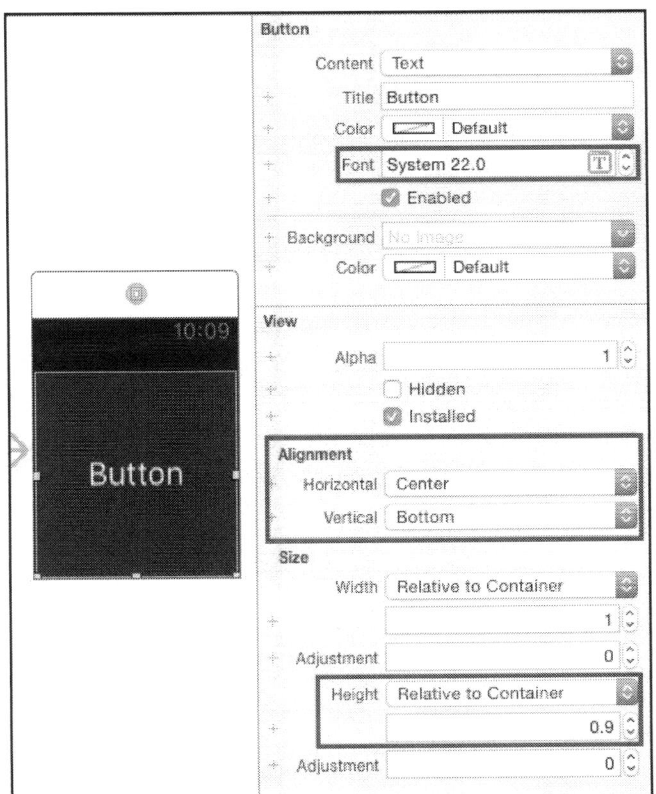

When you tap the button, the code that you put into `willActivate()` should run.

Instead of writing it again, you'll pull it out into its own method so that both `willActivate()` and the button tap can call it.

Open **InterfaceController.swift**, and below `willActivate()`, add this empty `showFortune()` method:

```
func showFortune() {

}
```

Copy all the lines you added to `willActivate()`, below `super.willActivate()`, and paste them into `showFortune()`, then replace those lines in `willActivate()` with a call to `showFortune()`, so that your file looks like this:

```
override func willActivate() {
  super.willActivate()
  showFortune()
}

func showFortune() {
  let peopleIndex = emoji.people.count.random()
  let natureIndex = emoji.nature.count.random()
  let objectsIndex = emoji.objects.count.random()
  let placesIndex = emoji.places.count.random()
  let symbolsIndex = emoji.symbols.count.random()
  // 2
  label.setText("\(emoji.people[peopleIndex])
    \(emoji.nature[natureIndex])\(emoji.objects[objectsIndex])
      \(emoji.places[placesIndex])
        \(emoji.symbols[symbolsIndex])")
}
```

`label.setText()`? But you deleted the label from the interface controller! Keep calm, you'll change this code as soon as you connect the button, in the same way that you connected the label. Open **Interface.storyboard**. With the **assistant editor** showing **InterfaceController.swift**, **Control-drag** from the button to just above the `label IBOutlet`. In the pop-up window, check that **Type** is `WKInterfaceButton`, then name the outlet **button** and click **Connect**.

OK, now replace `label.setText` with `button.setTitle`, in the last line of `showFortune()`: the emoji fortune will replace the Button title that you see in **Interface.storyboard**. Delete the `label IBOutlet`.

Next, you'll connect the button to an *action* that happens when the user taps it. **Control-drag** from the button to an open line below `showFortune()`. This time, in the pop-up window, be sure to change **Connection** from **Outlet** to **Action**. Name the action `newFortune` and press **Connect**.

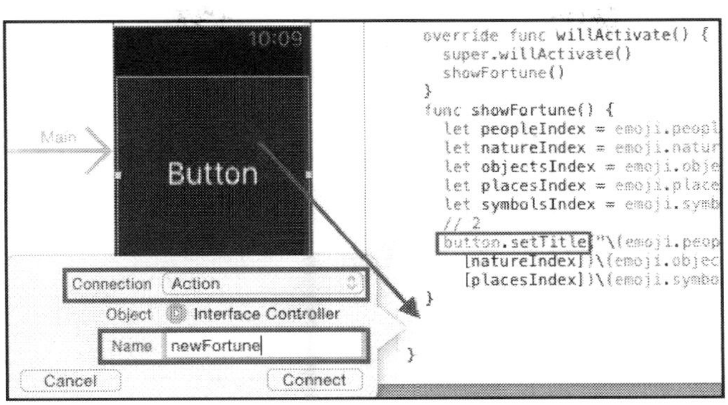

You'll see this empty method:

```
@IBAction func newFortune() {
}
```

> **Note**: If you create another `IBOutlet` instead, just delete it to get rid of the Xcode error. Control-drag again, making sure to change **Connection** to **Action**.

The only thing `newFortune()` needs to do is call `showFortune()`, so add this line in `newFortune()`:

```
showFortune()
```

Dressing up your app

One last thing: add a fortune cookie background image, for the finishing touch! Open **HelloAppleWatch WatchKit App\Assets.xcassets** and the Attributes Inspector. Click the **+** button and select **New Image Set**. Change the **Name** to **Cookie**, check **Devices \watchOS\Apple Watch**, and drag **38mm.png** and **42mm.png** from this chapter's folder into the corresponding spots:

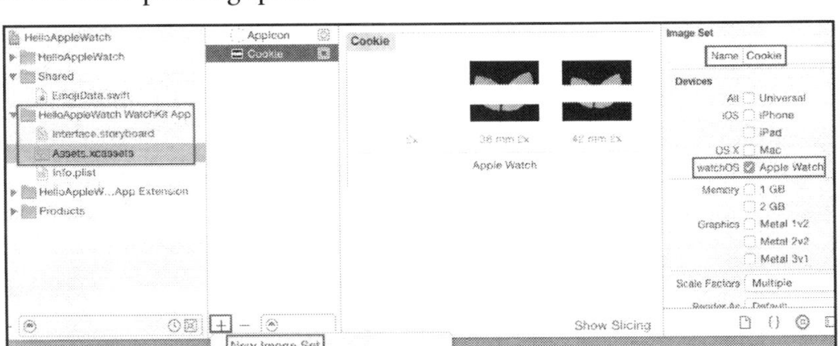

Open **Interface.storyboard**, select the **Interface Controller**, and in the Attributes Inspector, set **Background** to **Cookie**:

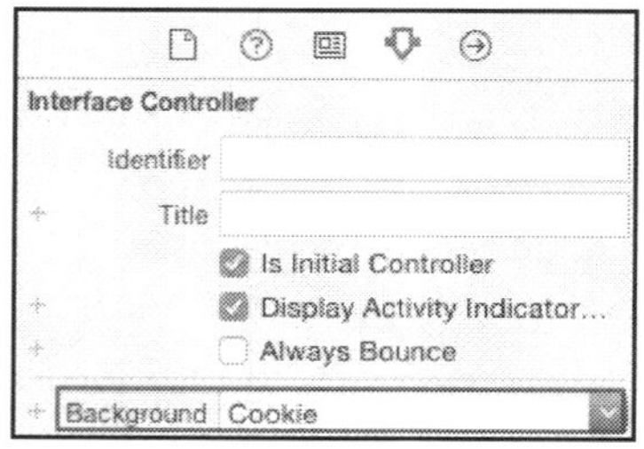

Build and run, and let your Watch tell your fortune over and over until you get *exactly* the one you want!

Where to go from here?

At this point, you have hands-on experience making a simple WatchKit-based app.

If you're new to iOS, you've also learned how to set up and use storyboard outlets—these work exactly the same way in plain old iOS apps—and you've learned a few tricks while making your way around Xcode.

I hope this chapter has whetted your appetite to try out all the cool stuff in the rest of this book, as well as boosted your confidence that *you can do this*!

In the next few chapters, you'll learn about design, architecture, basic UI controls and layout, all of which will get you started using the watchOS 2 SDK to build more complex interfaces and apps.

Chapter 2: Architecture

By Ryan Nystrom

The Apple Watch provides a unique challenge for engineers due to its form factor and the fact that it's the first version of a major product. Developers who used the first version of the iPhone OS SDK can recall how limited, buggy and *different* it was. Instead of AppKit, developers had to learn how to use this shiny new framework called UIKit. They also found themselves confined to a strange, foreign space known as the app sandbox.

Of course, most of what was puzzling then is now commonplace for iOS developers, and the OS itself is considerably improved. The tools and frameworks are more robust, the app sandbox is widely accepted and devices are faster and more efficient.

The WatchKit framework for watchOS 2 is in a situation similar to the early days of iOS. There are new tools, frameworks and methods for building Apple Watch apps. To build quality Watch apps now and in the years and updates to come, you'll need a solid foundation in the architecture of both the Watch and the WatchKit framework, and that's what this chapter aims to provide you.

Exploring the Watch

Before jumping into WatchKit, take a few minutes to familiarize yourself with what the Apple Watch is, and—more importantly—what it isn't.

Operating system

Here's a niggling question: What is the power behind the face of the Apple Watch? Is it iOS? Is it another flavor of OS X, like iOS is?

Apple is calling this new software *watchOS*, which turns out to be built on top of iOS!

While outside the scope of this book, a quick Goggle search for "PepperUICore" will return several articles detailing what's running under the Watch's hood, and the differences between the more elaborate, bundled Apple Watch apps and those you're able to build using WatchKit.

Interaction

Among the coolest features of the Apple Watch are the ways users can interact with it. Taken from the Apple Watch Human Interface Guidelines (apple.co/1IIMtDZ), there are four ways users can interact with your apps:

- **Action-based events**: These are what you're likely already familiar with: things like table row selection and tap-based UI controls.
- **Gestures**: The gesture system for the Apple Watch is a lot more limited than the bountiful gesture options developers have in iOS, supporting only vertical and horizontal swipes and taps. Currently, the Watch *does not* support multi-touch gestures like pinching.
- **Force touch**: This is an interesting new gesture. The Apple Watch has special tiny electrodes around the display to determine if a tap is light or has more pressure and force behind it. This is a nice trade-off for losing multi-finger gestures.
- **The digital crown**: The excellently designed crown on the Apple Watch lets users navigate without obstructing the screen. For example, as with the pinch gesture, scrolling on the Watch screen is impractical because your fingers would likely hide the visual input you need to determine how far to scroll. You also have the option of using the crown to zoom and even input some forms of data.

The Watch display

Right out of the gate, you'll need to support multiple screen sizes for the Apple Watch.

- The **38mm** Watch screen is 272 pixels wide by 340 pixels tall.
- The **42mm** Watch screen is 312 pixels wide by 390 pixels tall.

Luckily for developers, both Watches share an aspect ratio of 4:5, so, at least for the time being, you won't have to do a ton of extra work to support both screen sizes.

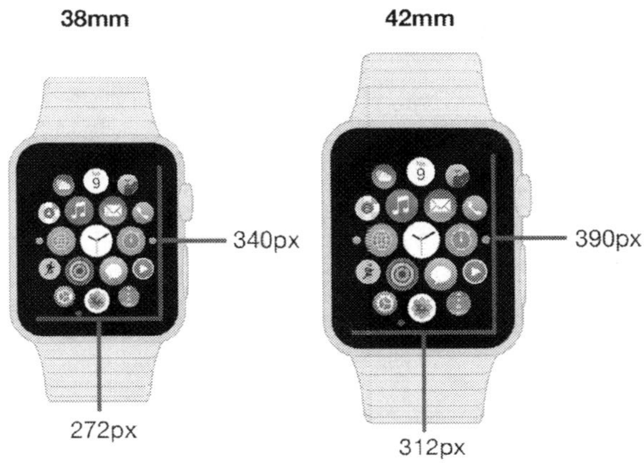

> **Note**: That doesn't mean you should hardcode your interfaces for this aspect ratio. Apple is notorious for adding additional screen sizes to their products. Always design and build your interfaces to be screen-size agnostic!

Introducing WatchKit

A couple of months after announcing the Apple Watch, Apple provided eager developers the tools to start building Watch apps. Apple bundled the primary framework, called WatchKit, with Xcode 6.2.

Even though Apple released Swift only a few months before it released WatchKit, the framework had both Swift and Objective-C support.

What it is

Viewed from a high level, WatchKit is nothing more than a group of classes and Interface Builder additions that you can wire together to get an Apple Watch app working. Some of the important classes are:

- **`WKInterfaceController`**: This is the WatchKit version of `UIViewController`. Later in this chapter, you'll learn more about this class and how to use it.
- **`WKInterfaceObject`**: Instead of shipping with a Watch version of UIKit, WatchKit provides what could best be described as proxy objects for dealing with the user interface. This class is the base from which all of the Watch interface elements, like

buttons and labels, inherit.

- **`WKInterfaceDevice`**: This class provides all of the information about the Watch, like screen size and locale.

You'll be building all of your user interfaces in storyboards, whether you love them or hate them.

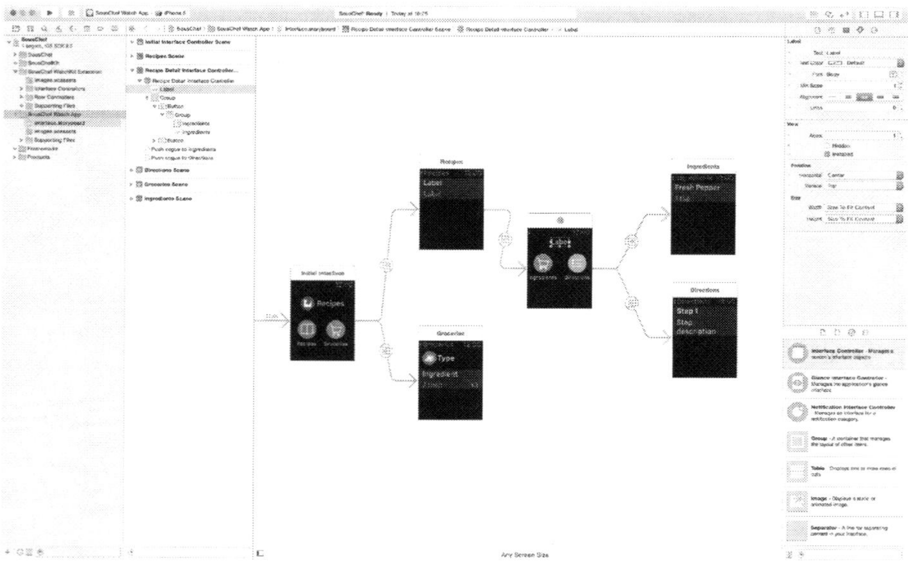

What it isn't

You'll build watch apps for watchOS 2 as extensions, just as you might build a share extension. These are dependent apps—the Apple Watch can't install them without a paired iPhone.

That may sound weird, but carry on reading to learn more about how to compose Watch apps.

> **Note**: If you're interested in reading about how to build regular app extensions, check out this tutorial on building an iOS 8 Today extension: bit.ly/1wOP4Vd

WatchKit apps

There are three main parts to a Watch app:

- **iOS app**: This is the "host" application that runs on an iPhone or iPad. You can never run an app on the Apple Watch without a host app.

- **Watch app**: This is the bundle of files and resources that is included with the host app but then installed on the Apple Watch. The bundle includes the app's storyboard and any images or localization files used *in the storyboard*.
- **Watch extension**: The last piece of the puzzle is the actual code that you write. This gets compiled and transferred to the Watch for execution. Any images or localizations accessed *in code* should be bundled with the extension.

In Xcode, these are all different targets. Creating a watchOS app or adding the target will create all of the Watch targets for you.

As you can see below, the app and menu icons require several sizes because the 38mm and 42mm Watches have different widths and heights.

Image	Apple Watch 38mm	Apple Watch 42mm
Notification center icon	29 pixels	36 pixels
Long Look notification icon	80 pixels	88 pixels
Home screen icon and Short Look icon	172 pixels	196 pixels
Menu icon canvas size	70 pixels	46 pixels
Menu icon content size	80 pixels	54 pixels

WatchKit classes

WatchKit consists of a set of entirely new classes. `WKInterfaceController` acts as the controller in the familiar model-view-controller pattern, and instances of `WKInterfaceObject` are used to update the UI. All of the new WatchKit classes follow typical Apple class-naming conventions and are prefixed with `WK`. Try to figure out what that stands for. :]

WKInterfaceController

`WKInterfaceController` is essentially WatchKit's `UIViewController`—only this time, Apple engineers have taken notice of all the `UIViewController` pain points developers have struggled with, like passing data between controllers, handling notifications, and managing context menus, and improved the lot!

Lifecycle

`WKInterfaceController` has a lifecycle, just like `UIViewController`. It's much simpler, though—there are only four methods you need to know.

- **`awakeWithContext(_:)`** is called on `WKInterfaceController` immediately after the controller is loaded from a storyboard. This method has a parameter for an optional context object that can be whatever you want it to be, like a model object, an ID or a string. Also, when you call this method, WatchKit has already connected any `IBOutlets` you might have set up.
- When **`willActivate()`** is called, WatchKit is letting you know the controller is about to be displayed onscreen. Just as with `viewWillAppear(_:)` on iOS, you only need to use this method to run any last minute tasks, or anything that needs to run each time you display the controller. This method can be called repeatedly while a user is interacting with your Watch app.
- If there is anything you need to do once the system has finished initializing and displaying the controller, you can override the method **`didActivate()`**. This is analogous to `viewDidAppear(_:)` on iOS.
- Finally, there's **`didDeactivate()`**, which is called when the controller's interface goes off-screen, such as when the user navigates away from the interface controller or when the Watch terminates the app. This is where you should perform any cleanup or save any state.

Segues

Since you're using storyboards to build your interfaces and connect your controllers, you're probably not surprised to hear that segues play a big part in managing the transition between two instances of `WKInterfaceController`.

Segues work in WatchKit very similarly to the way they work in iOS: They are still "stringly" typed, meaning they each need their own identifier string, and you create them by Control-dragging between controllers in Interface Builder.

Instead of `performSegueWithIdentifier(_:sender:)`, WatchKit provides several amazingly convenient new methods you can override to pass context data in between controllers:

- **`contextForSegueWithIdentifier(_:)`** returns a context object of type `AnyObject`. Use this to pass custom objects or values between controllers.
- **`awakeWithContext(_:)`** is called when your `WKInterfaceController`'s UI is set up. Controllers can receive context objects from methods like `contextForSegueWithIdentifier(_:)`.

With these methods, you can simply check the identifier of the segue that's being performed and then return a relevant context object, which could be a model object, a string or just about anything else you might want!

Here's an example of using a segue to pass a context object to the next controller:

```
override func contextForSegueWithIdentifier(
  segueIdentifier: String) -> AnyObject? {
  if segueIdentifier == "RecipeIngredients" {
    return recipe?.ingredients
  }
  return nil
}
```

Interface objects

For dealing with user interfaces in iOS, UIKit provides an assortment of controls and objects that all seem to inherit from classes like `UIView`, `UIControl` and eventually `UIResponder`. This provides each view with basic functionality like touch handling, while allowing classes to add their own advanced features and overrides.

WatchKit is somewhat of a different story. There are only 11 interface-related classes available, and they all inherit from `WKInterfaceObject`, which then inherits from... `NSObject`?

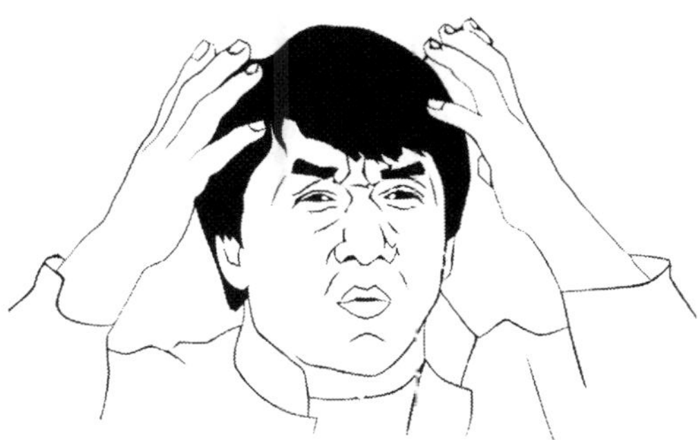

This is because you're not dealing with real objects in the usual sense, but rather with *proxy objects.*

Proxy objects

Instead of having some sort of `WKView`, you'll be working with instances of `WKInterfaceObject` that act as proxy objects for the view state on the Watch. These objects are *write-only*, which means you can only set state, like background color or text.

Each class that inherits from `WKInterfaceObject` gets a handful of helpful methods:

- **`setHidden(_:)`** hides and shows the object. This method works by collapsing the space the object was taking up in the Watch layout system. More on this later.

- **`setAlpha(_:)`** changes the alpha of the object.
- **`setWidth(_:)`** and **`setHeight(_:)`** manually set the width and height of the object, respectively.
- **`setAccessibilityLabel(_:)`**, **`setAccessibilityHint(_:)`** and **`setAccessibilityValue(_:)`** configure the accessibility options for each object.

WatchKit views and controls

You will never add a `WKInterfaceObject` directly to any of your interfaces. Instead, you'll use these 11 subclasses:

- **`WKInterfaceButton`**: Your standard button. These come stocked with a background and a label, but through the use of groups and layouts, you can make really complex button styles.

- **`WKInterfaceDate`**: This class, unique to WatchKit, is a label built to display dates and times. That means no more fussing with `NSDateFormatter`!

- **`WKInterfaceGroup`**: This is another special WatchKit class that handles all of the interface layout and grouping. You can add other objects to a group to lay them out horizontally or vertically and adjust their spacing and padding.

- **`WKInterfaceImage`**: This subclass is almost exactly the same as `UIImageView`. The one special quality of `WKInterfaceImage` is that it lets you set multiple images and animate them. The GIF is dead, *long live the GIF*!

- **`WKInterfaceLabel`**: This is your run-of-the-mill label, just like `UILabel`. You'll use this class anywhere you need to display text.

- **`WKInterfaceMap`**: This is a peculiar object. Maps on WatchKit are not interactive. In your controllers, you'll set an `MKCoordinateRegion`, which is simply a latitude, longitude and zoom level, and the map will configure a static view of that location. You can still add things like pins and custom annotations, but they won't be interactive.

- **`WKInterfaceSeparator`**: If you've been making iOS apps for a while, you've probably run into the scenario where you add a `UIView` or `CALayer` just to change the appearance of a table's separators. Now you have a fully-configurable `WKInterfaceSeparator` that you can use in tables and views, and that even works for vertical separation!

- **`WKInterfaceSlider`**: This is a slimmed-down version of `UISlider` in that it offers more limited functionality and shouldn't be subclassed. You can still customize the slider with min and max values, min and max icons and the number of steps. There is a new `continuous` property that you can set in Interface Builder to make the bar solid. With this property turned off, the bar is etched in the number of steps.

- **`WKInterfaceSwitch`**: This object is also similar to its iOS counterpart, `UISwitch`, except now you get a handy built-in label.

- **`WKInterfaceTable`**: Tables in WatchKit are quite useful, and it's likely you'll use them all over the place. An instance of `WKInterfaceTable` is automatically paired with it's owning `WKInterfaceController` for interaction events and segues. Tables are row-based and have no notion of sections. You'll make a relatively complex table later in this book and get a feel for how to use multiple row styles.

- **`WKInterfaceTimer`**: This is another special WatchKit interface object. Since watches traditionally handle time, Apple created a class that is basically a label that counts up or down to a specific date. You can configure what units to display: seconds, minutes, hours, days, weeks, months and even years.

- **WKInterfaceMovie**: New in watchOS 2 is the ability to play videos. You'll have to include a video file, or download one, in order to play it. There isn't a way to play videos via storyboards. You can, at least, provide a placeholder cover photo.

- **WKInterfacePicker**: Another new interface element in watchOS 2 is the counterpart to the iOS UIPickerView. You have to add items to the picker in code, but you can configure it as a scrolling picker or as a sequence of images in the storyboard.

Layout

Auto Layout has been a controversial tool among developers because of its coupling with Interface Builder, verbose syntax and foreign-looking visual format language. But with the introduction of varying device sizes and size classes, Apple has been pushing Auto Layout heavily.

Most developers were expecting Apple to force us to use Auto Layout in WatchKit. Just by looking at the methods on `WKInterfaceObject`, you can see that there isn't any way to change the position of the object, so that must mean you're going to have to brush up on Auto Layout, right?

Auto Layout be gone! WatchKit provides its very own layout system that abstracts away most of the pain of layout and sizing and lets you focus on building your app. The WatchKit layout system defaults to sizing objects based on their content size and puts every object into either a horizontal or a vertical layout group.

This works in much the same way as HTML and CSS layout. Content is king, and interface elements are spaced and laid out relative to the content that comes before them.

Things like the number of lines in a label, the font size and the image size are all automatically calculated to lay out surrounding objects and even to size table row heights!

No more calculating text height for table views! Take a look at this more complex interface for a `WKInterfaceTable` with multiple row types. You're going to build this exact interface later in the book.

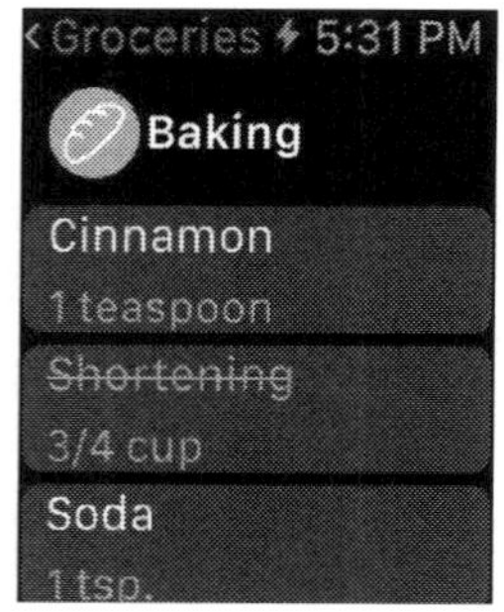

In this interface, all of the work is done in the storyboard, and the `WKInterfaceController` code only has to worry about wiring the data to the interface objects.

Notifications and glances

Alongside your typical Watch apps built with controllers and segues, WatchKit includes two other ways that users can interact with the Watch and your apps.

Notifications

Notifications have been around since iOS 3 was introduced in 2009. On Apple Watch, notifications work in almost exactly the same way they do in iOS. If the Watch receives a local or remote notification, it displays an alert, along with a vibration and an optional noise, and it lights up the screen.

WatchKit introduces two new types of notifications: the **short look** and the **long look**. While both notification types are triggered by a remote or local notification, the source of the notification can determine which, or both, of the notification types you'll want to use.

The short look

A short look is a very simple notification. It's comparable to the notifications that were available in iOS prior to iOS 8: The user sees only your app's icon, some text and the title of your app. If the user taps on the short look notification, then the Watch, like the iPhone, launches the full app.

The only real differences between the short look and pre-iOS 8 notifications are in layout and appearance.

The long look

A long look notification has a more complex interface that is completely customizable. The top part of the notification is called the **sash** and contains the name of your app and the icon, on top of a translucent, blurred bar.

Beneath the sash, you can add any content you want. Text content is driven by the notification and is either dynamic or static. With static notifications, you must bundle any image resources as part of the WatchKit extension. With dynamic notifications, you can customize the interface a bit more, but if you take too long, the system will fall back to the static notification.

You can also add any action items to the notification, so the user can jump into your app immediately and have it carry out the corresponding action. The user can dismiss your notification or simply tap anywhere in the content area to open your app.

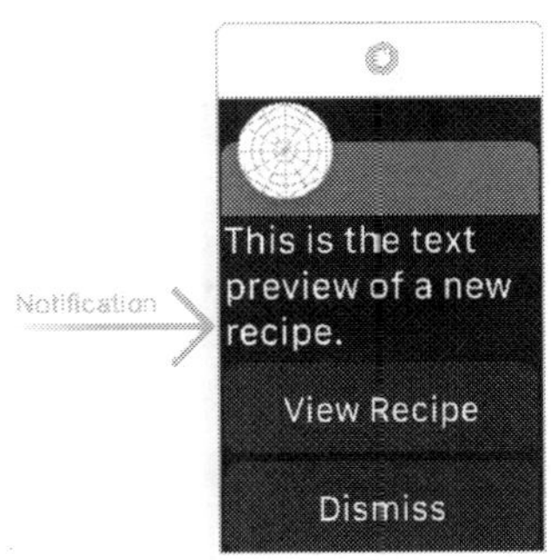

One interesting feature of short and long look notifications is that if you've made both types available for your app, users can toggle between them using a wrist-based gesture. After receiving a notification, the Watch will first display the short look, and if the user brings her wrist up to look at the notification, the Watch will switch to the long look.

This feature can provide more context and flexibility to your users, so they don't have to fumble around navigating the tiny screen.

> **Note**: You'll have the opportunity to build your own custom notifications in Chapter 11, "Notifications".

Glances

Another interaction point in WatchKit is the glance, which provides a "quick look" into your app, similar to Today extensions in iOS 8. The user gets a consumable, single-screen interface that tells her something about the state of the app, like the temperature outside or how much time is left before the roast in the oven is cooked to perfection.

In the **WatchKit Programming Guide**, Apple gives a couple of great examples of appropriate uses for glances:

"The glance for a calendar app might show information about the user's next meeting, while the glance for an airline app might display gate information for an upcoming flight."

Glances use `WKInterfaceController` just like a normal WatchKit interface controller. Apple recommends you keep glances simple, though: scrolling, and any interactive interface objects like buttons and switches, aren't permitted.

You can also use `updateUserActivity(_:userInfo:)` to advertise contextual information, so your Watch app knows what to do when the user taps your glance. Using this method in your glance, and `handleUserActivity(_:)` in your app, you'll be able to open the app and configure its interface accordingly. These two methods are collectively known as **Handoff**.

> **Note**: If you're eager to jump into making your own glance, skip to Chapter 10, "Glances", to learn what's involved!

Complications

Complications is a new API for watchOS 2 that lets you add third-party customizations to Watch faces. These are like the battery life, current temperature and next appointment widgets you're probably used to seeing, as below:

The `ClockKit` framework includes the functionality required to create custom complications, including the `CLKComplicationDataSource` protocol. An object that conforms to this protocol determines what the complication displays, and which features it supports. You can provide a basic complication, or you can take advantage of advanced features like timeline data and use the shared `CLKComplicationServer` object.

> **Note**: You will learn more about `ClockKit` in Chapter 12, "Complications".

WatchKit limitations

The first versions of the Apple Watch and WatchKit are exciting, but there are a few things these newcomers cannot and should not do. These limitations are important to keep in mind as you're contemplating your first app.

Intended for lightweight apps

From the Apple Watch Human Interface Guidelines:

"Apps designed for Apple Watch should respect the context in which the wearer experiences them: briefly, frequently, and on a small display."

You should look at building an Apple Watch app as literally extending an iPhone app to the user's wrist. The Watch is meant for quick and ephemeral interactions.

Small in size

Developers are used to having at least 320 points in width, amazingly sharp Retina displays and a screen big enough for four-finger gestures. But the Apple Watch is small—really small.

Remember that the Apple Watch takes extremely limited input and is strapped to the user's wrist. Your interfaces should be big and simple. Make your fonts and buttons large and use very few of them.

Where to go from here?

This has been an overview of the design and features of WatchKit—what it can and cannot do. There are many exciting, new and unique tools for building Apple Watch apps, and the best way to get familiar with them is to try them for yourself. What's more, I think we all know this is just the beginning for WatchKit!

In the following chapters, you will indeed get to try out many of the different interface controls and objects in WatchKit, as well as begin construction of a larger Apple Watch app that will take you through building custom layouts, navigation, tables and much more!

Chapter 3: UI Controls

By Ryan Nystrom

Apple delivered 13 interface controls with WatchKit, all of which inherit from `WKInterfaceObject`, which itself inherits from `NSObject`. Many of the interface controls have UIKit counterparts, but some are unique to WatchKit.

In this chapter, you'll get your hands on two new interface controls provided by WatchKit and experience how to begin piecing together a functional Apple Watch app. Indeed, you'll build such an app: a cooking companion that will do all the timing and calculating so you can prepare the perfect steak!

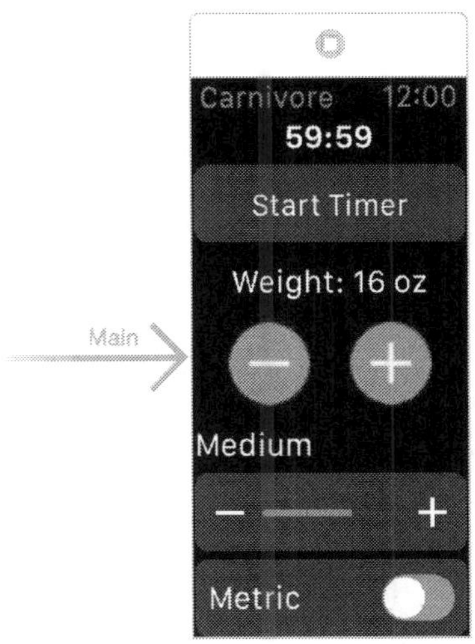

Note: If you want a detailed review of each of the new controls, please refer to Chapter 2, "Architecture".

Getting started

To jump right into building and using the new interface objects, grab the **Carnivore** starter project. This is mostly bare, but we've provided it so you don't have to waste any time on setup and configuration.

Open **Carnivore.xcodeproj** and have a poke around. Take a look at the targets and the project files. You'll see that we've already created the WatchKit App **scheme** for you, as well as **groups** for the Carnivore WatchKit Extension and the Carnivore WatchKit App.

There's also **CarnivoreKit** that simply contains an `enum` that both the iPhone app and the Watch app you're about to build will use.

Select the **Carnivore WatchKit App** scheme and build and run to launch the Watch app in the Apple Watch simulator. You'll see a lot of empty space for you to work with.

> **Note**: If you want to know how to create a Watch app from scratch, please see Chapter 1, "Hello, Apple Watch!"

Next, take a look at the **Carnivore WatchKit Extension** and **Carnivore WatchKit App** groups in the project navigator. You'll see the following files and groups in each:

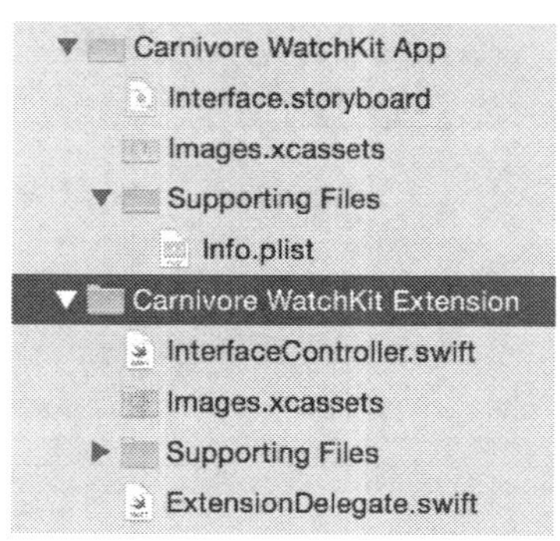

Each group of files corresponds to an individual app target with the same respective name. This helps organize your files while also keeping them accessible. It's a much cleaner setup than having a bunch of different Xcode projects crammed into a single workspace.

Make sure you understand the purpose of each group or target:

- **Carnivore WatchKit Extension**: This target houses all of the code that runs as an extension on your iPhone. Refer back to Chapter 2, "Architecture", for more.
- **Carnivore WatchKit App**: This target is for all of the resources that are physically stored on the Watch, including images, files and the interface storyboard.

Open **Interface.storyboard** from the **Carnivore WatchKit App** group and take a look at the default, blank interface controller:

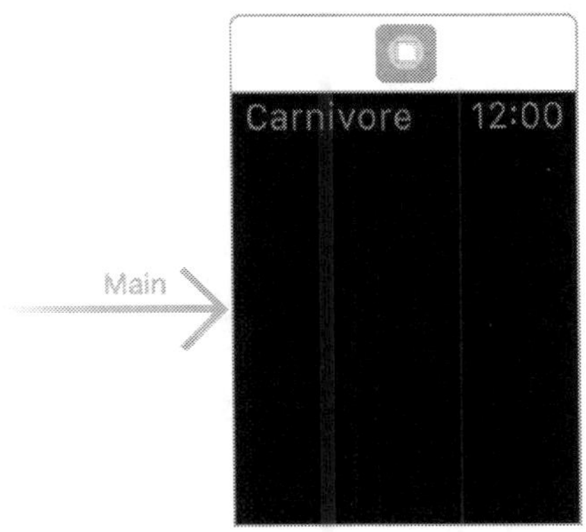

If you've worked with iOS storyboards, this should look pretty familiar. There is a main entry point arrow designating that this is the controller that the OS will load when the app launches.

Enough poking around—it's time to put some stuff on the screen!

The timer object

Throughout the rest of this chapter, you're going to create all of the interface elements for the app, one by one. While you won't use all 13 UI controls provided by WatchKit, pay attention while you're working and you'll see just how powerful WatchKit storyboards can be.

To cook the perfect steak, you need to know a couple of things about your meat and the preferences of whomever is going to eat it, so that you can determine just the right amount of time to leave the meat in the oven—and for the sake of simplicity, we are assuming you are cooking with an oven!

All in all, you're going to need to be able to:

- Start and stop a timer;
- Increase and decrease the weight of the meat;
- Select the diner's cooking preference, from rare to well done;
- Toggle between metric and imperial units.

With **Interface.storyboard** open, find **group** in the Object library and drag one onto the interface controller.

You'll see a dashed border with the word "Group" in the middle. This is just a placeholder. If you were to run the app now, you wouldn't actually see anything new on the screen.

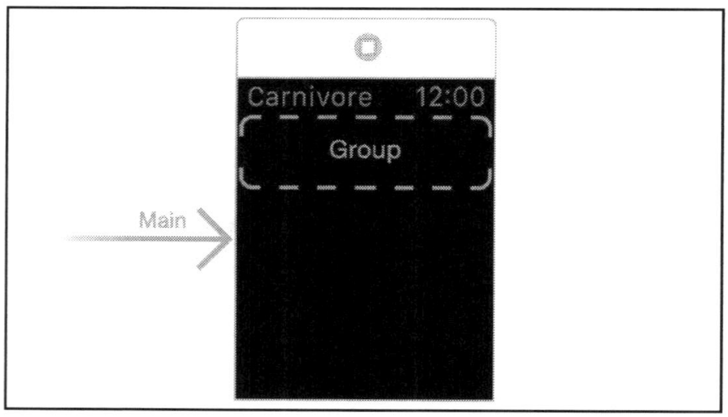

> **Note**: Groups are unique interface objects in that they occupy the space of their contents. You can specify a width and height for a group, but the real magic is in how they automatically lay themselves out. You can read more in Chapter 6, "Layout".

Next, drag a **timer** into the group. Timers also have placeholder text to give an idea of how their contents will be formatted.

With your new timer selected, open the **Attributes Inspector** and change the following attributes:

- In **Units**, select only **Second** and **Minute**;
- Change **Font** to **Text Styles – Headline**;
- Set **Alignment** to **Center** (the middle of the five buttons);

- Change the **Horizontal** position to **Center**.

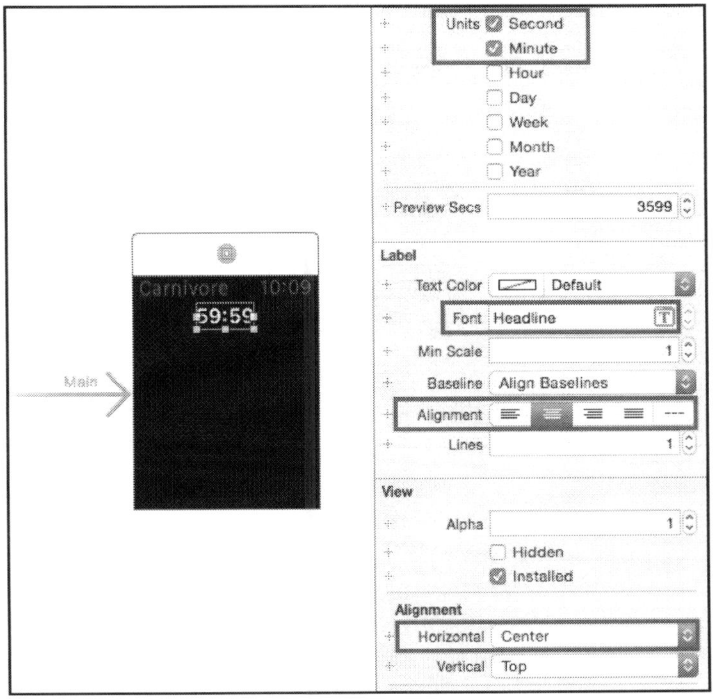

Wow, that's a lot of setup for such a tiny interface element! What exactly did you do?

The **Units** attribute configures what time units the timer will display. If you were to select Day, Month, Year and set a date of two months, three days and one year into the future, then the timer would read "1y 2m 3d". The timer is *really* smart in how it displays the time, which means no more fussing around with `NSDateFormatter`.

Position is a new type of attribute that's unique to WatchKit and is extremely powerful. It lets you lay out objects to the left, center or right of their container.

It might seem like a lot of setup, but take a look at all the steps you would have to do in an iOS app to get a similar interface object:

- Use `NSDateFormatter` to get a string representation of an `NSDate`;
- Subclass `UILabel`;
- Set up the necessary Auto Layout constraints on the label;
- Use an `NSTimer` to update the label every second.

Using `WKInterfaceTimer` saved you from writing a whole lot of code and from running any number of tests!

With the Carnivore WatchKit App scheme selected, build and run the app to see your new timer:

Hmm. That looks kind of... *lame*. Why isn't it doing anything? Well, in your storyboard you've given the timer a placeholder number of seconds, but this doesn't carry over when you run the app; it's purely for design purposes. For the timer to work, you need to wire it up and trigger it in code.

First, you need something to trigger the timer. Find **button** in the Object Library and drag it next to the timer, or just below it if you're dragging it into the document outline. Make sure you add the button to the same group that contains your timer. You can confirm this by checking the document outline.

But wait! Where did your timer go?

The problem is, all groups have a horizontal layout by default. You need to change your group to make it vertical.

Select the **group** in the document outline. Then in the **Attributes Inspector**, change the **Layout** to **Vertical**.

Double-click on the text in the button and change it to **Start Timer**. You can also do this by selecting the button and changing the text in the **Title** field of the Attributes Inspector.

Build and run your Watch app to see the new button:

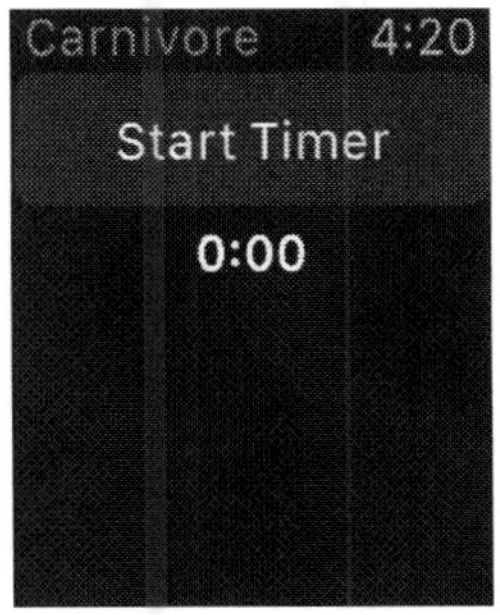

You'll be able to tap on the button and see the app both highlight it and depress it in 3D space. Now you're going to make that button do something!

Wiring the timer

Option-click on **Carnivore WatchKit Extension\InterfaceController.swift** to open the controller in the assistant editor. You should see the storyboard's and controller's Swift code side by side.

Control-drag from the timer in **Interface.storyboard** into **InterfaceController.swift** to create a new `IBOutlet`. In the pop-up, name the outlet `timer`, make it of type `WKInterfaceTimer` and give it a **weak** connection.

Now **Control-click** the **button**. Click on the **selector** option under **Sent Actions** and drag over to **InterfaceController.swift**. In the pop-up, name the new action `onTimerButton`.

Inside `onTimerButton()`, add a print statement to test that this method is wired up and working. Your method should look like this:

```
@IBAction func onTimerButton() {
  print("onTimerButton")
}
```

Build and run your app. Tap on the **Start Timer** button a couple of times and make sure you see some output in your console log:

```
onTimerButton
onTimerButton
onTimerButton
```

Now that you're confident you've wired up the button properly, how about using it to make the timer work?

Replace the contents of `onTimerButton()` with the following code:

```
// 1
let countdown: NSTimeInterval = 20
let date = NSDate(timeIntervalSinceNow: countdown)
// 2
timer.setDate(date)
timer.start()
```

Here's what you're doing with the above code:

1. You set a 20-second countdown variable and use it to instantiate an `NSDate` object. `WKInterfaceTimer` always uses date objects, not primitives, to count time.
2. You set the date for the timer and then start the timer. A timer won't do anything until you call `start()` on it. Any time that passes between setting the date and calling `start()` will be subtracted from the timer.

Build and run the app and then tap on the button. Now, instead of some boring console output, you'll see the timer start and count down all the way to zero!

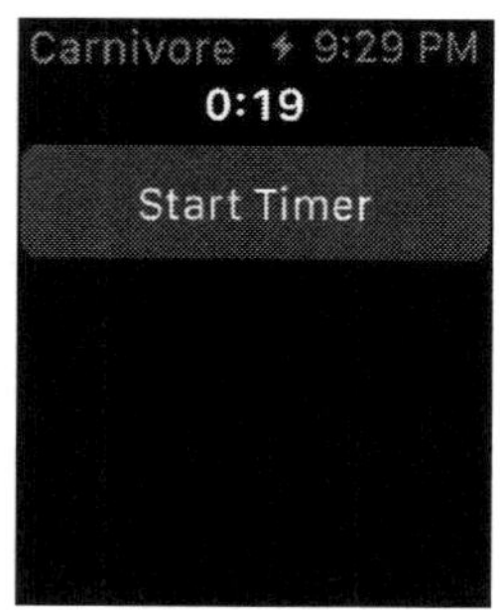

Using a label and buttons to control weight

You've seen how to add interface objects to your storyboard as well as how to wire them into your controller. It looks like it's time to build out this app!

Open **Interface.storyboard** and drag a **label** from the Object Library to just below the first group that contains the timer and button. That's *below* the group, not inside it! Change the **Text** to **Weight: 16 oz** and the **Horizontal** position to **Center**.

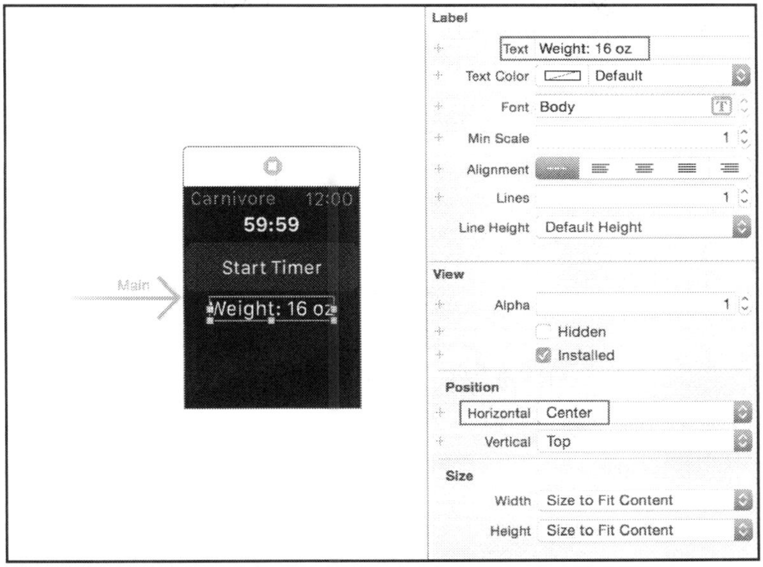

Next, drag another **group** beneath the label you just added. You can leave the Layout setting of this group as Horizontal.

Now drag a **button** into the group. With this new button selected, change the following attributes in the Attributes Inspector:

- Clear the **Title** field;
- Set the **Background** image to **minus**;
- Change the **Horizontal** position to **Center**;
- Set the **Width** size to **Size to Fit Content**.

You'll end up with a button that looks just like the following:

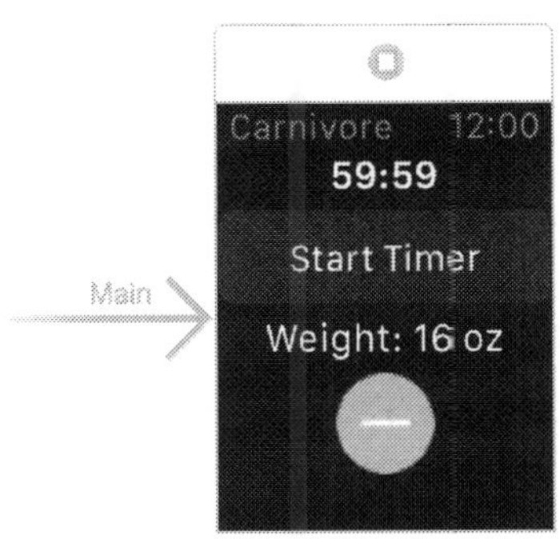

Next, click on your new button, **copy** and then immediately **paste**. This will paste a new button with the same configuration directly after the selected button, and within the same group.

Select this new button and change the **Background** image to **plus**.

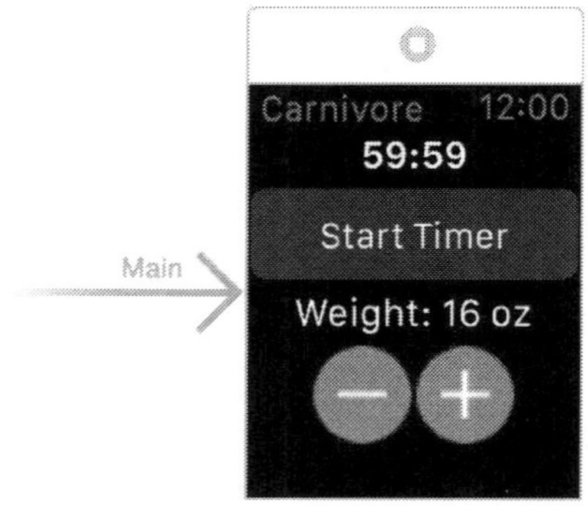

If you're a fan of Apple design and documentation, you've probably run across the Human Interface Guidelines at least a couple of times. Apple puts a lot of emphasis on interactive element sizes and spacing. You can probably tell that those two blue buttons are way too close for comfort.

Groups have powerful attributes that make layout extremely easy. In the case of items being too crowded, there's an attribute called **Spacing** that fixes just this.

Select the **group** that contains your two blue buttons. You might have to use the document outline to select it. Change the **Spacing** attribute from Default to **20**. Press the Return key to commit the change and watch Interface Builder update automatically.

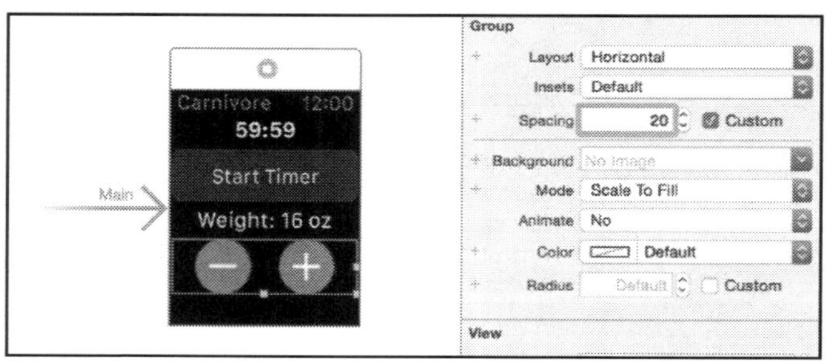

While you're at it, all of the items are getting a little tight vertically. Well, it turns out that the contents of `WKInterfaceController` are already in one big layout group! You know this because `WKInterfaceController` can contain other interface objects, are aligned vertically, and even have spacing and inset options.

Select the interface controller by clicking on the white header above all of your interface objects. In the **Attributes Inspector**, change **Spacing** to **10** and press Return. This will add a little vertical padding so your interface doesn't feel too crammed.

Open **InterfaceController.swift** in the assistant editor so you can see both it and **Interface.storyboard** at the same time. You're going to add a couple of outlets and actions.

Control-click on the **weight label** and drag to create an IBOutlet. Name it weightLabel, give it a type of WKInterfaceLabel and make it a **weak** connection.

Next, just as you did for the Start Timer button, add an IBAction for both the **plus** and **minus** buttons. Name them onMinusButton and onPlusButton, respectively.

If you did this correctly, you'll have added the following code to InterfaceController:

```
@IBOutlet weak var weightLabel: WKInterfaceLabel!

@IBAction func onMinusButton() {

}

@IBAction func onPlusButton() {

}
```

Now it's time to make the buttons functional. Close the assistant editor and open **InterfaceController.swift** in the main editor. Add a new variable to the top of the class:

```
var ounces = 16
```

This will keep track of the selected weight for your meat. A default of 16 ounces, or one pound, is a good starting point.

Add a new method just below awakeWithContext(_:):

```
func updateConfiguration() {
  weightLabel.setText("Weight: \(ounces) oz")
}
```

This simple function updates your label with the current weight. You'll be adding a lot to this function in due course to update the interface to reflect the app's current state.

In onMinusButton(), add the following code:

```
ounces--
updateConfiguration()
```

And in onPlusButton(), add the following code to increase the current weight:

```
ounces++
updateConfiguration()
```

Thanks to Swift, this code is short, clean and very readable!

Lastly, to make sure the app updates the interface with the proper state from the beginning, add a call to updateConfiguration() to the end of awakeWithContext(_:):

```
override func awakeWithContext(context: AnyObject?) {
  super.awakeWithContext(context)
  updateConfiguration()
}
```

Build and run the Watch app. Click on the plus and minus buttons to see your label update accordingly:

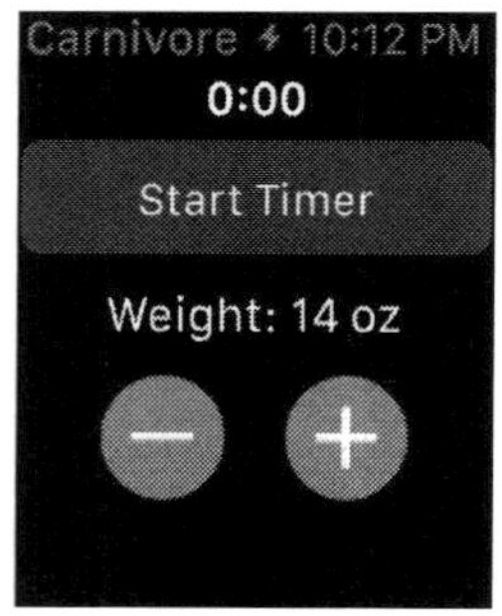

> **Note**: If you want, you can add minimum and maximum values to the weight. As it stands, you can choose a steak that's the weight of an entire cow! Except it won't fit in your oven...

Using a slider object to control doneness

People have their own preferences when it comes to cooking meat, from rare to well done to cremated. To please your diners, you need to be able to regulate the cooking temperature.

Open **Interface.storyboard** and drag another **group** from the Object Library to just below the group containing the two blue buttons. Make sure it's in the same hierarchy level as the buttons, weight label and timer groups.

Drag a **label** and a **slider** into your new group. Since the group is horizontal by default, select the group, open the Attributes Inspector and change **Layout** to **Vertical**.

You'll have four cooking temperatures: rare, medium rare, medium and well done. For the user to select one of these options, you'll have to configure the slider appropriately.

Select your new slider and, in the Attributes Inspector, make the following changes:

- Change the **Slider Value** to **2** to select medium by default;
- Change the **Slider Minimum** to **0** for rare;
- Change the **Slider Maximum** to **3** for well done;
- Set the number of **Slider Steps** to **3**. There is also an empty state, which actually makes four steps, but you need to set the number of values in *addition* to the value zero.

Make sure that **Continuous** is **unchecked**. This will give you step dividers on the slider to make the available options and means of selection more obvious to the user.

Open **InterfaceController.swift** using the assistant editor. **Control-drag** from the new label to create an `IBOutlet`. Name the outlet `cookLabel`, make the type `WKInterfaceLabel` and make it a weak connection.

Control-click on the **slider** and drag the **selector** option into InterfaceController.swift to create an `IBAction`. Name the new action `onTempChange`.

To represent the cooking temperature, you could simply remember that rare is the integer 0, medium rare is 1 and so on, but Swift makes creating an `enum` to represent data structures like this too easy to pass up!

Open the file **MeatTemperature.swift** and take a look around. You should see possible values, like `.Rare` and `.Medium`, and helper methods to turn a value into a string or associate a cook time modifier.

Great! Not only do you have a way to represent cooking temperatures, but now you're supplying a readable string and a time modifier. Let's plug this into the app.

Go back to **InterfaceController.swift** and add another variable just under the ounces variable you added earlier:

```
var cookTemp = MeatTemperature.Medium
```

This sets your default cooking temperature to `.Medium`, which in my experience is a popular choice.

Find the `onTempChange(_:)` method that you connected to the slider earlier and add the following code:

```
if let temp = MeatTemperature(rawValue: Int(value)) {
  cookTemp = temp
  updateConfiguration()
}
```

This code does two things:

- It creates a `MeatTemperature` variable. `WKInterfaceSlider` changed values are always of the type `Float`, so you have to cast it to an `Int` before initializing.

- The code also sets the current cooking temperature and updates the interface if a `MeatTemperature` variable was created.

To update the interface, add the following line to `updateConfiguration()`:

```
cookLabel.setText(cookTemp.stringValue)
```

Build and run, swipe down to the slider and tap around to change its value. Watch the label update every time you tap the plus or minus button on the slider!

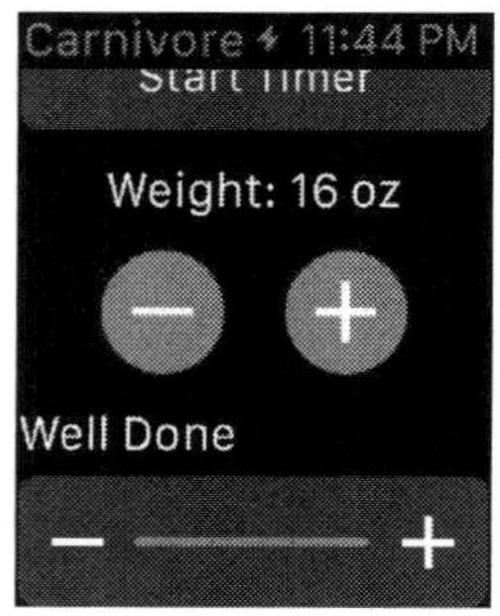

Integrating the timer

What good are these interface objects if they don't tell you how long to cook your meat? Looks like it's time to make the timer functional.

One interesting feature of `WKInterfaceObject` is that it doesn't have very many ways to get the current state. This is because, as you read in Chapter 2, the code is executed on the phone. The state of the UI might have changed in the time that the phone has spent executing, so you need to keep track of any state yourself, like whether your timer is running.

Near the top of **InterfaceController.swift**, where your other properties are declared, add another to track the status of the timer:

```
var timerRunning = false
```

Your timer is not running when the controller is initialized, so it's safe to set its default value to `false`.

The timer counting down isn't enough to reflect the state of your app. It's a good idea to update the Start Timer button when the user taps it.

Open **Interface.storyboard** in the main editor and **InterfaceController.swift** in the assistant editor. **Control-click** and drag from the **Start Timer** button to create an outlet named `timerButton`.

Replace everything inside `onTimerButton()` so that it looks like this:

```
@IBAction func onTimerButton() {
  // 1
  if timerRunning {
    timer.stop()
    timerButton.setTitle("Start Timer")
  } else {
    // 2
    let time = cookTemp.cookTimeForOunces(ounces)
    timer.setDate(NSDate(timeIntervalSinceNow: time))
    timer.start()
    timerButton.setTitle("Stop Timer")
  }
  // 3
  timerRunning = !timerRunning
}
```

1. Upon a user tap, if the timer is already running, you stop it and update the button title. This causes the timer to stop updating its UI.
2. If the timer isn't running, you create a cooking time interval using `cookTimeForOunces(_:cookTemp:)`, found in the `MeatTemperature` `enum`, and use it to create an `NSDate`. Then you start the timer and update the button title.
3. As the timer state has changed with the user tapping the button, you reflect that in your variable.

Build and run your Watch app. Change your cooking configuration, then tap the Start Timer button and watch the title change and the timer begin to count down. You can stop and restart the timer as many times as you like:

Using the switch to change units

Since only three countries in the world use imperial units, it would be best to be able to toggle between imperial and metric. This is a perfect use-case for a `WKInterfaceSwitch`!

> **Note**: Liberia, Myanmar and the United States, if you were curious, although in the US, they are called United States customary units.

Open **Interface.storyboard** and drag in one last **group** beneath the slider you added earlier. Make sure you add the group to the same hierarchy as your other groups.

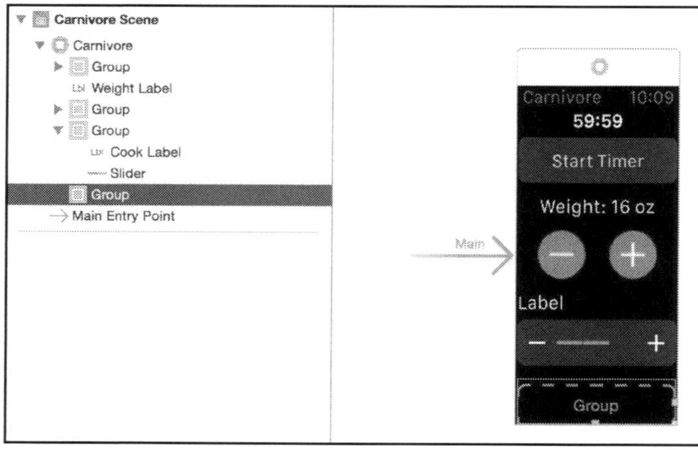

Drag a **switch** object into the new group. Open the Attributes Inspector and change the **Title** attribute to **Metric**. Also change the **State** to **Off**. Remember, you're using imperial units by default.

Open **InterfaceController.swift** in the assistant editor, and just as you've been doing, **Control-click** the new switch and **drag** from the **selector** option to create a new `IBAction`. Name this action `onMetricChanged`.

Near the top of **InterfaceController.swift**, where your other variables are in `InterfaceController`, add another variable:

```
var usingMetric = false
```

This variable will keep track of which unit system, imperial or metric, your user prefers.

Go back to the `onMetricChanged(_:)` method you just added and make it look like the following:

```
@IBAction func onMetricChanged(value: Bool) {
  usingMetric = value
  updateConfiguration()
}
```

In the code above, you simply change your new variable whenever the user taps the switch and then tell the app to update the interface accordingly.

Find `updateConfiguration()` and change it to look like the following:

```
func updateConfiguration() {
  // 1
  cookLabel.setText(cookTemp.stringValue)

  var weight = ounces
  var unit = "oz"

  if usingMetric {
    // 2
    let grams = Double(ounces) * 28.3495
    weight = Int(grams)
    unit = "gm"
  }
  // 3
  weightLabel.setText("Weight: \(weight) \(unit)")
}
```

1. The measurement system doesn't affect the cooking temperature, so you don't alter this line.
2. There are 28.3495 (roughly) grams per ounce, so if you're in metric mode, you need to convert your units. Notice that the ounces variable is *always* in ounces; you only use the metric state when it comes to configuring the interface objects.
3. You set the text of the `WKInterfaceLabel` with the converted weight and the proper unit abbreviation.

Build and run the Watch app. Play around with the different settings. You should see your cooking weight change whenever you tap the switch!

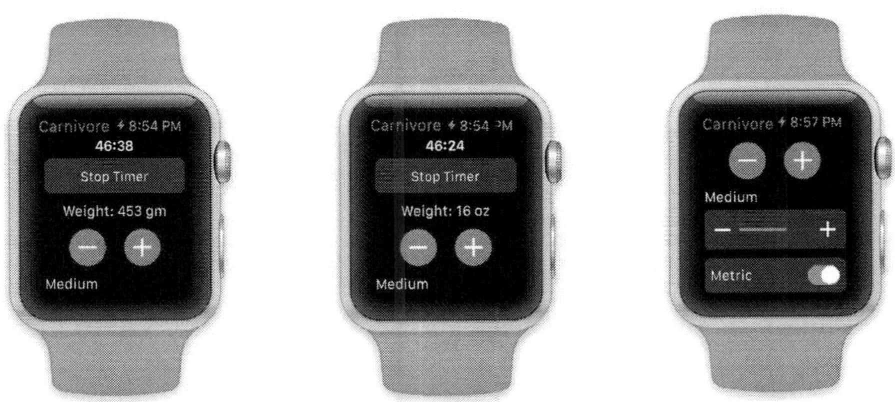

Where to go from here?

You've learned a ton about new and familiar interface controls in this chapter: groups, labels, buttons, images, switches, sliders and timers. There are still several other controls you can explore, like `WKInterfaceMap` and `WKInterfaceSeparator`.

You could also extend the app by adding interface objects to change the oven temperature, which will affect the cooking time, or even to select between different meats and vegetables. Make the app work to accommodate just how you like to cook!

In the next few chapters, you're going to take a look at some of the more interesting aspects of Watch app interface design, including pickers, layout, and navigation.

Chapter 4: Pickers

By Ryan Nystrom

The first version of WatchKit came with a decent starter kit of UI controls. There were buttons, switches, and tables... but this toolbox fell short when it came to interactions with some of the Apple Watch's physical interfaces. Most notable was the lack of controls that used the digital crown: one of the physical features most touted by Apple.

In watchOS 2 and the much improved WatchKit framework, Apple has introduced `WKInterfacePicker`. If you're familiar with iOS development, this control is functionally similar to `UIPickerView`, which is a sort of spinner control used to select an item from a long list.

One of the most common pickers is the `UIDatePicker` subclass which lets you easily select date components like days, months and years.

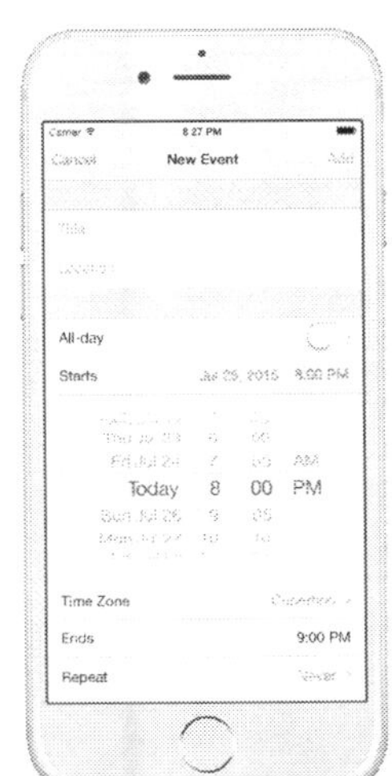

WKInterfacePicker provides the same functionality and usability for the Apple Watch. It enables you to give your users a large list of items to pick from without eating up the entire interface with buttons and options.

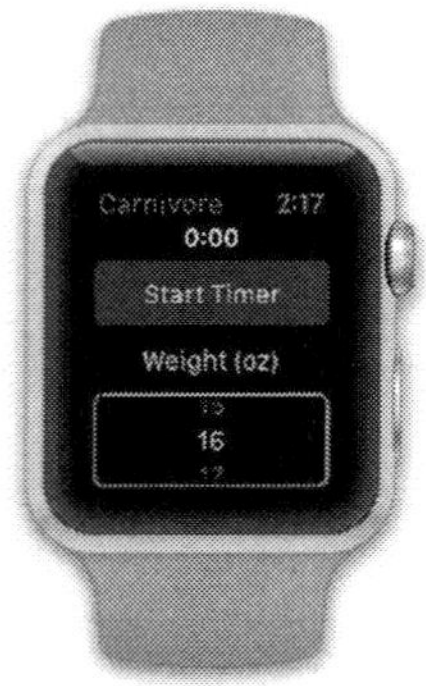

Using WKInterfacePicker is super simple:

1. Provide the picker a list of data. This can be text, images, or both!
2. Setup an IBAction and handle changes to the selected picker value.

That's it!

Another amazing feature of WKInterfacePicker is that it gives you access to the Digital Crown. The crown frees the user from covering up the watch's screen while they select options; so they can view more interface elements.

Since you use pickers to select from large lists of options, using the crown to see more of the screen is perfect! You can save your users from extra scrolling or add other features that are easy to get to.

In this chapter, you'll retool and enhance the previous chapter's Carnivore app to incorporate two styles of pickers, one simple and one advanced. Along the way, you'll acquaint yourself with the basics of `WKInterfacePicker` and get a taste of what this new control can do for your apps.

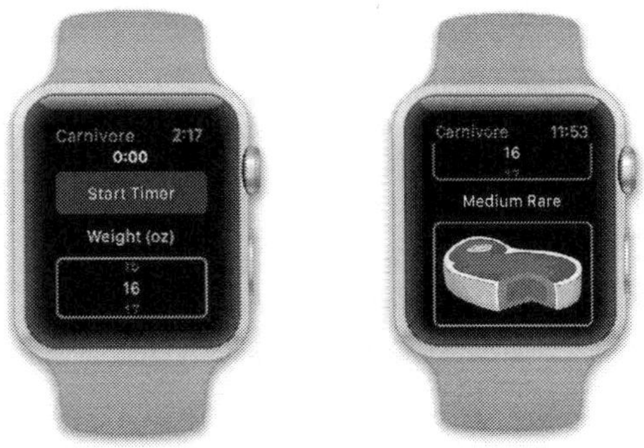

Getting started

If you completed the previous chapter on UI Controls, simply open that same project, **Carnivore.xcodeproj**, to pick up right where that chapter left off. If you got stuck or skipped the previous chapter, then open the **Carnivore.xcodeproj** starter project from this chapter's resources.

Build and run the **Carnivore WatchKit App** target and make sure you see something like the screenshot below. The Watch app should be fully functional: You should be able to start the timer, change the weight and cycle through cook times.

> **Note**: If you haven't read the UI Controls chapter, we suggest you skim through it first to familiarize yourself with the Carnivore app.

Code slayer

Before you begin building pickers, you first need to rip out the old ways of selecting weights and temperatures for cooking your meats. Instead of using buttons, `WKInterfacePicker` can make your app even more user-friendly.

Using buttons to make a selection from a range of data is much more cumbersome than quickly swiping through a list. Every change requires a tap, and that can get annoying! Plus, being able to use the digital crown makes selection even easier.

Open **Carnivore WatchKit App\Interface.storyboard** and select the following interface elements:

- The **weight label**;
- The **group** housing both the **increase and decrease buttons**;
- The **group** with the **temperature label and slider**;
- The **group** containing the **metric switch**.

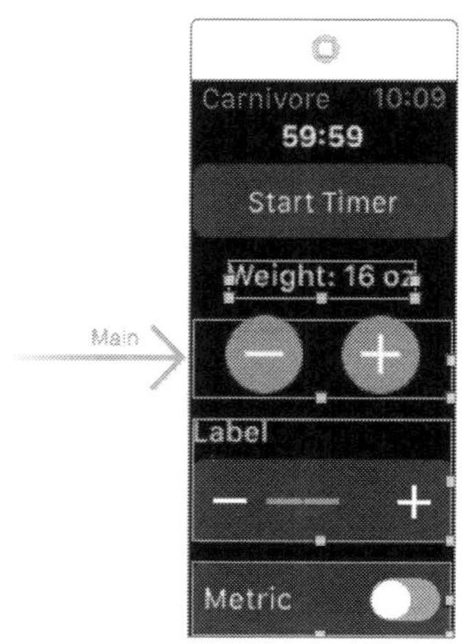

Once you have all of these elements selected, **delete** them! You can also remove the elements one at a time, if you prefer.

Your storyboard should now look like this:

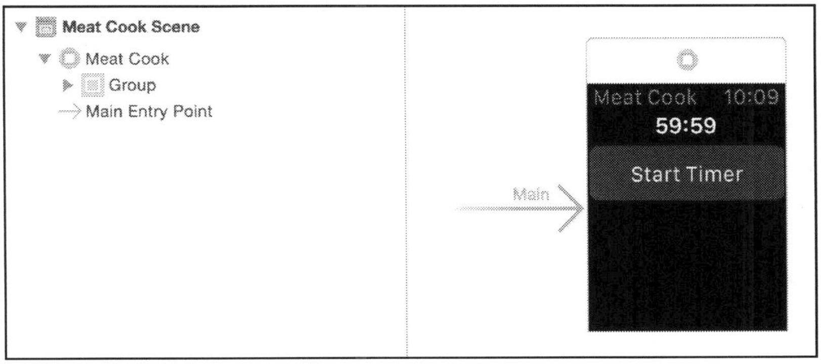

You're going to have to remove some code as well. Open **Carnivore WatchKit Extension\InterfaceController.swift** and find your `IBOutlets`.

Delete `weightLabel` and `cookLabel`, since you just removed those elements from the storyboard.

Remove the entire `updateConfiguration()` method as well. From now on, you're going to be updating your state based on picker events!

While you're in the mode for culling code, remove a few more methods:

- **`onTempChange(_:)`**
- **`onPlusButton()`**
- **`onMinusButton()`**
- **`onMetricChanged(_:)`**

You removed all of these elements from the storyboard, so none of this code is going to do any good!

Lastly, to make the compiler happy, delete the call to `updateConfiguration()` in `awakeWithContext(_:)`.

Build the app—you don't need to run it. Everything should compile just fine.

If you've slain your code with thoroughness and precision, your implementation of `InterfaceController` will still have the following `IBOutlets` and variables:

- **`timer`**, as an outlet to the `WKInterfaceTimer`;
- **`timerButton`**, which is your start and stop button;
- **`ounces`** to keep track of the selected ounces for your steak;
- **`cookTemp`**, which is your desired cooking temperature;

- **timerRunning**, a flag that determines whether or not the timer is running.

Also, you'll have only the following functions:

- **awakeWithContext(_:)**, which simply has a call to `super`;
- **onTimerButton()**, which contains logic about what to do when the user taps the timer button.

You've made space for a few pickers, but you have more than one style of picker to choose from. Let's learn about them now.

Picker display styles

The `WKInterfacePicker` API comes with three different display styles for data, each with its own purpose. You can use your finger or the digital crown to navigate through all of the different picker styles.

The list style

The **list** style is the most common of the three. You'll use it when you want to display a series of vertically stacked elements consisting of titles and/or images.

You can mix and match to display just text, just images, or both! This style is the most similar to that of `UIPickerView`.

You would want to use this style to pick from things like dates, times, or small icons.

The stacked style

The second available style, called **stacked**, requires that all of the items you give to the `WKInterfacePicker` have an image; otherwise, nothing appears. The images are displayed in full screen, and when you scroll through the options, you'll notice a cool 3D fade-and-scale animation.

The following screenshot shows a stacked picker in the middle of a transition.

You use the stacked style to select from a set of larger images. A good rule of thumb for using the stacked style would be for any data that could be displayed on a card.

The sequence style

The last available picker style, called **sequence**, is similar to the stacked style in that both display full-screen images. But the sequence style doesn't use an animated transition. Instead, the images simply replace each other as you scroll through the items.

At first this might sound super boring, but sequence-style pickers exist so you can design a control that involves more than merely swiping through a list. This is where the digital crown comes into play. Imagine something like the circular progress control in the Activity app that you can scroll to fullness with the crown.

Start End

To achieve this effect, all you have to do is provide a series of progressive images. Once assigned to your `WKInterfacePicker`, the picker will automatically scroll through the images you gave it.

But don't limit your image sequence imagination to just filling circles. You can combine all sorts of images in a series and scroll through them almost as if they were stills from an animation: weather effects, facial expressions, you name it!

If you put time and effort into designing your image sequences, you can achieve some really amazing controls!

But for your first picker, you'll start with the simplest and most familiar display style: the list.

Your first picker

Since you already removed the buttons to select a cook temperature, you're going to add a picker so that selecting the weight of your steak is much faster.

Open **Carnivore WatchKit App\Interface.storyboard** and in the Object Library, find the **picker** element. Drag and drop it beneath the **Start Timer** button.

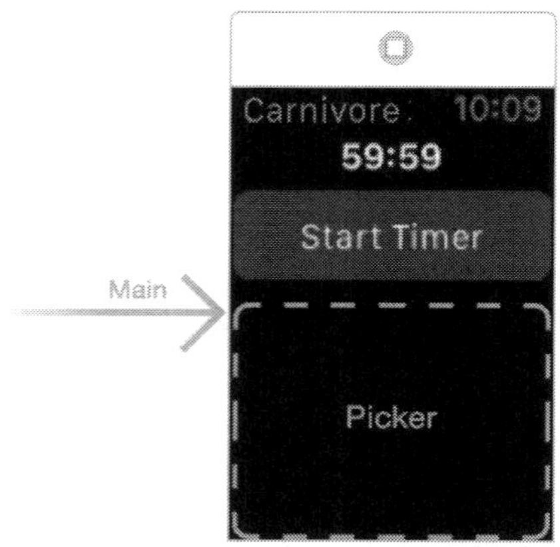

With the new picker still selected open the Attributes Inspector. Notice that there isn't a way to add any items, text or images to the picker. Configuration of items in `WKInterfacePicker` has to happen entirely in code, much the same way that tables and collections views with dynamic data must be set up in code.

> **Note**: Oddly, while all data configuration **must** be done in code, a `WKInterfacePicker` must be initialized via the storyboard. Likewise, the style of the picker must be determined in the storyboard; it cannot be changed at runtime.

To configure your picker's items, you first need to create an `IBOutlet` for it. Open **Carnivore WatchKit Extension\InterfaceController.swift** in the assistant editor and Control-drag from the **picker** to `InterfaceController` to create an outlet. Name this outlet **weightPicker**.

Next, you will add a series of `WKPickerItems` to `weightPicker` to configure it. Unlike using a delegate for `UIPickerView`, instances of `WKInterfacePicker` are configured with a first-class object. Picker items hold the strings and images that are displayed by the picker. Find `awakeWithContext(_:)`. It will be empty aside from a call to `super`. Add the following code:

```
// 1
var weightItems: [WKPickerItem] = []
for i in 1...32 {
  // 2
  let item = WKPickerItem()
  item.title = String(i)
  weightItems.append(item)
}
// 3
weightPicker.setItems(weightItems)
// 4
weightPicker.setSelectedItemIndex(ounces - 1)
```

Here's what happening:

1. This code first creates a mutable array that can only accept instances of `WKPickerItem`.
2. To cover a wide array of steak sizes, you iterate 32 times and create an item for each step. You simply use a string format of the integer as the title of the `WKPickerItem`.
3. The last step to populate the `WKInterfacePicker` is to call `setItems(_:)` with an array of `WKPickerItems`. If you were to run the app at this step, you would see a functional picker.
4. To make sure your picker is in sync with the current state of your controller, you use the `ounces` variable to set the index of the selected item.

Build and run the Watch app, and you'll see something like this:

> **Note**: If you're using the simulator, clicking and dragging will replicate scrolling the entire view. To scroll through a picker, use your laptop's trackpad or the scroll-wheel of a mouse. If you're running the app on your watch you can scroll with your fingers or the digital crown.

There it is: your first working `WKInterfacePicker`! However, it's not very usable yet. For starters, what's it for?

Go back to **Carnivore WatchKit App\Interface.storyboard** and drag a **label** element directly above the picker. Change the label's text to **Weight (oz)** and change its **Horizontal Position** to **Center**.

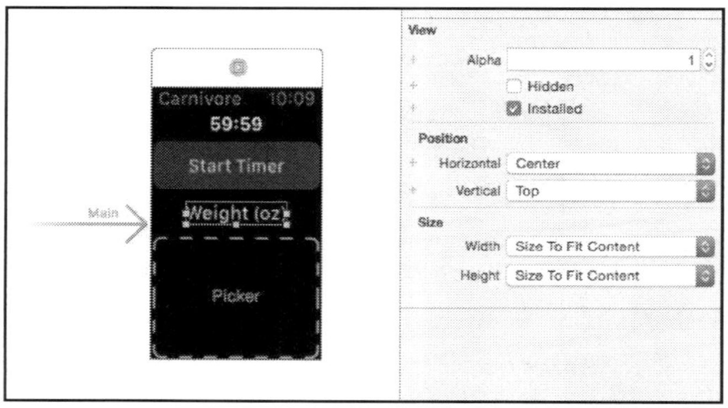

Notice that you can't scroll through the items unless you first tap on the picker. Wouldn't it be great to be able to tell when the picker is selected?

Apple's engineers have it covered! Still in **Interface.storyboard**, select the **picker** you just added and open the **Attributes Inspector**. Change the **Focus Style** to **Outline**.

While you're at it, make the picker a little shorter by changing the **Height (Fixed)** to **55**.

Build and run the Watch app again, and try to use the picker. Now, selecting your picker surrounds it with a bright green indicator. Much more intuitive!

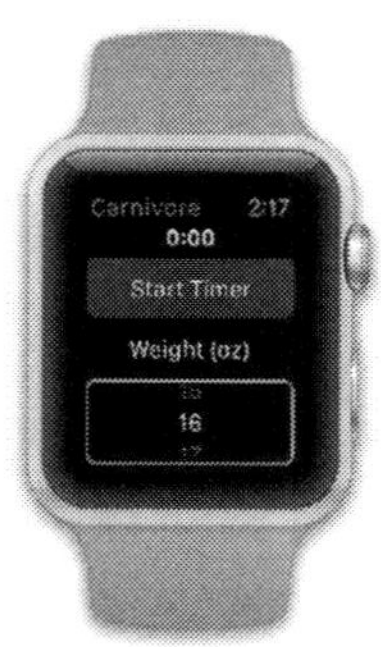

While your new picker is now easy to use, if you play around with the picker selection and the timer button, you'll notice that the cook time never deviates. That's because whenever `onTimerButton()` is triggered, `ounces` is always going to be the value to which it was initialized!

To fix this, you need to wire up an `IBAction` from your picker to the controller. Open **Carnivore WatchKit App\Interface.storyboard** in the main editor and **InterfaceController.swift** in the assistant editor.

Right-click the picker and drag from **selector** in the popup dialog to `InterfaceController`. Name your action `onWeightChanged`.

Add the following code to your new method:

```
@IBAction func onWeightChanged(value: Int) {
  ounces = value + 1
}
```

The `value` parameter is the *index* of the item that is currently selected in your picker. Remember that when you set up your items, you used the range `1...32`, so your indices will actually be `0...31`.

Build and run. Your timer will now adjust based on the weight of the steak you're going to cook:

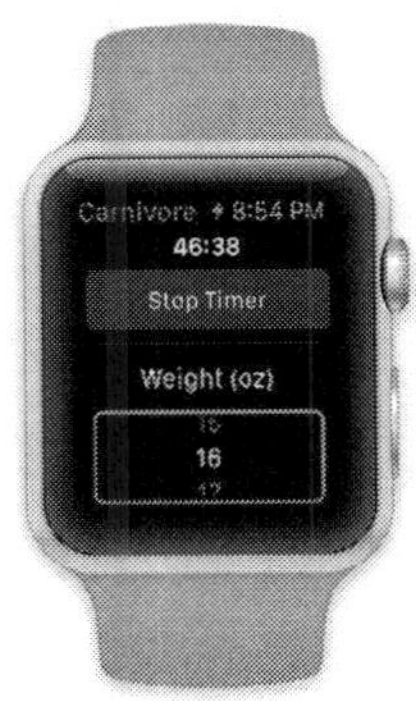

A sequence-style picker

Weight isn't the only factor when it comes to cooking the perfect steak. People prefer their food cooked in a variety of ways, from a light sear all the way to charred. To determine how long to cook a steak, you also need to know how done the diner wants it.

Recall from the previous chapter that the original Carnivore app let users select a doneness level ranging from rare to well done. `WKInterfacePicker` provides another convenient means of selecting an item from a set: a set of doneness levels based on the internal temperature of the meat while it's cooking, or the "cook temperature."

Knowing what "medium rare" means when actually cooking is much clearer if you can see an image that explains the concept! To accomplish this, you will add another picker to make selecting a doneness level more visual. This is done using the *sequence* picker style.

Open **Carnivore App\Interface.storyboard** and drag a **label** beneath the picker you previously added. Change your new label to have a **Horizontal Position** of **Center**, just like the weight label. This label will display the currently selected cook temperature.

Next, add another picker beneath that label. Change its **Style** to **Sequence**. Also, set its **Focus Style** to **Outline** so you can clearly tell when the picker is active. You'll use this picker to display a sequence of images representing the various cook temperatures or doneness levels.

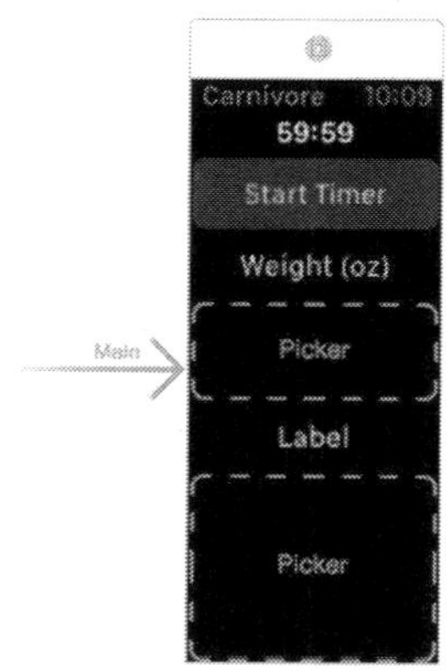

Open **InterfaceController.swift** in the assistant editor and add an `IBOutlet` for both the label and the picker you just added. Name them `temperatureLabel` and `temperaturePicker`, respectively.

While you're adding outlets, **right-click** the **new picker**, drag from the **selector** option to `InterfaceController` and add a new `IBAction` named `onTemperatureChanged`.

Change the code in `onTemperatureChanged(_:)` to the following:

```
@IBAction func onTemperatureChanged(value: Int) {
  let temp = MeatTemperature(rawValue: value)!
  cookTemp = temp
  temperatureLabel.setText(temp.stringValue)
}
```

This function takes the selected index in the picker and creates a `MeatTemperature` `enum` from it. It then sets the current `cookTemp` state variable and updates the `temperatureLabel` outlet you just created with the text that represents the cook temperature or doneness level.

> **Note**: If you don't remember what temperatures and strings are available, check out **CarnivoreKit\MeatTemperature.swift**.

The last step to set up your picker is to assign an image to each `WKPickerItem` to create a sequence. Before wiring it all up, open **Carnivore WatchKit App\Images.xcassets** and take a look at the numbered **temp** images.

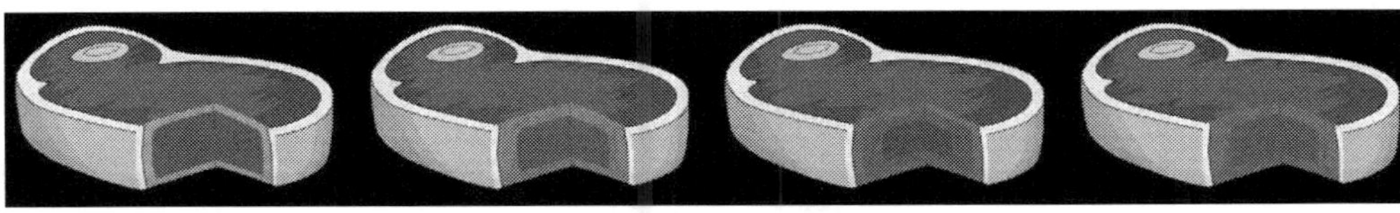

These four images represent the cross section of a steak when cooked to various temperatures. As long as all of your images have the same dimensions, `WKInterfacePicker` will be able to cycle through them as you scroll with the digital crown.

> **Note**: All of the images have a black background because removing the transparency channel conserves image size. Apple recommends in the Apple Watch Human Interface Guidelines that you optimize your images as much as possible for the Watch's limited graphics processing power.

Go back to **InterfaceController.swift** and at the end of `awakeWithContext(_:)`, add the following code:

```
// 1
var tempItems: [WKPickerItem] = []
for i in 1...4 {
  // 2
  let item = WKPickerItem()
  item.contentImage = WKImage(imageName: "temp-\(i)")
  tempItems.append(item)
}
// 3
temperaturePicker.setItems(tempItems)
// 4
onTemperatureChanged(0)
```

This should look familiar, but let's walk through it:

1. You create a mutable array to hold your instances of `WKPickerItem`, and iterate the range `1...4`.
2. You initialize a new `WKPickerItem` and assign a `WKImage` using the current step's value.
3. You set up the picker's items, just like you did with the previous picker.
4. Finally, you call `onTemperatureChanged(_:)` to initialize your controller and your label's state as if the first item had been selected.

Build and run the Watch app. Scroll through the meat selections. Your timer calculations will update according to the temperature and weight you select. Now that's well done!

Where to go from here?

In this chapter, you worked with two styles of `WKInterfacePicker`, each of which made use of the digital crown which lets you scroll through different picker items. You also got a glimpse of the creative possibilities of using pickers with image sequences.

Remember, there's also the stacked picker style. That style is best used for animating through a series of images that don't necessarily need to be in sequence but deserve their own images: things like cards or a photo album.

Pickers aren't the answer to fix every user-experience, but whenever you need to select from any amount of data, `WKInterfacePicker` will make it incredibly easy to do so!

Chapter 5: Layout

By Ryan Nystrom

In 2008, when Apple first released the iOS SDK, layout was driven by *springs and struts*, a primitive layout system that automatically resizes views based on their parents' edges. With the release of the iOS 6 SDK in 2012, Apple delivered a powerful new system called Auto Layout that it continues to improve, most recently in iOS 8. Auto Layout is driven by *constraints*—relationships between views' sizes, positions or edges.

Fast forward to today, and WatchKit has introduced an entirely new layout system. Instead of deriving layout from constraints, WatchKit relies heavily on content size and spacing to position interface elements.

In this chapter, you'll learn the reasoning behind this new layout system, as well as beginning to build an interface that's far more complex than the one in the previous chapter.

The app you'll make will display a photo along with details about it, such as the time it was taken and the name of the photographer. You will focus only on the layout portion during this chapter — the remaining functionality is left as an exercise for the reader. :]

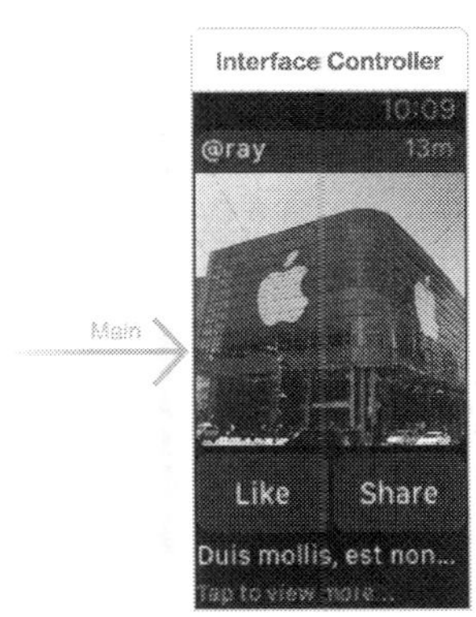

Getting started

Before jumping into building your first complex layout, you should take a look at the starter project's iPhone app to get a feel for what the Watch version will be like.

Open **Layout.xcodeproj** and build and run the scheme for the iOS app. You'll see something like the following screenshots:

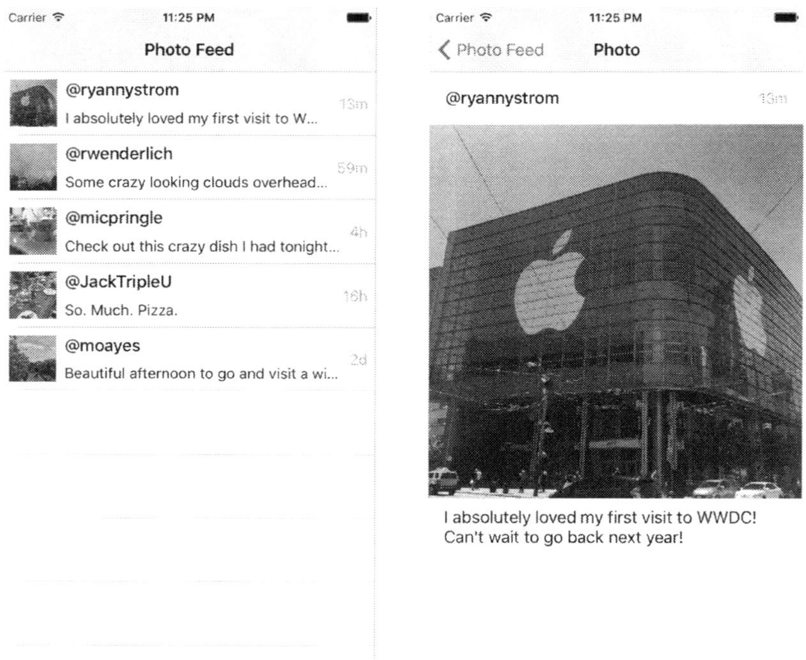

Full-screen images look great when viewed on the iPhone. The larger screens on the 6(s) and 6(s) Plus give you very detailed, super high resolution photos. Your designers also have significant *screen real estate* to add other metadata, like the name of the person who posted the photo and any comments he or she might have about it.

But what happens when you shrink to only 272x340 pixels on the 38mm Apple Watch? Keep reading to find out how to use WatchKit layouts to transform a complex design into something simple and responsive.

> **Note**: Remember that both the 38mm and 42mm Apple Watches have Retina screens, so the 38mm is really 136x170 *points* and the 42mm is 156x195. You can read more about dealing with different Watch screen sizes in Chapter 15, "Advanced Layout".

Understanding layout in WatchKit

Before you start dragging, dropping and clicking in Interface Builder, you need a quick tour of the features of this new layout system provided by WatchKit.

There are only three new concepts you need to understand to get started building sophisticated interfaces: **groups**, **content sizing** and **relative spacing**.

Layout groups

You'll remember using several interface elements called **groups** in the previous chapter. Groups are instances of `WKInterfaceGroup`, which inherits from `WKInterfaceObject`, just like `WKInterfaceLabel` or `WKInterfaceTimer`.

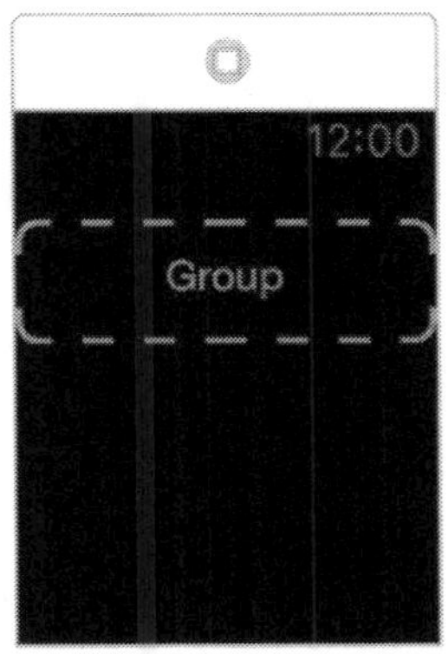

If you've ever used an empty view in iOS as nothing more than a container to group and lay out other views, then groups in watchOS will feel instantly familiar. And just like `UIView`, `WKInterfaceGroup` is much more than a simple container for other interface elements. You can configure the appearance and behavior of a group in many different ways!

Open the header file **WKInterfaceGroup.h** and get a feel for all the things you can do with a group.

> **Note**: To open **WKInterfaceGroup.h** in Xcode, open the **Open Quickly** dialog (**Command-⇧-O**) and type **"WKInterfaceGroup"**. When the autocomplete shows **WKInterfaceGroup.h**, press Return to view the file. Notice that the class is in Objective-C!

In addition the functionality that they inherit from `WKInterfaceObject`, the appearance of groups can be highly customized:

- **`setBackgroundColor(_:)`** changes the background color.
- **`setCornerRadius(_:)`** changes the corner radius. No more fumbling with the `CALayer` property of a `UIView`!
- **`setBackgroundImage(_:)`** sets the background image using an image from the extensions asset catalog. It's nice to not have to add a `UIImageView`.
- **`setBackgroundImageData(_:)`** sets the background image data, usually when adding a series of images to animate.
- **`setBackgroundImageNamed(_:)`** sets the background image using an image from the Watch app's asset catalog.
- **`startAnimating()`** begins animating through the background images, if there's more than one.
- **`startAnimatingWithImagesInRange(_:duration:repeatCount:)`** is like `startAnimating()` but gives you a lot more control.
- **`stopAnimating()`** stops any image animations.

Look at the group-specific attributes in the Attributes Inspector in Interface Builder, and you'll see even more options you can use to create compelling layouts.

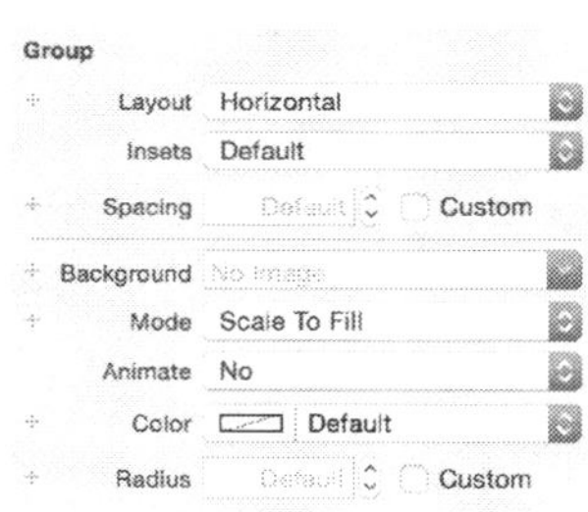

Layout is one of the most important attributes of a group, controlling the axis along which the interface elements inside the group are laid out. You can use either **Horizontal** or **Vertical**.

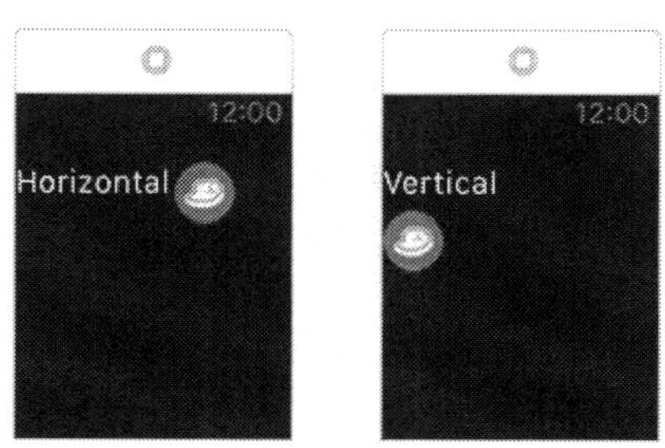

> **Note**: If you use a horizontal layout, make sure to pay attention to the sizes of any dynamic interface elements like labels. If they grow too big, they'll push any sibling elements off-screen.

Insets let you create a margin between the group and its contents. If you've ever worked with `UIEdgeInset` in classes such as `UIScrollView`, this will feel familiar. You can change the top, bottom, left and right insets independently for groups.

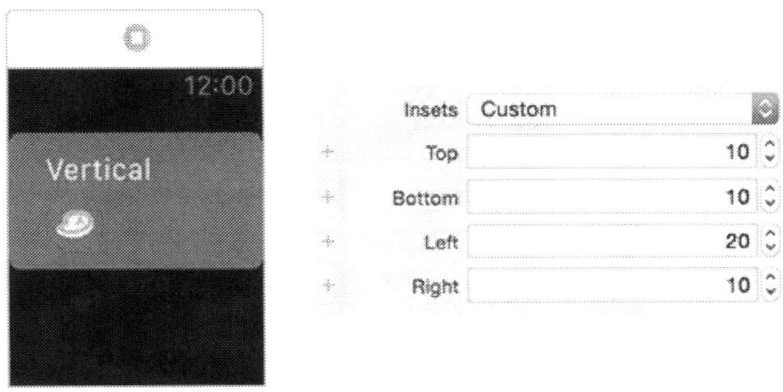

The Apple Watch Human Interface Guidelines recommend that interface elements in your interface controllers hug the side of the screen, because there's a black bezel around the physical screen that affords a natural margin. However, content towards the middle of the screen can sometimes benefit from a little extra padding, to prevent your interfaces becoming too cramped.

Spacing adjusts the distance *between* the elements within a group. Horizontal and vertical spacing add space to the x- and y-axes, respectively.

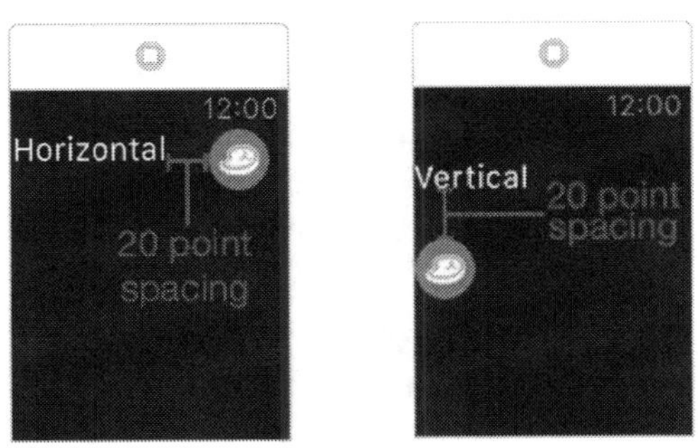

The attributes in the next section of the inspector are more self-explanatory. You can change the **Background** image, the drawing **Mode**, decide whether to **Animate** the background image, or simply select a background **Color**.

The last attribute in the section is **Radius**, which changes the corner radius of the group. The default radius value is 6 points, but this is only applied when you set either a background color or a background image; otherwise the group doesn't use rounded corners at all.

> **Note**: When changing the radius attribute, pay attention to the layout and size of your content. Groups will automatically clip anything that falls outside the bounds of clipped corners. This is a great example of when it would be useful to adjust the insets.

Content size

Another interesting feature of this new layout system is that it's driven by content size, the combined size of all the content within each group in the interface.

In WatchKit, the space taken up by text is determined by an `NSAttributedString`, which contains attributes like the font, line spacing and color. WatchKit renders the text off-screen, determines the height and width based on the string's bounding box and then applies that to the layout.

Unlike in iOS, WatchKit automatically handles all of the layout for you.

Take a look at the example below. Instead of fussing with text bounding sizes, the groups are simply set to **Size To Fit Contents** and WatchKit takes care of the rest! To achieve the same effect in iOS, you'd have to create a number of constraints between your views and an outer scroll view.

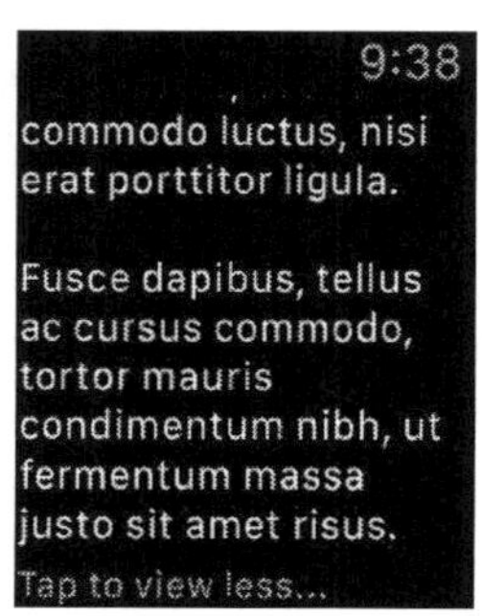

The **Lines** attribute is important when configuring any interface element that contains text, such as a label. This attribute informs the element to truncate any text where the number of lines exceeds the value you set here. Setting this property to 0 will allow as many lines as needed to lay out the text without truncating.

Relative spacing

The last important feature of the layout system provided by WatchKit is the way it allows you to size and position an interface element based on its parent's size and position. In WatchKit, the parent will always be a group.

Even when you're in Interface Builder, the root interface element of `WKInterfaceController` is a group.

Below, you can see the available attributes when editing any type of `WKInterfaceObject` in Interface Builder:

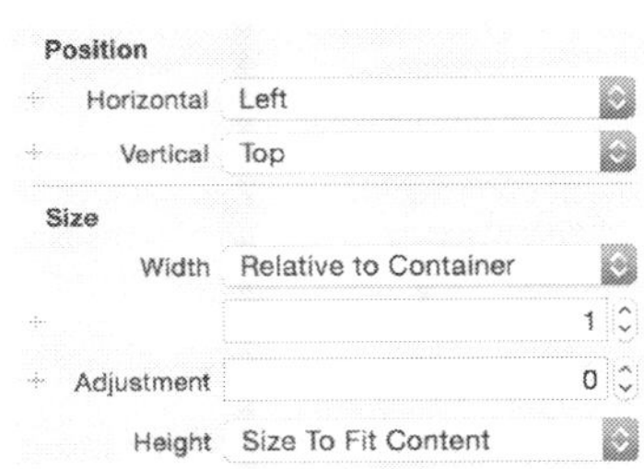

You can change both the Horizontal and Vertical position attributes. You can align the Horizontal position to the left, right or center and the Vertical position to the top, center or bottom.

The layout system updates the position of any interface elements at three major points:

- When the interface is first loaded;
- Any time the content, such as label text and background images, changes;
- Any time sibling elements are hidden or unhidden.

You can change the **Height** and **Width** attributes of an interface element to fit their content, be relative to their container or be fixed to a certain value.

If you change either height or width to **Size To Fit Content**, the layout system decides how tall and wide the interface element needs to be to fit its content. With a label, if you set the width to fit its content, the label won't grow beyond the size of its containing group.

For images, you should almost exclusively use **Size To Fit Content** along with appropriately sized images. This results in pixel-perfect layout of your interfaces.

The setting **Relative to Container** allows you to specify a multiplier between 0 and 1, which represents the size of the interface element as a proportion of its parent's size. You can also change the adjustment value, which offsets the final size.

```
Parent[width|height] * multiplier + adjustment = [width|height]
```

For example, if you had a parent group with a width of 250 points and you wanted equally-sized images side by side, you would set their multipliers to 0.5 (or 50%), making each image 125 points wide. If you then realized the images needed to shrink a bit to account for padding, you could set each image view's adjustment to -10, making each image 115 points wide.

The last size setting, **Fixed**, allows you to manually set a width or height value to which the interface element will adhere, no matter its content size.

The below image demonstrates a label nested in a group with a fixed width and height. Notice the label is truncated because the group is too small to fit the text on a single line.

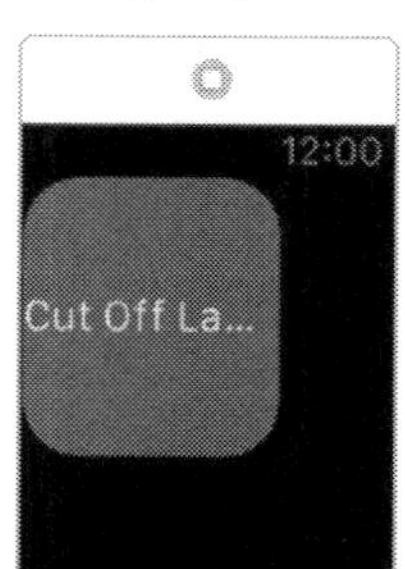

Fixed size is a good option to have in your tool belt, but use it with caution. Remember the Watch comes in two different sizes with two different pixel dimensions. A fixed size on one screen may not look right on another.

Laying it all out

It's time to grab the starter project, crack your knuckles and get down to business.

For this chapter, you're going to build the layout block for a single post. There won't be much code. Most of what you'll learn is how to compose groups and other `WKInterfaceObject` elements to create a more complex layout in Interface Builder.

Open **Layout WatchKit App\Interface.storyboard** and find the default controller; it will have the default Xcode project class of `InterfaceController`. The controller will look something like this:

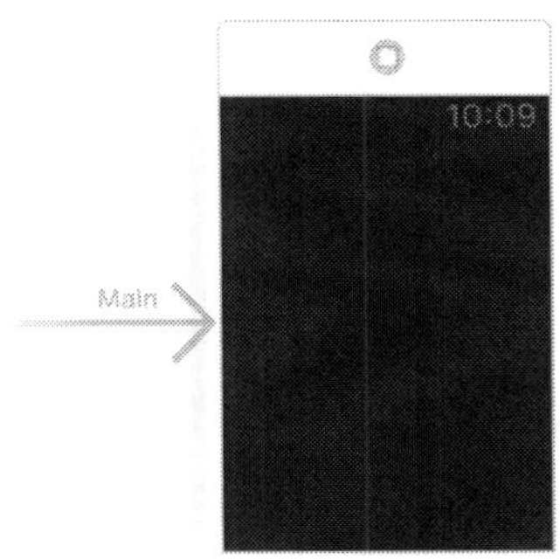

That's not very exciting is it? To spice it up, add your first **group** by finding it in the Object Library and dragging it into the controller. Inside this group, add an **image** element, once again dragging it from the Object Library.

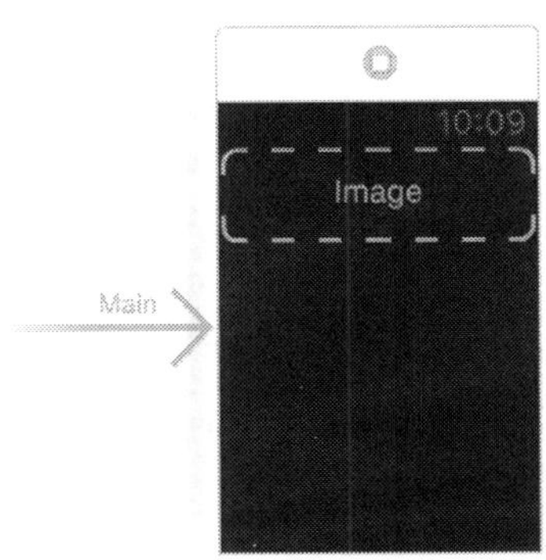

Select the image element you just added and open the Attributes Inspector; you'll see that the height and width are set to **Size to Fit Content**.

However, the image has the gray, dashed border because there isn't any content! Likewise, if you were to build and run the app now, you'd still have a black screen.

With the **image** still selected, change the **Image** property to **wwdc**.

The corners of the image are *rounded* automatically because `WKInterfaceGroup` has a default corner radius of 6 points and automatically clips its contents.

Collecting metadata

Now that you've added the main attraction—the photo—it's time to add some of the other information included in a post. Remember, for now you're only adding user interface elements!

You need to add the username and time so that it's right above the image, just like in the iPhone app.

Go back to **Interface.storyboard** and add a new group inside the first group, above the image. You're going to add two labels, one for the username and one for the time the image was taken, so you'll need something to contain them.

But wait a minute, where did your image go?

Look at the document outline, and you'll clearly see that the WWDC image element hasn't gone anywhere.

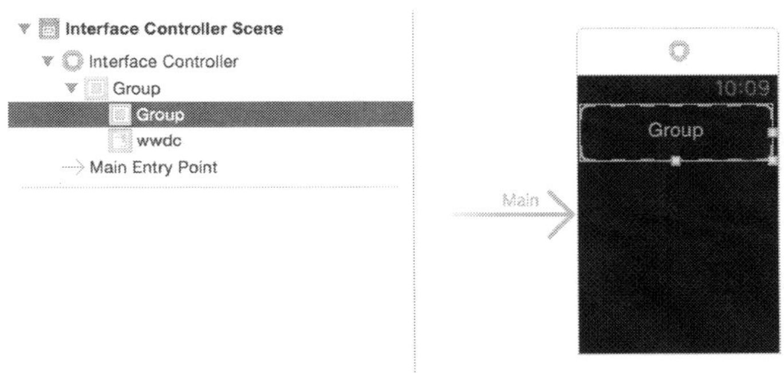

`WKInterfaceGroup` elements default to a *horizontal* layout. To add a header group, you're going to have to change that!

Select the group you added first, which contains both the group you just added and the WWDC image. Open the Attributes Inspector and change the **Layout** to **Vertical**:

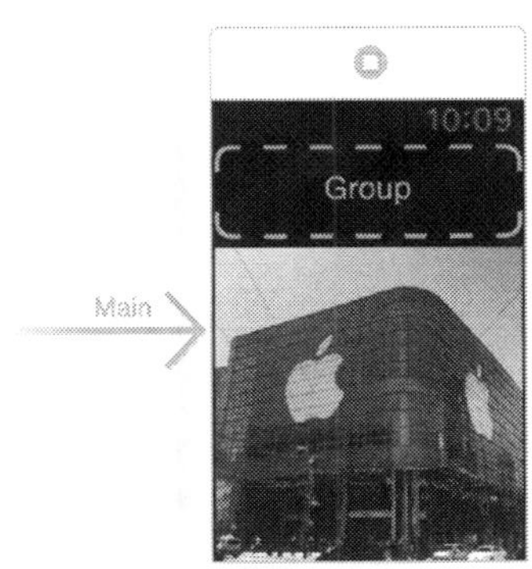

That looks *much* better!

Drag two **labels** into this new group, and change the text to something more representative of the label, **@gruber** for the left and **13m** for the right.

Select the **rightmost label** that you just added and change its **Horizontal Alignment** to **Right**. This will make the label stick to the right edge of its container.

> **Note**: Any instance of `WKInterfaceObject`, including any descendants, default to having left horizontal alignment and top vertical alignment.

The nicely clipped corners are now gone from the image. This is because the new group has pushed the image down from the top of its parent, which was doing the clipping. However that was a nice visual touch, and `WKInterfaceGroups` make rounded corners very simple!

Select the **parent group** that contains the header and image, and change its **Background Color** to **#1F2124**.

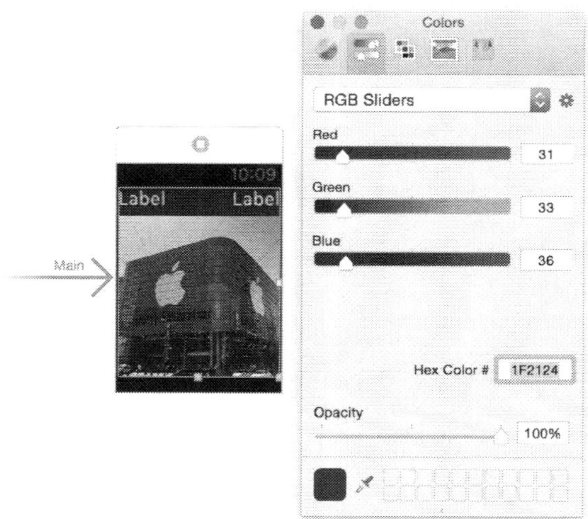

It's starting to look good! But the header looks a little... *tight*, doesn't it? It would be nice to have room for longer usernames.

Select **both** of the **labels** in the header and change the font to **Text Styles - Subhead**. This will shrink the text a bit but still respect the user's font scaling preferences.

While you're at it, select the **rightmost label** and change its **Text Color** to **Light Gray**.

Finally, the labels are still sitting too close to the edge of their container group. The text lined up to the left and right edges is a little hard on the eyes. Let's cinch that in!

Select the **group** containing both of the labels and change the **Horizontal Alignment** to **Center** and the **Width** to **Relative to Container** with a value of **0.95**. This will pinch the group to 95% of its parent's width and center it horizontally.

Build and run. Behold your progress on the Watch!

Laying out buttons

Images and text are all well and good, but what use is an app that you can't interact with? Using buttons is an easy way to add interactive features to your app.

> **Note**: Check out Chapter 3, "UI Controls" to learn about other awesome interactive elements in WatchKit—maps, sliders and more!

Still in **Interface.storyboard**, drag a new **group** into the controller, just under the group that contains the image and labels, and then drag two **buttons** inside your new group.

You can only see one button. Remember how the WWDC image disappeared when you added the header group? That was because the group was set to a *horizontal* layout and the image was pushed off-screen. But this time, instead of switching to a vertical layout, for each **button**, change the **Width** to **Relative to Container** with a value of **0.5**.

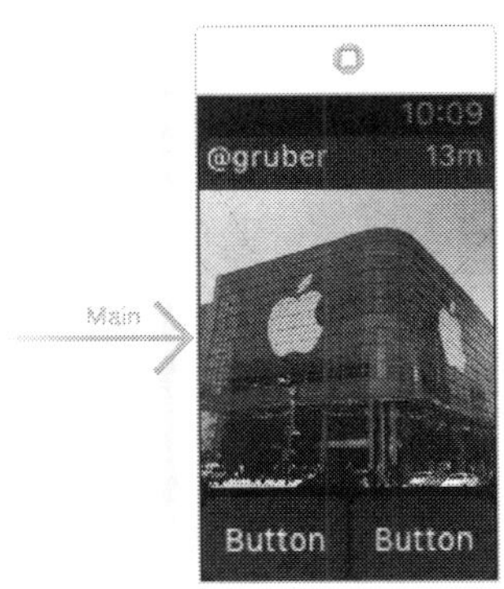

Using relative layouts is an easy way to squeeze all of your content into its container. It's like Auto Layout without the pain!

> **Note**: Just because it's simple to cram all your elements into their containers doesn't mean you should. Interactions on the Apple Watch are *extremely* brief, and you want to make it as easy as possible for your users to do things like tap buttons. It's OK to make them big!

You're not going to wire up the buttons in this chapter, but for aesthetic purposes, change the **Text** of the labels to **Like** and **Share**, respectively.

Dynamic layouts

While you're restricted to using `WKInterfaceObject` elements and you have to use storyboards, but that doesn't mean you can't get fancy with your layouts. There are a couple of properties that you can change on the fly, like height, width, alpha and hidden.

With the introduction of watchOS 2, you can even animate these properties—all of them apart from hidden!

In **Interface.storyboard**, drag a **button** element beneath the group that holds both of the buttons you added in the previous section. You might have to use the document outline to sneak it in there.

One nice thing about buttons in WatchKit is that they can either use the template background and label *or* act as their own group! This means you can stuff all sorts of other elements inside them and make the entire group interactive.

In the Attributes Inspector for the button you just added, change **Content** to **Group**. While you're there, change the new group's **Layout** to **Vertical**.

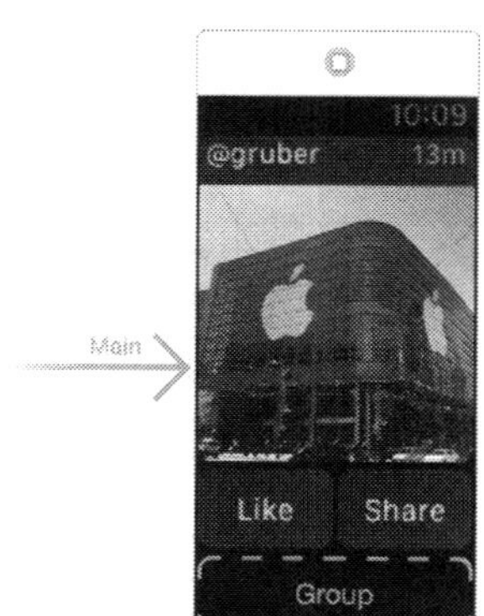

Drag three **labels** into your new button group.

Now come up with a quote to add for the WWDC image, something like, "My first WWDC was awesome! Can't wait for next year!" Set this as the text of the **first two labels**—yes, the same text for both labels. This will make sense in a minute!

Next, change each of the labels' attributes:

- Give the **first label** a **Font** of **Footnote**.
- Also give the **second label** a **Font** of **Footnote**, set **Lines** to **0** for an unlimited number of lines, and **check** the **Hidden** box.
- Lastly, change the **Text** of the **last label** to **Tap to view more...**, give it a **Font** of **System 11.0** and set **Text Color** to **Light Gray Color**.

Your document outline and storyboard will look something like this:

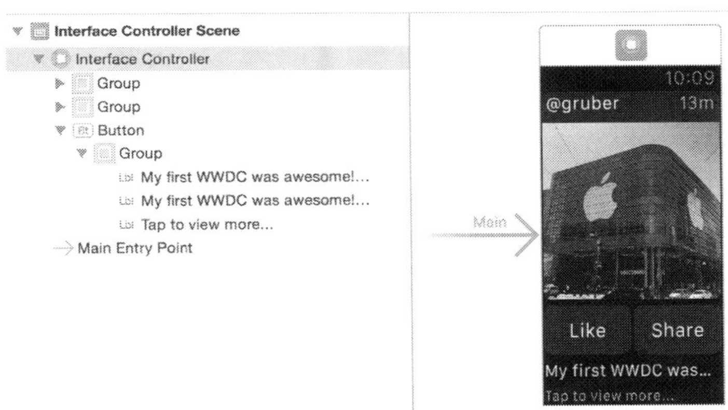

You're going to be using the button's tap interactions to toggle between the single and unlimited line labels to make it appear as if you're expanding and collapsing the text!

But to make this work, you're going to have to leave the storyboard and write...

In the assistant editor, open **InterfaceController.swift**. Drag and create an `IBOutlet` for each of the three labels that have your comment text. Name them `expandedCommentLabel`, `collapsedCommentLabel` and `moreLabel`, from top to bottom. You'll have to use the document outline to make an outlet for the hidden label.

While you're at it, **right-click** the **button** in the **document outline** and drag from the **action** option to `InterfaceController`. Name the action `onMoreButton`.

Open **InterfaceController.swift** in the main editor and add a variable named `expanded` just beneath your outlets, and initialize it to `false`. Your class will now have the following variables and method:

```
@IBOutlet var expandedCommentLabel: WKInterfaceLabel!
@IBOutlet var collapsedCommentLabel: WKInterfaceLabel!
@IBOutlet var moreLabel: WKInterfaceLabel!
var expanded = false

@IBAction func onMoreButton() {}
```

Add the following code inside `onMoreButton()`:

```
// 1
expanded = !expanded
// 2
collapsedCommentLabel.setHidden(expanded)
expandedCommentLabel.setHidden(!expanded)
// 3
moreLabel.setText(
  "Tap to " + (expanded ? "view less" : "view more") + "...")
```

1. You toggle the expanded flag to the opposite of what it was.
2. You hide or show the collapsed and expanded label, depending on the current state of `expanded`.
3. You change the label's text to reflect the expanded or collapsed state.

Build and run the Watch app. Scroll down to the comment, then tap the comment and see how easy it is to not only add a simple interaction, but also to get automatic layout based on content size!

Where to go from here?

This app currently represents the layout for one screen of what could be a fully functional app. Adding a new screen with a table that lists the posts and links the user to the interface you've created during this chapter would make a very usable app.

You can also wire up the Share and Like buttons, even if only to change some fake state. You'll definitely want to make sure you're comfortable with dynamically changing your interfaces with WatchKit.

If you're itching for even more layout, be sure to check out Chapter 15, "Advanced Layout" to learn how to bend layouts in WatchKit to your will!

Chapter 6: Navigation

By Ryan Nystrom

To build anything more than a single-screen app for the Apple Watch, you're going to need some means of navigating around the Watch app itself.

You're likely used to the many ways of navigating in iOS—navigation controllers, modal presentations, tab controllers, page controllers and so forth. On top of the built-in means of navigation, you can also take matters into your own hands and build custom `UIView` and `UIViewController` containers.

Navigation in WatchKit uses familiar concepts and takes the following forms:

- **Hierarchical**: similar to `UINavigationController`.
- **Page-based**: similar to `UIPageViewController`.
- **Modal**: any type of presentation or dismissal transition.

In WatchKit, unlike in UIKit, you are strictly limited to these three navigation methods. There is no custom navigation. In fact, you can't even mix and match hierarchical navigation and page-based navigation.

Well, not strictly. You can, however, use modals with either type—that is, you can modally present one type from the other. All you need to do is pick a base navigation type for your app and then decide whether mixing with modals is appropriate.

In this chapter, you'll first take a closer look at each of the three forms of navigation in WatchKit. After that, you'll dive into implementing a mixed navigation hierarchy in an app designed to help you navigate a color palette!

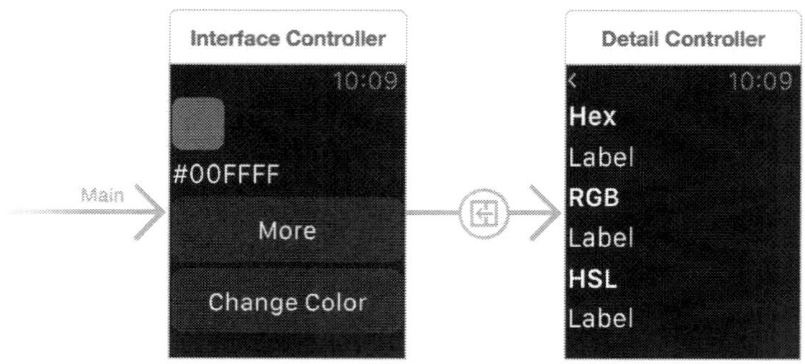

Getting around in WatchKit

Since the navigation systems in WatchKit are so limited, it's worth taking a moment to familiarize yourself with each type of navigation before turning to an app.

Hierarchical navigation

Hierarchical navigation will be one of the concepts most familiar to developers coming from iOS. In UIKit, `UINavigationController` manages pushing and popping child controllers and their animations.

WatchKit has a very similar system:

- You can push instances of `WKInterfaceController` onto the navigation stack.
- Swipe gestures and back buttons are built-in.
- You can use storyboards to set up the navigation, or you can do it in code.

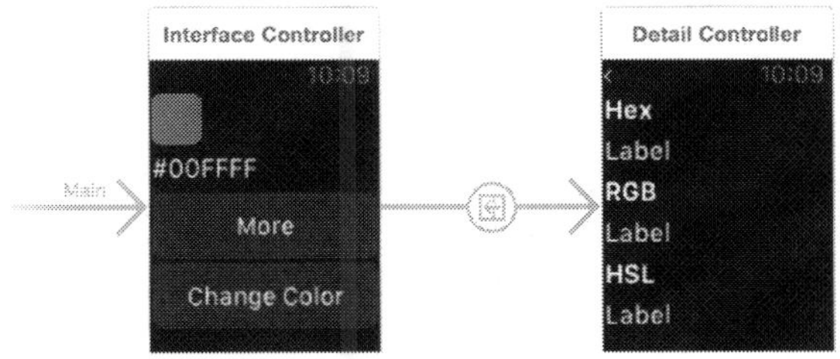

Instead of having a master navigation controller, WatchKit handles all of the navigation for you. You can simply Control-drag from a button to a controller, or simply call `pushControllerWithName(_:context:)` in your code.

There is an important concept that Chapter 2, "Architecture", touched on briefly: when using a hierarchical navigation system, WatchKit gives you an optional `context` parameter that you can pass between controllers as you navigate.

You'll most commonly use the `context` parameter when you're pushing from a master controller to a detail controller in the navigation stack. Instead of intercepting "stringly"-typed segues or adding lots of custom methods and properties, you can simply pass context objects between controllers.

UIKit has a great architecture for creating views, laying out their subviews and separating the concerns between controllers and views. However, communication between controllers has always been difficult. Using context-passing in WatchKit will keep your app's architecture clean and expressive.

> **Note**: You'll get your hands on context objects later in this chapter, and throughout the rest of the book!

Page-based navigation

This is the second main form of navigation in WatchKit. A page-based navigation structure is essentially a group of `WKInterfaceController` instances strung together laterally, between which you can swipe. Each page should contain a unique chunk of information and perform a unique function. In UIKit, this would be most similar to a `UIPageViewController`, which manages several instances of `UIViewController`, as seen in the Weather app.

When building a page-based WatchKit app, you aren't able to pass a context object between the different controllers in the group, nor are you able to use a hierarchical navigation within its pages, *ever*. It's one or the other.

> **Note**: You *can* get a mix of page-based navigation and hierarchical navigation by presenting either one modally from the other.

Apple presented an example of a page-based Watch app at the Apple Watch announcement—a timepiece app that has pages containing different representations of time, like digital, analog and solar.

To wire up a page-based interface, you simply have to connect each `WKInterfaceController` in Interface Builder, defining it as the next page. You'll have an initial controller—the one shown first—and a list of other controllers between which you can swipe back and forth.

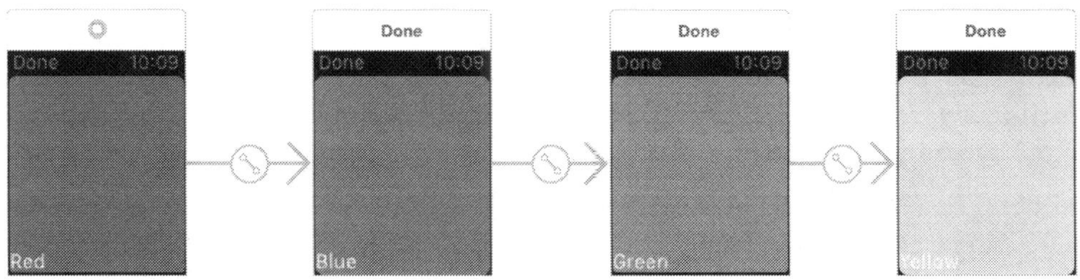

You do have limited control of a page-based app's hierarchy in code. There are two methods you can call:

- **`becomeCurrentPage()`**: Call this from within an instance of `WKInterfaceController` to animate that controller into view.
- **`reloadRootControllersWithNames(_:contexts:)`**: You can use this method to dynamically load different controllers into your interface. This can be useful for enabling or disabling certain controllers, based on data availability or user settings.

Modal navigation

The last possible means of getting around in WatchKit is by modal navigation. This is a familiar concept to anyone who's built iOS and Mac apps: think full screen pop-ups.

When you present a `WKInterfaceController` modally, it animates into view from the bottom of the screen, taking up the entire interface. Controllers presented modally have a built-in cancel button for getting back to the underlying controller. You can change the title of this button to something such as "Done" or "Finished", depending on the context of your modal:

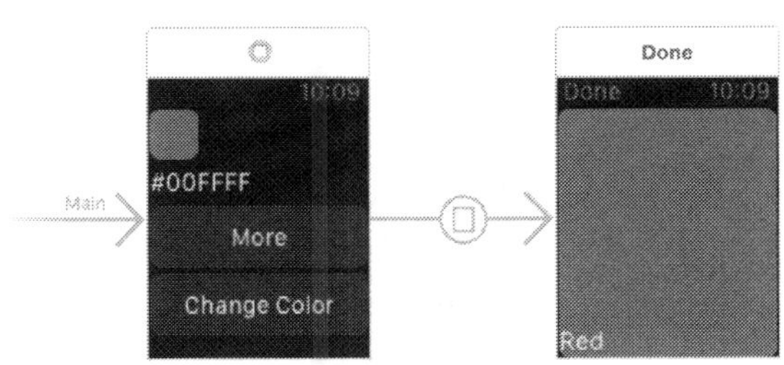

You can display a `WKInterfaceController` modally by either wiring it up in Interface Builder or calling one of the following methods in code:

- **`presentControllerWithName(_:context:)`**: This method displays a single `WKInterfaceController` modally. Note that you can pass a context object just as you can in hierarchical navigation.

- **`presentControllerWithNames(_:contexts:)`**: This method lets you display several instances of `WKInterfaceController` modally using page-based navigation, as previously discussed. In the event that your modal has multiple pages, use this method to provide easy access. This is an example of how you can combine multiple types of navigation.
- **`dismissController()`**: Use this method to dismiss the modal interface controller.

You should reserve modal navigation for context-specific interfaces, option selection or quick actions, all of which allow you to interrupt the current workflow for a specific purpose.

Getting started

Open the **ColorPicker.xcodeproj** starter project included with this chapter. You'll see several groups, including:

- **ColorPicker**: This group has basic functionality to run the app on an iOS device. You won't be adding anything here, but instead making the Watch app more functional than this version.
- **ColorPicker WatchKit App**: This group contains the storyboard and resources you'll need to navigate throughout the app.
- **ColorPicker WatchKit Extension**: This group contains all the classes and code requried to run the Watch app.
- **ColorPickerKit**: This is simply a single shared file that the iOS app and extension use to share models and logic. `ColorManager` is a singleton that knows about the colors available to your app, as well as the state of the selected color.

Build and run the Watch app. You'll see the screen below:

Right now, the app isn't very functional—neither of the buttons do anything! This app is intended to serve as a color picker, where users can select from a palette and view details about the chosen color, like its red, green and blue (RGB) values, or its hue, saturation and light (HSL) values. The standard hex color format should also be visible.

You can tell just by looking at the buttons that this app is, at root, going to have a hierarchical navigation structure. Each button will either push to a child controller or present a modal.

You'll be making this app fully functional by wiring up these buttons to navigation controllers to access the color palette, change colors and view a color's details. By the end, you'll have had a taste of all three forms of navigation in WatchKit.

A modally-presented, paged-based palette

Open **ColorPicker\WatchKit App\Interface.storyboard** and drag in a new **Interface Controller**. Go to the Attributes Inspector and change your new controller's **Identifier** to **ColorPalette**.

Drag in a new **group** element onto this controller and set its **Width** and **Height** size attributes to **Relative to Container**. Change the group's **background color** to **red** so you can confirm it's sized correctly.

While you're setting up interface elements, add a **label** as a child element to the group you just added. Change the label's **Vertical Position** to **Bottom**.

Your storyboard will now look something like this:

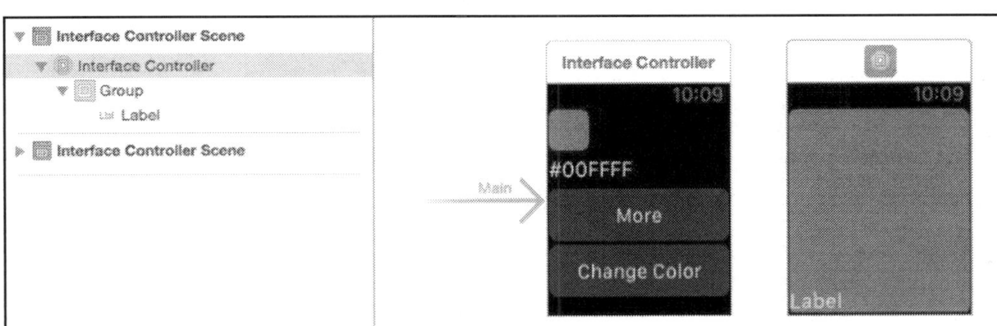

This controller will act as a template for a series of color swatches. You'll end up with a paged group of controllers that each has a background color of a swatch you can select, along with the hex value of the color.

Before you can start using the controller, you need a new class. Create one by selecting **ColorPicker WatchKit Extension** and selecting **File\New\File...**. Add a **Cocoa Class** named **ColorController**, and make sure it's subclassing `WKInterfaceController`:

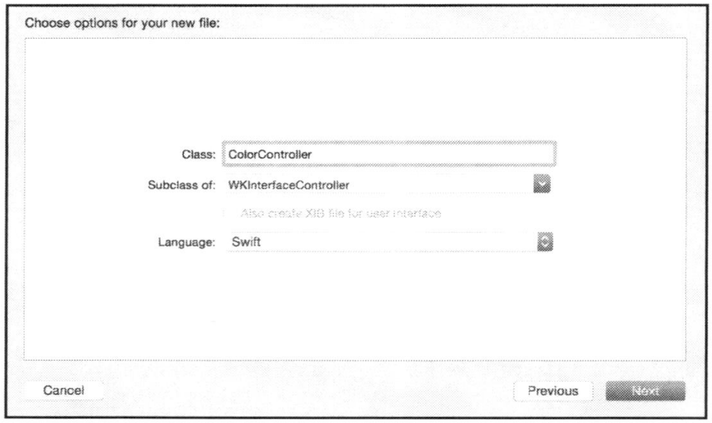

Open **ColorController.swift** and make sure that the file imports WatchKit. Sometimes Xcode will decide to import `Cocoa` in Watch app projects.

Open **Interface.storyboard** in the main editor and **ColorController.swift** in the assistant editor. In the storyboard, change the class of the new controller you created above to `ColorController`.

Drag an `IBOutlet` from both the **group** and **label** that you added previously and name them `backgroundGroup` and `label`, respectively.

Also, in **ColorController.swift**, add a variable to capture the current controller's color value:

```
var activeColor: UIColor?
```

Remember from the previous section that you can pass a `context` object to a presented or pushed controller in WatchKit. This object is of type `AnyObject`, so you can really make it whatever you want.

With **ColorController.swift** still open, replace the `awakeWithContext(_:)` definition with the following:

```
override func awakeWithContext(context: AnyObject?) {
  super.awakeWithContext(context)
  if let color = context as? UIColor {
    activeColor = color
    backgroundGroup.setBackgroundColor(color)
    label.setText("#" + color.hexString)
  }
}
```

This code checks that the `context` object that it receives is a `UIColor`, and if so, sets it as the `activeColor` as well as updates the state of the interface by changing the background color and the label's text.

> **Note**: `hexString`, an extension of `UIColor` in `ColorManager.swift`, simply converts the RGB values of the color to a hexadecimal representation.

Presenting the modal

Having a modal controller is great, but it's not of much value if your app doesn't present it!

Open **ColorPicker WatchKit App\Interface.storyboard** in the main editor and **InterfaceController.swift** in the assistant editor. **Right-click** the **Change Color button** and drag from the **selector** to your `InterfaceController` class. Create an `IBAction` named `changeColors`.

Update `changeColors()` to have the following implementation:

```
@IBAction func changeColors() {
  let colors = ColorManager.defaultManager.availableColors
  let names: [String] = colors.map { c in "ColorPalette" }
  presentControllerWithNames(names, contexts: colors)
}
```

This function takes the array of available colors from the `ColorManager` singleton, maps it to an array of strings that represent the identifiers you previously gave the `ColorController` in your storyboard, and then calls `presentControllerWithNames(_:contexts:)`, which modally presents a series of paged controllers.

Build and run the Watch app. Tap the Change Colors button. You'll now have a modal presentation of a paged list of color controllers. Try swiping left and right through the controllers.

Isn't it amazing how, with very little setup, you have both a modal and a paged navigation in one?

Notice how the title of the color controller is "Cancel". That's a little harsh, isn't it? The idea is to present a list of colors and *select* one, not cancel.

To change the title of the modal return button, open **Interface.storyboard** and select the **ColorPalette** controller. Change the **Title** attribute to **Done**.

Build and run again, and check the title of the modal return button. It should be a little more user-friendly:

Maintaining color selection

You've probably noticed that when you tap the "Done" button, nothing really changes with the root controller. You're still stuck on whatever color and text the storyboard is configured with.

To change that, open **ColorController.swift** and add the following code:

```
override func didAppear() {
  super.didAppear()
  if let color = activeColor {
    ColorManager.defaultManager.selectedColor = color
  }
}
```

didAppear() is called as soon as the controller is displayed on the Watch's screen. As you swipe between pages, you move from one controller to another, and didAppear() is called each time. Thus, you can assume that when this function is called, it is presenting the "selected" color. All you have to do is update the value of the ColorManager singleton, which is what you do above.

That will update your app's state, but what about getting the root controller to update its user interface?

Open **InterfaceController.swift** and add the following implementation of willActivate():

```
override func willActivate() {
  super.willActivate()
  let color = ColorManager.defaultManager.selectedColor
  colorGroup.setBackgroundColor(color)
  label.setText("#" + color.hexString)
}
```

Since this function is called *just before* the controller is displayed, it's a good place to update your interface before the color controllers are dismissed.

> **Note**: willActivate() is a good double-whammy, in that it's called on first run of your controller as well as any other time that the controller is about to be presented. This will feel familiar to anyone who's worked with viewWillAppear(_:) in UIViewController; it's a great opportunity to update your interface's state before you show it to the user.

Build and run the Watch app. Xhange to another color and dismiss. You'll be able to cycle through colors and see your UI update:

Pushing a child controller

You've saved the most common and familiar type of navigation for last: hierarchical navigation, with its typical *push and pop* style of interface.

Open **ColorPicker WatchKit App\Interface.storyboard** and add a new interface controller. Drag and drop **6** new **labels** into the controller. Change the **Font** of the **first**, **third**, and **fifth** labels to **Headline**. Also change the text of the same three labels to **Hex**, **RGB** and **HSL**, respectively.

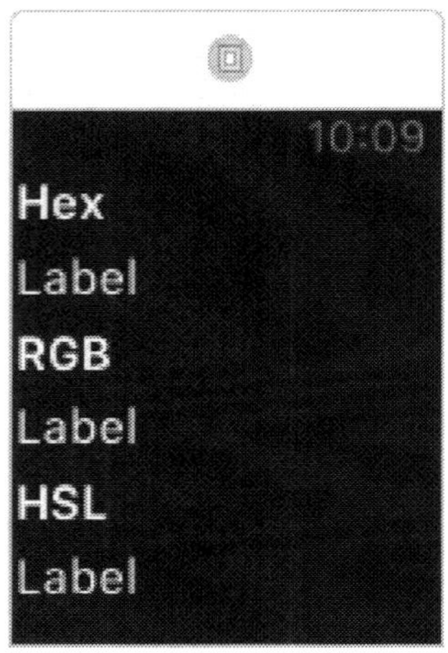

Add a new file to **ColorPicker WatchKit Extension**. Make it a **Cocoa Class** named **DetailController**, which subclasses `WKInterfaceController`.

Open **Interface.storyboard** and change your new controller's **class** to `DetailController`.

Open **DetailController.swift** in the assistant editor and create an `IBOutlet` for the second, fourth and sixth labels:

- Name the second label `hexLabel`
- Name the fourth label `rgbLabel`
- Name the sixth label `hslLabel`

Like so:

```
class DetailController: WKInterfaceController {

  @IBOutlet var hexLabel: WKInterfaceLabel!
  @IBOutlet var rgbLabel: WKInterfaceLabel!
  @IBOutlet var hslLabel: WKInterfaceLabel!

  override func awakeWithContext(context: AnyObject?) {
    super.awakeWithContext(context)
      // Configure interface objects here.
  }
```

Open **DetailController.swift** in the main editor and replace `willActivate()` with the following:

```
override func willActivate() {
  super.willActivate()
  let color = ColorManager.defaultManager.selectedColor
  hexLabel.setText("#" + color.hexString)
  rgbLabel.setText(color.rgbString)
  hslLabel.setText(color.hslString)
}
```

This code takes the currently selected color from the `ColorManager` singleton and configures the interface elements according to its values.

Now that you have your new controller, there's only one tiny step required to display it. Open **Interface.storyboard**, **right-click** and **drag** from the **More** button to your new detail controller. Let go, and then select the **push** option from the popup:

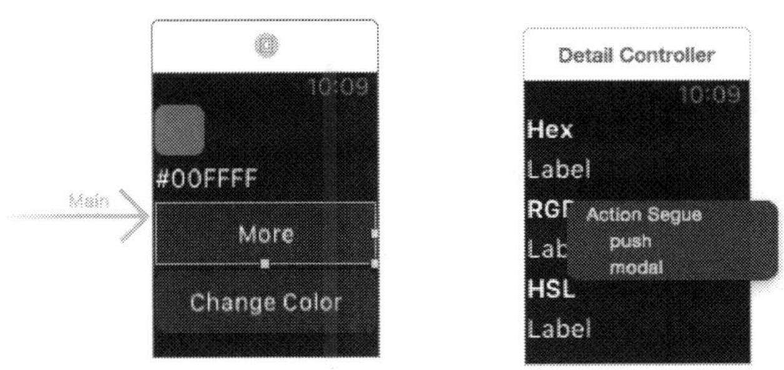

Build and run, select a different color and then tap the **More** button. You'll see hex, RGB and HSL values for the currently selected color. It's as simple as that!

Where to go from here?

Take a moment to reflect on your app's final navigational structure: beginning with an initial controller, you can either push a new controller or modally launch a series of page-based controllers. In other words, you were able to use all three navigation methods in one app by leveraging modals!

Remember that at root, your app needs to stick to either hierarchical or page-based navigation. And just because there are multiple and complex ways to navigate throughout a Watch app doesn't mean you should take every opportunity to use them all. The best apps for the Apple Watch have extremely limited navigation. Design your apps to be used for seconds, not minutes, which means very shallow navigation hierarchies.

There are a few more types of interface elements that aid in navigation, like tables and menus. Keep reading to learn more about how to get around in your apps!

Chapter 7: Tables

By Ryan Nystrom

When building any type of software application, you'll almost always find yourself needing to handle a dynamic amount of data. Typically, data sets are structured into arrays, sets or dictionaries, and often tables are the best way to display these collections.

Ever since the first proto-developer created the first program, we've had to build tools to abstract the handling and display of these data sets. `UITableView` in UIKit is an example of such a tool: a dynamic view that Apple has optimized to display an infinite amount of data in an efficient manner.

When creating apps for the Apple Watch, you'll undoubtedly run into the same scenario: You've got a dynamic collection of data and you need to display it on the tiny 38mm screen. This chapter will show you how to do just that.

Tables in WatchKit

Even if you've never built an app for iOS, as an iOS user you've experienced table views... everywhere. From Settings to Mail, `UITableView` is one of the staple views in iOS.

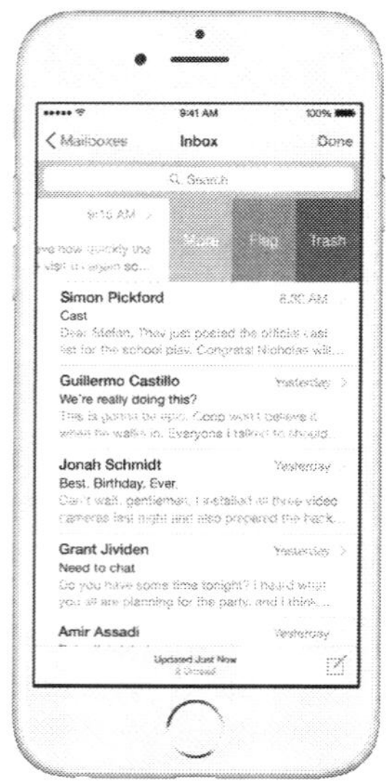

`UITableView` isn't available in WatchKit, but Apple has your back — in the form of `WKInterfaceTable`.

WatchKit's table class

`WKInterfaceTable` is similar to `UITableView` in that it manages the display of a collection of data, but the similarities pretty much end there.

For starters, `WKInterfaceTable` can only display a single dimension of data—no sections. This forces you to give your interfaces simple data structures.

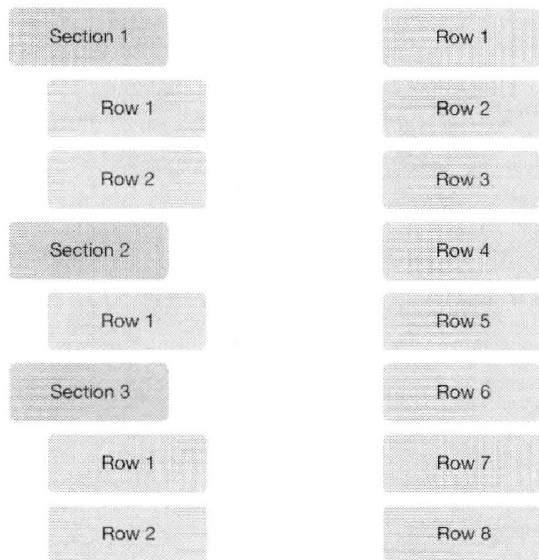

Tables in iOS Tables in WatchKit

Just like other `WKInterfaceController` and `WKInterfaceObject` classes, `WKInterfaceTable` works perfectly with storyboards. Once you've connected a table from your storyboard to an `IBOutlet`, you simply set the number of rows to display and the row type, like this:

```
table.setNumberOfRows(10, withRowType: "IngredientRow")
```

This single line sets up a table with 10 rows. You don't need to implement any data source or delegate protocols or override any methods. That's pretty sweet.

The **row type** in the code above is an identifier that behaves just like a `UITableViewCell` reuse identifier.

Enough with the theory—let's get cracking!

Getting started

Open **Recipes.xcodeproj** and build and run the iPhone app to get a feel for your Watch app's companion. This app is a simple recipe list that lets you browse each recipe's ingredients and directions.

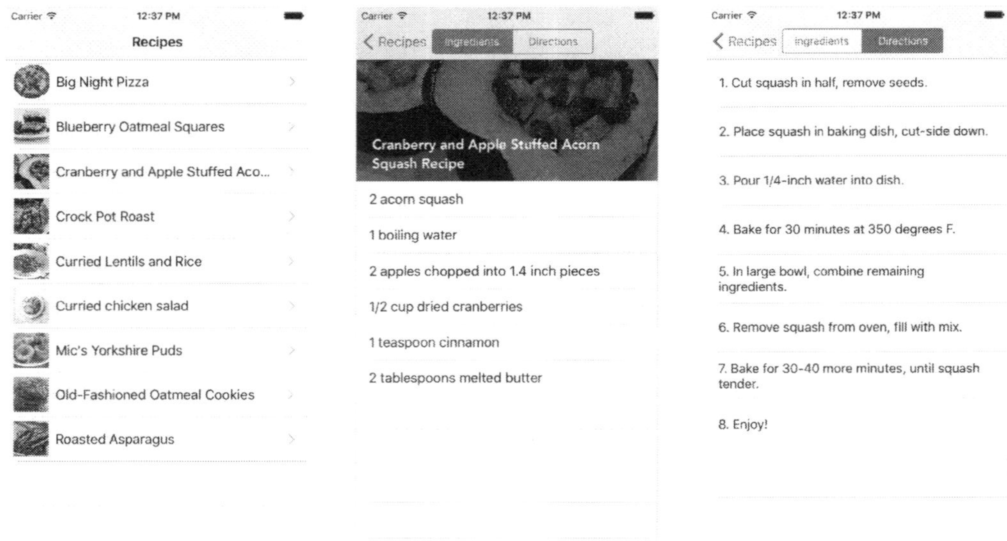

Notice how the iPhone app takes advantage of `UITableView`: there are a dynamic number of recipes, ingredients and directions—exactly what a table is meant to handle.

Open **Recipes WatchKit App\Interface.storyboard** and find the only controller in the scene. It's completely blank, waiting for you to fill it out.

First you need to display a list of all the recipes you have available. From the Object Library, drag a **table** into the controller.

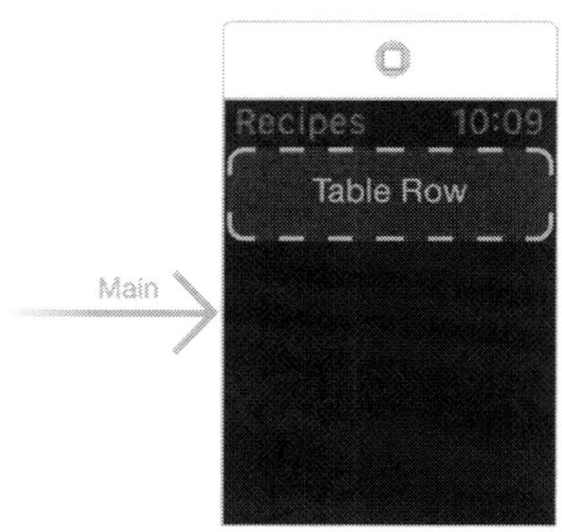

A new table gives you a placeholder row with an etched outline. You'll recognize this as almost identical to the placeholder for a `WKInterfaceGroup`, as you found in Chapter 5, "Layout". Take a look at a side-by-side comparison of the two placeholders:

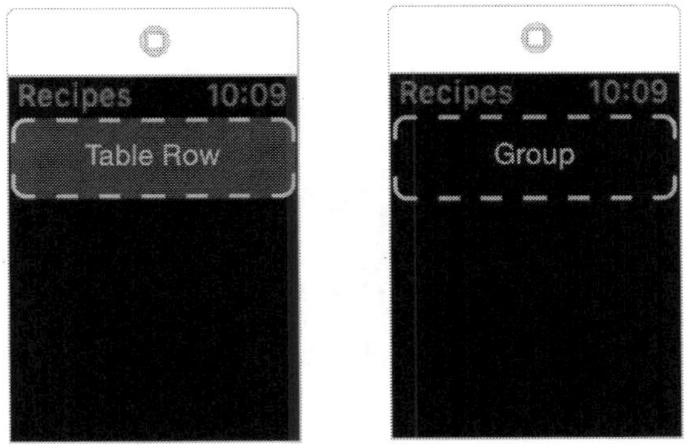

Click on the **Table Row** and notice in the document outline that it *actually is* a group! Each row in a `WKInterfaceTable` gets a base group interface element.

Drag two **labels** into the placeholder table row group. The labels will align themselves horizontally, but since the text will quickly expand, a vertical layout would be more manageable.

Select the **group** of the table row and change the **Layout** to **Vertical**. The row is now cutting off a little bit of the bottom label.

There's an easy fix. Since the base element of a table row is a group, it too can automatically size itself based on its content. With a couple of clicks in Interface Builder, Xcode will size all of your table rows *automatically*. No more mucking with dynamic cell heights or doing manual calculations!

Select the **group** of the table row and set the **Size Height** to **Size To Fit Content**. This will expand your table row to fit both labels.

The topmost label will display the name of the recipe, while the bottom label will display the total number of ingredients, which will give the user a clue about how much time they'll need to spend on the recipe. It might not be the night for an elaborate meal!

Select the **top label** and change **Lines** to **0**. This will allow the label to word wrap for as many lines as it needs. Since you've already set the group to size itself relative to its content, this means all the layout and sizing will happen automatically.

Next, select the **bottom label** and change the **Font** to **Footnote** and the **Color** to **Light Gray Color**, so the label has less visual prominence:

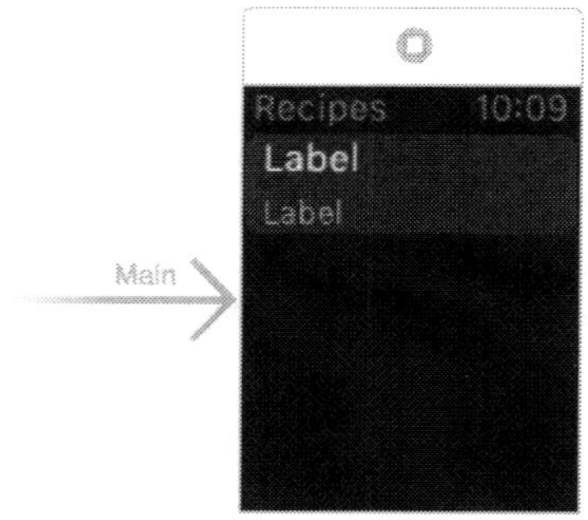

Controlling each row

Just as each cell in a `UITableView` is powered by a `UITableViewCell` subclass, `WKInterfaceTable` requires you to create what's called a **row controller** to represent each row.

A row controller has outlets and actions that are wired to the row in the storyboard. The `WKInterfaceController` that owns the table is then responsible for setting up and configuring your row controllers.

> **Note**: There is no row controller class. Each row controller only needs to inherit from `NSObject` to work with `WKInterfaceTable` rows. Remember that WatchKit interface objects are *proxy objects*, and not views themselves. Refer back to Chapter 2, "Architecture", for more information about proxy objects in WatchKit.

Right-click the **Recipes WatchKit Extension** group and select **New File...**. Create a new **Cocoa Class** that inherits from `NSObject` and name the file **RecipeRowController**.

Open **Recipes WatchKit App\Interface.storyboard** in the main editor and select the **Table Row Controller** from the document outline.

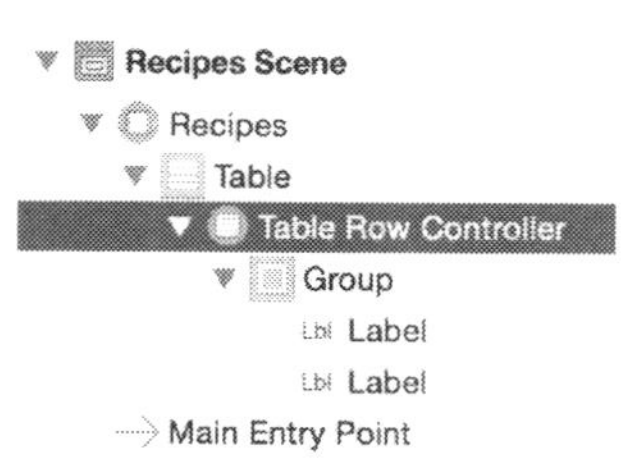

In the Identity Inspector, change the **Class** of the row to `RecipeRowController`. Then in the Attributes Inspector, change the **Identifier** to `RecipeRowType`.

Open **Recipes WatchKit Extension\RecipeRowController.swift** in the assistant editor.

Right-click and drag from the **top label** in the row to `RecipeRowController` and create a new outlet named `titleLabel`.

Repeat this for the bottom label and name the outlet `ingredientsLabel`.

While you have **Interface.storyboard** open in the main editor, open **RecipesController.swift** in the assistant editor. **Right-click** and drag from the **table** in the storyboard to `RecipesController` to create a new outlet named `table`.

Filling the table with data

Unlike `UITableView`, `WKInterfaceTable` has no delegate or data source protocols that you have to implement. Instead, there are only two main functions you need to use to add and display data:

- **`setNumberOfRows(_:withRowType:)`** specifies the number of rows in the table as well as each row controller's **identifier**, which in this case would be the string `RecipeRowType` that you added to the row controller in your storyboard. Use this method if all the rows in the table have the same identifier.
- **`rowControllerAtIndex(_:)`** returns a row controller at a given index. You must call this after adding rows to a table with either `setNumberOfRows(_:withRowType:)` or `insertRowsAtIndexes(_:withRowType:)`.

Open **Recipes WatchKit Extension\RecipesController.swift** and add an instance variable so you have access to recipe data:

```
let recipeStore = RecipeStore()
```

You can find `RecipeStore` in the `Shared\Storage` group; it reads recipe data in a specific scheme from `Recipes.json` and loads it into memory. Once you've initialized it, you can access available data through the `recipes` property.

Next, implement `awakeWithContext(_:)` for `RecipesController`:

```
override func awakeWithContext(context: AnyObject?) {
  super.awakeWithContext(context)
  // 1
  table.setNumberOfRows(recipeStore.recipes.count,
    withRowType: "RecipeRowType")
  // 2
  for (index, recipe) in recipeStore.recipes.enumerate() {
    // 3
    let controller =
      table.rowControllerAtIndex(index) as! RecipeRowController
    // 4
    controller.titleLabel.setText(recipe.name)
```

```
    controller.ingredientsLabel.setText(
      "\(recipe.ingredients.count) ingredients")
  }
}
```

Taking this step by step:

1. Use the `count` of the recipes to set the number of rows in the table. This table only has one type of row, so you pass `RecipeRowType` for the identifier.
2. Iterate through the rows with the handy Swift `enumerate()` function, so you can get the object *and* the index in one pass.
3. Next, get a row controller for each row in the table. You can force-unwrap to `RecipeRowController`, since you're only using one type of row in the table.
4. Finally, set the title to the recipe's name, and the ingredients to a count of the total number of ingredients in the table.

Build and run the Watch app. Check out your new list of recipes, now conveniently available on your wrist!

Getting directions

You have the recipes available in a list, but the app isn't *useful* yet. What good is the name of a recipe without any directions? If you're hungry, it might be a mild form of torture.

To include the directions, you need another controller to display all the steps in a recipe. With the dynamic nature of each recipe's list of steps, a table would be an excellent choice here, just like in the iPhone app counterpart.

Open **Recipes WatchKit App\Interface.storyboard** and drag a new **interface controller** into the scene.

From the document outline, select the **RecipeRowType**, right-click and drag to your new controller. When you let go, a modal will appear. Select the **Push** option to create a segue between the two controllers:

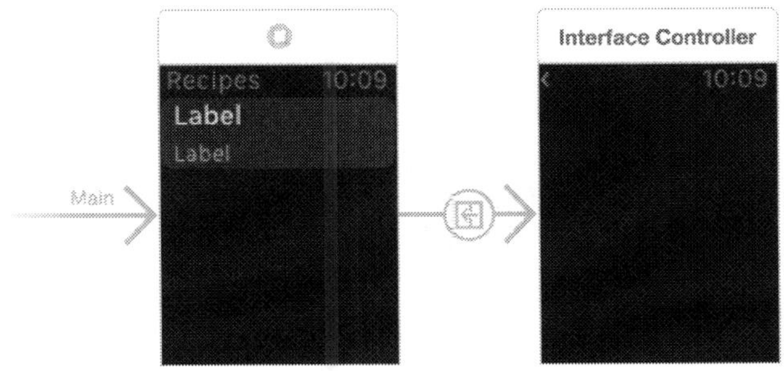

`WKInterfaceTable` rows have the ability to trigger navigation events when someone selects them. In this case, you're implementing a *push* navigation to the new controller from the selected row.

> **Note**: To learn more about different navigation types, like modals and pages, check out Chapter 6, "Navigation".

Open **RecipesController.swift** and add the following method:

```
override func contextForSegueWithIdentifier(
  segueIdentifier: String, inTable table: WKInterfaceTable,
  rowIndex: Int) -> AnyObject? {

  return recipeStore.recipes[rowIndex]
}
```

Overriding this `WKInterfaceController` method lets you decide what context to pass to the receiving controller, via `awakeWithContext(_:)`, when you trigger a segue from a table row selection. This method is *incredibly* convenient, because it gives you all the information you need: the identifier of the segue and the index of the selected row.

Since you only have one row and one segue, you can safely assume this method is called only when someone taps a recipe!

Go back to **Interface.storyboard** to start setting up your new controller.

Drag a **table** into the new controller. In the Attributes Inspector, change the **Prototype Rows** to **2**. You're going to use the first row as the "header" of the recipe and then add a row for each step in the recipe's directions.

Drag a **label** element into the **first row group**. Change this label's **Lines** to **0** so it will word wrap, as you did for the previous table; also, change the **Font** to **Headline**. This label will display the name of the recipe.

Drag another **label** into the **second row group** and change the **Lines** to **0**. You don't need to do anything else for this label, which will contain the text for one of the recipe's directions.

Select the **first row's group** and change the **Color** to **Clear Color** to help the header stand out from each of the steps.

For both of the **row groups**, change the **Size Height** to **Size To Fit Content**.

Your interface should now look like this:

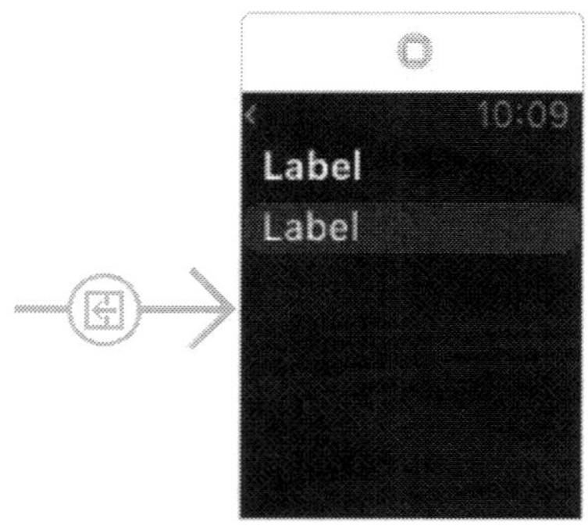

Using multiple rows

As you did in the previous section, you need to make row controller classes for each row, so that you can connect interface element outlets and relate a class to a specific identifier.

Right-click **Recipes WatchKit Extension** and select **New File...**. Create a new **Cocoa Class** that subclasses `NSObject`, and name it **RecipeHeaderController**.

Do this again to create a class named **RecipeStepController**.

Back in **Interface.storyboard**, select the **first row controller**. Change its **Class** to `RecipeHeaderController` and its **Identifier** to `RecipeHeader`. Also, since you can't tap these rows, **uncheck** the **Selectable** option.

Repeat this process for the **second row controller** using the class `RecipeStepController` and the identifier `RecipeStep`.

Open **RecipeHeaderController.swift** in the assistant editor. Create an outlet from the label in the row and name it `titleLabel`.

Next, open **RecipeStepController.swift** in the assistant editor, create an outlet for that row's label and name it `stepLabel`.

You need a class for your new controller, so right-click **Recipes WatchKit Extension** and select **New File...**. Create a new **Cocoa Class** that inherits from `WKInterfaceController` and name it **RecipeDetailController**.

Back in **Interface.storyboard**, change the **Class** of your new controller to `RecipeDetailController`. Make sure that the **Module** is set to **Recipes_WatchKit_Extension** and *not* to the main app.

Finally, select the **table** in the new controller and, with **RecipeDetailController.swift** open in the assistant editor, create an outlet named `table`.

Just to recap, you should now have:

- `RecipeDetailController`, created with a `WKInterfaceTable` outlet and set to the new controller's class;
- `RecipeHeaderController`, created with one `WKInterfaceLabel` outlet and connected to the first row in the table;
- `RecipeStepController`, created with one `WKInterfaceLabel` outlet and connected to the second row in the table.

Good work setting everything up! Now let's get cooking.

Open **RecipeDetailController.swift** and add the following code:

```
override func awakeWithContext(context: AnyObject?) {
  super.awakeWithContext(context)
  // 1
  if let recipe = context as? Recipe {
    // 2
    let rowTypes: [String] = ["RecipeHeader"]
    table.setRowTypes(rowTypes)
    // 3
    for i in 0..<table.numberOfRows {
      // 4
      let row = table.rowControllerAtIndex(i)
      if let header = row as? RecipeHeaderController {
```

```
        header.titleLabel.setText(recipe.name)
      }
    }
  }
}
```

1. You make sure that whatever context is being passed exists and is of type `Recipe`.
2. Next, you create an array of the row controller identifiers and set it on the `WKInterfaceTable`. You have to use `setRowTypes(_:)` when dealing with multiple row controller types. For now, you simply set up the header row controller. The number of rows in the table will directly correlate with the length of the array passed in this method.
3. Next, you iterate the rows in the table by using the convenience `numberOfRows` property on the table.
4. Finally, you get the row controller at each index, and if the controller is of type `RecipeHeaderController`, you set up the `titleLabel` with the recipe's name.

Build and run, and select a recipe to view your one cell!

Go back to **RecipeDetailController.swift** and update the `if`-statement inside `awakeWithContext(_:)` to the following:

```
if let recipe = context as? Recipe {
  // 1
  let rowTypes: [String] =
    ["RecipeHeader"] + recipe.steps.map({ _ in "RecipeStep" })
  table.setRowTypes(rowTypes)
  for i in 0..<table.numberOfRows {
    let row = table.rowControllerAtIndex(i)
    if let header = row as? RecipeHeaderController {
      header.titleLabel.setText(recipe.name)
    // 2
    } else if let step = row as? RecipeStepController {
```

```
      step.stepLabel.setText("\(i). " + recipe.steps[i - 1])
    }
  }
}
```

1. Swift makes dealing with arrays incredibly simple. Here you create an array of `"RecipeStep"` identifiers for each `step` in the recipe. You also append the mapped array of identifiers to the header identifier array, giving you a list of strings—the first string is for the header and the rest are for the steps.
2. You add an `else-if` statement to check if the row controller is of type `RecipeStepController`. If it is, you set the text of the step label to the step number and the step text. Remember, because you added a header, you need to subtract 1 from the index to map the row index back to your data.

Build and run the watch app. Now you'll see the name of the recipe as well as all the cooking instructions. It's time to go make yourself lunch!

Where to go from here?

What you've seen here is just the beginning of what you can do with tables. For instance, because row controllers each have their own sizeable groups, you can get creative by adding lots of interface elements with as much dynamic content as you like.

`WKInterfaceTable` is designed to be simple, but you can definitely bend it to your will. In Chapter 16, "Advanced Tables", you'll learn how to add more dynamic data types to your tables, like sections and headers, as well as use editing features like updating, inserting and deleting rows.

Chapter 8: Menus

By Ryan Nystrom

If you've ever wanted to present a context menu or alert view for a particular action in iOS, you've had to create a `UIAlertView` or `UIActionSheet` (iOS 7 or earlier), or create a `UIAlertController` (iOS 8 and later). Whether picking an action from a menu or confirming a more permanent action like deletion, creating menus in iOS has always taken some time.

For WatchKit, Apple introduced a new and simple API for creating context menus. Instead of creating menus from scratch and wiring up delegates or closures, you simply create menu items in Interface Builder and wire up their actions just like you would with buttons or other interface objects.

Wiring up outlets and code can sometimes be confusing when you don't know where the action is initiated. With the menu system in WatchKit, you can create your button actions and menu actions in the same way.

The one pitfall is that if your interfaces are generally dynamic, creating static context menu items in Interface Builder does limit the functionality of your application, as these can't be changed at runtime. But on the plus side, no code!

In this chapter, your starter project is a timer app for race car drivers, one that badly needs a few menus. Working with the Watch app, you'll learn how to create simple-yet-powerful menu items, both statically using Interface Builder and dynamically through code. You'll also learn how to wire up menus, create their icons and respond to different actions.

Understanding WatchKit menus

Before diving into creating your first menu, you need to understand how menus work in WatchKit and how you can create them.

Gestures

iOS has a gesture called a “long press” that you can represent in code by using a `UILongPressGestureRecognizer`. WatchKit has a similar gesture, but its semantics are hidden from you. Instead of a long press, you have what's called a “force touch” gesture.

When the user presses firmly on the screen, it’s considered a force touch. The Apple Watch hardware takes care of determining the difference between a hard force touch to bring up a menu, and a softer tap. You can’t change the behavior of a force touch; it will always bring up the context menu, if one exists.

Menu interface

To create a menu, you first need to set up menu items. Each menu item has a title that's displayed as text in the interface and an image that's displayed as a vibrant image over a blurred background.

The Apple Watch comes with a selection of stock icons you can use, shown below:

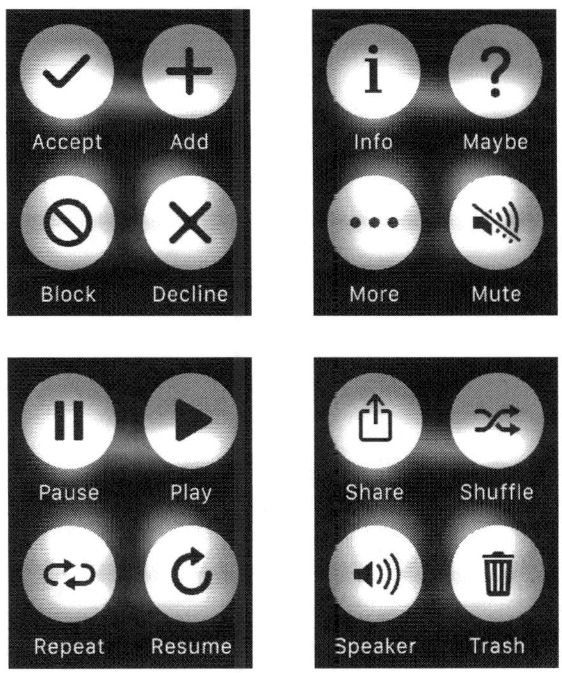

Since the 38mm and 42mm Watches have different screen densities, if you want to create a custom icon, you'll need to create differently sized icons for each device. The **Apple Watch Human Interface Guidelines** includes recommendations for designing your custom icons:

- For 38mm icons, you'll want to make your icon canvas size 70 pixels and the content size 46 pixels. When you're making lines for glyphs, keep them between 4 and 8 pixels.

- When making icons for the 42mm Apple Watch, make your icon canvas size 80 pixels and the content size 54 pixels. When you're making lines for glyphs, keep them between 5 and 9 pixels.

> **Note**: The **canvas size** of an icon is the entire size that it occupies. The **content size** is the actual bounds of the icon: its height and width. When creating WatchKit icons, you can simply fit your icons into the content size and the system will scale the images appropriately.

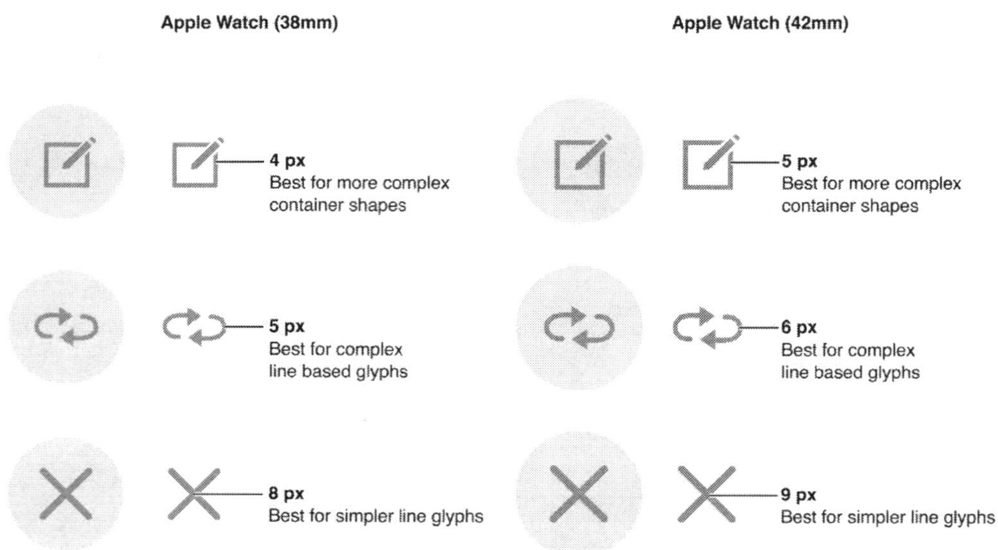

At most, you can only fit four menu icons onto the screen at once. Usually, one icon is reserved for a Cancel button, leaving you only three icons for your custom actions. Be careful to choose only actions and icons that pertain to the interface controller that the user is currently viewing.

> **Note**: Menu interfaces don't scroll or allow you to add arbitrary interface objects. If you add more than four objects, WatchKit will only show the first four and discard the rest.

Default actions

Unlike `UIActionSheet` or `UIAlertView`, you don't have to conform to any protocols or wire up any delegates to get WatchKit menus working. Instead, you simply create menu items in Interface Builder or in code and then connect the items to actions in your

`WKInterfaceController` using the familiar target-action pattern.

By default, menu items are Cancel actions. If you don't connect an action, either through Interface Builder or through code, tapping on a menu item will simply dismiss the context menu. This makes creating Cancel buttons a breeze!

Getting started

Open **TrackTimer.xcodeproj** and build and run the **TrackTimer** iOS scheme on an iPhone or the simulator. This simple app is for any racetrack enthusiast or gear-head;

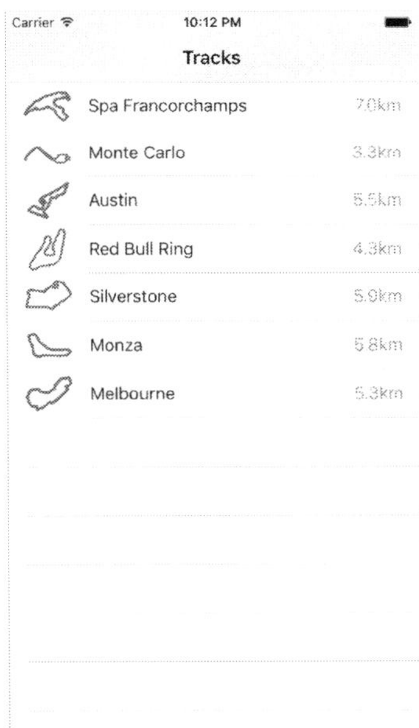

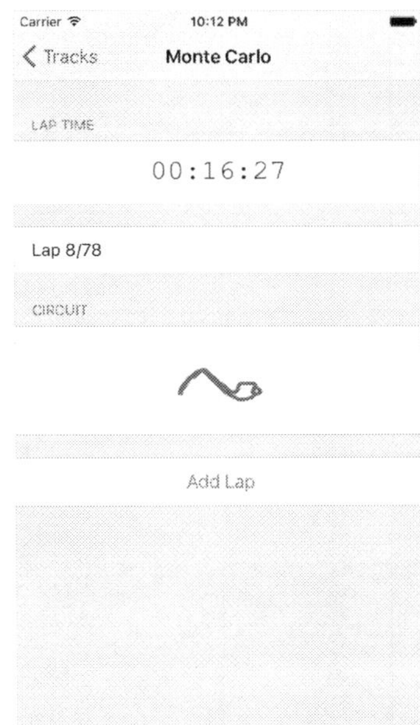

You can select from many of the world's most famous racetracks, and then time each of your laps on the track.

However, if you're driving a multi-million dollar car at hundreds of miles per hour, you don't have time to take out your phone! Your hands are going to be a little busy with the steering wheel.

Maybe you could make something that would track your lap times but still let you *watch* the road...

OK, OK, enough with the bad puns—let's get to building something!

Sorting with menus

Switch to the **TrackKit WatchKit App** scheme, and build and run to take a look at the starter Watch app:

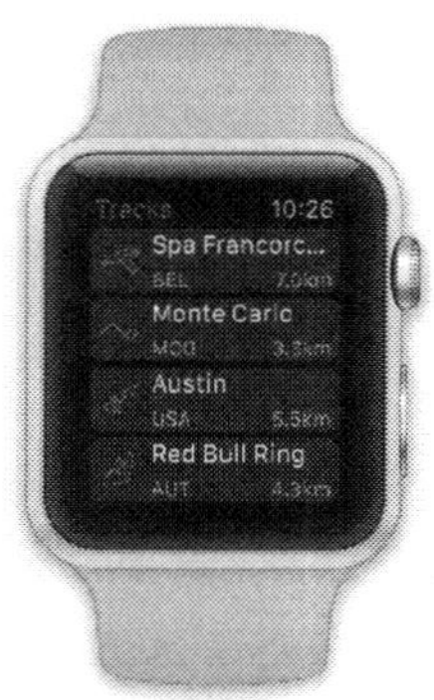

Right now it's not very useful; all of the tracks are sorted in seemingly random order and the timer controller only lets you add laps.

First of all, it would be handy if you could sort the tracks. The most obvious way to do this would be alphabetically, but more diehard racers might know the tracks by length.

Providing quick access to options that swap between states and toggle switches is exactly what menus were made for! Menus are simple to use and don't clutter up the user interface with things that aren't always needed.

Open **TrackTimer WatchKit App\Interface.storyboard** and find the only interface controller in the Watch app. In the Object Library, find and drag a **menu** to on top of the only controller.

Nothing shows up in the controller, but the document outline should have a new item in it named **Menu**.

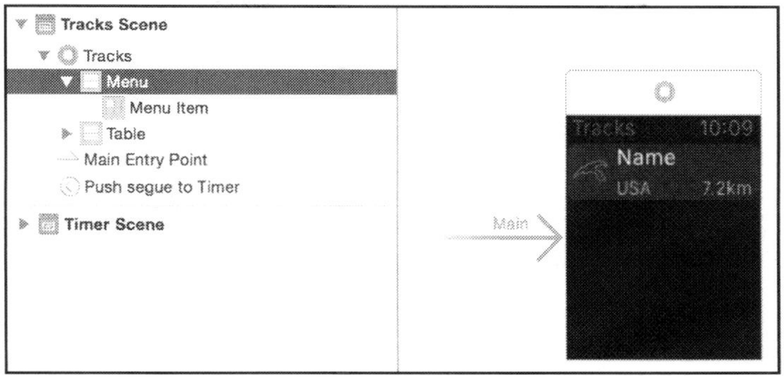

Select the new **menu** and in the Attributes Inspector, change **Items** to **2**. This will give you two menu items that you can use to toggle between alphabetical and track-length sorting.

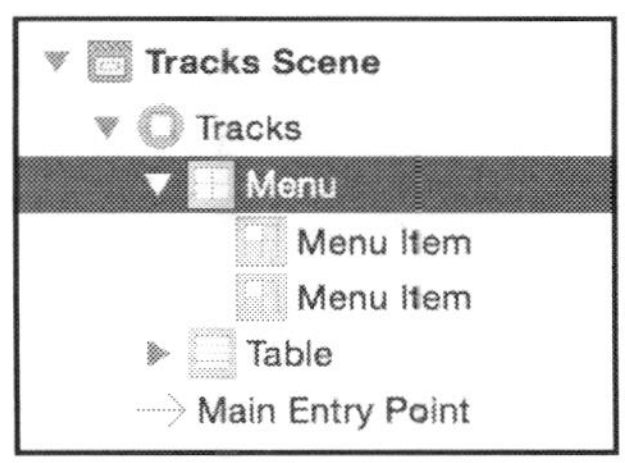

There are now two menu item elements inside the menu. Each of these items represents an option that will be displayed over the tracks controller after you force-touch.

Select the **first menu item** and change the **Title** to **Alphabetical** and the **Image name** to **alpha**:

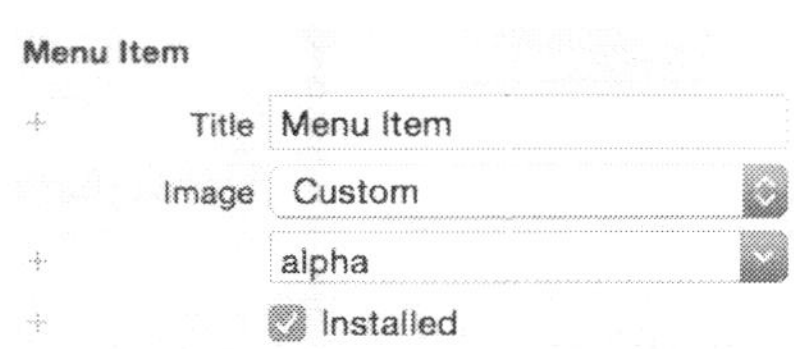

Do the same for the second **menu item**, but change the **Title** to **Circuit Length** and the **Image name** to **ruler**.

> **Note**: Both the **alpha** and **ruler** images are supplied for you in TrackTimer WatchKit App\Assets.xcassets, with just a single size. If you wanted to better support both the 38mm and 42mm Watches, you could use the + button next to **Image name** to provide *different* images for the different Watch sizes.

Build and run your app, and force-touch the controller. In just a short space of time you have two menu items set up and working. How easy was that?

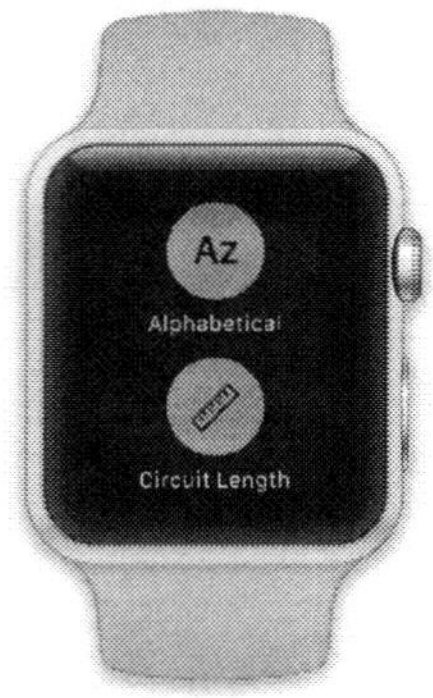

> **Note**: If you're using the Watch simulator, toggling between force-touch and normal touches is a little cumbersome. Use **Command-Shift-2** to enable force-touch when you click the mouse. To go back to normal touches, use **Command-Shift-1**.

Wiring up menus

It may have been easy to get menus on the screen, but you probably noticed they don't *do anything*. However, getting them to work is just as easy as adding a `WKInterfaceButton` or any other control!

With **TrackTimer WatchKit App\Interface.storyboard** still open in the main editor, open **TrackTimer WatchKit Extension\TrackTableController.swift** in the assistant editor.

Select the **first menu item** labeled **Alphabetical**, right-click and drag from the document outline to `TrackTableController` and create a new `IBAction` named `onAlphaSort`.

Do the same for the other **menu item** labeled **Circuit Length** and create an action named `onCircuitSort`.

Open **TrackTableController.swift** in the main editor and find the method `updateTable()`.

Replace the first two lines of the method:

```
func updateTable() {
  tracks = Track.famousTracks
```

With the following:

```
// 1
func updateTable(alphaSort: Bool) {
  // 2
  let sort: ((Track, Track) -> Bool)
  // 3
  if alphaSort {
    sort = { $0.name < $1.name }
  } else {
    sort = { $0.circuitLength < $1.circuitLength }
  }
  // 4
  tracks = Track.famousTracks.sort(sort)
```

1. You change the method signature to take in a `Bool` parameter to indicate whether or not you want to do alphabetical sorting.
2. You create a closure called `sort` that takes in two `Track` objects and returns a `Bool`.
3. Based on the `alphaSort` parameter, you set the `sort` closure to check either the order of the string `name` or the number `circuitLength`.
4. You use the Swift `sort(_:)` function and the `sort` closure to drive the sorting order of the tracks.

Call this new method from inside `onAlphaSort()` by adding the following statement to the bottom of the method:

```
updateTable(true)
```

And again in `onCircuitSort()`:

```
updateTable(false)
```

Notice you're alternating the `alphaSort` parameter in each method.

If you try to build, you'll still get a compiler error. Find `awakeWithContext(_:)` and change the call to `updateTable()` to this:

```
updateTable(true)
```

This will initialize the table with an alphabetically sorted list.

Build and run the Watch app. Try selecting either of your new menu items. `updateTable(_:)` simply rebuilds the `WKInterfaceTable` in response to a menu tap. It's as simple as that!

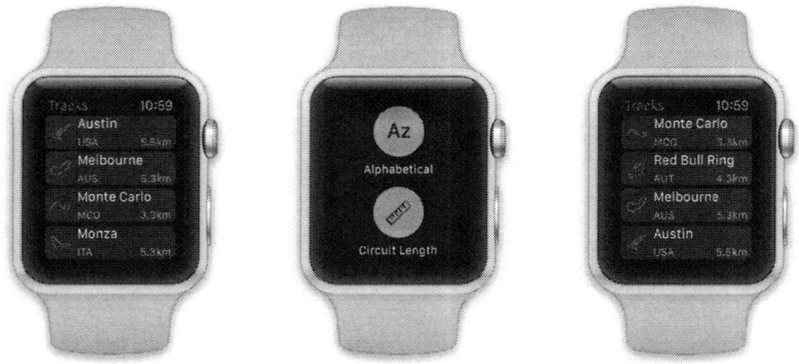

Dynamic menus

Creating menus in your storyboards is a quick and easy way to accomodate different options or settings, but what if your menu items should reflect different states of an app?

The bundled **Workout** Watch app shows different menus according to whether you've paused or resumed your workout.

Since the Watch app already makes it easier to safely blast through racetracks, it would be great to have a similar ability to pause, resume and end, in case you were to get an important phone call.

Open **TrackTimer WatchKit Extension\TimerController.swift** and take a moment to get familiar with a couple of properties and methods in the class:

- **`TrackTimer`** is a class that takes a `Track` and contains data and functionality about a single race: the current lap and start/pause times. It also has several methods to mutate the state of the current race: `addLap()`, `resume()` and `pause()`. Finally, the helpers `hasStarted` and `isPaused` check the state of a race.
- **`awakeWithContext(_:)`** tries to restore a race that's already in progress.
- **`updateState()`** updates the interface based on the current status of the `TrackTimer`. It toggles the text of the Start button and the lap counter.
- **`startTimer()`** is called to kick off the `WKInterfaceTimer`.
- **`onTimerButton()`** is the `IBAction` wired up to the Start button.

You're going to add menu items based on the state of the existing race. If a race is in progress, you want End and Pause options. If you're already paused, you want to swap the Pause item with one named Play.

Since your menu items are dynamic, you can't use storyboards to accomplish menu item swaps, because there's no way to connect an `IBOutlet` to an item and hide or show it. Instead, you're going to rely on the `TrackTimer` to tell you the race's state, and build your menus *in code*.

Open **TimerController.swift** and add a new method:

```
func updateMenuItems() {
  // 1
  clearAllMenuItems()
  // 2
  if trackTimer.hasStarted {
    // 3
    addMenuItemWithItemIcon(.Decline, title: "End",
      action: "reset")
    // 4
    if trackTimer.isPaused {
      addMenuItemWithItemIcon(.Play, title: "Resume",
        action: "startTimer")
    } else {
      addMenuItemWithItemIcon(.Pause, title: "Pause",
        action: "pauseTimer")
    }
  }
}
```

1. Each time you update the menu items, you need to clear the existing items because the menu API in `WKInterfaceController` only lets you add new items.
2. You only add menu items if the race has started; otherwise, there isn't anything to

end, pause or resume!

3. You add the End menu item using the `.Decline` system icon (the big X). The action "reset" is a Swift shortcut for using a `Selector`. You'll add this method in a bit.
4. You check if the race is paused and add a Pause or Play item accordingly. Notice that the Play menu item uses the existing `startTimer()` method.

> **Note**: There are two other methods you can use to add menu items to your controllers: `addMenuItemWithImageNamed(_:title:action:)` to use a custom image included in your image assets, and `addMenuItemWithImage(_:title:action:)` to use a `UIImage` for your custom icon.

Next, you need to add implementations for the two methods, `reset()` and `pauseTimer()`, that your menu items will call. Add this code to `TimerController`:

```
func pauseTimer() {
  trackTimer.pause()
  updateState()
}

func reset() {
  trackTimer.end()
  updateState()
}
```

Each method calls the respective `TrackTimer` method and then calls `updateState()` to update the user interface.

Lastly, add the following to the bottom of `updateState()`:

```
updateMenuItems()
```

This will update your menu icons any time the state of the race changes.

Build and run the Watch app. Select a track, and then tap the Start! button to trigger a race. You can now force-touch to show the menu after the race starts in order to toggle between ending, pausing and resuming the race!

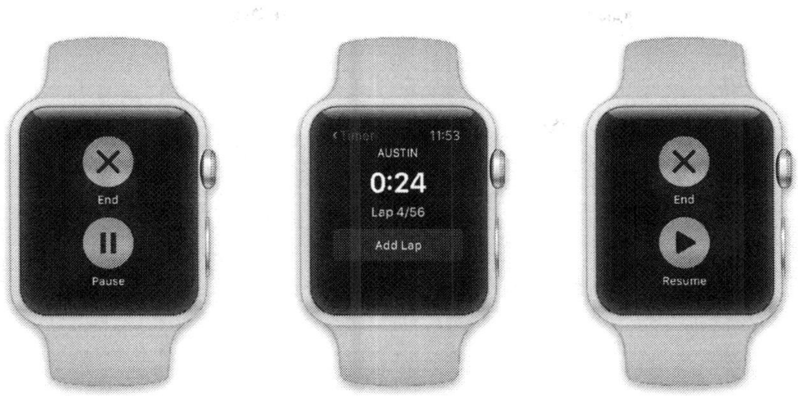

Where to go from here?

One of the most challenging aspects of using a menu in your `WKInterfaceController` subclass is deciding what needs to be shown. Make sure you spend time upfront deciding why a certain action should be a menu instead of a button or a table row.

Once you decide that a menu is necessary, you've seen in this chapter just how easy it is to add, configure and hook up your menu items using either storyboards or code. Remember that apps on the Apple Watch are used for very brief periods of time, so take advantage of menus to make toggling options a breeze.

Chapter 9: Animation

By Jack Wu

When Apple originally released watchOS, WatchKit offered only one way to perform your own animations—by flipping through image frames like a GIF. Even with such a limited API, developers sprang into action, creating some truly impressive animations. However, deep down, we weren't satisfied; the dream of the ability to captivate users through animations lived on.

Now, watchOS 2 has arrived and grants *one* additional animation API. Just one—but a very good one. It's once again time to bring all of your creativity to bear and make the absolute most of this new API.

This chapter will get you going by first introducing the three main ways you can perform animations in watchOS 2 and the different effects achieved by each method. Then, you'll use these methods in practice by creating some basic animation effects for a beautiful—but not yet animated—app called Woodpecker.

Later, in Chapter 17, "Advanced Animations", you'll discover a few more techniques to make the most of the APIs and create some dazzling animations in Woodpecker. So let's get started!

Getting started

No one really knows how long it takes to form a habit. Some say three weeks, others say three months. In reality, most people don't care how long it takes—unless it takes too long!

Woodpecker is an app that focuses on what you know for sure: habits are formed through repetition. That's all there is to it. A woodpecker doesn't say "I'll peck this wood for 3 hours"; it pecks until it finds the food. The Woodpecker app takes this and applies it to your habits.

Simply add a task, set a goal for the habit-forming repetition count, and peck away! Can't think of a task? How about "complete a raywenderlich.com tutorial"? 800 times should be enough, right? :]

Now that you're excited to work on this app, locate the starter project for **Woodpecker** and open **Woodpecker.xcodeproj** in Xcode.

Build and run the iPhone app. Get a feel for the app and how it works. Create a few tasks and finish them. It's very simple, and a bit delightful, even if I do say so myself. :]

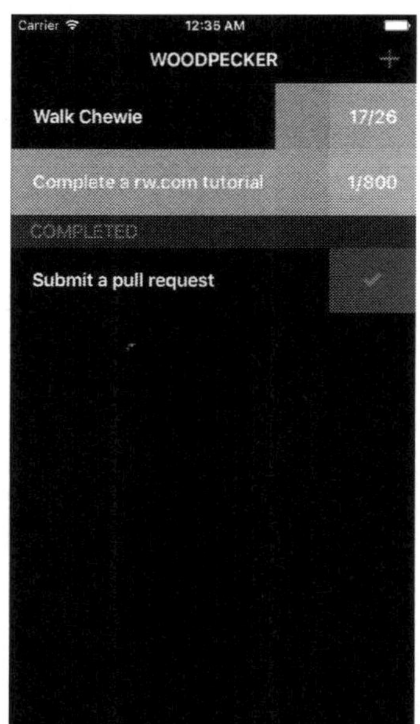

Now build and run the Watch app. Again, create a few tasks and finish them.

The simplicity is there, but the delightfulness? Well, you're about to add that. :]

> **Note**: You need to use Force Touch to add multiple ongoing tasks. This is a bit of a pain on the simulator. Press **Command-Shift-2** to perform a force touch, then press **Command-Shift-1** to perform a regular touch on the menu item.

Take a moment and browse through Woodpecker's source code. Pay extra attention to the two interface controllers in the WatchKit extension—that's where you'll be adding the magic.

Animation overview

The animation APIs, like most things in WatchKit, are extremely simple yet very powerful. There are three main types of animations in WatchKit: *free* animations, property animations and animated images.

Free animations

WatchKit performs free animations for you implicitly, for free! Did I mention these are my favorite? :]

WatchKit performs most of these animations for you when updating tables, which animate the insertion and deletion of rows whenever you use either of these two methods:

```
func insertRowsAtIndexes(_ rows: NSIndexSet,
  withRowType rowType: String)
func removeRowsAtIndexes(_ rows: NSIndexSet)
```

The best free animation—and thus, my favorite of favorites—occurs when you update a table row. That is correct—whenever you make an update to the contents of a table row that changes the height, WatchKit reloads the row for you with an implicit, free animation.

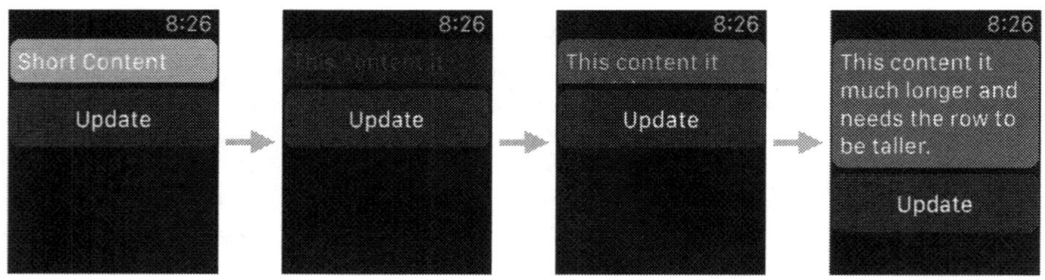

This is quite powerful, and sometimes even justifies placing an *entire* Watch interface into a single table row.

Property animations

These are new to WatchKit with watchOS 2. Without further ado, here's the new method on `WKInterfaceController`:

```
func animateWithDuration(_ duration: NSTimeInterval,
  animations animations: () -> Void)
```

Does this look familiar? It might, because it's identical to a method that `UIView` has in UIKit! But this is all you get in WatchKit. No completion handlers, options, springs—just the animation duration.

If you aren't very familiar with UIKit, don't worry; this method is simple to use. In the `animations` block, you perform all the changes you want to animate, and WatchKit will animate them for you. For example, if you want to animate the `alpha` of `ghost` to `1` over `0.4` seconds, you simply have to type:

```
animateWithDuration(0.4) {
  ghost.alpha = 1
}
```

That's it! As you can see, the method works beautifully with trailing closure syntax, resulting in very readable code.

Not everything is animatable, though, so disappointingly you can't just throw any change into that block and be done with animations in your Watch app.

The following properties are animatable on anything that descends from `WKInterfaceObject`:

- Alpha
- Width and height
- Horizontal and vertical alignment
- Color and background color (*not* text color)

And on `WKInterfaceGroup`:

- Content inset

It might not seem like a lot of power, but with a few tricks, this one method will cover the vast majority of your WatchKit animation needs!

Animated images

Last but definitely not least, WatchKit can display animated images. These can be thought of as flip-books—you provide several images as frames and then *flip* through them. If you do it fast enough, you get an animation.

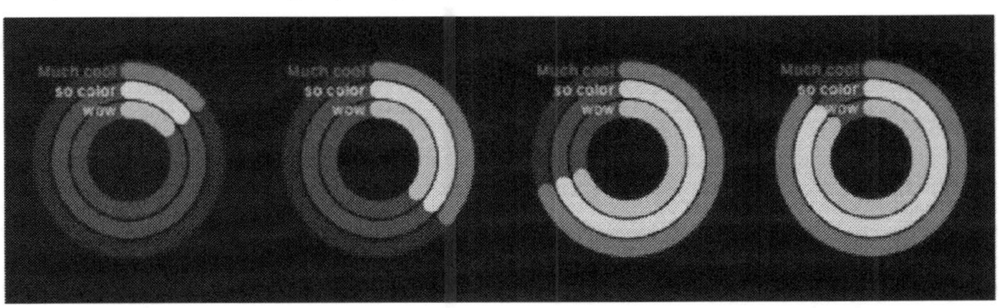

You can display animated images on interface objects that conform to the new `WKImageAnimatable` protocol. Currently, only `WKInterfaceGroup`, `WKInterfaceButton`, and `WKInterfaceImage` conform to `WKImageAnimatable`.

That's it for now; you'll learn how to use animated images later in this chapter.

With that, you know the basics of creating animations in WatchKit. In the remaining sections, you'll implement each of these animation methods in the world's best habit creation app—Woodpecker!

Animations in practice

It's time to create some animations! In this section, you'll see in action all the animation methods described earlier, starting with my favorite—free animations.

Shuffling rows

Open **TaskInterfaceController.swift**. You can see that `TasksInterfaceController` is implemented using two tables, `ongoingTable` and `completedTable`.

After the user adds a new task, the app dismisses `NewTasksInterfaceController` and calls `updateOngoingTasksIfNeeded()` on `TasksInterfaceController`. Currently this method simply reloads the entire table. That definitely sounds inefficient, since you know the only change that *can* happen is adding a new row.

Delete the `loadOngoingTasks()` call in `updateOngoingTasksIfNeeded()` and replace it with the following snippet:

```
// 1
let newRowIndex = tasks.ongoingTasks.count-1
ongoingTable.insertRowsAtIndexes(NSIndexSet(index: newRowIndex),
  withRowType: OngoingTaskRowController.RowType)

// 2
let row = ongoingTable.rowControllerAtIndex(newRowIndex) as!
  OngoingTaskRowController
row.populateWithTask(tasks.ongoingTasks.last!,
  frameWidth: contentFrame.size.width)
```

Here's a breakdown of what's happening:

1. You use `insertRowsAtIndexes(_:withRowType:)` to add a new row to the end instead of reloading the entire table.
2. Since you added a new row, you must populate it. This is similar to when you populate the table for the first time.

This looks a lot more efficient. Build and run. When you create a new task, notice you also get an animation for the new row, *gratis*.

Awesome! I'm sure you want more free animations now, and luckily there's another great place for them.

When the user completes a task, the app removes the task from `ongoingTable` and adds it to `completedTable`. Currently, you do this by simply reloading both tables after the task is completed. These two actions are also perfect candidates for free table row animations.

Still in **TaskInterfaceController.swift**, find `table(_:didSelectRowAtIndex:)` and then find the two lines of code inside the `if task.isCompleted` block:

```
loadOngoingTasks()
loadCompletedTasks()
```

Replace these lines with the following snippet:

```
// 1
ongoingTable.removeRowsAtIndexes(NSIndexSet(index: rowIndex))

// 2
let newRowIndex = tasks.completedTasks.count-1
completedTable.insertRowsAtIndexes(
  NSIndexSet(index: newRowIndex),
  withRowType: CompletedTaskRowController.RowType)

// 3
let row = completedTable.rowControllerAtIndex(newRowIndex) as!
  CompletedTaskRowController
row.populateWithTask(task)

// 4
self.updateAddTaskButton()
self.updateCompletedLabel()
```

Here's what's going on:

1. Instead of reloading the entire table, you can take advantage of the fact that you know exactly what's changed and use `removeRowsAtIndexes(_:)` to remove the completed row.

2. Similarly, for `completedTable`, you're always adding the new row to the end, so you can use `insertRowsAtIndexes(_:withRowType:)` to do so.
3. Since you're adding a new row, you must configure it. Here you're grabbing the newly created row and populating it with the newly completed task.
4. You want to update the state of the add task button and completed label for the changes that just occurred. These two methods will handle that for you.

Notice, again, that these changes are *not* animation-related. They're simply best practice. Your performance will increase, since you're not reloading entire tables and best of all, you get free animations!

Build and run. Complete a few tasks and observe the animations.

The row removal is noticeable when there's more than one ongoing task in the table after you complete one. When there's only one, the appearance of the new task button covers up the nice animation. Hmm... If only that button came in slowly... over time... like an animation!

> **Note**: You can use **Command-T** in the Watch simulator to slow down the animation speed. This works in the iPhone simulator as well!

Fading in, changing size and more!

In Woodpecker, when you complete the last ongoing task, the Add Task button simply pops out. This is quite confusing for users—they might think that this is a bug or that they did something wrong.

Animations to the rescue! The button should appear with an animation to reassure the user. But *how* should it appear?

The safest animation in most cases is the fade-in, which is easy to implement with property animations. Find `updateAddTaskButton()` in **TasksInterfaceController.swift** and replace its implementation with the following snippet:

```
// 1
addTaskButton.setHidden(ongoingTable.numberOfRows != 0)

if (ongoingTable.numberOfRows == 0) {
  // 2
  addTaskButton.setAlpha(0)
  // 3
  animateWithDuration(0.4) {
    self.addTaskButton.setAlpha(1)
  }
}
```

1. You use `setHidden(_:)` to show and hide the button appropriately. If the button should be shown, you want to perform an animation.
2. The button needs to be fully transparent in the beginning, before it fades in.
3. Inside the `animateWithDuration(_:animations:)` block, simply set the `alpha` of the button to `1` to animate the fade-in. Note how you use the trailing closure syntax here.

That's all you need! Build and run. Complete a task again and watch the Add Task button fade in. Much better!

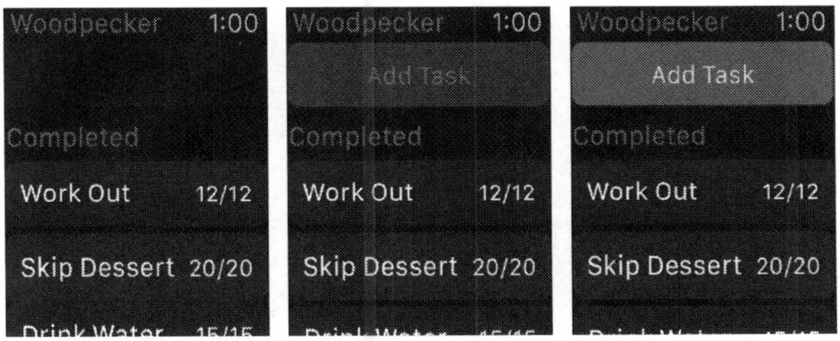

Animations can also provide the user with important feedback. When you perform a task in Woodpecker, the progress bar is just *begging* for some action. You don't want to leave it hanging, do you?

Return to `table(_:didSelectRowAtIndex:)` in **TasksInterfaceController.swift**. In the `else` statement after the code you previously added, wrap the call to `updateProgressWithTask(_:frameWidth:)` in an animation block, so it looks like this:

```
animateWithDuration(0.4) {
  row.updateProgressWithTask(task,
    frameWidth:self.contentFrame.size.width)
}
```

Could it be that easy? Build and run the Watch app. Yes, it is indeed *that* easy:

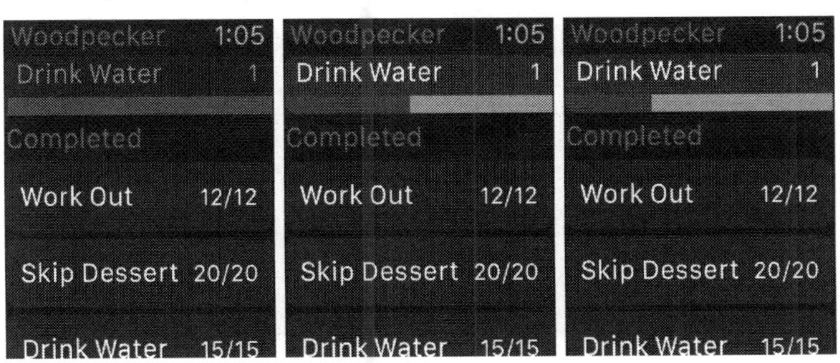

You must be getting the hang of this, so you can try the next one yourself. In **NewTaskInterfaceController.swift**, find `selectColor(_:button:)`. This is what gets called when you tap on a color button. See if you can animate the `alpha` change of the two buttons *and* the `backgroundColor` changes that occur when you choose a color.

Done already? The trick here is to use a single animation block for all the property changes. Here's the resulting function's body:

```
selectedColor = color

self.animateWithDuration(0.4) {
  if let previous = self.selectedColorButton {
    previous.setAlpha(0.3)
  }
  self.selectedColorButton = button
  button.setAlpha(1)
  self.addNameGroup.setBackgroundColor(
    color.color.colorWithAlphaComponent(0.3))
}
```

Build and run the Watch app again. Such a small change, but what an awesome effect:

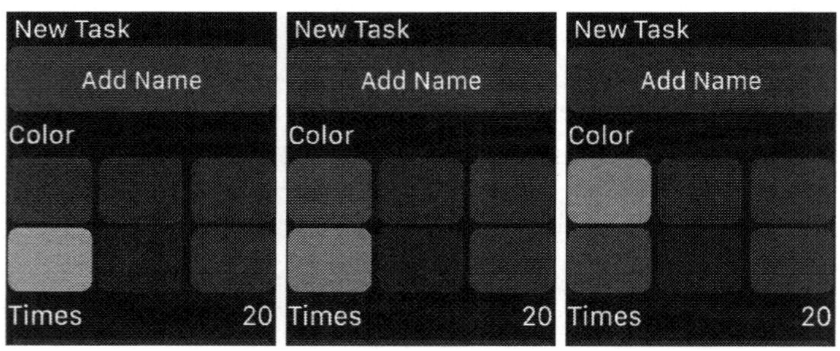

Now for the last one! This one is going to be a bit more complicated than the previous ones.

By now, you might have noticed that if you attempt to create a task without choosing a name or a color, the app displays a little error image:

It's pretty cool, but also a bit jarring. I bet you know what it needs. :]

There's a small challenge here, because there are two stages in displaying the error. You must show it and *then* hide it later.

Without access to completion blocks like in UIKit, the best way you can chain animations together in WatchKit is to use `dispatch_after()` from Grand Central Dispatch.

Find `displayError()` in **NewTaskInterfaceController.swift** and perform your magic on it, without looking below!

I'm sure you got it right, but here's the resulting `displayError()`:

```
errorImage.setHidden(false)

animateWithDuration(0.4) {
  self.errorImage.sizeToFitHeight()
}

let delayTime = dispatch_time(DISPATCH_TIME_NOW,
  Int64(1 * Double(NSEC_PER_SEC)))
dispatch_after(delayTime, dispatch_get_main_queue()) {
  self.animateWithDuration(0.4) {
    self.errorImage.setHeight(0)
  }
}
```

Build and run. Force an error and boom, magic:

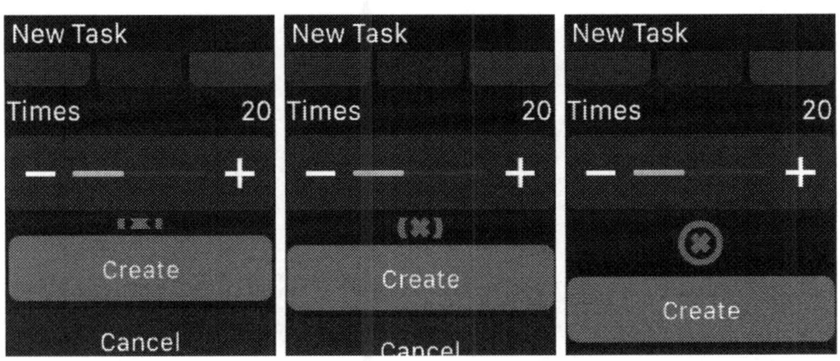

When using animations, you never want to add one *just for the effect*. Animations can serve many functional purposes in apps. Here, you've used them to draw the user's attention to changes and provide context.

That's it for now for property animations. You'll learn more cool tricks later in the book —there's so much more you can do with them! :]

Animated images: a paradox?

That error animation was cool and all, but could it be even better? Of course it can! In this section, you'll use an animated image to make the error "x" spin around... and around and around and around. But first, a primer on animated images, as promised.

What *are* animated images? Does the term even make sense? Well, sort of... In WatchKit, an **animated image** is made up of a sequence of images. You can package all the images in the entire sequence into one animated image.

Yes, animated images are *just* images.

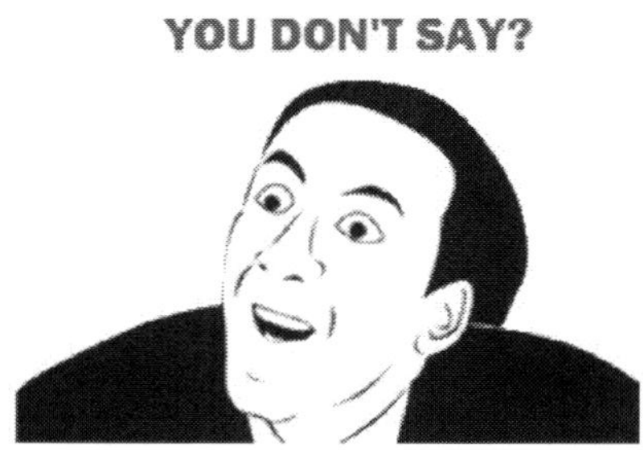

It may sound obvious, but this is quite important—it means you display an animated image just as you would a normal image, using the same APIs.

Animated images are even stored the same way, by using `UIImage`. `UIImage` has had this functionality since iOS 5, but it didn't receive much attention until WatchKit came around.

You can create an animated image in two ways:

1. You can use the `UIImage` method `animatedImageWithImages(_:duration:)` to create an animation from a sequence of images. This is also how you should cache animations on the Watch. Do not send over all the frames individually; it won't work!
2. To create an animated image from images that are already in your Watch app's bundle, you first need to number the frames by appending an integer to them, starting from 0, such as **frame0.png**, **frame1.png** and so on. You set the animated image on an instance of `WKInterfaceImage` by using `setImageNamed(_:)` and passing in the filename prefix, which in this case is **frame**.

After you've set the animated image on an interface element, you can control the animation using these methods from `WKImageAnimatable`:

- **`startAnimating()`** starts the animation with the default values set in the storyboard.
- **`startAnimatingWithImagesInRange(_:duration:repeatCount:)`** starts the animation with the specified range, duration and repeat count. A repeat count of `0`

will make the animation repeat forever.

- **stopAnimating()** stops the animation. No surprises here!

An animated image: the error spin

Animated images are the most *powerful* in terms of what they can achieve. They are also the most *expensive* to use. They take up more disk space, more memory *and* have lower performance than all the other animation methods.

Thus, you should use them conservatively.

Back to Woodpecker. If you've been poking around, perhaps you've noticed the **X-Animation** folder in the Watch app's image assets. Look in there and you'll see a series of image frames representing a rotating "x". You've probably guessed it by now—you're going to make the error spin!

Find `displayError()` in **NewTaskInterfaceController.swift** again and update the body to the following:

```
errorImage.setHidden(false)

// 1
errorImage.setImageNamed("x")

// 2
errorImage.startAnimating()
animateWithDuration(0.4) {
  self.errorImage.sizeToFitHeight()
}

let delayTime = dispatch_time(DISPATCH_TIME_NOW,
  Int64(1 * Double(NSEC_PER_SEC)))
dispatch_after(delayTime, dispatch_get_main_queue()) {
  self.animateWithDuration(0.4) {
    self.errorImage.setHeight(0)
  }
}
```

There are only three new lines here, as marked:

1. Since the images in the sequence are named **x1**, **x2** and so forth, you set the image to the `WKInterfaceImage` by using the common prefix `x`.
2. You call `startAnimating()` to start the animation from the beginning.

That's all you need to do! Build and run the Watch app one final time. Trigger an error again and enjoy the spinning X. I'm sure you'll want to do that a few more times!

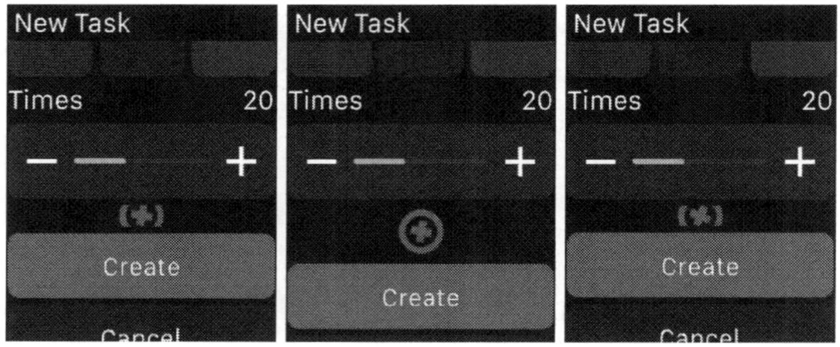

Where to go from here?

You've now learned about, and used, the three main ways of creating animations in WatchKit for watchOS 2. Congratulations! I bet you're aching to use these methods in your own apps, so knock yourself out.

You also may be starting to see the vast number of possibilities these simple APIs provide. Feel free to jump on to Chapter 17, "Advanced Animations" to see a few more animation techniques you might not have thought of. You'll also get to continue working on Woodpecker!

Chapter 10: Glances

By Ben Morrow

Interactions with the Apple Watch are supposed to be simple and brief. You want your users to have immediate, single-touch access to the most important information from your apps—and that's the purpose of the glance.

A glance is an extension of your Watch app that presents information the user can consume straightaway, without first having to launch your app. Glances in WatchKit are the equivalent of Today extensions in iOS.

To help you understand and make the most of glances, this chapter will walk you through creating a glance for an app called Breakout. If you've ever felt the need to get away from your desk for a spell—perhaps your eyes are glazing over from too many online tutorials—then you'll appreciate Breakout, which will give you a super-quick workout to get the blood pumping.

The best way to use Breakout will be through its glance, which will work like this:

- The glance will display a single exercise to do.
- If you tap the glance, the Watch app opens where a timer will start immediately, telling you how long to do the exercise.

- During the workout, you'll also be able to use the glance to check the timer's status.
- If you happen to be looking at the glance when the timer finishes, you can tap to mark the workout as don'll see your earned trophy and you can tap it to see your all-time stats.
- The next time you look at the glance, another exercise will queued up and at the ready!

A glance wouldn't be much use if it displayed the same information all the time. Glances show the current data from your app and in this chapter you'll take that to the next level by building different interfaces for different states of the app: inactive, active, and just finished.

Here's what Breakout's glance will look like by the time you've finished this chapter:

The Breakout starter project includes both the iOS and watchOS 2 apps. In this chapter, you'll design the glance interface and implement the Handoff feature that will open the app and start the timer. Let's get started!

Getting started

To access glances, a user swipes up from the watch face—the same, familiar gesture that launches the Control Center on the iPhone and iPad. There's one big difference, though: glances are *only* available from the watch face, not from inside apps nor from the Home screen.

The Watch presents glances as a queue through which users can navigate by swiping horizontally; page indicator dots at the bottom of the screen show the user where they are in the queue. Tapping anywhere on a glance launches the corresponding Watch app.

Glances can make use of Handoff to inform the Watch app what was being displayed before the user tapped the glance. The Watch app can then use this information to display a contextually relevant interface upon opening. In this chapter, you'll get a brief introduction to Handoff and learn how it works with glances. You'll then take a deep dive into Handoff once you reach Chapter 20.

If you have an Apple Watch, try out your available glances to get a feel for how they work.

Glances come packaged with Watch apps; you can install or uninstall them using the Apple Watch app on the iPhone, with a maximum of 20 glances installed at a time. You'll learn how to uninstall and reinstall the Breakout glance a little later in the chapter.

Designing a glance

Apple intends for users to experience glances with just a quick glance—hence the name! That means there are some restrictions as to what you can do with a glance:

- Each Watch app can only contain a single glance.
- The content is read-only; interactive components like buttons and switches aren't allowed.
- A glance isn't scrollable, so you need to make sure all your content fits within a single screen. This means you must be selective about the information you choose to display, making sure it's absolutely relevant in the current context.

Don't despair, though! These limitations actually make it much easier to design glances for their intended purpose—to enhance your app and provide a rich user experience measured in fractions of a second.

Fire up Xcode and open the starter Breakout project. Select the **Breakout for watchOS** scheme and build and run. To get a feel for the app, start a workout on the first page and allow it to finish. When the workout completes, the app will pop to the second page. Force tap the trophy interface for the "Undo last" button.

Note: To force tap in the simulator, use **Hardware > Force Touch Pressure**.

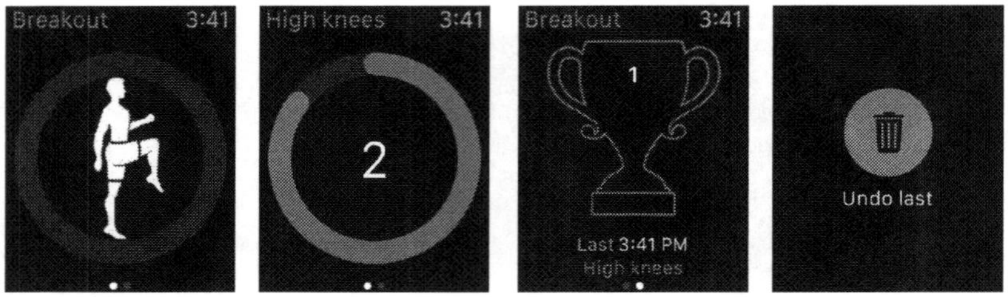

Creating the glance interface controller

You'll use Interface Builder to construct your glance interface, laying it out in the storyboard and connecting it to the data provided by your WatchKit extension.

There are two different ways you can add a glance to your Watch app:

- When you first add the Watch app target to your Xcode project, there's an option you can check called **Include Glance Scene**. This will add a glance interface controller to your storyboard and a suitably-named `WKInterfaceController` subclass to your WatchKit extension.

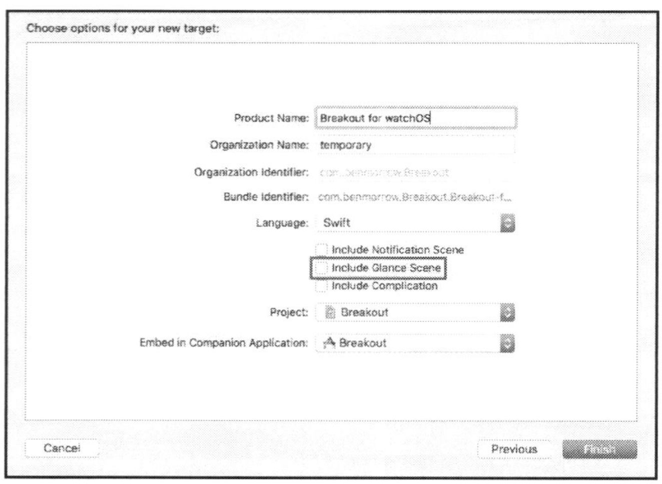

- Or, you can choose to add a glance to an existing project, which is what you'll do here.

To create a glance for this app, first you need a controller. To create a new controller, right-click on the **Breakout for watchOS Extension** group in the project navigator and choose **New File...**, then select the **iOS\Source\Cocoa Touch Class** and click **Next**. In the **Subclass of** field, type `WKInterfaceController` and for the **Class**, use **GlanceInterfaceController**. Click **Next** and **Create**.

Adding the glance to the storyboard

Now that you've got an interface controller ready to roll, it's time for the interface. Open **Interface.storyboard**. In the Object Library, locate **glance interface controller** and **drag** it onto the storyboard canvas.

You'll immediately notice it comes packed with a bunch of labels:

Glances are **template-based**, meaning you don't have total control over their appearance. The interface is split into upper and lower layout groups.

Select the **glance interface controller** in the document outline and then take a look at Attributes Inspector:

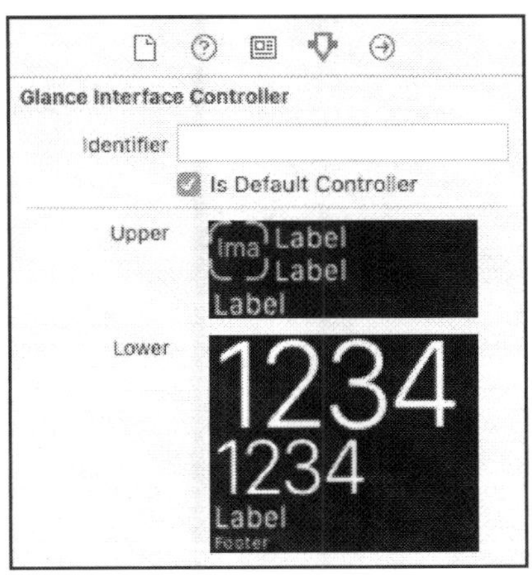

By choosing the appropriate templates, you can create glances for a variety of content that best matches the data in your app. Apple provides these templates so that your glance will fit in with the glances from other apps.

Creating the glance build scheme

When you're developing a glance, it can be useful to run it directly by itself in the Watch simulator. That way you don't have to worry about swiping up from the watch face; you simply build and run the correct scheme and the glance appears. To prepare for this, you'll need to create a custom build scheme.

Open the **Scheme** menu and choose **Manage Schemes…**:

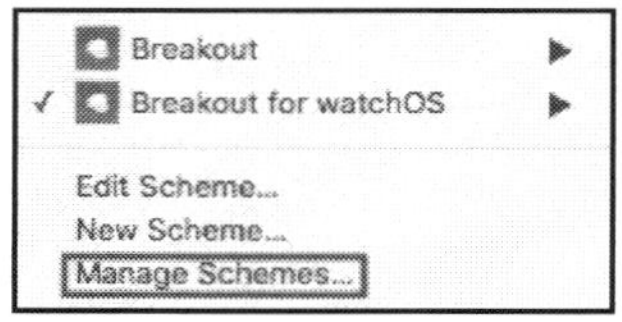

Next, select the **Breakout for watchOS** scheme and then click the **gear icon** at the bottom of the pane. Choose **Duplicate** from the pop-up menu:

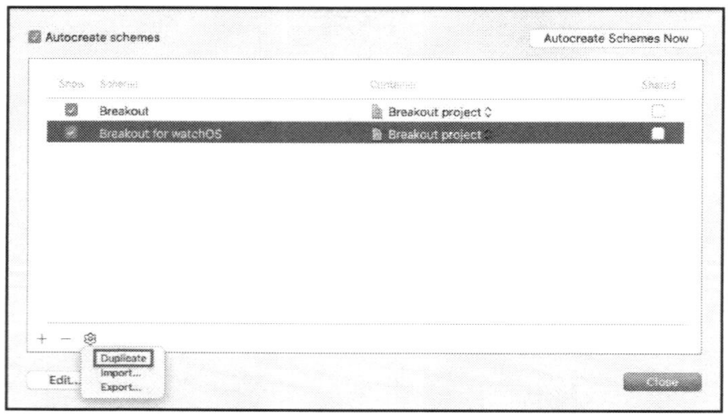

The name field will be highlighted. Call the new scheme **Glance**. Now you'll need to change the properties of the scheme to make it launch the glance instead of the full app. Select the **Run** build option in the left-hand pane. In the center pane, change **Watch Interface** to **Glance**:

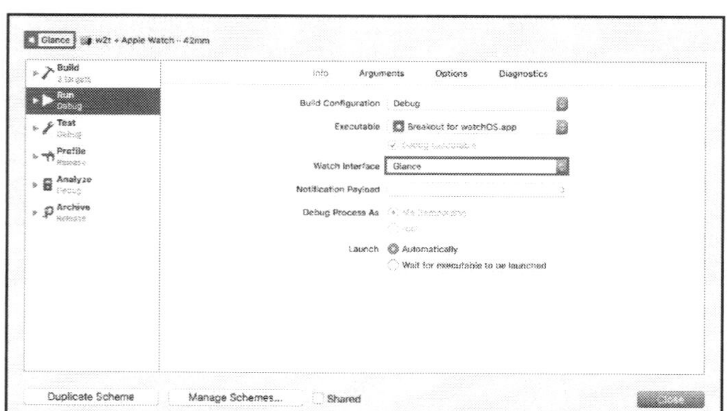

Click **Close** to save the changes and **Close** again to exit the scheme manager. change the scheme to **Glance** and build and run. You'll see your glance in the simulator, using the template you selected earlier.

Even though the glance doesn't show live data at the moment, the labels demonstrate that everything is working as expected:

Troubleshooting runtime bugs

The glance scheme, the app running in the simulator, and the app running on a device should all work. At the time of writing there are bugs in the current SDK that you may run into with glances. Anytime you're instructed to run the app during this chapter, you may see unexpected behavior. Hopefully these issues will be fixed by the time you read this chapter, but if they're not, read on.

If you get an error about the app, the glance, or an interface controller not being installed, you can uninstall and reinstall the Watch app and the glance. Press **Command-Shift-H** to go the Home screen on the iOS simulator. Navigate to the **Apple Watch** app and open the settings for **Breakout**. Toggle both switches off and back on:

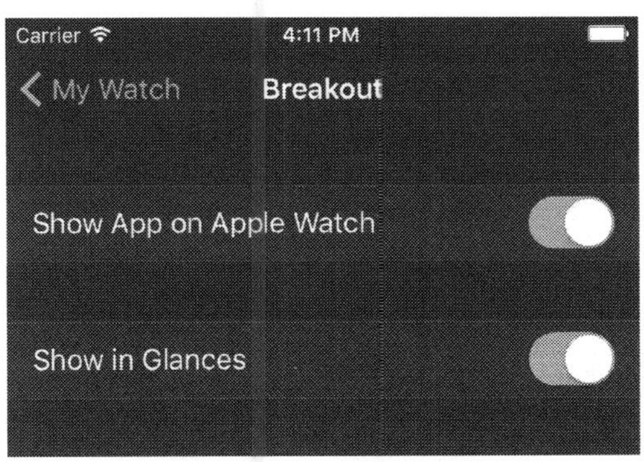

There is a bug in watchOS 2 that causes apps with glances to load erratically. You may see the loading spinner for unexpectedly long or the app might crash. Although frustrating, you need to simply run the app again over and over until you see the interface. This is a known issue (Radar **#22080322**) that affects both the watch simulator and the physical device:

If the glance never loads, try using **Reset content and settings** via the **Simulator** menu on both the iOS simulator and the watchOS simulator. Then build and run again. This last resort installs a clean copy of the app and usually fixes the unexpected behavior.

After you've confirmed the app is working, jump back to Xcode and get ready to build out the rest of your interface.

Designing the glance in the storyboard

First consider which glance templates you'll use. The image template provides maximum flexibility since you can swap out the images for standard group content.

In your storyboard, highlight the **glance interface controller**. From the Attributes Inspector, select the **Image** template for both sections:

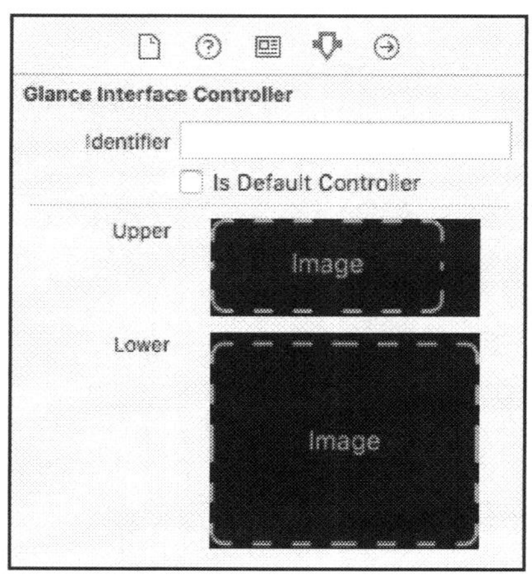

Now that you've got a cleaner slate, you're ready to add your own components.

> **Note**: If you have trouble seeing the popover to select a template, try changing the width of the inspector pane.

Drag a **label** from the Object Library to both of the **groups** in the the document outline, and **delete** the **image** from the upper group. Your upgraded document outline will look like this:

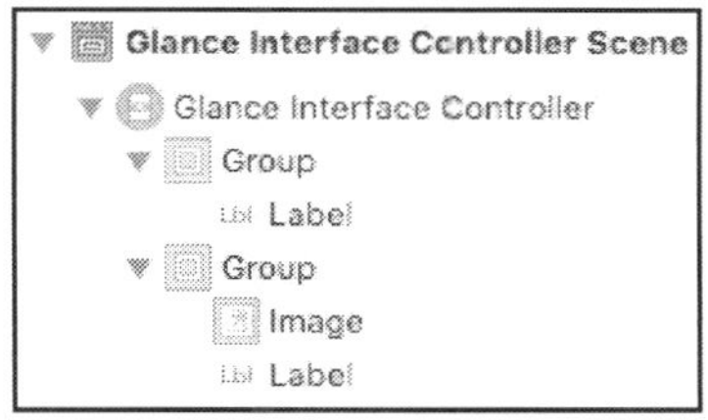

Select the **label** in the upper group and set its attributes to the following:

- Text: **Next breakout...**
- Text Color: **Dark Gray Color**
- Lines: **2**

Next select the **lower group** in the document outline and set its **Layout** to **Vertical**.

Then select the **image** in the lower group and set its attributes to:

- Image: **highknees**
- Mode: **Aspect Fit**
- Horizontal: **Center**
- Width: **Size To Fit Content**
- Height: **Fixed, 78**

Finally, select the **label** in the lower group and set its attributes to:

- Text: **High knees**
- Lines: **0**
- Alignment: **Center** (the second of the five toggles)
- Width: **Relative to container**

Build and run the **Glance** scheme. Your glance will now look like this:

Lookin' good! Now, if you noticed during the chapter introduction, your goal is to make the glance work for three different states: inactive, active and just finished. You've completed the preparation for the inactive state, so now you'll begin the work for the active state.

Adding components that will be hidden with code

You will now add some objects that can be toggled on and off in code depending on the state of the exercise timer.

Glance interface controllers don't automatically expand their height in the storyboard like standard interface controllers. Remember, glances don't scroll. To prepare the objects to toggle, you'll need to be able to see the new objects on while you're designing.

Select the **highknees** image and set its **Hidden** attribute to **checked**. The image will be hidden for now, but you'll reveal the image with code later.

Set the **Background** image of the lower group to **progress0** and set its **Mode** to **Aspect Fit**.

Drag a **timer** from the Object Library to the bottom of the same lower group. **Deselect** all **Units** options except **Second**. Set **Preview Secs** to **30**. You'll want the **Font** to be **System 36.0** and both **Horizontal** and **Vertical** alignment to be **Center**.

Build and run your glance. With all those attributes in place, you now have a polished glance design:

Your completed glance layout looks fantastic! With just a small amount of work up front, you can make a dynamic interface. Good work.

In the next section, you'll learn how to turn interface objects on and off when you need them. It's time to populate the glance with real data.

Programming the glance

To populate those labels with real data, you need to create some outlets. Select the glance controller in the storyboard, open Identity Inspector and set the **Class** to `GlanceInterfaceController`.

Hooking up the controller

With the storyboard still open, open the assistant editor and make sure it's displaying the `GlanceInterfaceController` class. Then **Control-drag** from each of the five elements in the glance storyboard into `GlanceInterfaceController`, and create an `IBOutlet` for each one, naming them as below. Your class will end up with the following outlets defined and connected:

```
@IBOutlet var titleLabel: WKInterfaceLabel! // Next breakout...
@IBOutlet var lowerSectionGroup: WKInterfaceGroup! // Ring image
@IBOutlet var workoutImage: WKInterfaceImage! // Running image
@IBOutlet var workoutNameLabel: WKInterfaceLabel! // High knees
@IBOutlet var timerLabel: WKInterfaceTimer! // 30
```

Note that you did not create an outlet for the upper interface group. You won't be interacting with it in code, so there is no reason to create an outlet for it. You're done creating outlets, so you can close the assistant editor. Now in the standard editor, open **GlanceInterfaceController.swift**.

Providing code to get current data

The `workoutManager` will keep track of when the workout started and when it's supposed to finish. It will also know how far along the timer is, so you'll need to have one of those for this class. Above the `IBOutlet` definitions, add the following:

```
let workoutManager = WorkoutManager.defaultManager
```

The `WorkoutManager` class uses the singleton pattern. The `defaultManager` property can be accessed from anywhere in the app and have access to the same shared data.

You need to compose the method that will hide what's unnecessary and show only the UI for when there is no breakout currently active, just a future one. Add this method to the bottom of the `GlanceInterfaceController`:

```
func showNextUpUI() {
  workoutImage.setHidden(false)
  workoutImage.setImageNamed(
    workoutManager.nextWorkout.imageName)
  workoutNameLabel.setHidden(false)
  workoutNameLabel.setText(workoutManager.nextWorkout.name)
  titleLabel.setText("Next breakout...")
  titleLabel.setTextColor(UIColor.darkGrayColor())
  lowerSectionGroup.setBackgroundImage(nil)
  timerLabel.setHidden(true)
}
```

There's nothing too complex going on here. You're specifically hiding and altering the interface objects in the glance for the specific state—like a magician directing attention to what they want to be seen at that moment.

So, since you've prepared for what happens when the timer is inactive, it logically follows that you'll need the code for an ongoing workout. Add this method just below the last:

```
// 1
func showActiveUI(remaining: NSTimeInterval) {
  // 2
  let location = Int(workoutManager.percentComplete *
    Double(circularProgressAnimationFrames))
  lowerSectionGroup.setBackgroundImageNamed("progress")
  lowerSectionGroup.startAnimatingWithImagesInRange(
    NSRange(
      location: location,
      length: circularProgressAnimationFrames
    ),
    duration: remaining,
    repeatCount: 1
  )
  workoutImage.setHidden(true)
  workoutNameLabel.setHidden(true)
  titleLabel.setTextColor(UIColor.whiteColor())
  titleLabel.setText(workoutManager.currentWorkout.name)
  // 3
  timerLabel.setHidden(false)
  timerLabel.setDate(NSDate(timeIntervalSinceNow: remaining))
  timerLabel.start()
  // 4
  NSTimer.scheduledTimerWithTimeInterval(remaining,
    target: self, selector: "showTrophy",
    userInfo: nil, repeats: false)
}
```

This method will show a nice circular countdown timer that represents the amount of time remaining in the breakout. This code introduces some new concepts. Here's what's happening:

1. Since it's possible that the user will view the glance in the middle of a breakout, the method gets called with a parameter called `remaining` that lets it know how much time is left on the clock.

2. The `length` constant is used to determine how many total frames of animation there are. Since all the ring progress animations use the same number of frames in this app, that number is set as a constant, called `circularProgressAnimationFrames` in Animation.swift. The `location` value determines where in the range of frames to start. These values will be used to create an `NSRange` that will be used to dictate which frames are animated in the group using `startAnimatingWithImagesInRange(_:duration:)`.

3. A `WKInterfaceTimer` is a special WatchKit interface object for which there isn't a UIKit analogue. When you provide it a future date, it will automatically update the interface for you as a nicely formatted countdown label.

4. Finally, it would be nice to know when the timer finishes so you can update the interface to a new state. This timer will call `showTrophy()` when it finishes.

Since you want something to happen visually when the clock reaches zero, you'll need to add the method you just called at the end of the previous method.

Do so now by add the following to the bottom of the class:

```
func showTrophy() {
  timerLabel.setHidden(true)
  workoutImage.setHidden(false)
  workoutImage.setImageNamed("trophy")
  lowerSectionGroup.setBackgroundImage(nil)
}
```

This method sets the state of the interface elements to hide the timer and show a congratulatory trophy. Put together, these three methods will produce quite a magic show!

One more thing before you're ready to test your glance. Each time the user invokes your glance, you want to show her the most current data and update the interface accordingly. To make the interface update each time, you'll add code to `willActivate()`. Remember that any code called outside of this method, like the code inside `awakeWithContext(_:)` or any class properties, will only be evaluated the first time a glance is run and won't be called on subsequent launches.

Add this code to the bottom of `willActivate()`:

```
if let remaining = workoutManager.timeRemaining {
  showActiveUI(remaining)
} else {
  showNextUpUI()
}
```

You made it! Each time a user navigates to the glance, this code will check if a workout is ongoing. If so, it will show the timer interface and if not, it will show what's coming next. Now you're ready to test.

This time, instead of launching the glance scheme, you're going to test it by navigating the simulator operating system. Select the **Breakout for watchOS** scheme and build and run:

1. Press **Command-Shift-H** to navigate to the watch face. This is the equivalent of pressing the digital crown on a physical device.

2. Swipe up on the display to show the glances. Navigate to the Breakout glance. All the work you put in to make sure to show only what was needed has paid off!

> **Note**: If you don't see your glance, stop the simulation. Go to the iOS simulator and from the Home screen (Shift-Command-H) open the Apple Watch app. Select the Breakout app and make sure to toggle on **Show in Glances**. Then, build and run the **Breakout for watchOS** scheme again.

3. Tap on the **glance** and you'll be taken to the app.
4. Tap on the main button and to start the 30-second breakout.
5. You want to check on the glance to see if it updated to the new state. After the 30-second timer starts, without delay press **Shift-Command-H** again. If you see the Home screen, press the key combination again. You'll end up at the watch face screen where you can swipe up for the glance.
6. Wow! The glance is completely transformed now that the workout is active.
7. Wait for it to complete so you can see what happens when the breakout timer finishes.

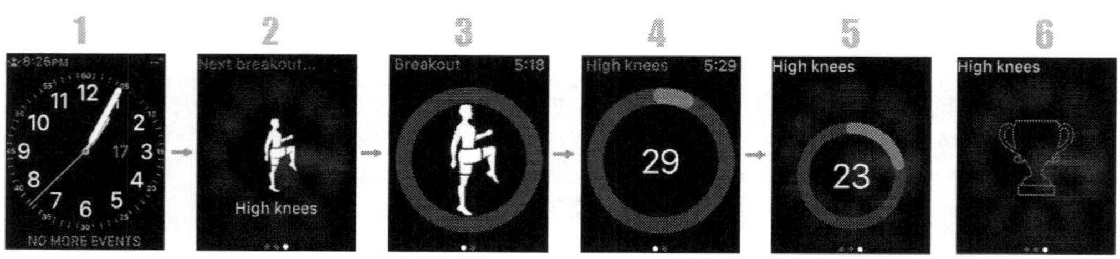

Congratulations on that maneuver! Your glance shows each of the three states, depending on the underlying data.

While this has been a success, you can go the extra mile by introducing Handoff. Imagine tapping the glance while it showed the next breakout and immediately starting the timer. Moreover, imagine tapping the glance after the workout and seeing your newly etched trophy.

Implementing Handoff

The first step to Handoff sorcery is to set up the initial interface to listen for a Handoff event. Open **InterfaceController.swift** and at the bottom of the class, add the following:

```
// 1
override func handleUserActivity(
  userInfo:[NSObject : AnyObject]?) {
  // 2
  guard let userInfo = userInfo,
    let action = userInfo["action"] as? String else { return }
  switch action {
    // 3
    case "startWorkout":
      prepareForWorkout()
    // 4
    case "showTrophy":
      WKInterfaceController.reloadRootControllers(
        [("InitialController",""),
        ("TrophyController","animate")])
    default:
      break
  }
}
```

Here's what's happening:

1. `handleUserActivity(_:)` receives a dictionary, which you can pack with just enough information to set a course of action.
2. Using optional binding, you check that the `userInfo` dictionary is not `nil` and that the `action` key is a `String`.
3. You use `pushControllerWithName(_:context:)` to trigger a new screen to launch and provide it with a `context` that you can handle on the new interface.
4. The way to redirect to a different page in code rather than by user action, is to use `WKInterfaceController.reloadRootControllers(_:)`. You pass the string "animate" as the context to `TrophyController`. `TrophyController` handles this context by calling `becomeCurrentPage()` in its `awakeWithContext(_:)`.

Now that you've got the listener in place, you need to prepare the event. Open **GlanceInterfaceController.swift** in the project navigator. You'd like to trigger the handoff in two of the different states; to do this, you use a method called `updateUserActivity(_:userinfo:webpageURL:)`.

At the end of `showNextUpUI()`, add this line:

```
updateUserActivity("com.rw.breakout.glance",
  userInfo: ["action": "startWorkout"],
  webpageURL: nil)
```

The first parameter isn't important for this app, but it's best practice to use a reverse domain notation to name the `type` of your handoff activity. The `webpageURL` is also not important for your purposes here, so you'll use `nil`. You'll learn much more about these parameters in the Handoff chapter later in the book. The `userInfo` dictionary is passing the "action" key and "startWorkout" value for which you set up a listener.

For the other state of the app, add this call to `showActiveUI(_:)`:

```
updateUserActivity("com.rw.breakout.glance",
  userInfo: ["action": "showTrophy"],
  webpageURL: nil)
```

Here you're using the `userInfo` dictionary again, but this time you pass the "showTrophy" value for which you set up a listener earlier.

Now build and run, and try the different states of the glance with its handoff.

1. Tapping the glance while it's showing the "Next breakout..." will open the app and start a timer.
2. Tapping the glance while a timer is running or finished will open the app and mark that exercise as complete.

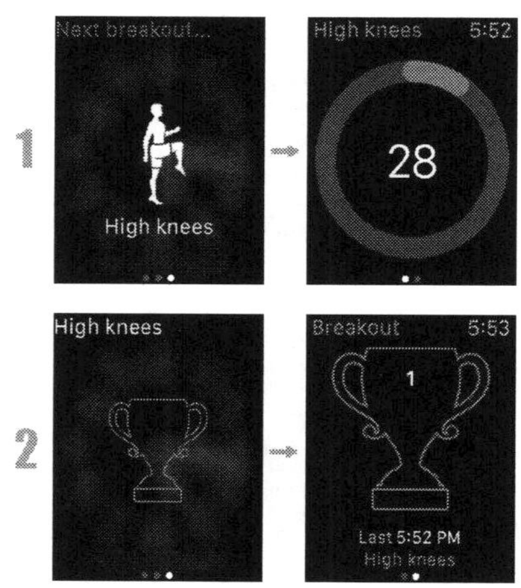

Superb work! You've built a glance that not only performs very useful functions for all the states of your app, it also looks great. You've made it easier than ever for your users to *breakout* of their desk jobs.

Where to go from here?

You now have a solid understanding of how to set up a glance, as well as a firm grasp of how to manipulate the glance interface.

Remember, you can configure the glance interface in much the same way as a Watch app. The only differences are these: you can't use any interactive elements like buttons or switches, and you have to keep all the objects within a single screen, since scrolling isn't supported.

With your glance looking polished, consider this—one way to make the experience even more seamless would be to push a reminder to take a breakout. In the next chapter, you'll learn just how to do that with notifications.

Chapter 11: Notifications

By Matthew Morey

Local and remote notifications let an app that isn't running in the foreground inform users about new, relevant information that's available.

iOS has had notification support since iOS 3, and its abilities have steadily increased over the years. With iOS 7, Apple added silent remote notifications support, allowing apps to wake up in the background and perform important tasks. Actionable notifications, added in iOS 8, allow users to take an action on a notification without first opening the app.

Existing iPhone apps that support notifications will work on the Apple Watch without any changes. watchOS uses a default system interface to show notifications.

However, with a little work, you can build beautiful, custom Watch notification interfaces. watchOS introduces two new types: the short look and the long look notification.

In this chapter, you'll add a custom long look notification interface to an iPhone and Watch app called Pawsome.

Pawsome is for all the cat lovers who procrastinate during the day by looking at cute cat pictures. The Pawsome app will make this easier by interrupting you throughout the day with cute cat pictures that are certain to trigger a smile.

> **Note**: If you're not familiar with the way notifications work in iOS or you find this chapter a little difficult, I recommend you read our Apple Push Notification Services tutorial: bit.ly/1fs7fok.

Getting started

Open the Pawsome starter project in Xcode and then build and run the **Pawsome** scheme. On first launch, you'll be told Pawsome wants to send you notifications; tap **OK**.

The existing Pawsome iPhone and Watch apps show a collection of cute cat pictures that you can easily browse.

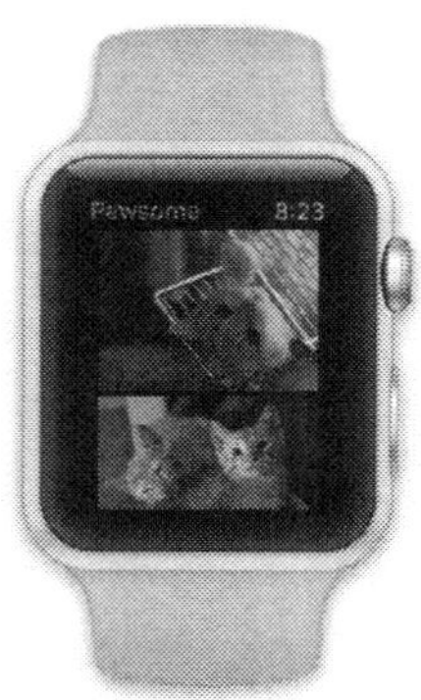

Unlike the iPhone version of Pawsome, the Watch version doesn't support custom notifications just yet. Don't worry— soon it will, but first you need to know how to test notifications on the Watch.

Testing notifications with the Watch simulator

Xcode 6.2 introduced the ability to test remote notifications on the Watch simulator using a local file to mimic the JSON payload file that's sent by Apple's Push Notification Service.

To use this feature, you simply need to add a new file with the extension ".apns" to your project.

In Xcode, show the project navigator. **Right-click** on the **Supporting Files** group in the **PawsomeWatch Extension** group and select **New File...**. Select the **Watch OS\Other\Empty** template and click **Next**.

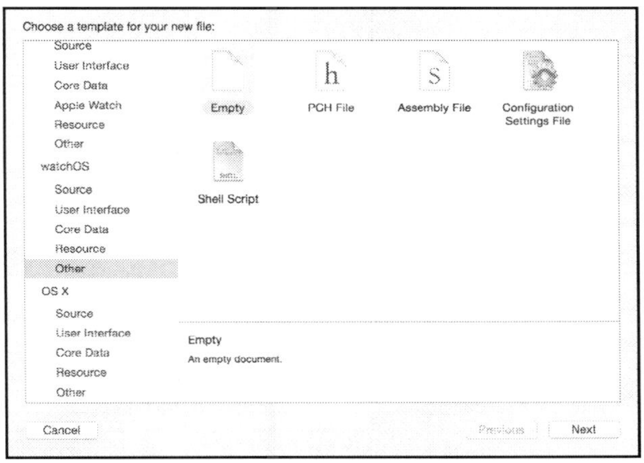

Name the file **PawsomeNotificationPayload.apns**, ensure no Targets are checked and click **Create**.

Now add the following JSON to the newly created **PawsomeNotificationPayload.apns**:

```
{
  "aps":{
    "alert":{
      "body":"Pawsome time!"
    },
    "category":"Pawsome"
  },
  "WatchKit Simulator Actions":[
    {
      "title":"More Cats!",
      "identifier":"viewCatsAction"
    }
  ]
}
```

If you've implemented remote notifications before, you know that the **aps** dictionary includes the notification title, body and optionally, a category. When the iPhone or iPad receives a notification and the app is in the background, the device displays a system dialog or banner showing the title and message.

Because the Watch simulator doesn't have access to the iPhone app's registered notification actions, the JSON payload includes a special key for testing, `WatchKit Simulator Actions`, which will come into play later when you implement the long look notification. The value of this key is an array of items, with each item representing a single action button that will be appended to the Watch's notification interface.

Even though the notification you're building is a local notification, you can pretend it's a remote notification for testing purposes. To the watchOS 2 SDK, there's no fundamental difference in the UI between a local and a remote notification, as it shows both to the user in the same manner.

Now that you have a sample JSON payload for testing notifications on the Watch, you need to create a new scheme to run the notification.

To add a new scheme, you'll first duplicate the current Watch app scheme. Choose **Product\Scheme\Manage Schemes...**, select the **PawsomeWatch** scheme, click on the **gear icon** and then click **Duplicate**.

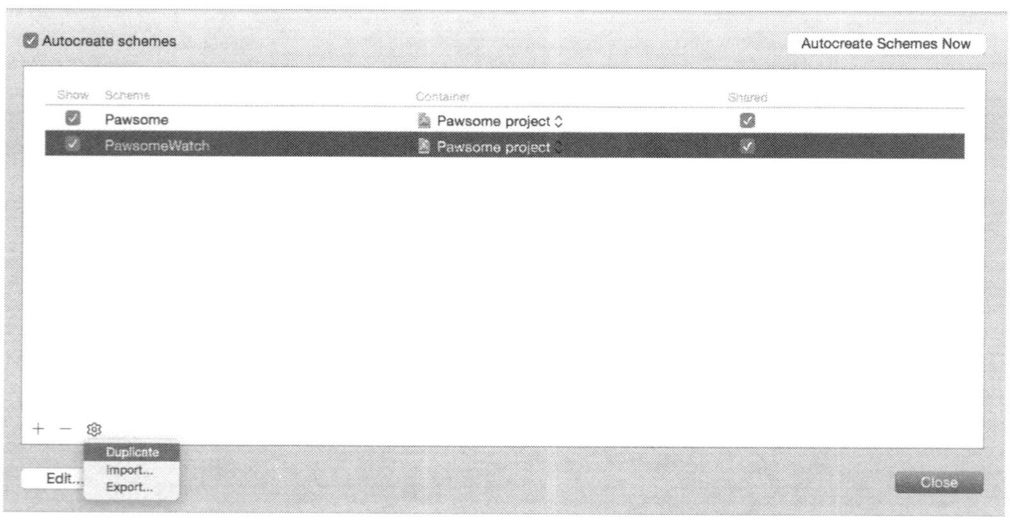

Name the scheme **Notification - PawsomeWatch** by selecting the new scheme and pressing the **Enter** key.

Next, click **Edit...** to edit the scheme. Select the **Run** option in the left-hand column of the scheme editor. In the **Info** pane, select the **Dynamic Notification** option from the **Watch Interface** drop-down. Xcode should automatically set the **Notification Payload** option to the **PawsomeNotificationPayload.apns** file.

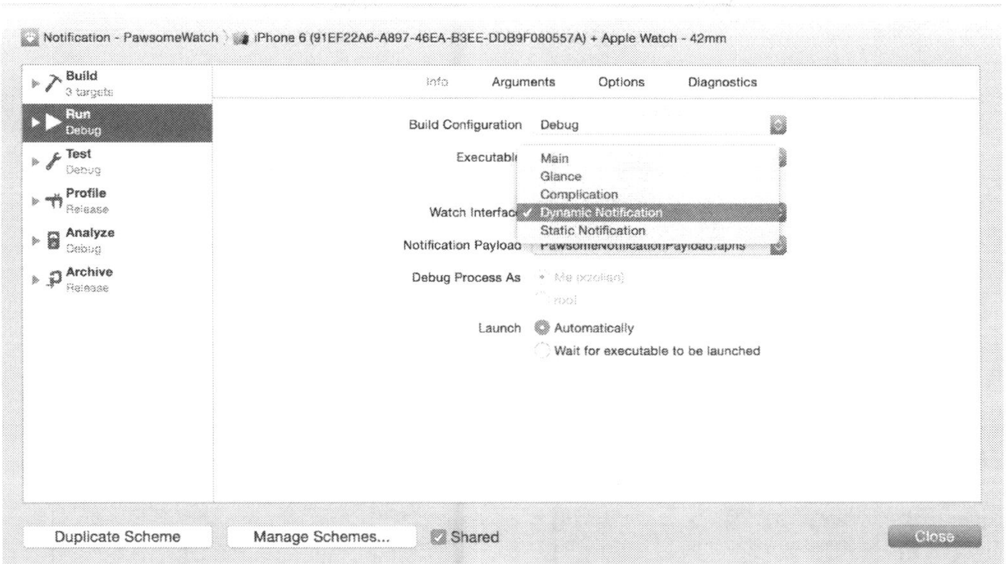

> **Note**: If your app supports more than one notification, you can add multiple APNS files and multiple schemes to make it easy to test each one. You can also select the **Static Notification** option to test the static version of a notification. Keep reading to learn more.

Close the scheme editor to return to the main Xcode interface. Build and run the new **Notification - PawsomeWatch** scheme. You'll see the short look notification on the Watch simulator for about a second, followed by the long look notification:

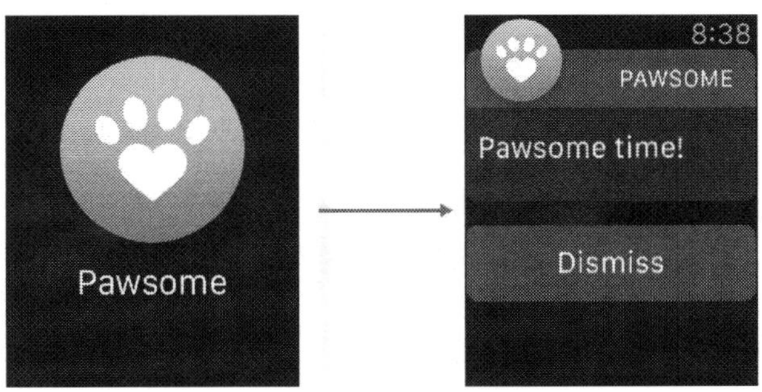

Xcode used the "Pawsome time!" string from **PawsomeNotificationPayload.apns** to populate the notification interface.

This feature in Xcode allows you to focus on the notification user interface without having to worry about servers, device tokens and the other complexities related to testing notifications.

Great job! It's not the *purrrtiest* but you will soon fix that.

Short looks

When the iPhone app receives a remote or local notification, iOS decides whether to display the notification on the iPhone or on the Watch. In general, the notification is shown on the device currently in use. If neither device is being actively used the notification will appear on the Watch.

If the Watch receives the notification, it will notify the user via a subtle vibration. If the user chooses to view the notification, which she'll do by raising her wrist, the Watch will show an abbreviated version called a short look. If the user continues to view the notification for more than a split second, the Watch will show a more detailed version, or a long look.

The short look notification is a quick summary for the user. Short looks show the app's icon and name, and the optional notification title, in a predefined layout.

The optional notification title is a very short blurb about the notification, such as "New Bill", "Reminder" or "Score Alert", and is added to the `alert` key's value. This allows the user to decide whether or not to stick around for the long look interface.

The Pawsome notification you're building doesn't need a title, as the app has only one type of notification, which also happens to be the name of the app.

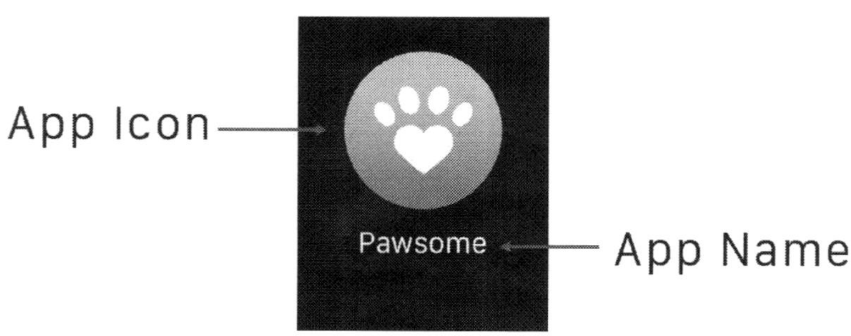

The text color of the app name is perhaps the only thing customizable about the short look notification interface. You can change it by setting the tint color in the Attributes Inspector for the notification interface controller.

Long looks

The long look is a scrolling interface that you can customize, with a default static interface or an optional dynamically-created interface. Unlike the short look interface, the long look offers significant customization.

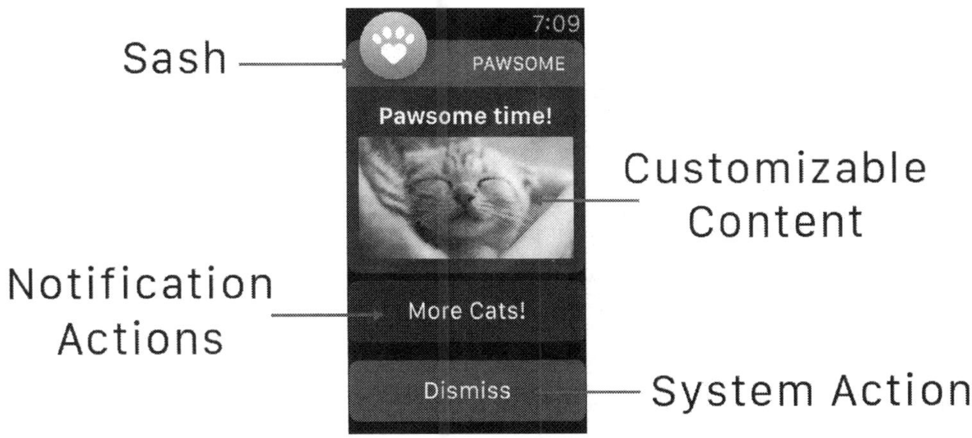

The sash is the horizontal bar at the top. It's translucent by default, but you can set it to any color and opacity value.

You can customize the content area as if it were a standard interface, but without any interactive controls such as buttons and switches.

Long look interfaces can show up to four custom notification actions. These actions need to be registered by the iPhone app. If they are, the long look interface displays them automatically, based on the notification's category.

The system-provided Dismiss button is always present at the bottom of the interface. Tapping Dismiss hides the notification without informing the iPhone app or the Watch extension.

You've just learned how to test notifications on the Watch using the special APNS file. You also now know the differences between a short look and a long look notification, and which parts of each you can customize.

In the next section, you'll learn how to create a custom long look notification by building one for Pawsome.

Creating a custom notification

Now that you've done all the prep work, you get to build the Pawsome custom long look static and dynamic notification, which will look like this when you're done:

Static notification

Open **Interface.storyboard** from the **PawsomeWatch** group and drag a **notification interface controller** from the Object Library onto the storyboard. Your storyboard will now look like this:

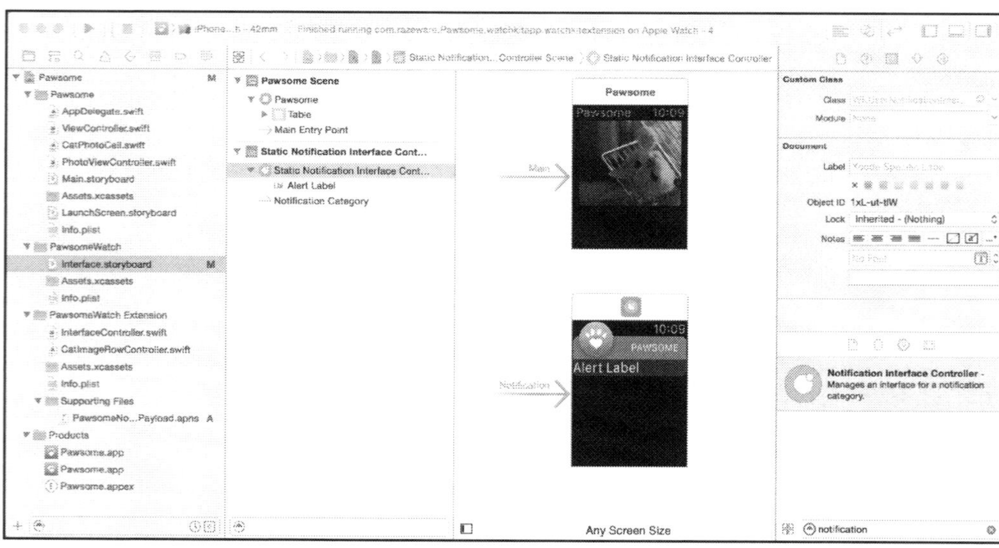

In your storyboard, notification categories are shown as arrows, or entry points, pointing to a notification scene. Since apps can have multiple notification types, categories are used to differentiate one notification scene from another.

Select the **notification category** for the notification scene you just created—that's the "Notification" arrow itself. Next, in the Attributes Inspector, set the notification category name to **Pawsome**, which is the same string you used earlier in **PawsomeNotificationPayload.apns**.

> **Note**: Notification categories are typically registered in the app delegate of the containing iOS app. If you're curious, open **AppDelegate.swift** to learn how and where Pawsome configures the notification category.

Select the **Alert Label** and then show the Attributes Inspector. Change the **Lines** parameter to **0** so that the label text will automatically wrap without truncating. Set the **Font** to **Headline** and the **Horizontal** position to **Center**.

Next, drag an **image** from the Object Library and place it under the label. This image will show the cute cat picture.

After selecting the image, open the Attributes Inspector and set the **Image** to **cat01**. Change the **Mode** to **Aspect Fill**. Finally, set the **Horizontal** position to **Center**.

Your storyboard will now look like this:

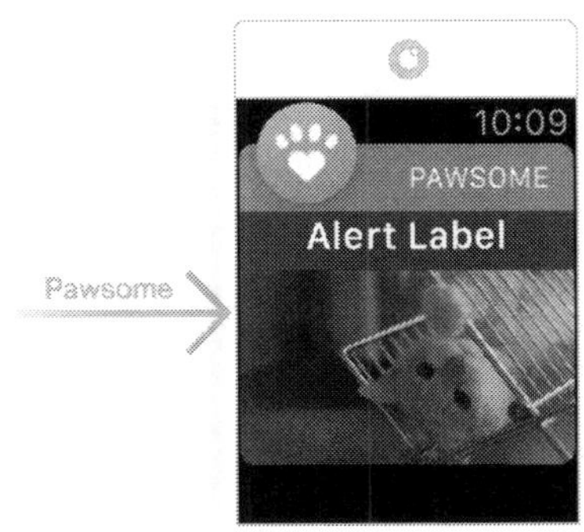

Build and run. As your joyful eyes can now see, the notification shows a cute cat picture.

Static notification interfaces such as this are important, as they provide a fallback in situations where dynamic interfaces are unavailable or fail to load.

You can only configure a static notification interface in the storyboard. That means you can't run any code to update its contents or configure its interface.

The only content that is dynamically updated in a static notification is the label, which is connected to a special outlet named `notificationAlertLabel`. The system automatically updates the text of this label with the alert message from either a remote or local notification or a test APNS file.

> **Note**: You might be wondering why a dynamic long look notification interface would fail to load. Imagine your dynamic interface receives an image URL from the notification payload and downloads the image for display. If the URL for the image is no longer valid or has been removed, the network request could potentially take a long time to fail.

Instead of making the user wait—or worse, not even showing the notification—watchOS will automatically fall back to using the static interface.

Now that you've completed the static long look interface, it's time to create the dynamic version.

Dynamic notification

With **Interface.storyboard** still open, select the **Pawsome** notification category. In the Attributes Inspector, enable **Has Dynamic Interface**.

Interface Builder will automatically create a new scene and add a segue from the static interface to the dynamic interface.

Interface.storyboard now looks like this:

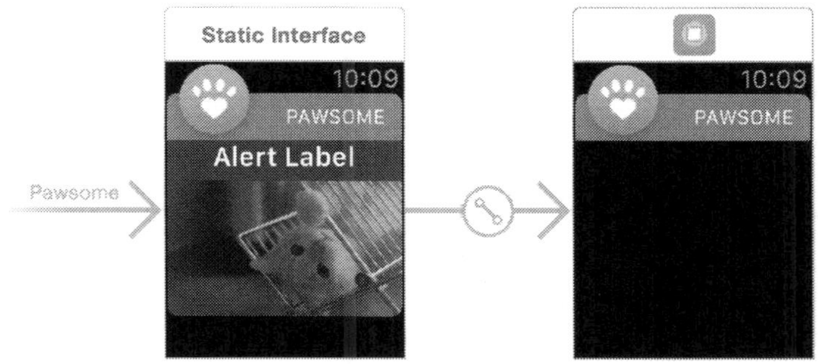

Next, drag a **label** from the Object Library onto the new dynamic interface.

This label will show the notification message. After selecting the label, open the Attributes Inspector and set the **Text** to **<message>**, the **Font** to **Headline**, the **Lines** to **0**, and the **Horizontal Position** to **Center**.

Next, drag an **image** from the Object Library and place it under the label. This image will show a random cute cat picture each time.

After selecting the image, open the Attributes Inspector and set the **Image** to **cat01**. Change the **Mode** to **Aspect Fill**. Finally, set the **Horizontal** position to **Center**.

> **Note**: You may be tempted to add interactive controls to the long look interface, such as buttons and switches. Don't do it; they won't work! Interactive elements aren't allowed in notification interfaces. You add buttons by setting up related notification actions when registering for notifications in the accompanying iPhone app. watchOS will always show them at the bottom of the long look interface.

Your dynamic notification scene will now look like this:

To update the label and show a random cat image each time a notification is received, you need to write some code.

With the project navigator visible, right-click on the **PawsomeWatch Extension** group and select **New File**. Select **watchOS\Source\WatchKit Class** and click **Next**.

Name the file **NotificationController**, set the **Subclass** to `WKUserNotificationInterfaceController`, and ensure you're adding the file to the **PawsomeWatch Extension** target.

Replace all the code in the new file with the following:

```
import WatchKit
import Foundation

// 1
class NotificationController:
WKUserNotificationInterfaceController {

  // 2
  @IBOutlet var label: WKInterfaceLabel!
  @IBOutlet var image: WKInterfaceImage!

  // 3
  func randomInt(min: Int, max:Int) -> Int {
    return min + Int(arc4random_uniform(UInt32(max - min + 1)))
  }

  // 4
  func updateDisplayWithNotificationUserInfo(
    userInfo: [NSObject : AnyObject]) {
    let catImageName = String(format: "cat%02d",
      arguments: [randomInt(1, max: 20)])
    image.setImageNamed(catImageName)
    if let aps = userInfo["aps"] as? NSDictionary,
      let alert = aps["alert"] as? NSDictionary,
      let body = alert["body"] as? String {
        label.setText(body)
    }
  }
}
```

Here's what you're doing with this code:

1. You create the class `NotificationController`, a subclass of `WKUserNotificationInterfaceController`.
2. This class includes an outlet for the notification message label of type `WKInterfaceLabel` and an outlet for the random cat image of type `WKInterfaceImage`.
3. `randomInt(_:max:)` returns a random integer between the passed-in minimum and

maximum integers. This method is used by the next method, `updateDisplayWithNotificationUserInfo(_:)`, to pick a random cat image for display.

4. `updateDisplayWithNotificationUserInfo(_:)` uses the passed-in `userInfo` dictionary to update the display. First, the method sets the cat image to a random cat using the previously mentioned `randomInt(_:max:)`. Next, it sets the <message> label to the `body` string from the `userInfo` dictionary.

Now add the following to the end of the class:

```
// 1
override func didReceiveRemoteNotification(
  remoteNotification: [NSObject : AnyObject],
  withCompletion completionHandler:
  ((WKUserNotificationInterfaceType) -> Void)) {

  // 2
  updateDisplayWithNotificationUserInfo(remoteNotification)

  // 3
  completionHandler(.Custom)
}
```

Let's go through this code step by step:

1. First, you override `didReceiveRemoteNotification(_:withCompletion:)`, which watchOS calls when it receives a remote notification or during testing when an APNS file is selected. watchOS calls the method before displaying the notification interface, allowing you to configure the interface.
2. Next, you call the helper method `updateDisplayWithNotificationUserInfo(_:)` to update the display.
3. Finally, you call `completionHandler()` with the `.Custom` parameter. If you were to call `completionHandler()` with the `.Default` parameter, the app would show the static interface.

Because the Pawsome notification you're building is a local notification, the app you ship will never call `didReceiveRemoteNotification(_:withCompletion:)` unless you added support for remote notifications. You're using it here for development and testing.

Now add the following to the end of the class:

```
// 1
override func didReceiveLocalNotification(
  localNotification: UILocalNotification,
  withCompletion completionHandler:
  ((WKUserNotificationInterfaceType) -> Void)) {
  // 2
```

```
    if let alertBody = localNotification.alertBody {
      let userInfo: [NSObject : AnyObject] = [
        "aps" : [
          "alert": [
            "body": alertBody
          ],
          "category": "Pawsome"
        ]
      ]
      // 3
      updateDisplayWithNotificationUserInfo(userInfo)
    }
    // 4
    completionHandler(.Custom)
  }
```

Let's go through this code step by step:

1. First, you override `didReceiveLocalNotification(_:withCompletion:)`, which does the same thing as `didReceiveRemoteNotification(_:withCompletion:)`, but for local notifications.
2. Because `updateDisplayWithNotificationUserInfo(_:)` expects the passed-in dictionary to match the standard push notification payload of a remote notification, you have to fake it by creating the `userInfo` dictionary. You populate the dictionary using the `alertBody` property of the local notification.
3. Next, you call the helper method `updateDisplayWithNotificationUserInfo(_:)` to update the display.
4. Finally, you call `completionHandler()` with the `.Custom` parameter.

Now open **Interface.storyboard**, select the dynamic notification interface and, in the Identity Inspector, set the **Class** to **NotificationController**.

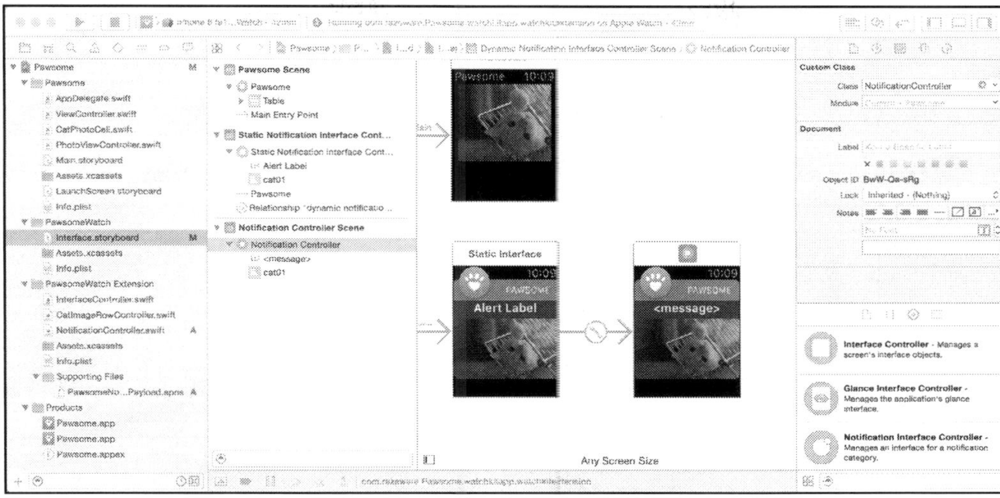

It's time to wire up the outlets for the <message> label and the cat image.

Show the assistant editor and Control-drag from the **<message>** label to the `label` outlet declared in the code.

Do the same thing for the cat image, but drag to the `image` outlet this time.

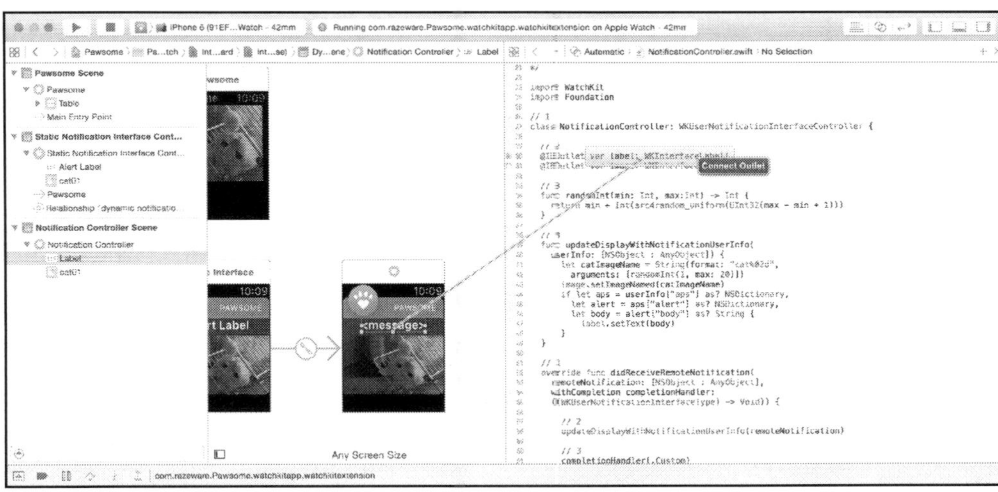

With the notification scheme selected, build and run. You'll see the following customized, dynamic long look notification.

It's so *purrrfect*!

Great work! Now you know how to add custom notification interfaces to your Watch apps.

Where to go from here?

You can find the final project in the folder for this chapter.

In this chapter, you tested Watch notifications, learned about short look and long look interfaces and how they differ, and most impressively, you built a custom, dynamically updated, long look local notification for the Apple Watch.

Now you know the basics of showing custom notifications on watchOS, but there's a lot more you can do from here, including handling actions selected by users from your notifications. A great place to go to for additional information is Apple's Local and Remote Notification Programming Guide: apple.co/1VFndEn.

Chapter 12: Complications

By Jack Wu

By now, you know that you should strive to make your Apple Watch apps *simple*. For you to accommodate user interactions that are measured in seconds, you need to give your users experiences that are uncomplicated and intuitive. Well, where's the fun in that? In this chapter, you'll go the extra mile and dare to add complications to your app.

Just kidding! Not *that* kind of complication—a watch complication. According to Wikipedia, a watch complication refers to any feature in a timepiece beyond the simple display of hours and minutes. That definition doesn't really work for the Apple Watch, since the vast majority of features don't involve displaying hours and minutes. By that definition, the Watch is full of complications!

On the Apple Watch, complications have been slightly redefined as elements on the Watch face that display small, immediately relevant bits of information. They are by far one of the most compelling and useful features of the Apple Watch. Unlike glances, they lie *right* on the Watch face, which makes accessing information as fast as raising your wrist.

With watchOS 2, developers are able to create custom complications for any app.

A new category of interaction

I repeat, *developers are now able to create custom complications for any app*. That means you.

Imagine the possibilities here. What's the score? *Raises wrist.* Is it time for tea? *Raises wrist.* Is this class over yet? *Raises wrist.* Should I use the washroom? Well... I guess you could follow a schedule for that. *Raises wrist.*

As a developer, complications give you a whole new way of engaging with your users. The closest relative to complications on the iPhone is the today extension, which similarly provides quick access to important info, but lacks the immediacy of a watchOS complication. To craft complications, you'll be using **ClockKit**, a new framework in watchOS 2.

Many questions arise just by pondering implementation: *How will the data be available so quickly? How can I update the data continuously? How can I make sure my data is displayed properly in such a small area?*.

This chapter and the subsequent Chapter 19, "Advanced Complications", will answer all of these questions and many more. You'll explore the architecture of ClockKit and learn how to take advantage of complications to give users the most concisely engaging experiences.

So yes, in this chapter, you'll add a complication to your app that doesn't complicate it. On the contrary, it will make your app even simpler to use!

Getting started

It's a well known fact that Apple Watch users love to surf—after removing the Watch, of course. It is thus crucial that you tell them the tide conditions of their favorite surfing spot so they can decide when to go surfing.

Luckily for your users, Tide Watch does exactly that. With Tide Watch, users can monitor tide conditions on their phones, their Watches, and once you're done, right on their Watch faces!

It's all in your hands now, so locate the starter project for **TideWatch** and open **TideWatch.xcodeproj** in Xcode.

Build and run the iPhone app and then the Watch app. Play around with both to get a sense of the data they show and how they display it. The data is pulled live from the Center for Operational Oceanographic Products and Services (CO-OPS) API for tide predictions.

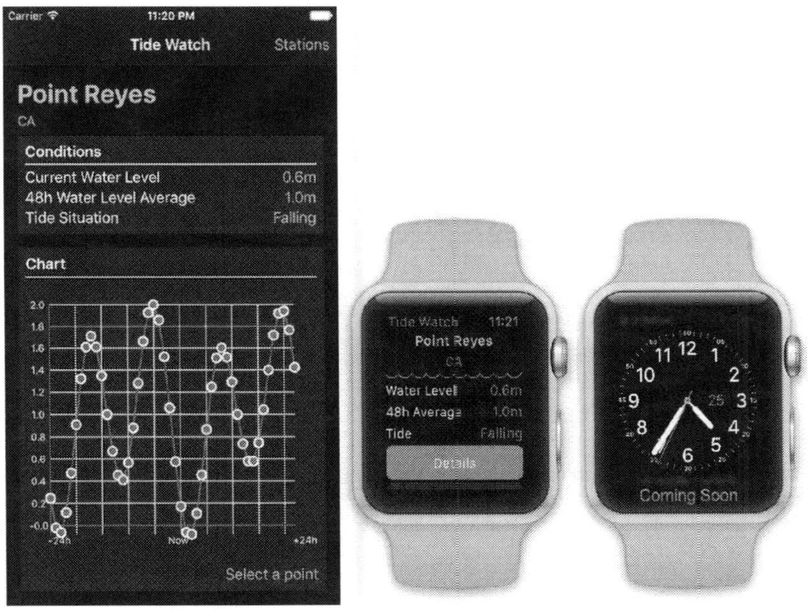

Take a few moments to browse the source code, paying extra attention to how the data is retrieved and modeled in **TideConditions.swift** and the other data models. That's the same data you'll display in the complication.

You don't want to keep the eager surfers waiting too long, though—it's time to complicate!

Adding a complication

In Xcode, open the project settings of the **TideWatch WatchKit App Extension** target. On the **General** tab, you'll see the **Complications Configuration** section:

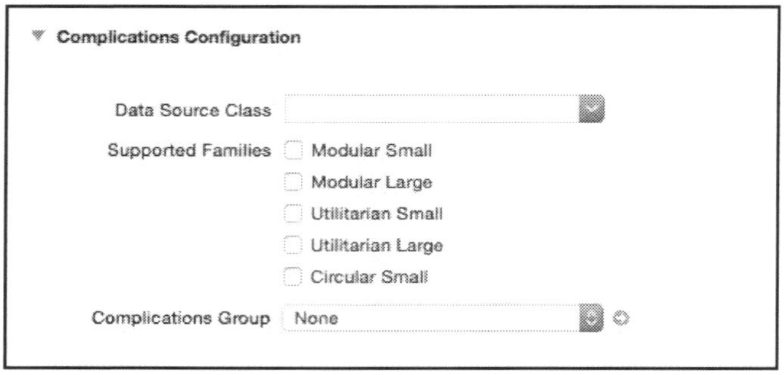

There are three fields here:

- **Data Source Class** will refer to a class that implements `CLKComplicationDataSource` to provide all the data.
- **Supported Families** is where you choose which Watch face families you'll support.
- The **Complications Group** stores the images for your complications within the assets file of your WatchKit extension target.

Most of this probably doesn't make sense yet, but it will soon. You'll fill in these fields one by one, beginning with the families.

Complication families

Three types of Watch faces can display complications: Modular, Utilitarian and Circular.

Look closely at the images below, and you can see the five different **complication families**, grouped by the type of Watch face on which they appear:

- **`ModularSmall`**

- `ModularLarge`
- `UtilitarianSmall`
- `UtilitarianLarge`
- `CircularSmall`

You can choose to support any number of these families, but it's best to support at least one from each Watch face. It's easy to add support for more families, so for your first foray into complications you'll add support for just **Utilitarian Small** and **Utilitarian Large** to Tide Watch. Select both of these options from the list of supported families:

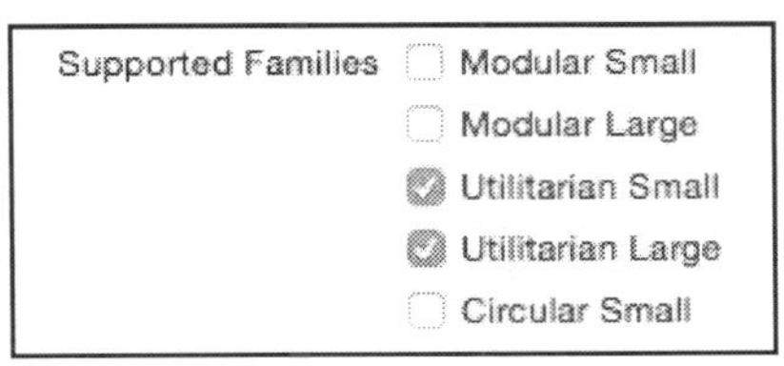

Creating the data source

The data source will provide the system with everything it needs to display a complication. The data source itself is simply an `NSObject` that conforms to `CLKComplicationDataSource`.

The main job of the data source is to package your complication's data into templates that the system can display. The system will request data from the data source to update the complication throughout its life cycle.

The data source needs to respond *as fast as possible*. It shouldn't perform any expensive network fetches or computations—the app should have already handled those—it should only be responsible for packaging that data for the system.

To begin, within the **TideWatch WatchKit App Extension** file group, create a new **Cocoa Touch Class** named **ComplicationController** that is a subclass of `NSObject`:

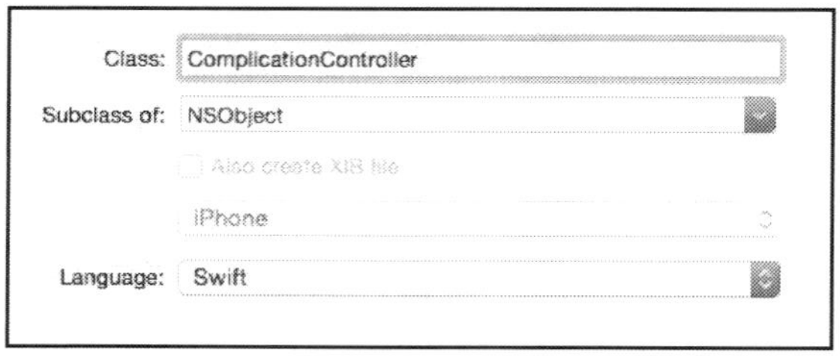

Click **Next** and add the class to the **TideWatch WatchKit App Extension** target:

Go back to the project settings and set `ComplicationController` as the **Data Source Class**:

Open the newly created **ComplicationController.swift** and replace its contents with the following:

```
import ClockKit

class ComplicationController: NSObject,
  CLKComplicationDataSource {

}
```

Here you import ClockKit and declare your new class as conforming to `CLKComplicationDataSource`. The compiler will complain that you don't conform to `CLKComplicationDataSource`. To fix this, copy the following method stubs into `ComplicationController`:

```
// MARK: Register
func getPlaceholderTemplateForComplication(
  complication: CLKComplication,
  withHandler handler: (CLKComplicationTemplate?) -> Void) {
  handler(nil)
}

// MARK: Provide Data
```

```
func getCurrentTimelineEntryForComplication(
  complication: CLKComplication,
  withHandler handler: (CLKComplicationTimelineEntry?)
  -> Void) {
  handler(nil)
}

// MARK: Time Travel
func getSupportedTimeTravelDirectionsForComplication(
  complication: CLKComplication,
  withHandler handler: (CLKComplicationTimeTravelDirections)
  -> Void) {
  handler(.None)
}
```

Here's what you've added:

- **`getPlaceholderTemplateForComplication(_:withHandler:)`** provides the template your Watch will display in the picker when the user is selecting a complication. This will return a sample to let the user know what they should expect.
- **`getCurrentTimelineEntryForComplication(_:withHandler:)`** provides the current template to display. You'll dive deep into what this means very soon. :]
- **`getSupportedTimeTravelDirectionsForComplication(_:withHandler:)`** enables an incredibly useful feature called **Time Travel** for your complication. You won't explore time travel until Chapter 19, "Advanced Complications", so you return a simple `.None` here to signal that you currently support none of the time travel directions.

Note how the data source methods don't return anything. Instead, they use the handler function passed in by the caller to return the data.

Before you go any further, you need to know all about these "templates" you keep reading about.

Complication templates

A complication template represents the types of data it can display and the arrangement of that data:

- The **data** is usually a combination of text and images but can sometimes be other things, such as the percentage to fill a ring.
- The **arrangement** describes how the template will display the data. Most arrangements are simple, such as the text positioned next to the image, but they can also be complex, such as a table layout.

Each subclass of `CLKComplicationTemplate` represents a single arrangement and uses properties to define what types of data it displays.

Glance at the documentation, and you'll notice over *20* different subclasses of `CLKComplicationTemplate` that you can use! Don't panic, though; you'll see that you can neatly organize them.

Complications are organized according to the family that can display them. Each complication family can display a number of different templates. You can further break down the templates by the types of data they display:

- **Only Text:** `SimpleText`, `StackText`, `Columns`, `Body`.
- **Only Images:** `SimpleImage`, `Square`.
- **Text and Image:** `LargeFlat`, `SmallFlat`, `StackImage`.
- **With Ring:** `RingImage`, `RingText`.

Tide Watch is a good example to demonstrate putting this all together. For small templates, Tide Watch can simply provide the current water level as text. For larger templates, Tide Watch can provide an icon, water level and tide condition. Thus, Tide Watch can provide the following templates:

1. `CLKComplicationTemplateModularLargeStandardBody`
2. `CLKComplicationTemplateModularSmallSimpleText`
3. `CLKComplicationTemplateUtilitarianLargeFlat`
4. `CLKComplicationTemplateUtilitarianSmallFlat`
5. `CLKComplicationTemplateCircularSmallSimpleText`

In most cases, you'll choose one template for each family, but you can use different ones at different times as well, if you need them. For example, if it makes sense in your app to show an image at certain times and no image at other times, you can use `SmallFlat` when you need to display the image and `SimpleText` when you don't.

Data providers

Templates don't directly take images and strings for display. ClockKit uses **providers** to help you display your data properly at all times. Providers are extremely convenient; they allow you to specify your *intentions* and leave the actual formatting to the system. You don't have to worry about shortening your strings or formatting your dates—the system will handle it all!

For text, there are a few providers to choose from:

- **CLKSimpleTextProvider** displays any text directly.
- **CLKDateTextProvider** displays a date using the calendarUnits you specify.
- **CLKTimeTextProvider** displays a time either within the user's current timezone or within an optionally specified timezone.
- **CLKRelativeDateTextProvider** displays the difference between a specified date and the current date. You can choose from many display styles, such as "2hrs 26mins", "2 hours" and "2:26".
- **CLKTimeIntervalTextProvider** displays a time interval between any two dates, such as "2:35—3:20PM".

For images, there is only CLKImageProvider, which has five properties you can set:

- **onePieceImage** is a template image to render if your image doesn't need two pieces.
- **tintColor** is the color you use to render onePieceImage or twoPieceImageBackground in.
- **twoPieceImageBackground** is a template image that is tinted with tintColor and displayed behind the foreground image.
- **twoPieceImageForeground** is a template image that you can display on top of twoPieceImageBackground. It is *always* tinted white.
- **accessibilityLabel** is a short string you can use to identify the purpose image for accessibility.

A template-image means that only the transparency of the image is taken into account when displaying. The color information will be ignored and the system will tint the image for you. The image provider will always resize your images properly for display, as well.

That's all you need to know to create a template. Now you're going to apply this knowledge to Tide Watch.

Providing a placeholder

The placeholder is simply a template that doesn't display any real data—it's shown when the user scrolls between complications to select one.

Back in **ComplicationController.swift**, replace the implementation of `getPlaceholderTemplateForComplication(_:withHandler:)` with the following snippet:

```
// 1
if complication.family == .UtilitarianSmall {
  // 2
  let smallFlat = CLKComplicationTemplateUtilitarianSmallFlat()
  // 3
  smallFlat.textProvider = CLKSimpleTextProvider(text: "+2.6m")
  // 4
  smallFlat.imageProvider = CLKImageProvider(
    onePieceImage: UIImage(named: "tide_high")!)
  // 5
  handler(smallFlat)
}
```

Here's what's happening:

1. You always need to check which family is requested so you can return the correct template.
2. You create the `CLKComplicationTemplateUtilitarianSmallFlat` template using the empty initializer.
3. Next, you create a `CLKSimpleTextProvider` that provides a sample of the data, and assign it to `textProvider`.
4. Then, you create a `CLKImageProvider` to provide a sample of an image and assign it to `smallFlat.imageProvider`.
5. Finally, you call the handler to return the data.

You're supporting *two* families here, so you need to check for the other one, as well. Add the following `else` statement right after the previous snippet:

```
else if complication.family == .UtilitarianLarge {
  let largeFlat = CLKComplicationTemplateUtilitarianLargeFlat()
  largeFlat.textProvider = CLKSimpleTextProvider(
    text: "Rising, +2.6m", shortText:"+2.6m")
  largeFlat.imageProvider = CLKImageProvider(
    onePieceImage: UIImage(named: "tide_high")!)

  handler(largeFlat)
}
```

The difference here is that since you have more room to display text, you can take advantage of the ability of `CLKSimpleTextProvider` to take both long and short versions of your text and display it appropriately.

Build and run the Watch app. Once it's running, return to the Watch face and **force**

touch (first pressing **Shift-Command-2**) to bring up the watch face chooser. Select the **UTILITY** watch face and tap **Customize** to begin customization (remember to return to normal touch mode with **Shift-Command-1** first). Scroll down in any of the complication slots and you'll see Tide Watch:

Don't select it, though; it doesn't display any data... yet!

> **Note**: Make sure you're on a Utilitarian Watch face—either Utility or Mickey—since Tide Watch currently only supports Utilitarian families.

Not bad for a few lines of code. To provide real data for your shiny new complication, you need a bit more information on top of the template. You're going to package this together into a timeline entry.

Timeline entries

You've chosen and created a few templates, and now it's time to provide real data. For this to happen, ClockKit needs to know *when* to display your templates. ClockKit uses a `CLKComplicationTimelineEntry` to represent a template for a certain time. This class has only three properties:

1. **date**: The `NSDate` on which to show the data.
2. **complicationTemplate**: Your packaged template, which you learned how to create above.
3. **timelineAnimationGroup**: This allows you to animate between entries.

Ignore the third one for now; you'll learn all about it in Chapter 19, "Advanced Complications". That means you only need to worry about the date.

Display time

The `date` is the first point in time the user will see the entry. For example, a time of 3 p.m. means that the complication will start displaying this entry at exactly 3 p.m., up until it's time to display the next entry.

The time that you should specify is greatly contextual to your data. Generally, your data is going to be useful for a certain period of time—but that doesn't necessarily mean you should provide the start time of that period as the `date` for the entry.

If you're displaying events in a calendar, you want the complication to show the upcoming event before it happens, not the one that just ended. To do so, you provide the end time of the *previous* event as the `date` for the current event. For example:

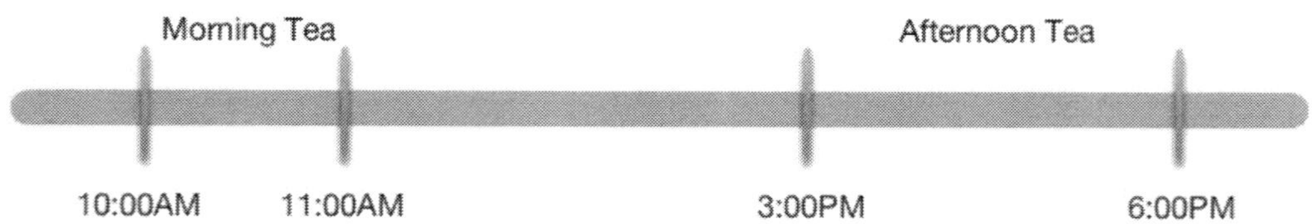

Here, at 12 p.m., the user should see "Afternoon Tea at 3PM" and not "Morning Tea at 10AM", since that's already happened. To achieve this, you should use 11 a.m. as the `date` for the "Afternoon Tea" entry.

On the other hand, if you're displaying up-to-date information as you are in Tide Watch, you want to display the latest data. In the case of Tide Watch, the user wants to see what the tide conditions are at that moment, and so you need to set `date` to the beginning of the time period when that tide condition is valid.

In summary, the `date` you select should be the answer to the question, "When should the user first see this entry?", which could well be different from the answer to, "When does this entry begin?"

Providing a timeline entry

Now that you know what's going into your timeline entry, you can build one—which is the last step in the process of creating your complication for Tide Watch.

To make it easier to package data into templates, add a few helper methods to Tide Watch's data models. Open **WaterLevel.swift** and add the following two methods to `WaterLevel`:

```
var shortTextForComplication: String {
  return String(format: "%.1fm", height)
}
```

```
var longTextForComplication: String {
  return String(format: "%@, %.1fm", situation.rawValue, height)
}
```

You'll use these methods along with `CLKTextProvider` to display the data.

Open **ComplicationController.swift** again—it's time to implement `getCurrentTimelineEntryForComplication(_:withHandler:)`. Replace the contents of the method with the following:

```
let conditions = TideConditions.loadConditions()
guard let waterLevel = conditions.currentWaterLevel else {
  // No data is cached yet
  handler(nil)
  return
}
```

First, you load the data from the cache. Here, you check if the data exists and simply exit if it doesn't. Remember that the data source's job is to return existing data as quickly as possible and it shouldn't attempt to fetch data over the network.

After you've confirmed the data exists, you want to determine which tide image to show. Add the following code to the end of `getCurrentTimelineEntryForComplication(_:withHandler:)`:

```
let tideImageName: String
switch waterLevel.situation {
  case .High: tideImageName = "tide_high"
  case .Low: tideImageName = "tide_low"
  case .Rising: tideImageName = "tide_rising"
  case .Falling: tideImageName = "tide_falling"
  default: tideImageName = "tide_high"
}
```

Here you simply do a `switch` on the tide situation to determine which image to use.

You've got all the information, so you can create the templates. Continue in `getCurrentTimelineEntryForComplication(_:withHandler:)` and add the following snippet to the bottom:

```
// 1
if complication.family == .UtilitarianSmall {
  let smallFlat = CLKComplicationTemplateUtilitarianSmallFlat()
  smallFlat.textProvider = CLKSimpleTextProvider(
    text: waterLevel.shortTextForComplication)
  smallFlat.imageProvider = CLKImageProvider(
    onePieceImage: UIImage(named: tideImageName)!)

  // 2
  handler(CLKComplicationTimelineEntry(
```

```
    date: waterLevel.date, complicationTemplate: smallFlat))
}
```

This is very similar to the way you created the placeholder:

1. First you check the family and create the template. You create the providers using the data you have and package it all up.
2. Here you create a `CLKComplicationTimelineEntry`, which includes the date along with the template.

Don't forget the other family. Add the following `else` statement right below the end of the previous `if` statement:

```
else {
  let largeFlat = CLKComplicationTemplateUtilitarianLargeFlat()
  largeFlat.textProvider = CLKSimpleTextProvider(
    text: waterLevel.longTextForComplication,
    shortText:waterLevel.shortTextForComplication)
  largeFlat.imageProvider = CLKImageProvider(
    onePieceImage: UIImage(named: tideImageName)!)

  handler(CLKComplicationTimelineEntry(
    date: waterLevel.date, complicationTemplate: largeFlat))
}
```

Once again, you can take advantage of the extra space by using the longer version of the text while keeping the shorter version as a backup.

That's it! Build and run the Watch app. Remember to let it finish loading the data that your complication will display. Activate your complication and observe your app instantly populate your data, right on the Watch face!

Where to go from here?

If this is your first complication, congratulations. Not only have you acquired the knowledge you need to add the convenience of complications to your Watch apps—you've made strides toward populating the world with very happy and efficient surfers.

Before you move on, play around with Tide Watch's complications. Try out the different templates and even add all the missing families, if you can.

The power of complications doesn't end here. Head over to Chapter 19, "Advanced Complications", to learn all about time travel and how to keep your data always up to date. See you there. :]

Chapter 13: Watch Connectivity

By Matthew Morey

One of the more difficult tasks in Watch app development is sharing data with the counterpart iPhone app. In the first version of watchOS, developers were limited to simple file or key/value pair sharing. In watchOS 2, Apple has provided a much more robust communication framework called Watch Connectivity.

Watch Connectivity lets an iPhone app and its counterpart Watch app transfer data and files back and forth. If both apps are active, live communication happens; otherwise, data transfers in the background so it's available as soon as the receiving app launches.

In this chapter, the iPhone and Watch versions of an app called CinemaTime will exchange data in the background using a mode of communication called "application context transfers".

CinemaTime is for patrons of a fictional cinema. It allows customers to view movie show times and buy tickets right from their iPhones and Watches.

Getting started

Open the CinemaTime starter project in Xcode and then build and run the **CinemaTimeWatch** scheme. Tap on **Purchase Ticket** and explore the app.

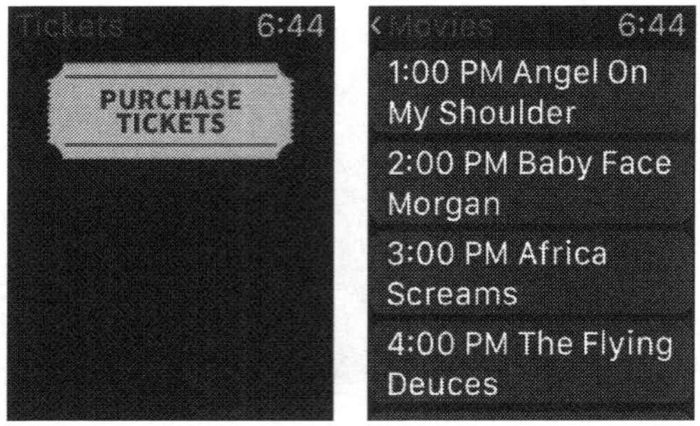

The existing CinemaTime apps show the movie schedule for a cinema. Customers can buy movie tickets from either app.

Build and run the **CinemaTime** scheme and explore the iPhone app.

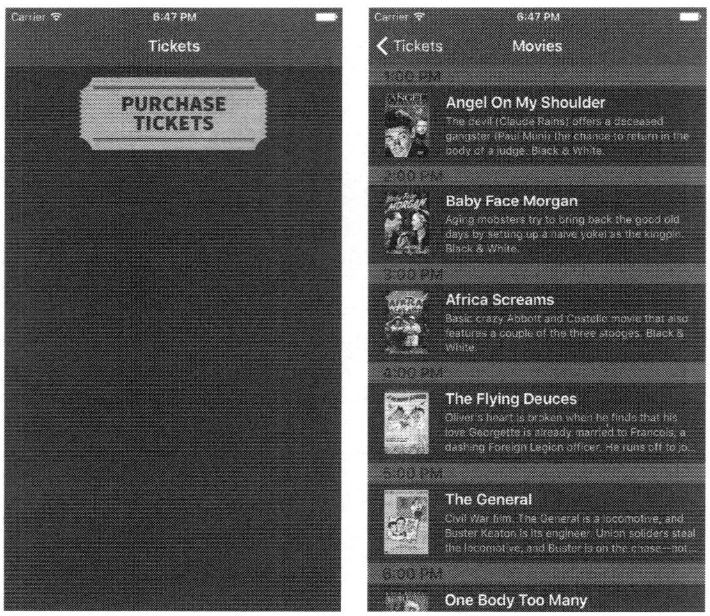

If you haven't already, buy a movie ticket in either app and then view the list of purchased movie tickets in the counterpart app. Do you see the issue?

Movie tickets purchased in one app are not shown in the other one. The apps are not sharing data.

Right now, when a customer buys a movie ticket in the iPhone app, it only exists there. If the customer then tried to use the Watch app to get into the cinema, they'd be turned away, as the Watch won't have the ticket.

Customers have a reasonable expectation that their data, movie tickets in this case, will be available from both versions of the app regardless of which app created the data.

In the rest of this chapter, you'll use the Watch Connectivity framework to sync the customer's purchased movie tickets between the iPhone and Watch versions of the app.

Setting up Watch Connectivity

Before you can transfer data between apps, you must first set up and activate a connectivity session. You should do this early in the app's lifecycle so any pending transfers can happen right away.

If the app launches in the background, a view controller's `viewDidLoad()` won't get called and any connectivity-related code located there won't run. In this case, you'll want to be sure your session is set up and activated outside of any view controller.

For CinemaTime you will add the setup and activation code to the iPhone's app delegate and the Watch's extension delegate in `application(_:didFinishLaunchingWithOptions:)` and `applicationDidFinishLaunching()`, respectively. These methods are executed even when the app launches in the background.

You use the `WCSession` class and `WCSessionDelegate` protocol to configure and activate connectivity sessions in both apps:

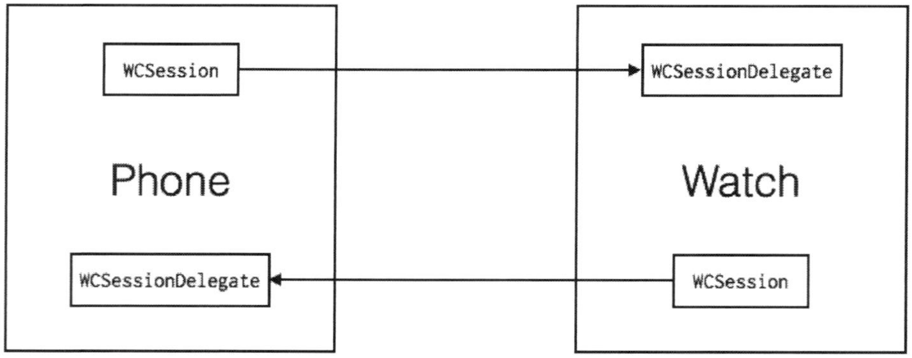

This is what you're about to do in the CinemaTime iPhone app.

iPhone connectivity setup

Open **AppDelegate.swift** and update the imports to include the Watch Connectivity framework:

```
import WatchConnectivity
```

The app delegate needs to conform to the `WCSessionDelegate` protocol to receive communication from the Watch. Update the class declaration to include the `WCSessionDelegate` protocol:

```
class AppDelegate: UIResponder, UIApplicationDelegate,
  WCSessionDelegate {
```

Before you can send or receive data via the Watch Connectivity framework, you must configure the session and assign a delegate. Locate `setupWatchConnectivity()`.

This method is called in `application(_:didFinishLaunchingWithOptions:)`. Setting up the Watch Connectivity framework right when the app launches ensures any pending communication happens right away. Now implement this method with the following:

```
private func setupWatchConnectivity() {
  // 1
  if WCSession.isSupported() {
    // 2
    let session = WCSession.defaultSession()
    // 3
    session.delegate = self
    // 4
    session.activateSession()
  }
}
```

Here's what you're doing with this code:

1. You check if the current device supports Watch Connectivity. This method returns `true` for all iPhones that support pairing with an Apple Watch running watchOS 2 or higher.
2. Next, you set `session` to the singleton session object `defaultSession` for the current device.
3. You set the session delegate to `self`. You must set the `delegate` property before calling `activateSession()`.
4. Finally, you signify that the app is ready to send and receive communication by calling `activateSession()`.

Calls to any `WCSession` communication methods must happen after the `WCSession` object has an assigned delegate and is active.

There is only ever one session object, `WCSession.defaultSession()`, per app — and only a single object can conform to the `WCSessionDelegate` protocol. These limitations mean that most of your Watch Connectivity-related code will need to exist in a single class. For simplicity, in the CinemaTime iPhone app, all the connectivity code is in the app delegate.

> **Note**: In general, avoid lumping too many things in a central location like the app delegate, and instead try to separate functionality by areas of concern. Because the amount of connectivity code you're writing is minimal, I've chosen to place this code in the app delegate, as it's easier to understand. If your connectivity code gets more complex than what you're writing for CinemaTime, you should consider moving it into a separate class.

You've finished setting up a connectivity session in the iPhone app, so now you need to add identical code to the Watch version. Prepare yourself — a lot of this will sound familiar!

Watch connectivity setup

Open **ExtensionDelegate.swift** and update the imports to include the Watch Connectivity framework:

```
import WatchConnectivity
```

Update the class declaration to include the `WCSessionDelegate` protocol:

```
class ExtensionDelegate: NSObject, WKExtensionDelegate,
  WCSessionDelegate {
```

Locate `setupWatchConnectivity()`. Yup, you guessed it. `setupWatchConnectivity()` is called in `applicationDidFinishLaunching()` to ensure any pending communication happens right away. Now replace the `TODO` with the following code:

```
private func setupWatchConnectivity() {
  if WCSession.isSupported() {
    let session  = WCSession.defaultSession()
    session.delegate = self
    session.activateSession()
  }
}
```

Are you experiencing déjà vu?

You should be, as the code to configure and establish a Watch Connectivity session is identical for both apps.

Build and run the **CinemaTimeWatch** scheme; this will launch the Watch app in the Watch simulator. Next, build and run the **CinemaTime** scheme to launch the iPhone app.

Both apps look and behave exactly as before, because all you've done is set up and activated the connectivity session.

Next, you'll send data — purchased movie tickets — back and forth between the iPhone and Watch apps.

Device-to-device communication

There are two types of device-to-device communication in Watch Connectivity: interactive messaging and background transfers.

Interactive messaging

When both apps are active, establishing a session allows immediate communication via interactive messaging. The `WCSession` methods `sendMessage(_:replyHandler:errorHandler:)` and `sendMessageData(_:replyHandler:errorHandler:)` send information. The `WCSessionDelegate` methods `session(_:didReceiveMessage:)` and `session(_:didReceiveMessageData:)` receive sent information.

Interactive messaging is best used in situations that need information transferred immediately. For example, if a Watch app needs to trigger the iPhone app to do something, such as tracking the user's location, the interactive messaging API can communicate the request from the Watch to the iPhone.

Before implementing interactive messaging, consider how likely your iPhone app and Watch app are to be active at the same time. Given the short lifespan of Watch apps, and the likelihood that they're used while the user's phone is tucked away in her pocket, your apps may get little opportunity to make use of interactive messaging.

> **Note**: To learn more about interactive messaging, see Chapter 18, "Advanced Watch Connectivity" and Apple's Watch Connectivity Framework Reference: apple.co/1JlPcnH.

Background transfers

If only one of the apps is active, it can still send data to the counterpart app using one of the background transfer methods.

Background transfers allow iOS and watchOS to pick the opportune time to transfer data. Both take into account the user's battery usage and other pending transfers to schedule all background communications. This has the benefit of reducing battery usage while still guaranteeing data transfers happen in a timely manner.

There are three types of background transfers: user info, file, and application context.

User info and file transfers

User info transfers send dictionaries of data to the counterpart app in first-in, first-out order (FIFO). Once a data transfer is started it's handled by the Watch Connectivity framework. The transfer will happen regardless of the state of the app that initiated it. The `WCSession` method `transferUserInfo(_:)` sends the dictionaries, and the counterpart app receives the dictionaries via the `WCSessionDelegate` methods `session(_:didReceiveUserInfo:)`.

A Watch game that needs to transfer the user's progress to the counterpart iPhone app would require a user info transfer. Using `transferUserInfo(_:)`, the iPhone app would receive notice of each completed level from the Watch app.

File transfers send a local file and optional dictionary to the counterpart app. Like user info transfers, file transfers allow you to queue up files in the background for sending. The `WCSession` method `transferFile(_:metadata:)` initiates a file transfer. The counterpart app receives the files via the `WCSessionDelegate` methods `session(_:didReceiveFile:)`.

A social app that allows you to favorite pictures would use file transfers to send the favorited images over to the counterpart app. For example, favoriting images on the iPhone would trigger a file transfer to the Watch via `transferFile(_:metadata:)`.

> **Note**: To learn more about user info transfers check out Chapter 18, "Advanced Watch Connectivity". Once you finish this chapter, I encourage you to work through Chapter 18 to achieve a holistic view of the Watch Connectivity framework.

Application context transfers

The application context transfer is the most appropriate method of communication for the CinemaTime apps. They are like user info transfers in that both allow you to transfer a dictionary of data between apps. The difference is that only the last dictionary of data, called a context, transfers over. For example, if one app starts multiple transfers, the counterpart app will only receive the last dictionary sent.

The `WCSession` method `updateApplicationContext(_:)` sends the context, and the `WCSessionDelegate` method `session(_:didReceiveApplicationContext:)` receives it in the counterpart app:

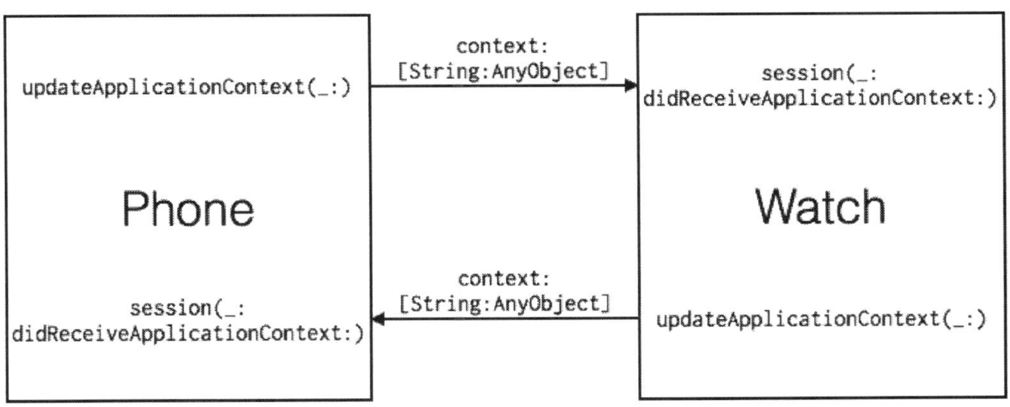

> **Note**: Although `updateApplicationContext(_:)` accepts a dictionary of type `[String : AnyObject]` this doesn't mean anything can be sent. The dictionary can only accept property list types such as arrays, dictionaries, and strings. See apple.co/1PZEPXD for a complete list of supported types.

You should use an application context transfer when you need to send a single set of the most interesting data from one app to its counterpart.

A cheap gas finding iOS app that tracks the user's location and suggests gas stations would use an application context transfer. For example, on the iPhone the cheapest gas stations near the user's current location would be packaged up and sent to the Watch via `updateApplicationContext(_:)`.

You'll use application context transfers to send purchased movie tickets first from the iPhone to the Watch. Then you'll complete similar steps to transfer tickets from the Watch to the iPhone.

iPhone-to-Watch communication

Find `sendPurchasedMoviesToWatch(_:)` in **AppDelegate.swift**. This function is called when the `NotificationPurchasedMovieOnPhone` notification fires, which is whenever the user purchases a movie ticket in the iPhone app.

Now replace the `TODO` with the following:

```
private func sendPurchasedMoviesToWatch(
  notification: NSNotification) {
  // 1
  if WCSession.isSupported() {
    // 2
    if let movies =
      TicketOffice.sharedInstance.purchasedMovieTicketIDs() {
      // 3
      let session = WCSession.defaultSession()
      if session.watchAppInstalled {
        // 4
        do {
          let dictionary = ["movies": movies]
          try session.updateApplicationContext(dictionary)
        } catch {
          print("ERROR: \(error)")
        }
      }
    }
  }
}
```

Let's go through this code step by step:

1. First you check if the current device supports Watch Connectivity.
2. Next, you set the `movies` constant to an array of strings representing all purchased movie tickets by calling `purchasedMovieTicketIDs()` on the `TicketOffice` singleton class. This array represents movie tickets purchased on the iPhone.
3. You set the constant `session` to the default connectivity session, and verify

installation of the counterpart Watch app. If the user hasn't installed the Watch app, there's no point in trying to communicate with it.

4. Finally, you call `updateApplicationContext(_:)` on the active session to transfer to the Watch a dictionary with the `movies` key set to the already-created `movies` array.

Now that the iPhone app is sending purchased movie tickets, you'll set up the Watch app to receive them.

Open **ExtensionDelegate.swift** and add the following to the end of the class:

```
// 1
func session(session: WCSession,
  didReceiveApplicationContext
  applicationContext:[String:AnyObject]) {
  // 2
  if let movies = applicationContext["movies"] as? [String] {
    // 3
    TicketOffice.sharedInstance.purchaseTicketsForMovies(movies)
    // 4
    dispatch_async(dispatch_get_mair_queue()) { () -> Void in
      WKInterfaceController.reloadRcotControllersWithNames(
        ["PurchasedMovieTickets"], contexts: nil)
    }
  }
}
```

Here's what you're doing:

1. Your code implements the optional `WCSessionDelegate` protocol method `session(_:didReceiveApplicationContext:)`. The active connectivity session calls this method when it receives context data from the counterpart iPhone app.

2. Next, you set `movies` to an array of strings representing all purchased movie tickets from the `applicationContext` dictionary. These are movie tickets purchased on the iPhone.

3. Next, you call `purchaseTicketsForMovies(_:)` on the `TicketOffice` singleton class with the `movies` array. Calling this method updates the list of purchased movies in the Watch app.

4. Finally, you reload the root view controller, which shows the purchased movie tickets, on the main queue. The delegate callback happens on a background queue, so the reload must happen on the main queue, as it's triggering UI updates.

Build and run the **CinemaTime** scheme to launch the iPhone app, and buy a movie. Next, stop the iPhone app and build and run the **CinemaTimeWatch** scheme. Voila! the movie you purchased on the iPhone app appears on the Watch app.

> **Note**: Notice that if you have both the iPhone app and the Watch app running at the same time, this use case will still work. While interactive messaging is the most immediate way to transfer data between two running apps, background transfers will work as well.

You've just added the ability to transfer purchased movie tickets from the iPhone to the Watch. Guess what you're going to do next?

Watch-to-iPhone communication

Open **ExtensionDelegate.swift** and locate `sendPurchasedMoviesToPhone(_:)`. When the `NotificationPurchasedMovieOnWatch` notification fires, the extension delegate calls `sendPurchasedMoviesToPhone(_:)`. This notification happens whenever the user buys a movie ticket on the Watch. Now replace the `TODO` with this code:

```
private func sendPurchasedMoviesToPhone(
  notification:NSNotification) {
  // 1
  if WCSession.isSupported() {
    // 2
    if let movies =
      TicketOffice.sharedInstance.purchasedMovieTicketIDs() {
      // 3
      do {
        let dictionary = ["movies": movies]
        try
WCSession.defaultSession().updateApplicationContext(dictionary)
      } catch {
        print("ERROR: \(error)")
      }
    }
  }
}
```

Although this code looks like what you just added in the iPhone-to-Watch communication section, there are some minor differences:

1. You check if the current device supports Watch Connectivity. On the Watch, this will always return `true`. Even so, it doesn't hurt to be careful in case this API behavior changes in future versions of watchOS.
2. Next, you set `movies` to an array of strings representing all purchased movie tickets by calling `purchasedMovieTicketIDs()` on the `TicketOffice` singleton class. This array represents movie tickets purchased on the Watch.
3. Finally, you call `updateApplicationContext(_:)` on the active session to transfer a dictionary to the iPhone with the `movies` key set to the already-created `movies` array.

This code is slightly different for the iPhone app because there, it checked to verify the installation of the counterpart Watch app. On the Watch, you don't need to check for iPhone app installation, because the only way the Watch app can exist is if there's an installed iPhone app.

Now that the Watch is sending purchased movie tickets, you'll set up the iPhone to receive them.

Open **AppDelegate.swift** and add the following code to the `AppDelegate` class:

```
// 1
func session(session: WCSession,
  didReceiveApplicationContext
  applicationContext:[String:AnyObject]) {
  // 2
  if let movies = applicationContext["movies"] as? [String] {
```

```
    // 3
    TicketOffice.sharedInstance.purchaseTicketsForMovies(movies)
    //4
    dispatch_async(dispatch_get_main_queue()) { () -> Void in
      let notificationCenter =
        NSNotificationCenter.defaultCenter()
      notificationCenter.postNotificationName(
        NotificaitonPurchasedMovieOnWatch, object: nil)
    }
  }
}
```

Here's what you're doing with this code:

1. The app delegate implements the optional `WCSessionDelegate` protocol method `session(_:didReceiveApplicationContext:)`. The active connectivity session uses this method to receive context data from the counterpart Watch app.
2. Next, you set `movies` to an array of strings representing all purchased movie tickets from the `applicationContext` dictionary. These are movie tickets purchased on the Watch.
3. Next, you call `purchaseTicketsForMovies(_:)` with the `movies` array on the `TicketOffice` singleton class. Calling this method updates the list of purchased movies in the iPhone app.
4. Finally, you post the notification `NotificationPurchasedMovieOnWatch` on the main queue signifying new purchases. The view controllers listening for this notification now know to update their views to show the newly purchased movie tickets. You use the main queue to post the notification, because the delegate callback happens on a background queue, and all UI updates need to happen on the main queue.

If you've made it this far, déjà vu must not phase you. If you've made it this far, déjà vu must not phase you. Oh, wait!

Build and run both apps, but this time, buy a movie ticket on the Watch app. After you purchase the ticket, the iPhone app will refresh and show the purchased ticket.

Congratulations! CinemaTime customers can now buy and view movie tickets from either app without worrying about where they made the purchase.

Where to go from here?

You can find the final project in the folder for this chapter.

In this chapter, you set up the Watch Connectivity framework, learned about the different ways to transfer data between counterpart iPhone and Watch apps, and finally, successfully implemented the application context transfer method.

Application context transfers provide a simple yet powerful way to share data between apps, but they aren't the be-all end-all solution. User info and file transfers, covered in Chapter 18, "Advanced Watch Connectivity", are also useful when you require more advanced communication.

Chapter 14: Playing Audio and Video

By Soheil Azarpour

In watchOS 2, Apple introduced a new API to play and record multimedia files on the Apple Watch, which wasn't possible in watchOS 1. Now the Watch runs the WatchKit extension natively, it has access to hardware-specific APIs. This is a great opportunity to create innovative apps and enhance the user experience with new interactive possibilities.

In this chapter, you'll learn about watchOS 2's audio and video APIs and how to use them in your code. You'll add audio and video playback, as well as audio recording, to a memo app so that users can record and review their thoughts and experiences right from their wrists. Let's get started!

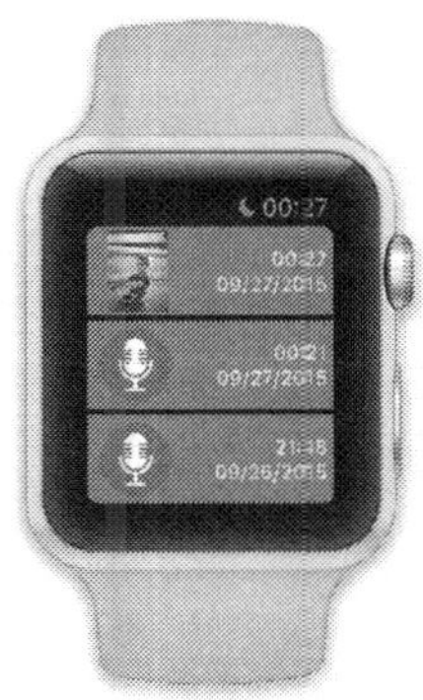

Getting started

The starter project you'll use in this chapter is called **Turbo Memo**. Open **Turbo Memo.xcodeproj** in Xcode and make sure the **Turbo Memo** scheme for iPhone is selected. Build and run in the iPhone simulator, and you'll see the following screen:

Users can record audio and video diaries by simply tapping the plus (+) button and then selecting either **Audio** or **Video** from the action sheet. The app sorts the entries by date, and users can play back an entry by tapping it.

Try adding audio and video entries to create some initial data.

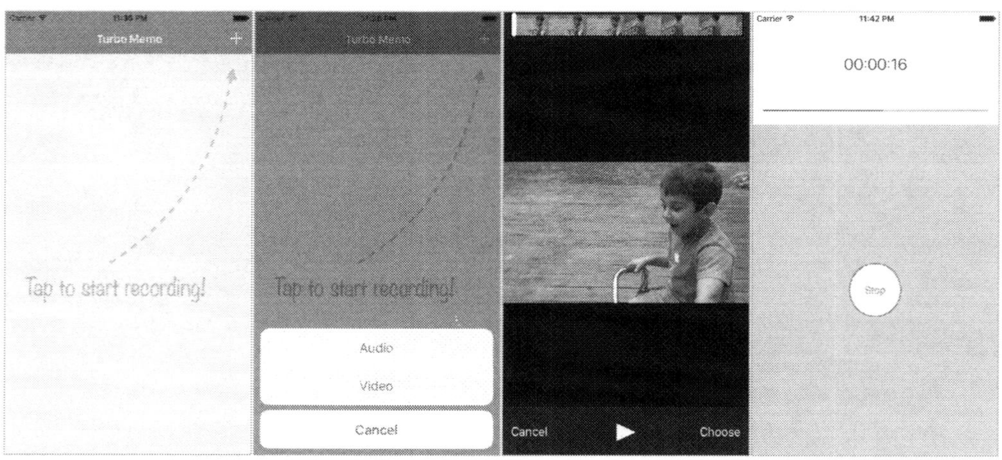

Now stop the app and change the scheme to **Turbo Memo Watch**. Build and run in the Watch Simulator, and you'll see the following screens:

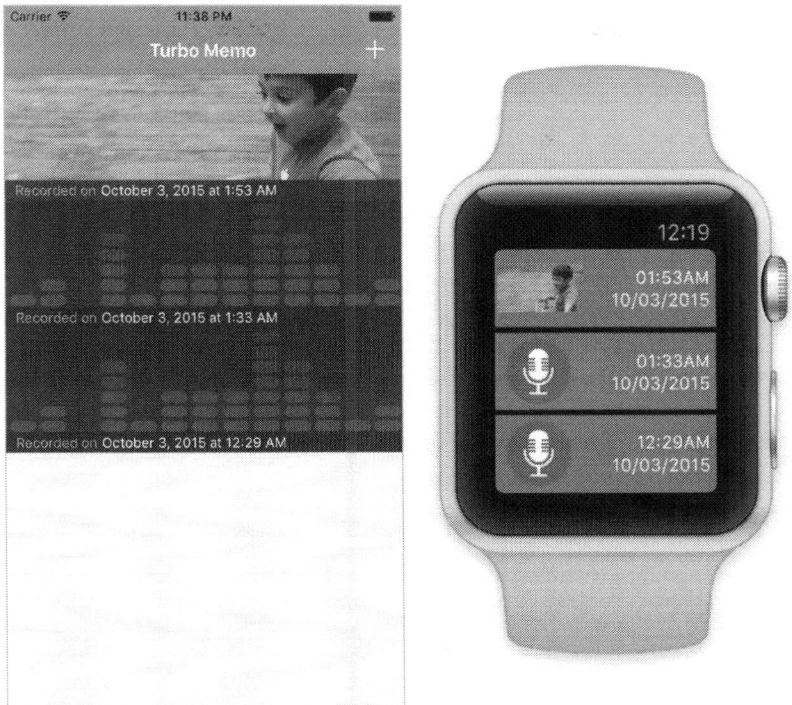

The Watch app syncs with the iPhone app to display the same entries, but it doesn't do anything else yet.

You're about to change that. Without further ado, let's play some media!

> **Note**: You may be wondering why you can add video memos only through the photo library and not by capturing them using the camera. The camera is available only on a device, so you won't be able to add video memos in the simulator. We chose the photo library as the source of video memos so that you can complete the entire chapter using the simulator.
>
> At the time of writing, the watchOS 2 media player has a bug preventing it from playing audio or video files on the device. If you want to enable adding video memos by capturing a video instead, open **MemosViewController.swift** in the project, find the implementation of `addMemoButtonTapped()` and update the `videoAction` block by replacing `.PhotoLibrary` with `.Camera`.

Playing audio and video

It would be satisfying if your users could play the memo entries on the Watch instead of just looking at a list of them. With the entries so easily accessible, the app would begin to live up to the "Turbo" in its name. In this section, you'll use new `WKInterfaceController` methods to play the audio and video files in the memos.

To play a media file, you simply have to present a built-in media player controller using the `presentMediaPlayerControllerWithURL(_:options:)` method on `WKInterfaceController`, passing in a file URL that you obtain from the `VoiceMemo` object the user selects from the `WKInterfaceTable`. It's that simple!

Open **InterfaceController.swift** and add the following:

```
override func table(table: WKInterfaceTable,
  didSelectRowAtIndex rowIndex: Int) {
    let memo = memos[rowIndex]
    // 1
    let options: [NSObject: AnyObject] =
      [WKMediaPlayerControllerOptionsAutoplayKey : true]
    // 2
    presentMediaPlayerControllerWithURL(memo.URL,
      options: options) { (didEndPlay: Bool,
      endTime: NSTimeInterval, error: NSError?) -> Void in
      // 3
      print("Finished playing \(memo.URL.lastPathComponent).
        Did end play? \(didEndPlay). Error?
        \(error?.localizedDescription)")
    }
}
```

Let's go through this step by step:

1. You create a dictionary of options to configure the media player. In this case, you'll start the playback automatically when the app presents the media player, by adding the `WKMediaPlayerControllerOptionsAutoplayKey` key.
2. Next, you present a media player controller by calling `presentMediaPlayerControllerWithURL(_:completion:)`and passing in the URL of the audio file and the playback options dictionary.
3. In the completion block, you check playback results based on your specific needs. Here, you simply log the results to the console.

That's it! Build and run the app. Make sure you've already created audio and video memos, and then verify that you can play both types.

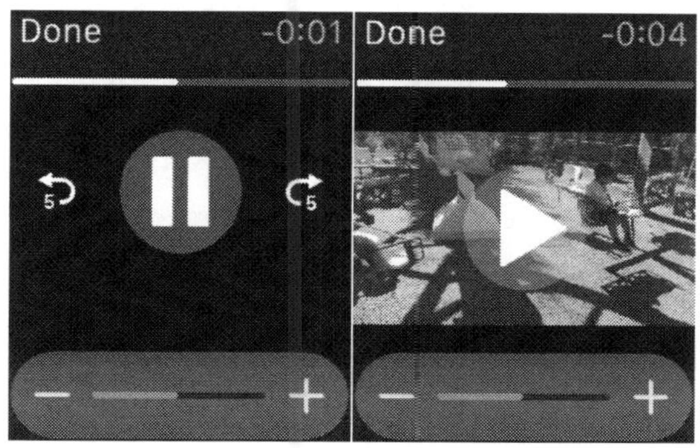

One simple API works for both audio and video playback! How handy is that? But there's more you can do.

Playback options

Besides `WKMediaPlayerControllerOptionsAutoplayKey`, there are a few other playback options you can specify:

- **`WKMediaPlayerControllerOptionsStartTimeKey`** specifies a point in time from which the media file will begin to play. This is particularly useful when you want to resume playback when the user returns to the app. Or, you can offer the user shortcuts to jump to certain timestamps in a clip.
- **`WKMediaPlayerControllerOptionsVideoGravityKey`** specifies how the video should be stretched to fit its container. The value should be a member of the `WKVideoGravity` enumeration. Possible values are `.ResizeAspect`, `.ResizeAspectFill` and `.Resize`.
- **`WKMediaPlayerControllerOptionsLoopsKey`** determines whether the content should loop.

Give the third option a try. Still in **InterfaceController.swift**, update the `options` dictionary so it loops:

```
let options: [NSObject: AnyObject] =
  [WKMediaPlayerControllerOptionsAutoplayKey: true,
  WKMediaPlayerControllerOptionsLoopsKey: true]
```

Build and run to make sure everything is still in order, and that the media player loops the content. If you want to break yourself of a habit by replaying an admonition until temptation subsides, now you can. :]

Supported formats

The watchOS 2 media player is very flexible and easy to use. In addition to the various playback options, it can play many common audio and video types. But, due to the Watch's limited processor and memory, Apple recommends the following formats:

- **Audio:** 32 kbps bit rate, AAC Stereo
- **Video:** H.264 high profile, 160 kbps bit rate, 30 FPS frame rate
- **Video:** full screen, 208x260 pixel resolution
- **Video:** 16:9 aspect ratio, 320x180 pixel resolution

Using a recommended format ensures your content is delivered to the user with the best possible outcome for the platform.

Movie player and more!

There are still more tools in the toolbox you can play with. Similar to `WKInterfaceImage`, watchOS 2 provides a `WKInterfaceMovie` object that displays a playback icon over a selected image. The app will automatically play an associated movie when the user taps the icon. You can specify the preview image by setting the `posterImage` property.

`WKInterfaceMovie` is particularly useful because it gives your video content a native look and feel, and the poster image helps users quickly understand the content of the video clip.

> **Note**: You can also pass a remote content URL to the media player. The media player will display a loading indicator and then display the file.

Look at the implementation of `updateInterfaceTableData()` in **InterfaceController.swift**, and you'll see a `VideoMemo` object with a `smallPreviewImage` property. The code sets that image on the `WKInterfaceImage` property of `MemoRowController`. Open **MemoRowController.swift** and add the following outlet:

```
@IBOutlet var interfaceMovie: WKInterfaceMovie!
```

Now open **Interface.storyboard**, and in the document outline, expand your **interface controller scene** to reveal `MemoRowController`. From the Utilities pane, search the Object Library for the **movie** object. Drag and drop one above your **preview image** inside the container group of `MemoRowController`, as shown below:

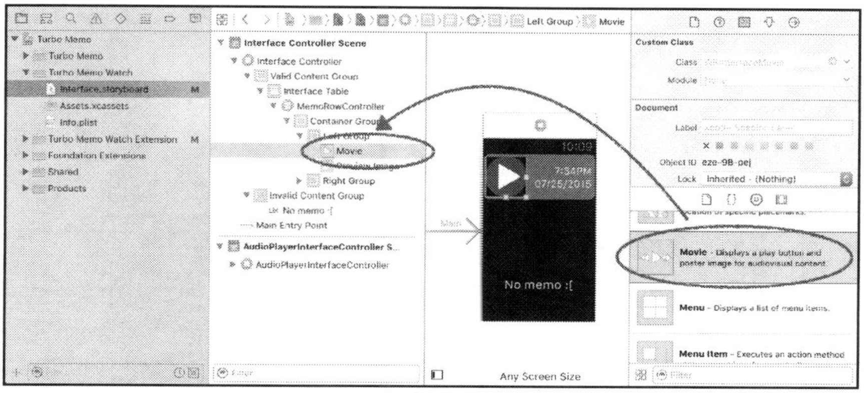

Next, **Control-drag** from `MemoRowController` in the view outline to the **movie** object to connect the outlet.

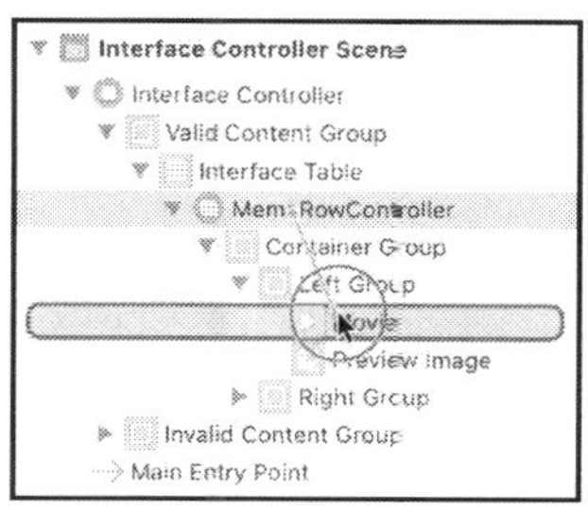

Open **InterfaceController.swift**, find the implementation of `updateInterfaceTableData()` and replace the optional unbinding of `videoMemo` with the following:

```
if let videoMemo = memo as? VideoMemo {
  controller.interfaceMovie.setHidden(false)
  controller.previewImage.setHidden(true)
  if let image = videoMemo.smallPreviewImage {
    let posterImage = WKImage(image: image)
    controller.interfaceMovie.setPosterImage(posterImage)
  }
  controller.interfaceMovie.setMovieURL(videoMemo.URL)
} else {
  controller.interfaceMovie.setHidden(true)
  controller.previewImage.setHidden(false)
}
```

You check the type of the memo and update the interface accordingly, using the new `WKInterfaceMovie` property.

Build and run! This time, you get a free play button on top of your video memo preview image. Tap the play button and the video will start to play.

Background audio playback

The media player controller in watchOS 2 has one limitation: As soon as the user dismisses the player, playback stops. This isn't necessarily a problem if the user is viewing a video memo, but if the user is listening to a long audio memo, you want to continue playing the file even when the user closes the media player.

In watchOS 2, very much like in iOS, you can specify that your app uses background audio. This lets the system prepare itself to take over and continue playing the audio file if a user dismisses your media player.

To declare support for background audio, you'll update the Info.plist for the Watch app. Open **Turbo Memo Watch\Info.plist**, select the **Information Property List** entry and tap the + button:

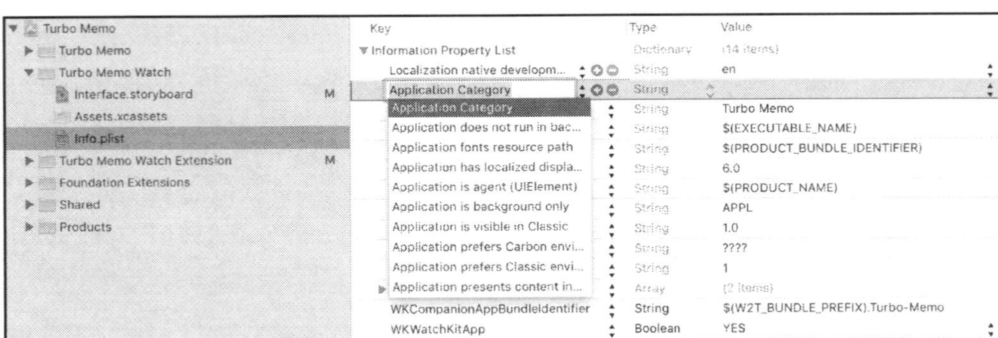

Change the value of the new key to `UIBackgroundModes`. Make sure its type is `Array` and then expand the key and add a new value named `audio`. Xcode will most likely change the values to more readable versions:

Key	Type	Value
▼ Information Property List	Dictionary	(14 items)
Localization native development re...	String	en
▼ Required background modes	Array	(1 item)
Item 0	String	App plays audio or streams audio/video using AirPlay
Bundle display name	String	Turbo Memo
Executable file	String	$(EXECUTABLE_NAME)

> **Note**: Apps can play long audio content through a connected Bluetooth headset in the background when the app is inactive. Your app initiates audio playback, but the system manages it.

You'll use `WKAudioFilePlayer` to play long audio files. `WKAudioFilePlayer` gives you more control over playback and the rate of playback. However, you're responsible for providing an interface and building your own UI.

The starter project includes `AudioPlayerInterfaceController`. You'll use `AudioPlayerInterfaceController` as a basis for your custom audio player.

Open **AudioPlayerInterfaceController.swift** and add the following properties at the beginning of `AudioPlayerInterfaceController`:

```
var player: WKAudioFilePlayer?
```

You'll use the `player` and `playerItem` variables to play back an audio file.

Still in **AudioPlayerInterfaceController.swift**, update the implementation of `awakeWithContext(_:)` as follows:

```
override func awakeWithContext(context: AnyObject?) {
  super.awakeWithContext(context)
  if let memo = context as? VoiceMemo {
    let asset = WKAudioFileAsset(URL: memo.URL)
    let playerItem = WKAudioFilePlayerItem(asset: asset)
    player = WKAudioFilePlayer(playerItem: playerItem)
  }
}
```

If the `context` you're passing to the controller is a `VoiceMemo`, you set up a `WKAudioFileAsset` to house the local `VoiceMemo` file. Both the `WKAudioFilePlayer` and the Now Playing glance use this asset. The glance uses metadata embedded in the audio file, or other properties you set on the asset to display file information. Once you create the asset, you use it to create a `WKAudioFilePlayerItem`, and use the item to track the playback state of the asset. Finally, you set up the player with the item.

Now that you have the player initialized with a player item, you need a way to play it.

Add the following to the end of the class:

```
private func play() {
  if player?.status == .ReadyToPlay {
    print("WKAudioFilePlayer is playing.")
    player?.play()
  } else {
    print("WKAudioFilePlayer failed to play.")
  }
}
```

Here, you check the status of the current item to play. If its status is `.ReadyToPlay`, you start the playback; otherwise, you log an error message to the console.

To start the playback automatically when the `AudioPlayerInterfaceController` appears, override `didAppear()` as shown below:

```
override func didAppear() {
  super.didAppear()
  play()
}
```

And finally, hook up the basic play and pause functions. Update the implementation of `playButtonTapped()` and `pauseButtonTapped()` in **AudioPlayerInterfaceController.swift** as follows:

```
@IBAction func playButtonTapped() {
  play()
}

@IBAction func pauseButtonTapped() {
  player?.pause()
}
```

That was easy!

Now, open **InterfaceController.swift**, find the implementation of `table(_:didSelectRowAtIndex:)` and update it as follows:

```
override func table(table: WKInterfaceTable,
  didSelectRowAtIndex rowIndex: Int) {
    let memo = memos[rowIndex]
    if let voiceMemo = memo as? VoiceMemo {
      presentControllerWithName(
        "AudioPlayerInterfaceController", context: voiceMemo)
    } else {
      // ... the rest of the code.
    }
}
```

Make sure you place the existing code within the `else` block. Here, if the selected memo is a `VoiceMemo`, you play it back using your new custom media player; otherwise, you use the system-provided media player.

Build and run, and select a voice memo from the list. The app will present your custom interface.

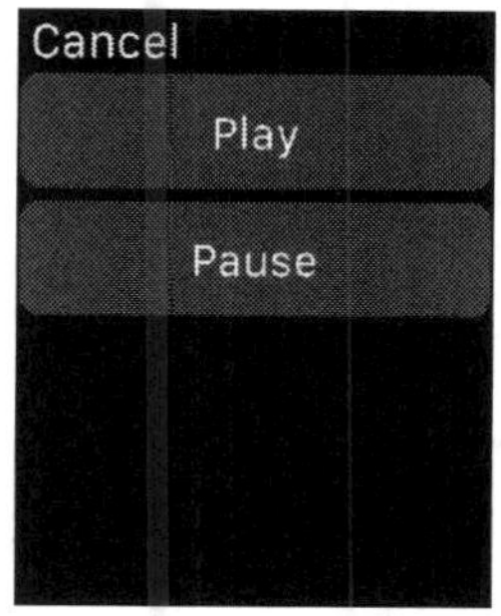

There's a lot more you can do with `WKAudioFileAsset`, `WKAudioFilePlayerItem` and `WKAudioFilePlayer`. You can use **Key Value Observing** to watch interesting properties, such as `currentTime` on `WKAudioFilePlayerItem`, and update an interface label to display lapsed time.

If you have more than one item to play, such as in a playlist, you'll want to use `WKAudioFileQueuePlayer` instead of `WKAudioFilePlayer` and queue your items. The system will play queued items back to back and provide a seamless transition between files.

Recording audio

One the most exciting features of watchOS 2 is its access to the microphone. Being able to add a voice memo to Turbo Memo on the Apple Watch is definitely something users will appreciate—so let's do it!

In watchOS 2, the WatchKit extension code is bundled and copied to the Apple Watch along with the Watch app itself. Even though the code now runs natively on the Watch, from the system's standpoint, it's still a separate process that's sandboxed within its own container. That means the Watch app and the WatchKit extension don't share the same sandbox!

When you start recording, it's the Watch app that does the recording and has access to the microphone. The WatchKit extension then needs to provide a shared container to which both can read and write, allowing the Watch app to write the audio and the WatchKit extension to grab it.

App groups

A container on the local file system that multiple processes can access... hmm, that sounds like an app group! Indeed, you need to enable app groups to share data between the Watch app and the WatchKit extension. Once you've done that, the OS creates a specific folder on the local file system, and anything you create or reference by the app group identifier will reside in this folder.

Apps groups require entitlements to work, but before you enable the entitlements, you need to make sure you've selected a valid team ID that matches your bundle identifier in Xcode.

In Xcode, select the project in the project navigator. Verify that the Watch app and extension targets have the same team selected:

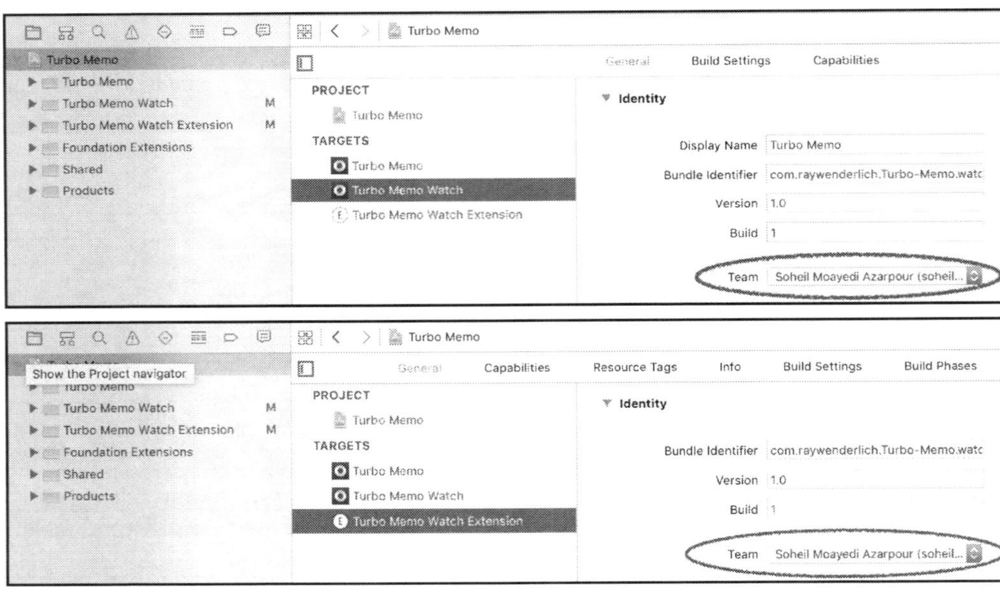

If you don't have any teams in the drop-down menu, make sure you've added a developer account in Xcode's preferences.

Now you need to change the bundle identifier of the project to one that's associated with your developer account. It should begin with com.<yourdomain> instead of com.raywenderlich.

It's an easy change to make, but unfortunately, there are far too many places where you need to make it, as is always the case with projects that have many targets. It could be a cumbersome process, and things could go wrong quickly! Fortunately, we've done the heavy lifting and provided you with a nice and easy shortcut.

A user-defined setting called **W2T_BUNDLE_PREFIX** has been created for you in the Turbo

Memo project build settings. As this is defined at the project level, all targets inherit it by default. You're going to update this setting in just one place, and it will automatically propagate everywhere you need it.

Make sure the Turbo Memo project is selected in the project navigator and select **Turbo Memo** under the **Project** heading in the middle pane. Select the Build Settings tab and scroll all the way down until you reach the **User-Defined** section, as shown below:

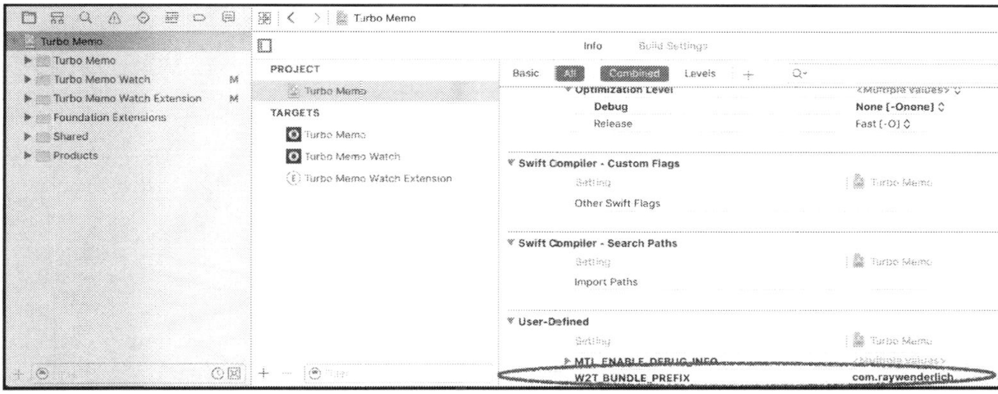

Find the `W2T_BUNDLE_PREFIX` entry and update the value to match your own domain.

Enabling app groups

Switch to the **Turbo Memo Watch** target and select the **Capabilities** tab. Enable **App Groups** by flicking the switch to **On**.

Make sure the App Groups section is expanded and tap the + button to add a new group. Xcode will then prompt you to enter a name for the new app group. Name it group.com.<YOUR_DOMAIN>.<GROUP_NAME>, replacing <YOUR_DOMAIN> with your actual domain, and <GROUP_NAME> with a meaningful name for your project, like `shared-container`.

When you're done, you'll see something that looks like this:

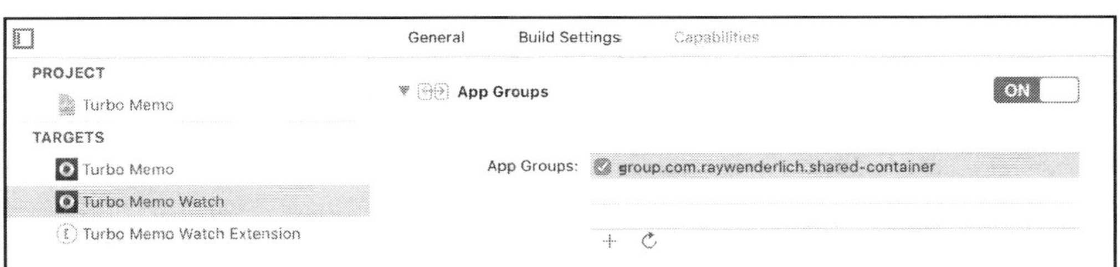

> **Note**: You must prefix all app groups with the word "group" followed by a period.

If you're a member of more than one development team, a modal dialog will likely appear asking you to select a team. Choose the one that's most appropriate for the Turbo Memo project—usually your personal team—and click Choose to continue.

Xcode will automatically add any required entitlements to your project. If you don't have an existing entitlements file, Xcode will create one:

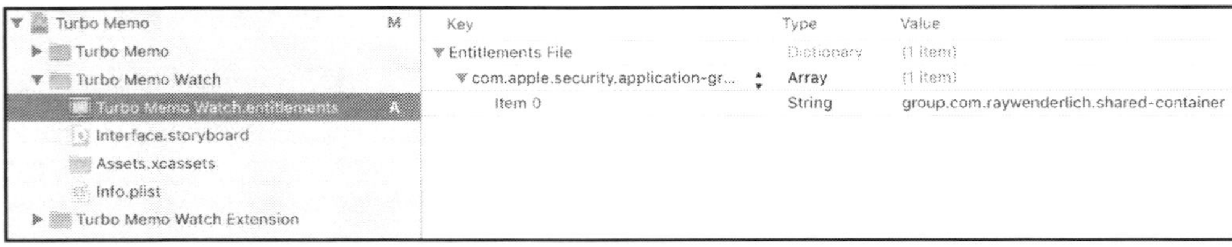

If everything goes well, you'll see the app group selected. If for any reason the creation process fails, the app group's name will appear in red, and you may have to go to developer.apple.com to create an app group manually. There are a couple reasons why this could happen:

- You don't have admin privileges on your developer account, or you don't have an active developer account.
- You used a name for the group that's already in use by you or another developer in your team.
- You added and removed a similar app group with a different casing—for example, `group.rw` versus `group.RW`—within the last few minutes. It usually takes a few minutes for the changes to propagate from Xcode to Apple's servers.

Now that you have a solid understanding of app groups and how they work, you're prepared to do a little hacking on Turbo Memo.

Recording

Open **InterfaceController.swift** and add the following at the end of the class implementation:

```
private func newOutputURL() -> NSURL? {
  // 1
  let appGroupIdentifier = "YOUR_APP_GROUP"
  guard let sharedContainerURL = NSFileManager.defaultManager().
    containerURLForSecurityApplicationGroupIdentifier(
    appGroupIdentifier) else { return nil }
  // 2
  let helper = MemoFileNameHelper()
  let dateFormatter = helper.dateFormatterForFileName
  let date = NSDate()
  let filename = dateFormatter.stringFromDate(date)
  // 3
```

```
    let output = sharedContainerURL.
      URLByAppendingPathComponent("\(filename).m4a")
    return output
  }
```

Make sure you replace `YOUR_APP_GROUP` with the reverse domain string you used earlier. It should be of the form `group.com.<YOUR_DOMAIN>.shared-container`. Let's break down this code:

1. You use the `containerURLForSecurityApplicationGroupIdentifier(_:)` method of `NSFileManager` to get a URL pointing to the shared container. If the app groups weren't properly set up, this method returns `nil`. Otherwise, it returns a URL that you can use like any other local file URL.
2. You create a consistently-named file name using the `MemoFileNameHelper` class.
3. Finally, you create a URL with the appropriate file name and extension to return. Note that the extension of the file determines the codec. The system uses an AAC codec for `.M4A` and `MP4` extensions, and an LPCM codec for `WAV`.

Now add a helper method, `processRecordedAudioAtURL(_:)`, to **InterfaceController.swift**:

```
  private func processRecordedAudioAtURL(URL: NSURL) {
    defer {
      do {
        try NSFileManager.defaultManager().removeItemAtURL(URL)
      } catch {}
    }
    guard let destination = NSFileManager.defaultManager().
      moveItemAtURLToUserDocuments(URL, renameTo: nil)
      else { return }
    let voiceMemo = VoiceMemo(filename: destination.
      lastPathComponent!, date: NSDate())
    MemoStore.sharedStore.addMemo(voiceMemo)
    MemoStore.sharedStore.save()
  }
```

Here, you try to move the recorded file from the shared container to the user's documents directory, simply to keep all the files organized and in one place. Once you've moved the file, you update the `MemoStore`.

Next, add the following method to **InterfaceController.swift**:

```
  @IBAction private func addVoiceMemoMenuItemTapped() {
    // 1
    guard let outputURL = newOutputURL() else { return }
      // 2
    let preset = WKAudioRecorderPreset.NarrowBandSpeech
    let options: [NSObject : AnyObject] =
```

```
      [WKAudioRecorderControllerOptionsMaximumDurationKey: 30]
    presentAudioRecorderControllerWithOutputURL(outputURL,
      preset: preset, options: options) {
      (didSave: Bool, error: NSError?) -> Void in
      // 2
      print("Did save? \(didSave) - Error: \(error)")
      if didSave {
        self.processRecordedAudioAtURL(outputURL)
      }
    }
  }
```

This is the action method you'll call when a user wants to add a new voice memo. Here's what you're doing:

1. You make sure you have a valid URL in the shared container where you can save the output.
2. Next, you configure presets for the recorder and present the system-provided audio recording controller. See below for more information on the presets you can use.
3. In the completion block, you log the result to the console and, if an audio file has been successfully saved, you pass it on to the helper method you implemented earlier.

When you present an audio recording controller, there are a number of things you can specify. First, the `preset` you select determines the sample and bit rates at which the audio will record:

- **`NarrowBandSpeech`**: As its name implies, this is a good preset for voice memos and voice messages. It has a sample rate of 8 kHz, and it records at a bit rate of 24 kbps with an AAC codec and 128 kbps with an LPCM codec.
- **`WideBandSpeech`**: This preset has a higher sample rate of 16 kHz, and it records at a bit rate of 32 kbps with an AAC codec and 256 kbps with an LPCM codec.
- **`HighQualityAudio`**: This preset has the highest sample rate at 44.1 kHz, and it records at a bit rate of 96 kbps with an AAC codec and 705.6 kbps with an LPCM codec.

You can also specify various recording options:

- **`WKAudioRecorderControllerOptionsMaximumDurationKey`**: You can set the maximum duration of recorded audio clips by passing in an `NSTimeInterval` value in seconds. There's no maximum recording time if you don't set a value for this key.
- **`WKAudioRecorderControllerOptionsAlwaysShowActionTitleKey`**: You can use this key to pass either `true` or `false` to modify the behavior for showing the action button. If you specify `false`, the audio recorder controller shows the button only after the user has recorded some audio. By default, the action button is always visible.

- **`WKAudioRecorderControllerOptionsActionTitleKey`**: You can use this key to pass in a `String` to customize the display title of the button that the user taps to accept a recording. By default, the button's title is **Save**.
- **`WKAudioRecorderControllerOptionsAutorecordKey`**: By passing a Boolean value for this key, you can change the automatic recording behavior of the audio recorder controller. If you set it to `true`, once the controller is presented, it automatically starts recording; otherwise, the user has to tap on the record button to start recording. The default value is `true`.

It's time to hook up the new action in the storyboard. Open **Interface.storyboard** and from the Object Library, drag and drop a **menu** into your **interface controller scene**:

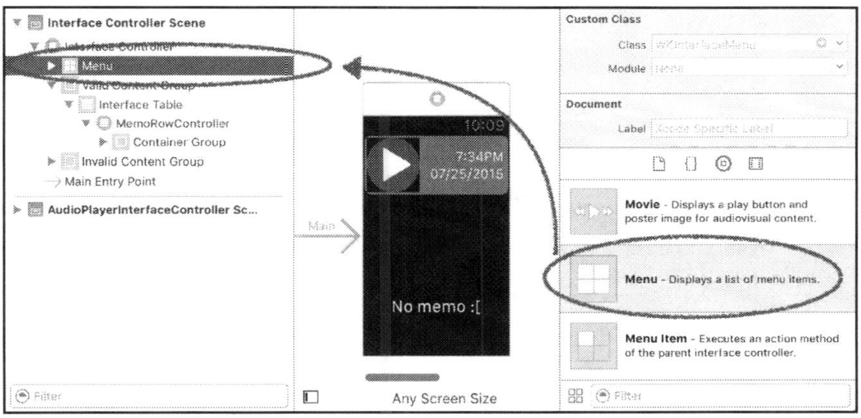

Expand the **menu** in the document outline and select the **menu item**. In the Attributes Inspector, change the menu item's **title** to **+ Voice** and its **image** to **Add**, as shown below:

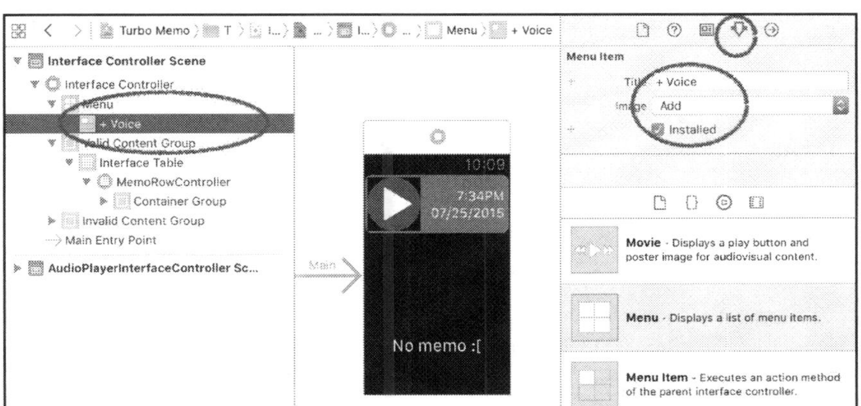

Now **Control-drag** from the menu item to the interface controller and connect the menu to `addVoiceMemoMenuItemTapped()`.

That's it! Build and run. Bring up the contextual menu using the force touch gesture and tap on the **+ Voice** button. The app will present you with an audio recording controller. Tap the **Save** button, and you'll have recorded your first voice memo on an Apple Watch, using your own code!

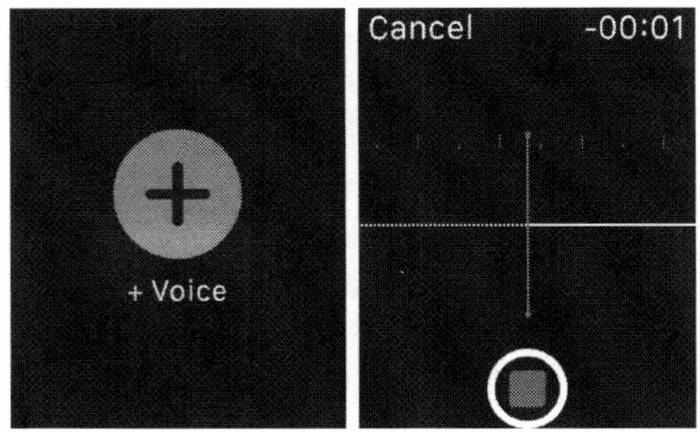

Where to go from here?

The audio and video API of watchOS 2 makes it possible to deliver a smooth multimedia experience on the Apple Watch even when the paired iPhone isn't in proximity. Whether recording audio or playing back audio and video, this is a technology with endless possibilities.

If you're curious to learn more about app groups, be sure you check out the "Sharing Data with Your Containing App" section of Apple's *App Extension Programming Guide*: apple.co/1I5YBtZ

Chapter 15: Advanced Layout

By Ryan Nystrom

WatchKit comes with a handful of amazing layout tools: `WKInterfaceGroup` with its spacing and padding; content-driven sizes; and versatile UI elements like `WKInterfaceLabel` and `WKInterfaceImage`. These tools let you whip together an interface without breaking a sweat.

However, the one thing that's missing is the precision layout and sizing we have in UIKit. Dynamically adding and removing views and nudging their frames and bounds are mostly out of the question in WatchKit, leaving designers scratching their heads every time Watch developers tell them, "that isn't possible".

But what if... it was?

That's right—with a little know-how, you can bend WatchKit's elements to your liking and build exciting, dynamic interfaces. In this chapter, you're going to build a powerful guitar-chord visualizer made entirely from groups and labels!

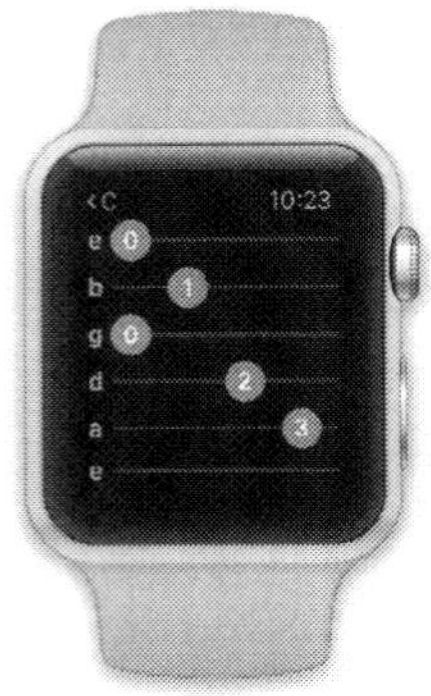

So tighten your headband, sheath your katana, and get ready to become a WatchKit layout ninja!

Getting started

Before you dive into building the Watch app, take a look at the iPhone version so you understand how the app works.

Open **ChordHelper.xcodeproj**, select the **ChordHelper target** and build and run. Try selecting a couple of different chords and look at how the blue indicators move, indicating which frets of the guitar your fingers should press for each string.

Take a look at the screenshot below, which shows how to play a standard C chord, along with a picture of someone playing the chord on a guitar.

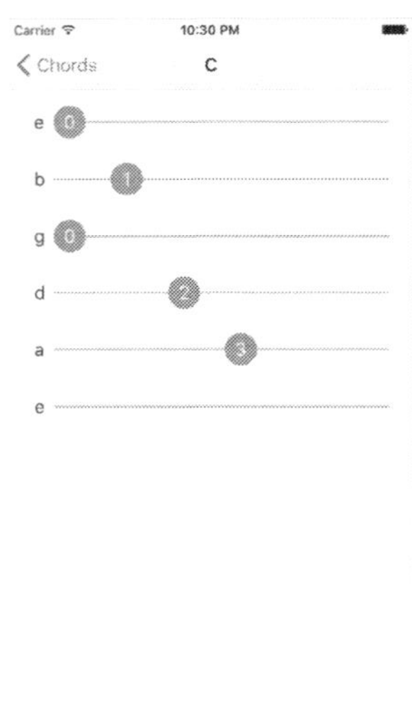

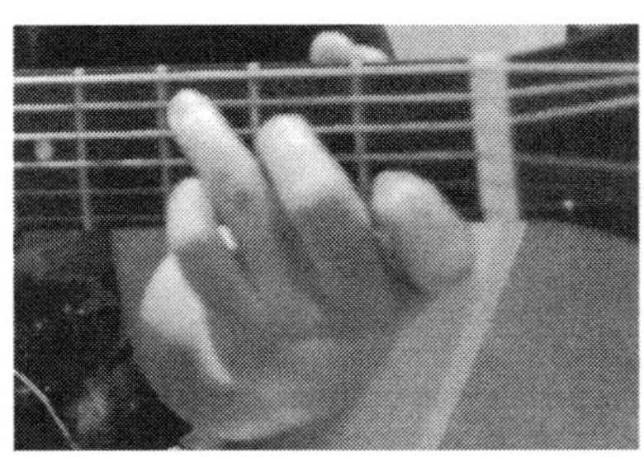

If you aren't familiar with guitar *tablature*, each line represents a string on the guitar, each with its own tuning (e.g. E, A, D, G, B, E). The dots and numbers correspond to a *fret* on the guitar neck. This is where you put your fingers. If the dot has a zero, that means that you play the string without putting your finger on a fret.

Typically you play chords near the base of the guitar neck, frets 0 to 5. Also, your hand can only stretch so far, so you will rarely see chords that span across more than five frets.

Open **ChordHelper\Main.storyboard** and find the view controller for the chord detail view. It's the one with six blue squares—the `CircleLabel` class makes them round. Drill down to the constraints on the blue squares and find the constraint that controls the x-position of the square.

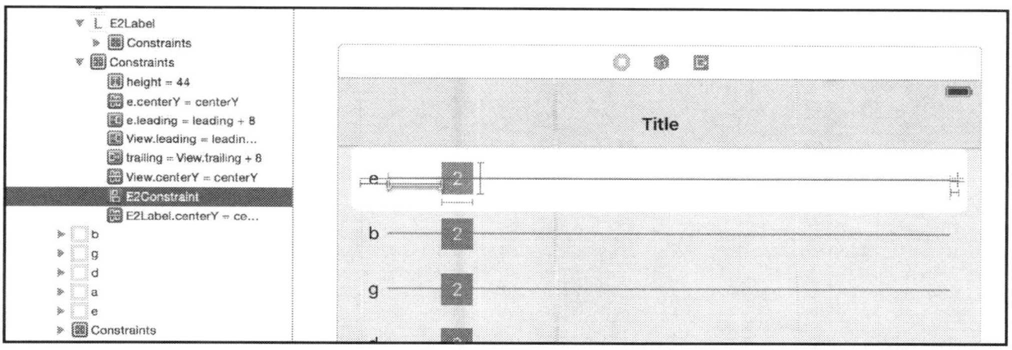

This constraint is connected to an outlet so that you can change the `constant` value to reflect the fret position.

> **Note**: "Frets" are raised metal strips on the neck of a guitar that divide the neck into semitone intervals. You press a guitar string against a fret to change the note of the string. There are typically 21 to 24 frets on electric guitars, and a **chord** is simply a combination of fret positions for one or more strings.

Through the rest of this chapter, you'll create a simple Watch version of the iPhone app that has a very similar dynamic layout.

The chord interface controller

Open the **ChordHelper WatchKit App target** with the **38mm Watch simulator** and build and run the Watch app. You'll see a list of chords, as shown:

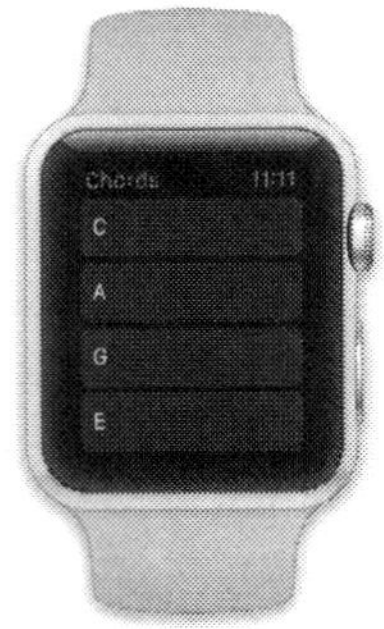

Try tapping on one of the items—nothing happens! That's because there aren't any segues or controllers set up for the WatchKit app. That's your job.

Open **ChordHelper WatchKit App\Interface.storyboard** and add a new **interface controller**. Right-click and drag from the prototype row in the table to the new controller you just added. Select **push** as the navigation type.

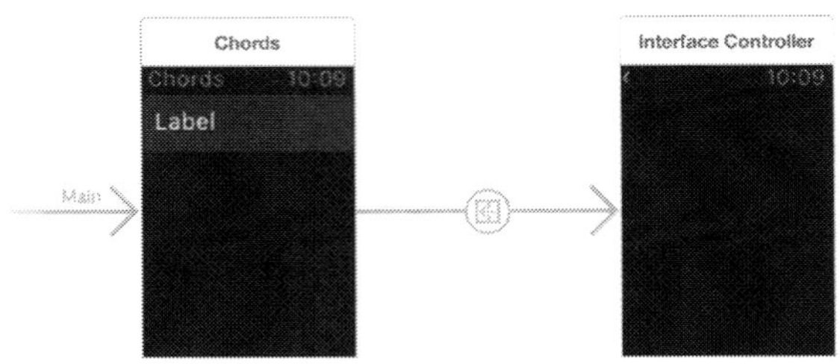

Select **File\New\File...** and add a new **Cocoa Class** named **ChordController** that subclasses `WKInterfaceController`. Make sure that **ChordHelper WatchKit Extension** is selected before you click Create.

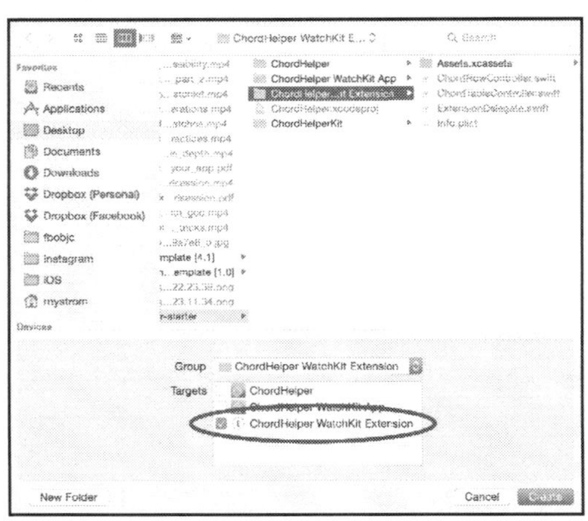

Still in **Interface.storyboard**, change the **class** of the new interface controller to **ChordController**.

Open your new **ChordController.swift** file and make sure the file imports `WatchKit`. Sometimes Xcode forgets to add it automatically!

Add the following implementation of `awakeWithContext(_:)` to the `ChordController` class:

```
override func awakeWithContext(context: AnyObject?) {
  super.awakeWithContext(context)
  if let chord = context as? Chord {
    setTitle(chord.name)
  }
}
```

You pass in a context object that is a `Chord` struct. You'll take a close look at this class soon; for now you're simply setting up the controller. Assuming you get a valid `Chord` object, you set the title of the controller to the `name` property of the chord.

Open **ChordTableController.swift** and add the following function:

```
override func contextForSegueWithIdentifier(
  segueIdentifier: String, inTable table: WKInterfaceTable,
  rowIndex: Int) -> AnyObject? {
    return Chord.standardChords[rowIndex]
}
```

This function simply returns a `Chord` object for the selected row, so it's passed as the context to the next controller.

> **Note**: If you need a refresher on navigation and context objects in WatchKit, check out Chapter 6, "Navigation".

Build and run the Watch app and select a chord. You'll see the app push an empty controller with the name of the selected chord onto the navigation stack.

Creating the fretboard layout

Displaying the fret position for each string requires several interface elements:

- A label for the string, typically the note to which it's tuned;
- A label that shows the fret number;
- A line to make it easier to identify the string label with the fret number.

Open **ChordHelper WatchKit App\Interface.storyboard** and drag a new **group** element into `ChordController`. Inside this new group, add a **label** and another **group**.

For the **label**, update it's attributes per the following:

- Change **Text** to **e**;
- Set **Text Color** to **Light Gray Color**;
- Set **Vertical Alignment** to **Center**;
- Finally, set **Width** to **Fixed** with a value of **10**.

Next, change the attributes of the **group** to the right of the label as follows:

- Set **Color** to a hex value of **2094FA**, which is a light shade of blue;
- Make **Width** and **Height** both **Fixed** with a value of **20**;
- Set **Radius** to **10**.

> **Note**: Setting the radius to a value of half the width and height turns any rectangular group into a circle. It's a very simple way to make dots and other circular containers. You can even nest circular groups to make borders!

So far, your controller looks like this:

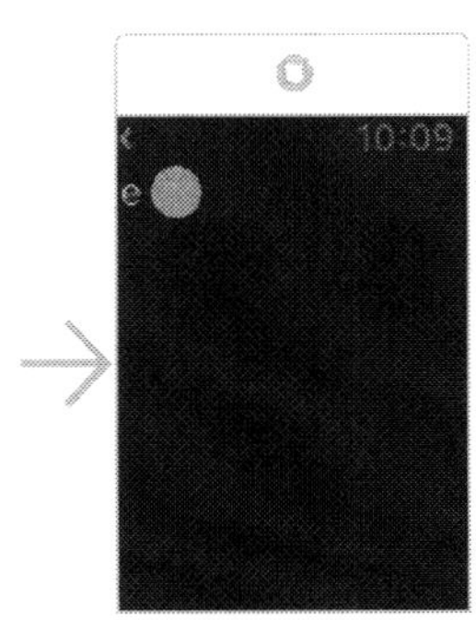

Drag another **label** element inside the blue group and change its attributes to the following:

- Change **Text** to a single-digit number to simulate a fret selection—**2**;
- Set **Horizontal** and **Vertical Alignment** to **Center**.

The last element your string group needs to look like the iPhone version is a line indicator. Stacking groups on top of each other can get tricky, so instead, you'll take advantage of the **Background Image** property to put an image behind the other interface elements.

Select the **group** that contains the label and the blue group. Set its **Background** to **line**, an image provided for you in Image.xcassets.

Build and run, and navigate to the chord controller to see your new group all laid out and looking pretty!

Positioning the fretboard dots

Recall from the first section that the blue dots move based on the fret position of each string. The iPhone app does this by dynamically changing the Auto Layout constraints.

In the absence Auto Layout, WatchKit provides a limited set of properties you can change dynamically on `WKInterfaceObject` using the following methods:

- **`setWidth(_:)`** adjusts the horizontal width of the element.
- **`setHeight(_:)`** adjusts the vertical height of the element.
- **`setAlpha(_:)`** changes the element's visibility without changing its size.
- **`setHidden(_:)`** hides or shows the element, by changing its size—either shrinking to nothing, or growing to full size. Consequently the size and position of surrounding elements will also change.

However, when you change the content size or the fixed size of an interface object, you're also adjusting the layout of all the surrounding objects, whether you want to or not.

This means you can use neighboring groups to move *other* objects onscreen. And remember, not every element needs to have content—you can use "invisible" groups to move things around.

In **Interface.storyboard**, drag a **group** into the string group, right between the **e** label and the blue group. Change the new group's **Width** to **Fixed 30** and its **Height** to **Relative to Container**.

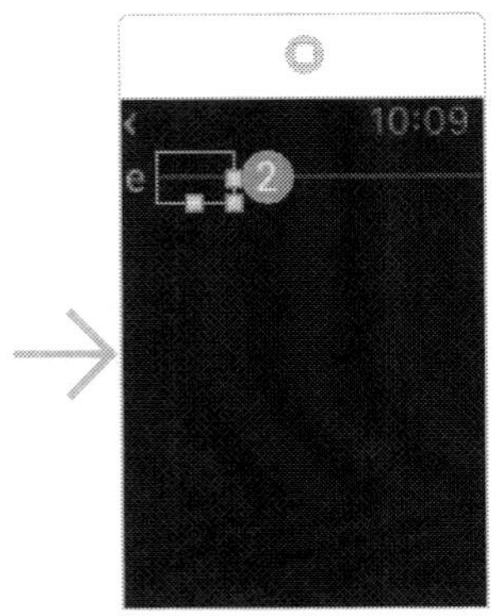

You can change the *fixed width* to whatever you want, and the blue label will move around! Remember how you can use `setWidth(_:)` to change the object's width? Now you have a way to move the blue label dynamically!

Creating the full chord interface

The chord interface currently displays just one string—but what about the other five? You need to set up interface elements for all six strings and connect them to the interface controller in code.

Still in **Interface.storyboard**, select the **group** that contains the string label, spacer and blue group in the **document outline**. **Copy** the group (Command-c) and **paste** (Command-v) **five** times.

Change the left-side labels of the strings to **e**, **b**, **g**, **d**, **a** and **e**, respectively. These represent the notes to which each string is tuned.

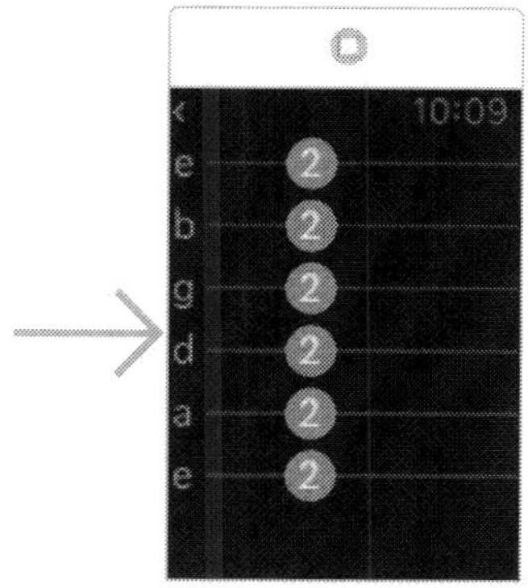

> **Note**: These string tunings are called "standard tuning" for six-string guitars. There are plenty of other tunings, as well as guitars with fewer or more strings!

Open **ChordHelper WatchKit Extension\ChordController.swift** in the assistant editor so you can create some `IBOutlet` connections.

Select the **spacer group** from the top e-string, **right-click** and drag to **ChordController.swift** and create an outlet called `e2Spacer`. Create an outlet for the blue group called `e2Circle`, and another outlet for the fret label called `e2Label`.

Do this again for each string, using the prefixes `b`, `g`, `d`, `a` and `e` in place of `e2` as you work down through the strings. In the end, you should have six spacer outlets, six label outlets and six circle outlets:

```
@IBOutlet var e2Spacer: WKInterfaceGroup!
@IBOutlet var bSpacer: WKInterfaceGroup!
@IBOutlet var gSpacer: WKInterfaceGroup!
@IBOutlet var dSpacer: WKInterfaceGroup!
@IBOutlet var aSpacer: WKInterfaceGroup!
@IBOutlet var eSpacer: WKInterfaceGroup!

@IBOutlet var e2Label: WKInterfaceLabel!
@IBOutlet var bLabel: WKInterfaceLabel!
@IBOutlet var gLabel: WKInterfaceLabel!
@IBOutlet var dLabel: WKInterfaceLabel!
@IBOutlet var aLabel: WKInterfaceLabel!
@IBOutlet var eLabel: WKInterfaceLabel!

@IBOutlet var e2Circle: WKInterfaceGroup!
@IBOutlet var bCircle: WKInterfaceGroup!
@IBOutlet var gCircle: WKInterfaceGroup!
@IBOutlet var dCircle: WKInterfaceGroup!
```

```
@IBOutlet var aCircle: WKInterfaceGroup!
@IBOutlet var eCircle: WKInterfaceGroup!
```

It would be pretty tedious to set up each of these outlets manually. Swift can make this process a lot easier with aliases and tuples.

In **ChordController.swift**, add the following alias and computed variable:

```
typealias GuitarString = (spacer: WKInterfaceGroup,
  label: WKInterfaceLabel, circle: WKInterfaceGroup)

var strings: [GuitarString] {
  return [
    (eSpacer, eLabel, eCircle),
    (aSpacer, aLabel, aCircle),
    (dSpacer, dLabel, dCircle),
    (gSpacer, gLabel, gCircle),
    (bSpacer, bLabel, bCircle),
    (e2Spacer, e2Label, e2Circle)
  ]
}
```

The `GuitarString` alias makes an easy-to-use tuple that includes the three main elements in every group you copied and pasted earlier. You initialize the `strings` array to hold six `GuitarString` tuples, representing each group from the bottom of your controller to the top.

Moving interface objects from code

To set up the chord, you have to iterate over the strings in the `Chord` object and configure each string group appropriately. Since you've already created the `strings` array, this will be simple!

Open **ChordController.swift** and in `awakeWithContext(_:)`, just beneath where you set the title of the controller and inside the `if` statement, add the following code:

```
// 1
let spacing: CGFloat = 30
let offset = CGFloat(chord.minimumFret) * spacing
// 2
for (string, fret) in zip(strings, chord.frets) {
  // 3
  string.label.setText("\(fret)")
  if fret == -1 {
    // 4
    string.circle.setHidden(true)
  } else {
```

```
      // 5
      string.spacer.setWidth(CGFloat(fret) * spacing - offset)
    }
  }
```

1. Since one can play chords at any place on a fretboard, you need to "normalize" the fretboard so that the minimum fret required for the specified chord is at the leftmost part of the screen. Remember that you have only a tiny Watch screen to work with!
2. You iterate through the frets on the chord object, using `zip(_, _)` so you have access to the `GuitarString` tuple and the `fret` position.
3. You set the white label inside the blue dot to the fret number.
4. The number `-1` represents an unplayed string, so hide the blue group when that's the case.
5. You set the width of the spacer group to the fret number multiplied by the spacing value, and subtract the offset so that the dots are all visible.

Build and run the Watch app, and select a chord. The blue dots will be positioned just as your fingers would be to play the chord!

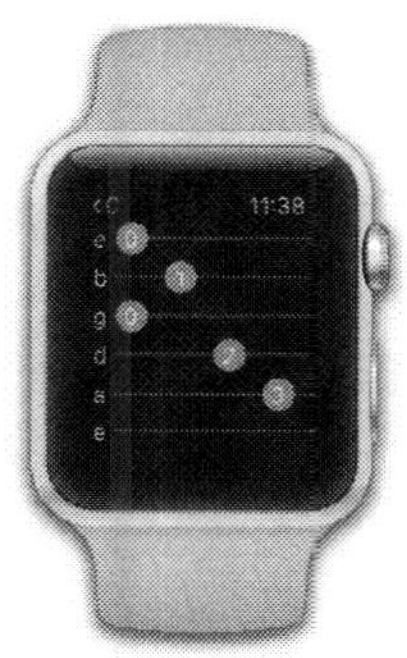

Responsive layout

Try running the app on the 42mm watch, and you'll find that the app is useable, but there's a slice of empty space at the bottom of the screen.

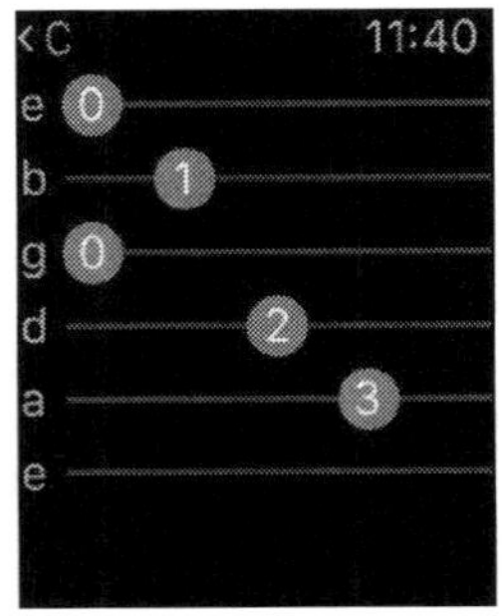

That's a lot of space you could be using to make the chords even more visible. This is the Watch—every bit of space counts!

By increasing the size of each string group, the dots and the spacing, you can take advantage of the extra width and height of the larger watch.

Open **ChordController.swift** and add a new variable to the top of the class:

```
let dimensions: (circleSize: CGFloat, spacing: CGFloat) = {
  let isBigWatch = WKInterfaceDevice.currentDevice()
    .screenBounds.size.width >= 156
  if isBigWatch {
    return (25, 35)
  } else {
    return (20, 30)
  }
}()
```

This function checks if the screen size is larger than 156 points, which is the width of the 38mm Watch screen, and then returns a tuple representing the size of the circle and the spacing for each fret.

In `awakeWithContext(_:)`, find the following line:

```
let spacing: CGFloat = 30
```

And replace it with the new width-based spacing:

```
let spacing = dimensions.spacing
```

Next, inside the for-loop where you set up the string groups, add the following code:

```
string.circle.setHeight(dimensions.circleSize)
string.circle.setWidth(dimensions.circleSize)
string.circle.setCornerRadius(dimensions.circleSize/2)
```

This sets the height and width to the new screen-based size, so that the dots are larger when there's more screen space. You also update the corner radius so that the dot is still a circle.

Since the `WKInterfaceGroup` strings have heights that are relative to their contents, the only height you explicitly have to set is that of the circle groups!

Build and run, and you can see how even a tiny size change makes the interface so much more useable on a 42mm device.

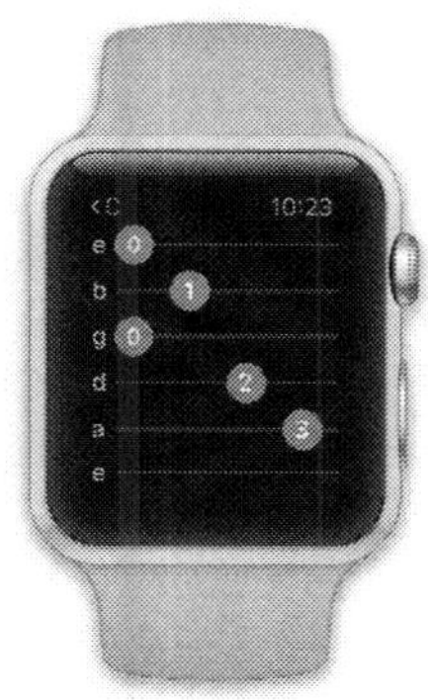

Where to go from here?

You've learned a couple of different ways to use groups that involve more than just placing items vertically or horizontally. By combining relative and fixed sizes and using "invisible" groups, you can create rich and complex layouts that will make your Watch apps sing!

If this chapter has struck a chord with you, there's much more you can do with WatchKit's layout tools. You could animate all of the properties that you changed on `WKInterfaceObject`, add support for instruments with more or less strings, or maybe add a button to play the selected note out loud.

Try Googling for other popular chord variations and you'll be taking the stage in no time!

Chapter 16: Advanced Tables

By Ryan Nystrom

Chapter 7, "Tables", covered topics such as basic lists, wiring together row controllers and using multiple controllers in a single table. That knowledge will let you build tables for the majority of Watch apps, but what if you want—or need—to go further?

There are a lot of instances in which your app can get a little... *advanced.* Let's say you're using Core Data, you're making network requests that add more data *and* you're loading large amounts of data, all at once—not to mention giving your users the power to add, remove and edit the contents of a table!

In this chapter, you're going to build a simple grocery list app that simulates table sections and integrates user interaction, demonstrating just how powerful a `WKInterfaceTable` can be.

Getting started

Open **Groceries.xcodeproj** and build and run the **Groceries iOS Target** on an iPhone or simulator.

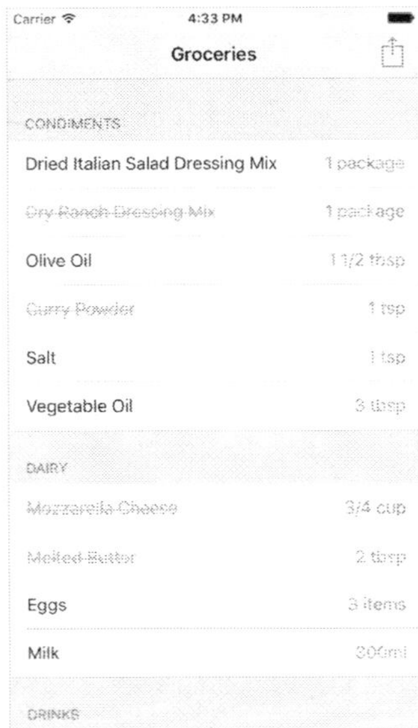

The app itself is very simple. It:

- Loads grocery files saved on disk as JSON;
- Parses the JSON and builds `Ingredient` model objects;
- Reloads the table using the **aisle** as the section and the **item** as the row;
- Marks an item as purchased when the user taps it;
- Clears purchased items using the action menu.

You're going to build an app with the same functionality but with the form-factor of the Apple Watch.

Adding row controllers

> **Note**: This section moves quickly through creating and configuring your table and outlets using multiple row controllers. If you find that it moves a little fast, take another look at Chapter 7, "Tables".

Open **Groceries WatchKit App\Interface.storyboard** to begin adding rows for your data.

Drag a **table** element onto the lone controller in the storyboard. Change **Prototype Rows** to **2**.

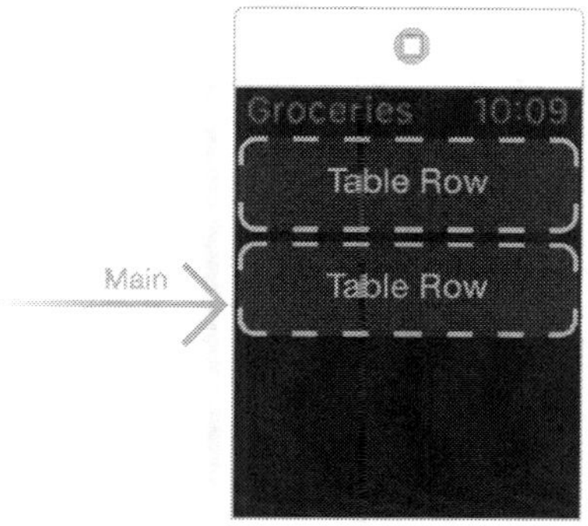

The first prototype row will represent the header for each of the grocery sections, while the second will represent the grocery items themselves.

Select the **first prototype row** and drag in an **image** and a **label**. Make sure the label is to the *right* of the image.

Select the **image** and set its image to **meat**. Since all the grocery category icons are the same size, you're using "meat" as a placeholder, so that the layout is correct within Interface Builder. Also, change **Vertical Alignment** to **Center** so the image sits in the middle of the containing group.

Next, select the **label** and change **Font** to **Headline** and **Vertical Alignment** to **Center**.

The **Apple Watch Human Interface Guidelines** state that `WKInterfaceTable` rows "*should present a consistent overall appearance*". Grocery item rows will make up the majority of your table and should have the default dark gray background color, similar to most table styles.

To help distinguish the headers from the grocery item rows, you are going to remove the background color. Select the **group** in the first row controller and change **Color** to **Clear Color**. Now, not only will the headers have an image and text, but will appear to have a black background, easily identifying them as different to the grocery item rows.

Lastly, your headers shouldn't be interactive. You don't want users tapping section headers that don't do anything! Use the **document outline** to select the **row controller** that houses the group and all of the elements you just added.

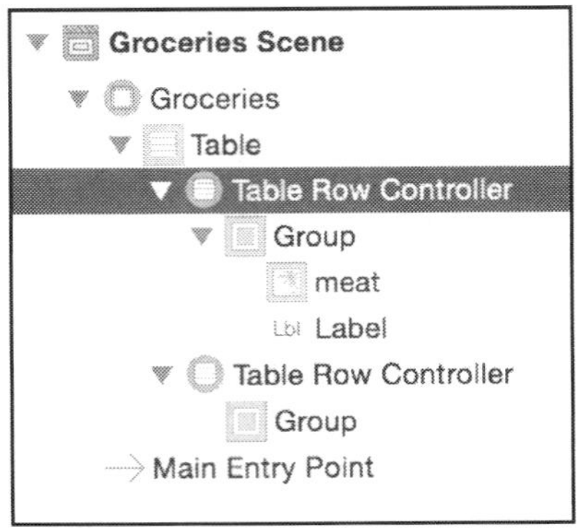

De-select the **Selectable** checkbox in the Attributes Inspector. Now your section header looks sharp!

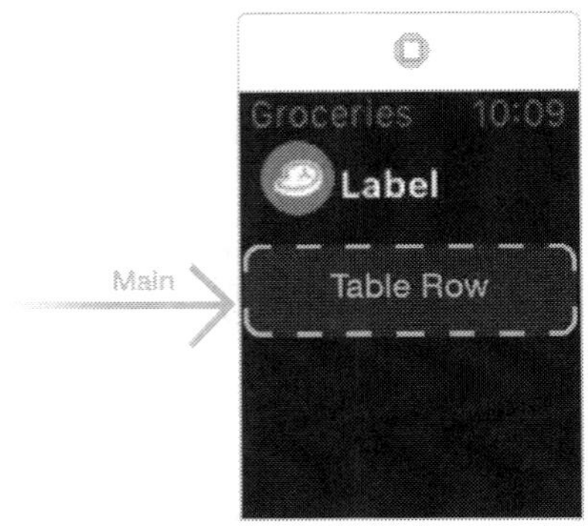

Next, you need to set up the row controller for the grocery items. Drag and drop two **label** elements into the **second row controller**.

The labels align horizontally, since that's the default for `WKInterfaceGroup`. Select the **group** that contains both labels and change its **Layout** to **Vertical**.

Also, your ingredient names will have varying lengths, and you want your row controller to size appropriately. Change its **Height** to **Size To Fit Content**.

To display all the text for longer ingredient names, select the **first label** and set **Lines** to **0** so it will word-wrap the entire string.

The second label will display the quantity of the ingredient to buy. Design-wise, it shouldn't be as prominent as the first label.

Select the **second label** and change **Font** to **Caption 1** and **Text Color** to **Light Gray Color**.

Before you can add data to your table, you need to wire up the row controllers and tables as outlets.

Right-click the **Groceries WatchKit Extension** group, click **New File...** and select **Cocoa Class**. Do this twice to create the following classes, both of which need to inherit from `NSObject`:

- `GroceryRowController`
- `GroceryTypeRowController`

Back in **Groceries WatchKit App\Interface.storyboard**, select the **first row controller**, change its **Class** to `GroceryTypeRowController` and set the **Identifier** to `GroceryTypeRow`.

Change the same settings for the second row controller, but use the class `GroceryRowController` and the identifier `GroceryRow`.

I know you did everything correctly, so your document outline will look like this:

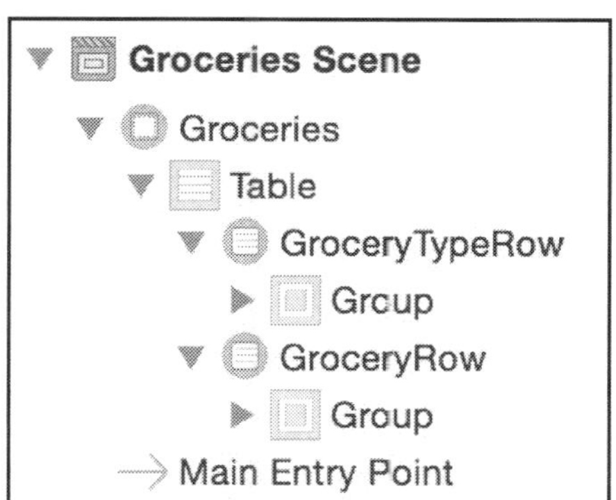

Note that Xcode generated a label for each row controller.

Open **GroceryTypeRowController.swift** in the **assistant editor** and connect the following outlets by control-dragging:

- Create an outlet for the **image element** named `image`.

- Create another outlet for the **label** named `textLabel`.

Next, open **GroceryRowController.swift** in the **assistant editor** and connect two more outlets:

- Add an outlet for the **first label** named `textLabel`.
- Create another outlet for the **second label** named `measurementLabel`.

Lastly, open **GroceryController.swift** in the **assistant editor** and create an outlet named `table` for the `WKInterfaceTable` in your storyboard.

> **Note**: The initial interface controller was already configured to be of the type `GroceryController` in the starter project.

Build the Watch app to make sure you've connected everything correctly, without any warnings or errors.

Creating multiple sections

Recall that the iOS app divides the grocery lists into *sections*. This is a familiar concept for most iOS developers: `UITableView` has a data source that has methods to return the number of sections, as well as the number of rows in each section—not to mention all of the convenient APIs in `UITableViewDelegate` that let you construct and configure section and row views.

`WKInterfaceTable` is conspicuously absent of any such APIs. All of the `WKInterfaceTable` methods expect a *single-dimensional* list of data—in other words, just an array. You can't use nested data types.

To work within this limitation, you somehow need to convert any *multi-dimensional* data structures into a flat structure.

You're going to simulate headers in a WatchKit table using the two different row prototypes you created in the previous section. The following image demonstrates how you can use the differently styled prototype rows to give the *appearance* of section headers:

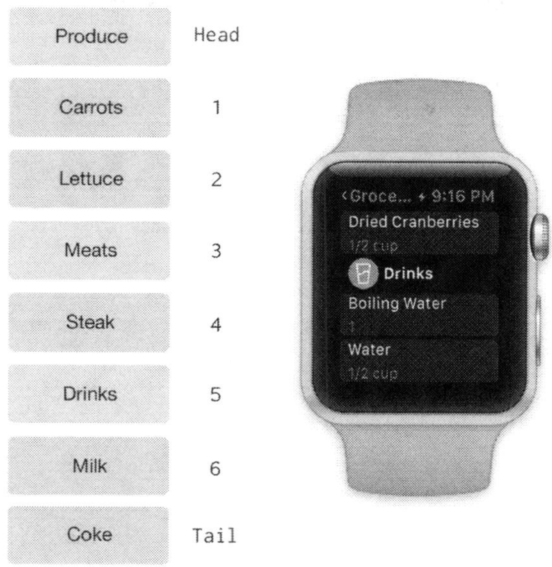

There are three methods that add data to a table:

- **`setNumberOfRows(_:withRowType:)`** adds rows that all have the same row controller identifier. This won't help you create sections, since you can only have a single row type!
- **`setRowTypes(_:)`** lets you pass in an array of varying row controller identifiers as strings. The identifiers need to match the ones configured in your storyboard, but they can be completely different from one another.
- **`insertRowsAtIndexes(_:withRowType:)`** inserts a single row type for the provided `NSIndexSet`. But, there's no limit to the number of times you can call this method. So in theory, you could iterate your sections and insert as you see fit!

Open **GroceryController.swift** and add the following method:

```
func loadIngredientsFile(file: String) -> [Ingredient] {
  let path = NSBundle.mainBundle()
    .pathForResource(file, ofType: "json")!
  let data = NSData(contentsOfFile: path)!
  let json = JSON(data: data)
  return Ingredient.fromJSON(json)
}
```

All of the data for your grocery list is stored in JSON files, grouped by grocery aisle. You can browse through the files in the `Shared` group. This function loads and parses the files in one pass.

Note: You'll notice that there are two force-unwrapped optionals in the code above. These will crash your app at runtime if something goes wrong. Typically you want to handle these cases, but for now, you're just loading bundled resources, so it's fairly safe.

You're going to use `insertRowsAtIndexes(_:withRowType:)` to simplify adding and configuring your sections, but since you're going to do this for *each file*, you'll want to abstract some of that work.

Open **GroceryController.swift** and add the following method to `GroceryController`:

```
func addGroceryAisle(name: String, items: [Ingredient]) {
  // 1
  let rows = table.numberOfRows

  // 2
  let headerIndex = NSIndexSet(index: rows)
  table.insertRowsAtIndexes(headerIndex,
    withRowType: "GroceryTypeRow")

  // 3
  let itemRows = NSIndexSet(
    indexesInRange: NSRange(location: rows + 1,
    length: items.count))
  table.insertRowsAtIndexes(itemRows, withRowType: "GroceryRow")

  // TODO configuring rows
}
```

1. First, you get the number of rows already in the table. Without this, every time you insert new data, you'll push the data to the front of your list when you want to push to the tail end.
2. Next, you create an `NSIndexSet` consisting of a single index for your header row controller, and insert it into the table.
3. Finally, you create a range of indices to represent the grocery item rows. The first index in this range immediately follows that of the header row, and you need the same number of rows as you have groceries in this aisle. You insert new rows into the table using the `GroceryRow` identifier you specified in your storyboard.

Next, replace the `// TODO configuring rows` comment with the following code:

```
// 1
for i in rows..<table.numberOfRows {
  let row = table.rowControllerAtIndex(i)

$[break]
```

```
    // 2
    if let row = row as? GroceryTypeRowController {
      row.textLabel.setText(name)
      row.image.setImageNamed(name.lowercaseString)
    } else if let row = row as? GroceryRowController {
      // 3
      let item = items[i - rows - 1]
      row.textLabel.setText(item.name.capitalizedString)
      row.measurementLabel.setText(item.formattedQuantity)
    }
  }
```

1. You iterate the range `rows..<table.numberOfRows` so that you're only acting on the header and item rows you just inserted. Remember that `rows` is the number of table rows *prior* to your inserting the new items.
2. Checking the type of `row` allows you to configure either the header rows, using the `name` parameter, or the grocery item rows, using the relevant ingredient from the `items` parameter.
3. Finding the correct ingredient in the `items` array requires offsetting `i` by the first row index of this aisle.

To load a single aisle of grocery items, add the following to **GroceryController.swift**:

```
override func awakeWithContext(context: AnyObject?) {
  super.awakeWithContext(context)
  let name = "Baking"
  let baking = loadIngredientsFile(name)
  addGroceryAisle(name, items: baking)
}
```

Here you simply override `awakeWithContext(_:)`, fetch the items in **Baking.json** and then insert them into the table.

Build and run the Watch app to see your data with its section header:

Looking good! But that's a single grocery aisle, and one can only eat so much bread.

In **GroceryController.swift**, add a constant near the top of the class:

```
let groceryFiles = [
  "Baking",
  "Condiments",
  "Dairy",
  "Drinks",
  "Meat",
  "Misc",
  "Produce"
]
```

This constant gives you access to each file included in your app's bundle.

Update `awakeWithContext(_:)` to the following:

```
override func awakeWithContext(context: AnyObject?) {
  super.awakeWithContext(context)
  for name in groceryFiles {
    let ingredients = loadIngredientsFile(name)
    addGroceryAisle(name, items: ingredients)
  }
}
```

Build and run the Watch app again. This time, scroll through the list to see all of your groceries loaded into the table:

But wait... why does the app take so long to start? See if you can come up with a reason it might take such a long time to load.

Performance-tuning tables

Just like in iOS, all interface operations performed in watchOS 2 happen on the *main queue*. If you do anything expensive on the main queue, that will block the interface from displaying, updating and responding to user touches.

This is a common problem in iOS, where the solution is to offload expensive work to *background queues* so that the main queue can carry on with its own business. It's the same with watchOS 2!

The problem with your Groceries app is that you're loading many files on the main thread. This is costly for a couple of reasons:

- Disk I/O is notoriously expensive;
- It takes time to deserialize the data and then convert it from JSON to models.

You only have 16ms to complete work on the main thread in order to maintain a responsive, 60-FPS app. Right now, loading all of these files takes too long.

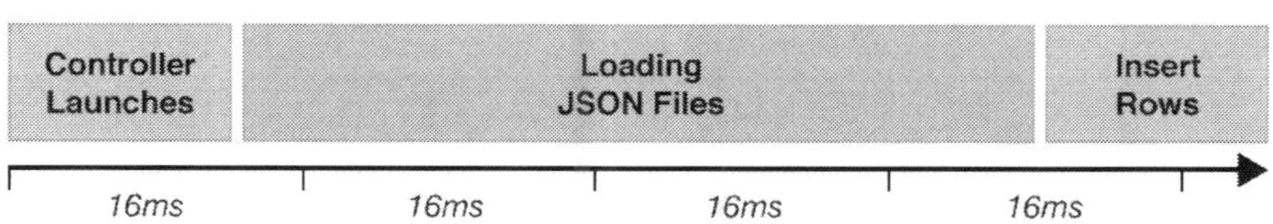

You can only use `WKInterfaceTable` on the main thread, but there's nothing stopping you from offloading all of the expensive work *and then* returning to the main thread to update the table.

Open **GroceryController.swift** and change `awakeWithContext(_:)` to the following:

```
override func awakeWithContext(context: AnyObject?) {
  super.awakeWithContext(context)
  let name = groceryFiles.first!
  let baking = loadIngredientsFile(name)
  addGroceryAisle(name, items: baking)
}
```

Instead of loading every single file on the main thread as soon as you create the controller, you load only the very first file so that you have content available immediately.

Override another `WKInterfaceController` method that gets called when the controller is *just about* to be shown:

```
override func willActivate() {
  super.willActivate()
  // 1
  dispatch_async(dispatch_get_global_queue(
    DISPATCH_QUEUE_PRIORITY_DEFAULT, 0)) {
    // 2
    var groceries = [(name: String, items: [Ingredient])]()
    // 3
    for file in self.groceryFiles {
      if file != self.groceryFiles.first {
        groceries.append((file, self.loadIngredientsFile(file)))
      }
    }
    // TODO update table
  }
}
```

1. You dispatch to one of the global concurrent queues to get off the main thread.
2. Next, you create a mutable array of tuples that have a `name` and an array of `Ingredient` objects. You'll use this array to collect all of the loaded files in the background and then transfer them to the main queue to use with the table.
3. You iterate over the files and load them from disk, and then add them to the `groceries` array so you can use them later. Make sure to skip the `first` item since you already inserted it in `awakeWithContext(_:)`.

> **Note**: `groceries` is a mutable array and thus not safe to use across multiple threads, which is why you're localizing any modifications of it to this one function. `groceryFiles` is *immutable* and thus safe to use across multiple threads.

Next, replace the `// TODO update table` comment with the following code:

```
dispatch_async(dispatch_get_main_queue(), {
  for grocery in groceries {
    self.addGroceryAisle(grocery.name, items: grocery.items)
  }
})
```

You dispatch asynchronously back to the main queue and then call `addGroceryAisle(_:items:)` using the items in the `groceries` array that you built in the background. This will insert the header and rows for your table.

Build and run to experience a much faster startup. You'll be setting the table in no time!

BA DUM TSSS

Updating table rows

Recall that in the iOS app, users have the ability to check off grocery items as they shop. This helps prevent users from getting the same item twice, or having to backtrack to the other side of the store for an item they already bought!

Luckily, `WKInterfaceTable` makes updating rows super easy. Open **GroceryRowController.swift** and add a couple of computed properties to `GroceryRowController`:

```
private var cellTextAttributes: [String: AnyObject] {
  return [
    NSFontAttributeName: UIFont.systemFontOfSize(16),
    NSForegroundColorAttributeName: UIColor.whiteColor()
  ]
}

private var strikethroughCellTextAttributes: [String: AnyObject]
{
  return [
    NSFontAttributeName: UIFont.systemFontOfSize(16),
    NSForegroundColorAttributeName: UIColor.lightGrayColor(),
    NSStrikethroughStyleAttributeName:
      NSUnderlineStyle.StyleSingle.rawValue
  ]
}
```

Both of these properties are attribute settings for `NSAttributedString`. `cellTextAttributes` is "normal" text, and `strikethroughCellTextAttributes` strikes through the text and makes it a light gray color.

Add two more properties with set observers to `GroceryRowController`:

```
var ingredient: Ingredient? {
  didSet {
    configureController()
  }
}

var strikethrough = false {
  didSet {
    configureController()
  }
}
```

`ingredient` lets you set an `Ingredient` object directly, upon which it calls `configureController()`. The `strikethrough` property controls whether or not to strike through the row.

You're getting compiler errors now because you're missing `configureController()`. Implement it now by adding the following to `GroceryRowController`:

```
func configureController() {
  // 1
  guard let ingredient = ingredient else {
    return
  }

  // 2
  let attributes: [String: AnyObject]
  if strikethrough {
    attributes = strikethroughCellTextAttributes
  } else {
    attributes = cellTextAttributes
  }

  // 3
  let attributedText = NSAttributedString(
    string: ingredient.name.capitalizedString,
    attributes: attributes)
  textLabel.setAttributedText(attributedText)
  measurementLabel.setText(ingredient.formattedQuantity)
}
```

1. You use Swift 2.0's `guard` to unwrap `ingredient` and return early if it doesn't exist. This protects `configureController()` from over-indentation.
2. You construct the attributes for the text string based on whether or not the cell

should have a strikethrough.

3. You build the NSAttributedString and set the textLabel to it. You also set the text for the measurementLabel.

Open **GroceryController.swift** and find addGroceryAisle(_:items:). Locate the following lines:

```
let item = items[i - rows - 1]
row.textLabel.setText(item.name.capitalizedString)
row.measurementLabel.setText(item.formattedQuantity)
```

And change them to this:

```
row.ingredient = items[i - rows - 1]
```

The GroceryRowController property observer on ingredient handles configuration of the row now, so all you need to do is set the value!

Now you need to respond to touch events in order to change and update the strikethrough-state of your rows.

Open **GroceryController.swift** and add the following code to GroceryController:

```
override func table(table: WKInterfaceTable,
  didSelectRowAtIndex rowIndex: Int) {

  if let row = table.rowControllerAtIndex(rowIndex)
    as? GroceryRowController {
    row.strikethrough = !row.strikethrough
  }
}
```

table(_:didSelectRowAtIndex:) is a method on WKInterfaceController that gets called any time the user taps a selectable row. You check if your row is a GroceryRowController and then toggle the strikethrough variable. Remember that this variable then internally re-configures the row controller.

Note: WKInterfaceController has other methods that deal with WKInterfaceTable objects, such as by aiding in navigation events. Check out Chapter 7, "Tables" for more info.

Build and run, and tap on a couple of ingredients to check off the rows as you pretend to shop!

Removing rows

Checking off all of these grocery items is useful and fun, but what happens when you have just one item left? Hunting for that last item out of the dozens of crossed-off ingredients could be a pain in the butt. It would be great if you could remove those crossed-off ingredients altogether.

`WKInterfaceTable` to the rescue! You can use `removeRowsAtIndexes(_:)` to remove a list of rows from your table.

However, you need to create an action in order to execute the deletion. Menus are exactly suited to this.

> **Note**: Chapter 8, "Menus", goes into much more detail about how and when to use menu items. Sometimes a menu isn't the answer, but when accessing a less-used option like item removal, a menu is the perfect element because it is seldom used but should be quickly accessible.

Open **Groceries WatchKit App\Interface.storyboard** and drag a **menu** element onto your controller.

Using the document outline, select the single **menu item** in your menu. Change **Title** to **Purchased** and **Image Name** to **clear-purchased**.

Open **GroceryController.swift** in the **assistant editor**. Right-click and drag from your lone **menu item** to `GroceryController` and create an `IBAction` named `onRemovePurchased`.

The `WKInterfaceTable` function `removeRowsAtIndexes(_:)` expects an instance of `NSIndexSet` to remove a list of rows. Currently, you're only changing the `strikethrough` property of rows that the user has tapped. Now you just need to collect all of the rows that have `strikethrough == true` and delete them!

In `GroceryController`, change the contents of `onRemovePurchased()` to the following:

```
// 1
let itemsToRemove = NSMutableIndexSet()
for i in 0...table.numberOfRows {
  // 2
  if let row = table.rowControllerAtIndex(i)
    as? GroceryRowController where row.strikethrough {
    itemsToRemove.addIndex(i)
  }
}
// 3
table.removeRowsAtIndexes(itemsToRemove)
```

1. First, you collect all of the indices in a `NSMutableIndexSet`. Notice that the variable is actually a constant, yet still a mutable object. Sometimes Swift is a bit silly! Sometimes when working with Apple frameworks, like WatchKit, base Swift classes aren't enough and Objective-C classes are either mutable or not.
2. If the row is a `GroceryRowController` and `strikethrough == true`, you add the index to the `itemsToRemove` collection. You take advantage of the Swift `where` clause to make this `if`-statement clean and simple.
3. You remove all of the collected rows from your table. `removeRowsAtIndexes(_:)` will automatically handle animation.

Note: Since `WKInterfaceTable` is powered by setting, inserting and deleting row controllers, there's no need to update a data source, as you would have to with `UITableView`. Instead, the table maintains it's own internal datastore of row controllers, which it keeps in sync with the interface.

Build and run the Watch app. Select a couple of rows, force-touch to show your menu and tap the icon to remove all of the items you already bought.

Works like a charm:

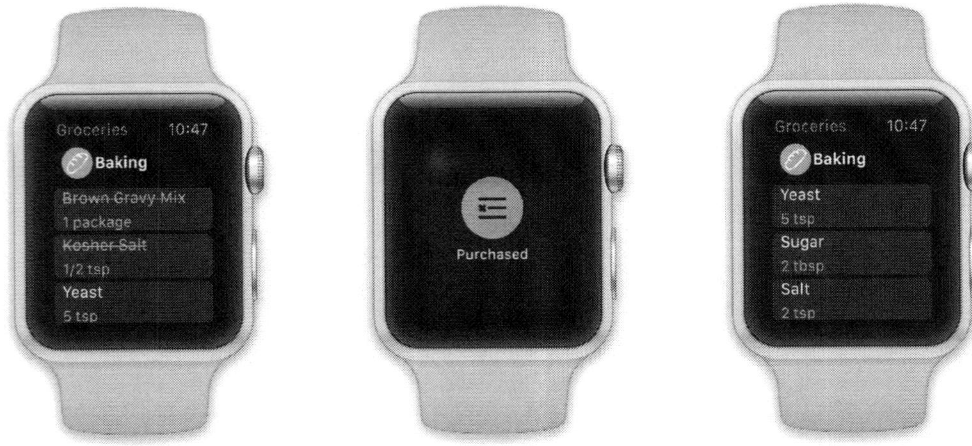

Where to go from here?

There are a lot of applications for `WKInterfaceTable`: network requests that come in after the app has started, notifications that trigger updates, and changes that may propagate from the parent iOS application—any situation in which you have dynamic data that requires editing your table.

An interesting challenge would be to get a table working alongside `NSFetchedResultsController`. If you've ever used this with Core Data, you've probably seen how well `NSFetchedResultsControllerDelegate` and `UITableView` work together. It isn't as simple with `WKInterfaceTable`, but all of the tools you need do exist!

You could also try updating the app to remove a section when a user has removed all of its items. This will take a little more data-structure logic to keep track of the number of sections and the number of items each contains, and then map their index paths back to the single-dimensional list structure of `WKInterfaceTable`. It's another good challenge to test your new table-making skills.

Chapter 17: Advanced Animation

By Jack Wu

watchOS 2 is filled to the brim with delightful animations. From the initial iPhone-Watch pairing process to the opening of apps, every corner of the operating system makes use of animations to provide an immersive experience.

As a developer, you want to create that same immersive experience for your users to make your app feel right at home in the rest of the operating system. In watchOS 1, this was close to impossible, and the difference between Apple's apps and third-party apps was very apparent. With the new watchOS 2 tools you learned about in Chapter 9, "Animation", you now have all you need to create the same kind of animations found in watchOS.

In this chapter, you'll learn how to take full advantage of the animation APIs in watchOS 2 to create gorgeous animations for your apps.

Getting started

If you completed Chapter 9, "Animation", then you're already familiar with Woodpecker, the app that helps you repeat tasks over and over until they're second nature. Woodpecker looked nice at the end of Chapter 9, but in this chapter, you'll take it to the next level.

Locate the starter project for this chapter and open it in Xcode. Build and run the Watch app, and add a few tasks before you move on. Here's a good one for you: "Pet a dog 50 times". You're welcome. :]

Note: Even if you completed Chapter 9, "Animations", and have the final project, use the starter project for this chapter. A few things were added to the starter project to help this chapter flow more smoothly.

Sequential animations

The first appearance of a view is a great opportunity to spice up your app with animations. You can see this in watchOS in a few places; for example, when you switch to an analog watch face from the app selector:

Here, the complications fade in a tiny bit after the watch face begins animating, and finish a few moments later. It's quite a nice effect.

The color buttons in Woodpecker are a great candidate for this type of animation. The first step is to set the initial values of the buttons. Open **Interface.storyboard** and select all the color buttons:

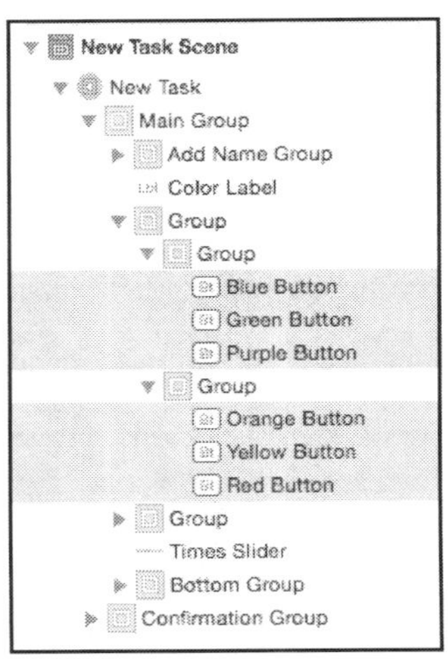

Set the **alpha** of all the buttons to **0** in the Attributes Inspector:

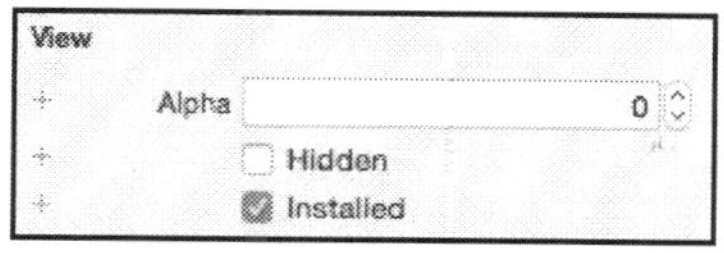

Note: As you will notice throughout this chapter, setting the initial values of interface elements in the storyboard makes them much less convenient for laying out your interface.

The alternative is to leave the values of the storyboard as-is and set up the initial values in `awakeWithContext(_:)`.

The trade-off should be seriously considered here since any task performed in `awakeWithContext(_:)` needs to be completed before the interface is displayed to users. In Woodpecker, there is quite a bit of set-up needed for each interface and so you will always be setting the initial values in the storyboard for the best performance.

Next, you want to add the code to animate the buttons into view. To do so, you need to take advantage of GCD's `dispatch_after()` function to start the animations one at a time, with slight delays in between. Open **NewTaskInterfaceController.swift** and add the following function to `NewTaskInterfaceController`:

```
func animateInColorButtons() {
  // 1
  let timeStep = Int64(0.1 * Double(NSEC_PER_SEC))
  // 2
  for (i, button) in colorButtons().enumerate() {
    // 3
    let delayTime =
      dispatch_time(DISPATCH_TIME_NOW, timeStep * Int64(i))
    dispatch_after(delayTime, dispatch_get_main_queue()) {
      // 4
      self.animateWithDuration(0.4) {
        if button === self.selectedColorButton {
          button.setAlpha(1)
        } else {
          button.setAlpha(0.3)
        }
      }
    }
  }
}
```

Here's the play-by-play of what's happening:

1. You define the delay between each animation's start time.
2. Next, you enumerate through each button, keeping track of its index.
3. For each button, the start time of the animation is `i * timeStep`. This allows the first one to start at time 0 and each subsequent one to follow suit.
4. You perform the animation, just like usual. :]

> **Note**: You want to keep tabs on the *total* animation time when creating sequential animations. The times accumulate quickly and you don't want your users to be waiting for your animations to finish.
>
> Here, the total animation time is when the last button finishes animating into view, which is 5 * 0.1 + 0.4 = 0.9 seconds, which is acceptable. A small change, such as increasing the delay between animations to 0.2, would result in a total time of 5 * 0.2 + 0.4 = 1.4 seconds, which feels a tad lengthy.

Almost done! Now you simply need to call your shiny new method. watchOS 2 has a new method in the `WKInterfaceController` lifecycle that's perfect for animations like this: `didAppear()`. The name speaks for itself!

> **Note**: As of Xcode 7.0, `didAppear()` is occasionally skipped upon the initial launch of the app. The filed radar (rdar://22874438) tracks this bug.
>
> This chapter will continue to use `didAppear()` to begin animations as it is the correct place to do so.
>
> If shipping an app, however, the workaround is to move all the code from `didAppear()` to `willActivate()`. The workaround may cut-off the animation a bit at times but should never leave the interface in an unusable state.

Add the following code to `NewTaskInterfaceController`:

```
override func didAppear() {
  super.didAppear()
  animateInColorButtons()
}
```

Build and run the Watch app. Add a new task and watch the magic happen:

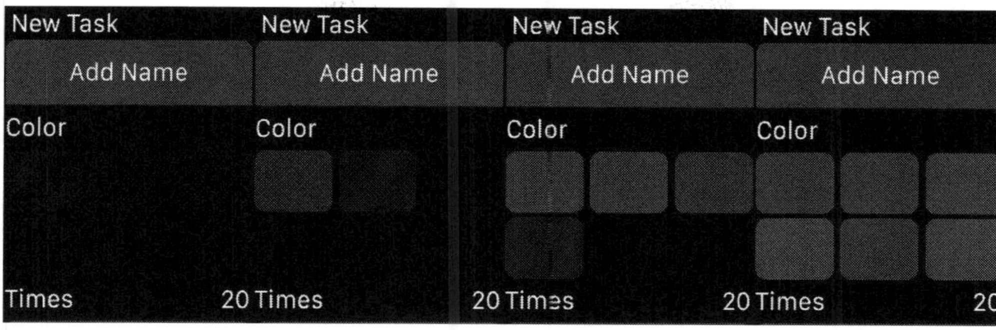

Sweet! That definitely makes me want to create more tasks. :]

Using groups in animations

Groups were the key to unlocking nice animations in watchOS 1, and they reprise their role in watchOS 2.

The main purpose of groups in watchOS 2 animations can be summarized in one word: **spacing**. With groups, you can add, remove and change the spacing between two interface objects:

If you then change the height of that group, you are effectively changing the spacing between the two labels.

> **Note**: You'll recognize this technique from Chapter 15, "Advanced Layout", where you used a group to reposition the dot on the guitar fretboard.

Sliding into view

Back to Woodpecker. Currently, when you add a new task, the new cell is already visible when you return to the tasks interface controller. It would be useful, and cool, if the cell animated to show the user that it's a new addition to the list. Hmm... using a spacer group here sounds like a great idea!

As with sequential animations, you want to set the initial state of the animation directly inside the storyboard. Open **Interface.storyboard** and find the **OngoingTaskRow** in the first scene.

Inside **Label Group**, add a new group as the first object:

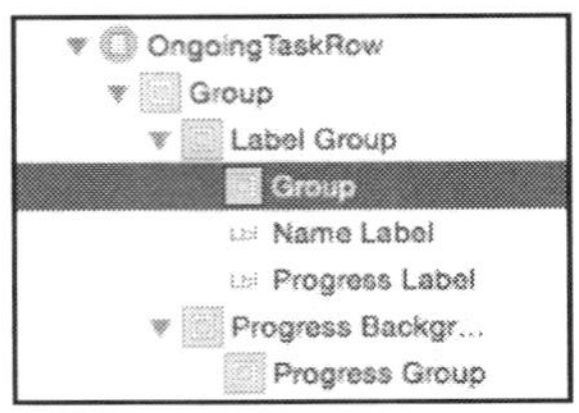

Configure the new group to have the following:

- Width: **Relative to Container**; **1**, **0** Adjustment
- Height: **Relative to Container**; **1**, **0** Adjustment

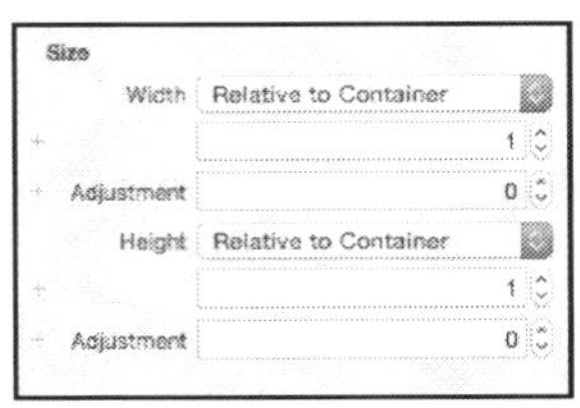

Since the labels will be sliding into view, the progress bar shouldn't be there in the beginning, either. Set the **alpha** of **Progress Background Group** to **0**.

The cell will now appear completely empty in the storyboard:

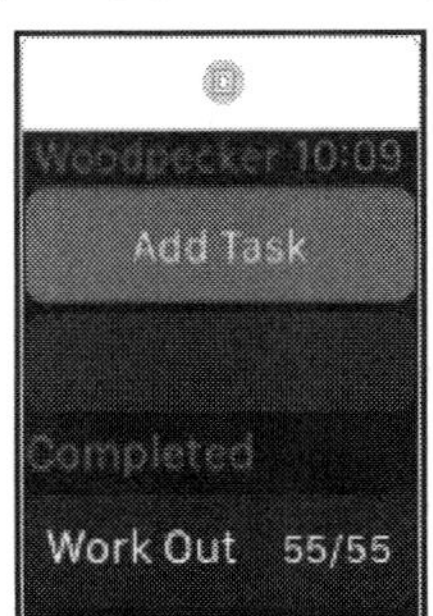

That's just how you want it! Now all you have to do to make the labels slide into view is set the width of the new spacer group to 0.

To do that, you first need an outlet connection to the new group. Open **OngoingTaskRowController.swift** in the **assistant editor**. You can do this by holding **alt** when clicking on the file.

Drag a connection from the new group into `OngoingTaskRowController` and name it `spacerGroup`:

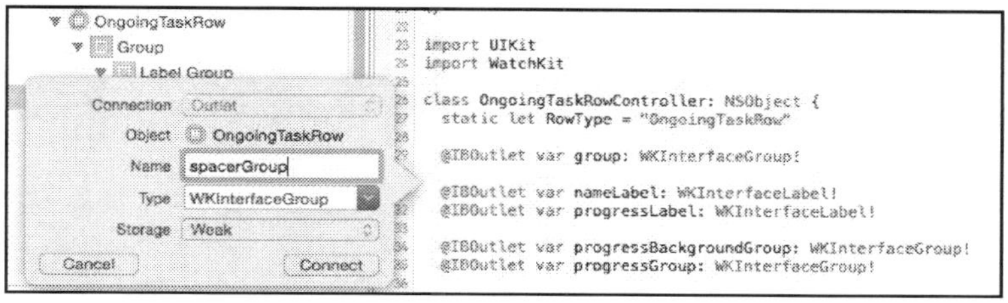

Now all the task rows are completely empty. All there is left to do is to fix that, with style!

Open **TasksInterfaceController.swift** and add the following method to `TasksInterfaceController`:

```
func animateInTableRows() {
  animateWithDuration(0.6) {
    for i in 0..<self.ongoingTable.numberOfRows {
      let row = self.ongoingTable.rowControllerAtIndex(i)
        as! OngoingTaskRowController
      row.spacerGroup.setWidth(0)
      row.progressBackgroundGroup.setAlpha(1)
    }
  }
}
```

There's nothing new here in terms of code. Inside an animation block, you iterate through all the rows of the ongoing table and set the width of `spacerGroup` to `0` and the alpha of `progressBackgroundGroup` to 1.

Lastly, you have to call `animateInTableRows()`. Again, `didAppear()` is provided for this exact purpose! Add the following method below `willActivate()` in `TasksInterfaceController`:

```
override func didAppear() {
  super.didAppear()
  animateInTableRows()
}
```

Again, there's nothing much that's new here. But since you call this code in `didAppear()`, you get the bonus of all the existing rows animating into view when the app launches.

Build and run the Watch app. Add a new task; now it's quite clear which row is new to the table:

This app keeps getting better and better!

More sliding into view

You may be asking, "Since the ongoing task rows are sliding in, why not have the completed ones do so as well?" That's a great idea! You should *totally* have the completed task rows animate in, just like the ongoing ones.

Since you came up with the brilliant idea, give it a try on your own.

Got it? Here are the steps:

1. Create a spacer group in the storyboard in the same group as the labels.
2. Set up the initial height and width of the spacer group to be the same as its parent.
3. Create a property for the new group in `CompletedTaskRowController`.
4. Inside `animateInTableRows()` in `TasksInterfaceController`, iterate through all the rows in `completedTable` and set the spacer group's `width` to `0` right after the loop for `ongoingTable`.

There's one final difference for the completed table—when the user completes a task, it is immediately added to the completed table. You need to slide in the labels when that happens, as well. To do so, find `table(_:didSelectRowAtIndex:)` in **TasksInterfaceController.swift**. Slide in the labels inside the `if (task.isCompleted)` block, right after you set up the new row. The body of the `if` statement will look like this:

```
ongoingTable.removeRowsAtIndexes(NSIndexSet(index: rowIndex))

let newRowIndex = tasks.completedTasks.count-1
completedTable.insertRowsAtIndexes(
  NSIndexSet(index: newRowIndex),
  withRowType: CompletedTaskRowController.RowType)

let row = completedTable.rowControllerAtIndex(newRowIndex)
  as! CompletedTaskRowController
```

```
row.populateWithTask(task)
animateWithDuration(0.6) {
  row.spacerGroup.setWidth(0)
}

self.updateAddTaskButton()
self.updateCompletedLabel()
```

Build and run the Watch app. Upon launch, both completed tasks and ongoing tasks will slide into view from the right. When you complete a task, the new row also animates in. Nice!

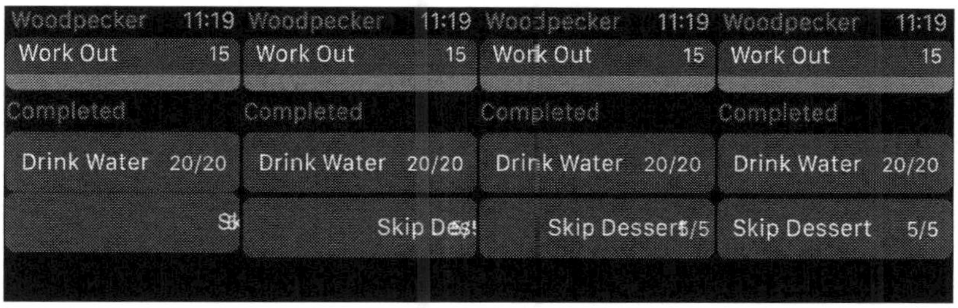

Interface transitions

You can also use groups to contain entire fullscreen interfaces, between which you can transition easily. You can use this to create nice prompts and alerts in your Watch app.

A confirmation prompt would be great in Woodpecker when the user finishes creating a new task, before the interface is dismissed. A nice checkmark sliding up from the bottom should do the trick!

The implementation is quite straightforward, and again, groups are going to be very handy. Open **Interface.storyboard** and find the **New Task Scene**.

To display the confirmation screen, you'll need to hide the entire current UI. To make that possible, you need to embed all the current elements into a group.

Xcode makes that extremely simple. Select all the top-level interface elements in the scene and select **Editor -> Embed In -> Vertical Group**. That's it! You'll now have a group that includes all the elements:

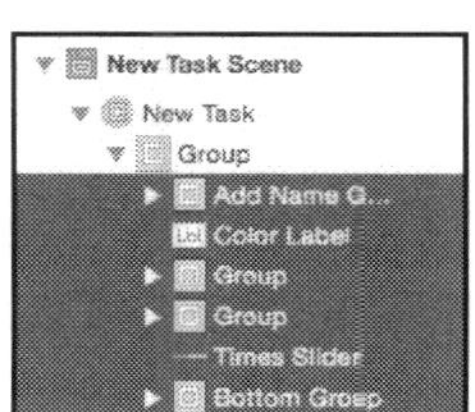

Next, add a new **vertical group** below this new group and add an **image** and a **label** to it. Set the image's attributes as per the following:

- Set Image to **check**;
- Set Horizontal Alignment to **Center**;
- Set Vertical Alignment to **Center**.

For the label, make the following changes:

- Set Text to **Done!**;
- Set Horizontal Alignment to **Center**;
- Set Vertical Alignment to **Center**.

Your scene will look like this:

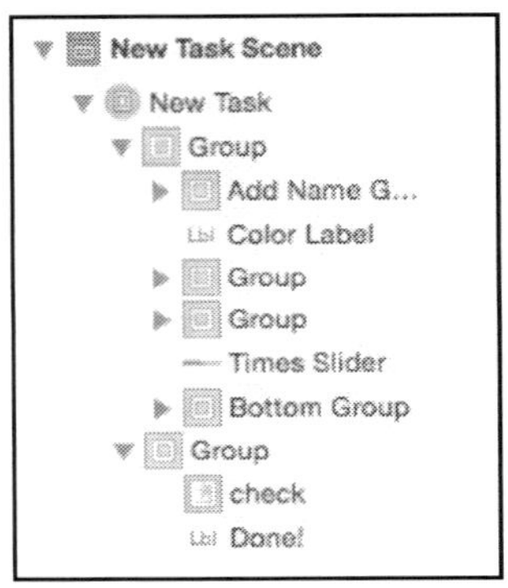

Remember, you always want the storyboard to have the initial state of the scene. Set the **Height** of the bottom group to **0** so that it's hidden in the beginning. After you set that, you'll notice a small space at the bottom of the scene. Set **spacing** to **0** on the **Interface Controller** itself to remove the gap:

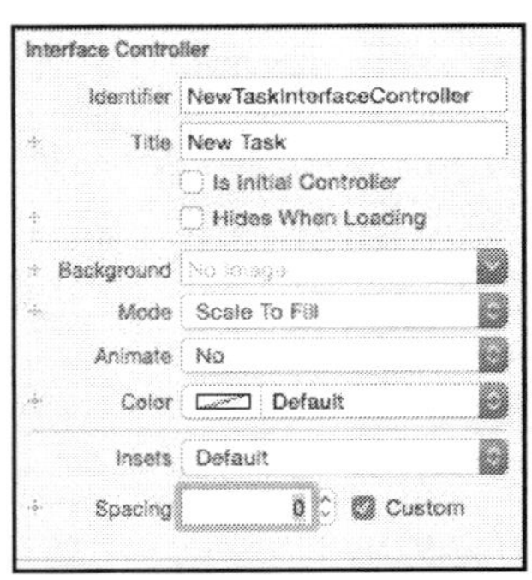

Next, you need to create outlet connections for the two top-level groups. Create the two new outlets inside `NewTaskInterfaceController`:

```
@IBOutlet var mainGroup: WKInterfaceGroup!
@IBOutlet var confirmationGroup: WKInterfaceGroup!
```

Now to put these groups to use. You want `confirmationGroup` to replace `mainGroup` after the task is created, but before `NewTaskInterfaceController` is dismissed.

Still in **NewTaskInterfaceController.swift**, find `onCreate()`. Replace `dismissController()` on the last line with the following snippet:

```
// 1
animateWithDuration(0.4) {
  self.mainGroup.setHeight(0)
  self.mainGroup.setAlpha(0)
  self.confirmationGroup.setRelativeHeight(1, withAdjustment: 0)
}
// 2
let delayTime = dispatch_time(DISPATCH_TIME_NOW,
  Int64(1.0 * Double(NSEC_PER_SEC)))
dispatch_after(delayTime, dispatch_get_main_queue()) {
  self.dismissController()
}
```

There isn't much new here:

1. Inside an animation block, you set both the height and alpha of `mainGroup` to `0`, and you set the height of `confirmationGroup` to take up the entire screen.
2. After `1` second, you dismiss the controller.

That's all there is to it! Build and run the Watch app. After you create a task, the confirmation group will slide into view as the main group fades out:

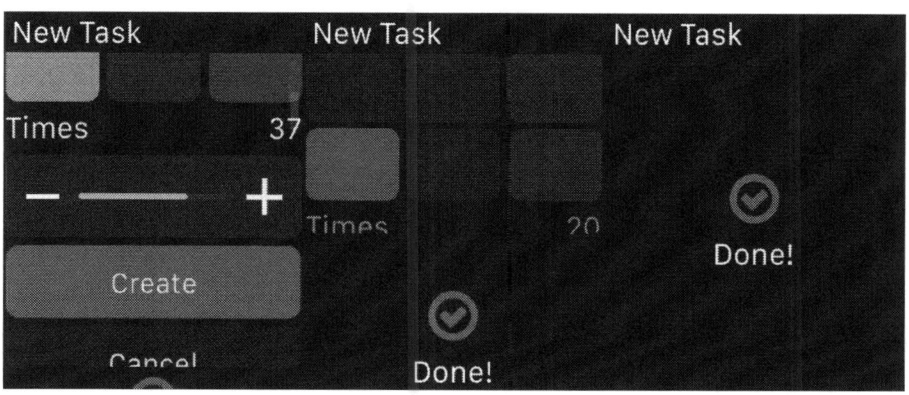

Simple, yet incredibly delightful!

Smoothing out text input

Woodpecker is looking really great now!

There's only one more place that could use some polish: the add name button.

After you enter a task name, you get a slightly jarring series of events. The text input dismisses, but you still see "Add Name" on the button. Then, after some arbitrary delay, the text immediately changes to the name you input. Just a tiny rough edge, and nothing a bit of polishing can't fix!

At the root of this problem, there are two issues at play:

1. The button should not display "Add Name" when you dismiss the view.
2. The name you input should not randomly appear.

The good news is, you can address both of these issues at the same time with the help of your old friend—groups!

The idea here is to slide the button's label out of view when the app presents the text input, and then slide it back into view after the app dismisses the text input.

The first step is, again, to set up the initial state in the storyboard. Open **Interface.storyboard** and find the **Add Name Button** in the **New Task Scene**.

In the Attributes Inspector, change **Content** to **Group**. Then select the new group inside the button and set the following properties:

- Layout: **Vertical**
- Spacing: **0**
- Height: **Fixed**, **40**

Next, add another group with a **Height** of **0** into the button group.

Lastly, add a label into the button group with these properties:

- Text: **"Add Name"**
- Text Alignment: **Center**
- Horizontal Alignment: **Center**
- Vertical Alignment: **Center**
- Width: **Relative to Container**; **1**, **0** adjustment

> **Note**: Here the label uses **Relative to Container** instead of **Size To Fit Content**, because you need to change the text in the label. A horizontal animation occurs when you change the width of the centered label in an animation block. Here you avoid this animation by keeping the label size independent of the text.

The resulting interface hierarchy will look like this:

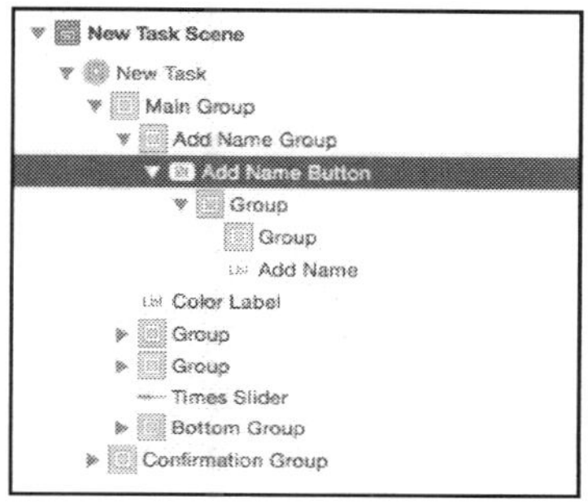

As always, you need to create connections for the spacer group and label. Add and connect the two outlets to `NewTaskInterfaceController` using the assistant editor, as before:

```
@IBOutlet var addNameSpacerGroup: WKInterfaceGroup!
@IBOutlet var addNameLabel: WKInterfaceLabel!
```

Now for the fun part! Find `addName()` and replace the method body with the following snippet:

```
let options = [
  "Work Out", "Express Love", "Drink Water", "Skip Dessert"
]
presentTextInputControllerWithSuggestions(options,
  allowedInputMode: WKTextInputMode.Plain) { results in
  if let result = results?.first as? String {
    // 1
    self.addNameLabel.setText(result)
    self.name = result
  }
  // 2
  self.animateWithDuration(0.4) {
    self.addNameSpacerGroup.setHeight(0)
  }
}
// 3
animateWithDuration(0.4) {
  self.addNameSpacerGroup.setRelativeHeight(1,
    withAdjustment: 0)
}
```

There are only three changes here, all familiar stuff:

1. The name is now displayed in `addNameLabel` instead of `addNameButton`.
2. When you dismiss the input text view, you set the height of the spacer group to `0`, so the label slides back in.
3. When you present the input text view, you make the spacer group take up the space, so the label slides out.

That's it: just a few simple components with a few simple method calls. But the result... Build and run and take a look:

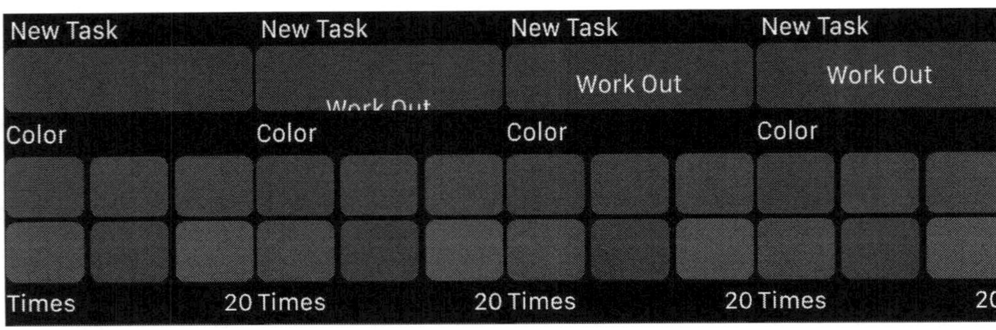

Not only does it look nice, it really smooths the user's experience when she goes to the text input controller.

Where to go from here?

Congratulations! You've put some polish on Woodpecker by adding smooth transitions and animations throughout.

I hope this chapter has demonstrated your ability to create enticing animations using only the simple animation APIs provided in watchOS 2. With enough creativity, your Watch apps will fit right in with the rest of the OS.

The next step is simple: Go polish your own apps! Find rough edges in the user experience and think about how you can smooth them out with animations. Good luck!

Chapter 18: Advanced Watch Connectivity

By Matthew Morey

In Chapter 13, "Watch Connectivity", you set up the Watch Connectivity framework, learned about the different ways to transfer data between iPhone and Watch apps, and successfully implemented the application context transfer method, all while working on an app for movie theater patrons called CinemaTime. By the end of Chapter 13, users could purchase a movie ticket from either the iPhone or Watch CinemaTime app and see their purchase on the other app.

In this chapter, you'll employ the user info mode of communication to transfer movie rating data between the CinemaTime apps. User info transfers are like the application context transfers you implemented in Chapter 13 in that both allow you to transfer a dictionary of data. The difference is that all dictionaries are transferred over, not just the last one.

You'll also use interactive messaging to transfer movie ticket QR codes from the iPhone to the Watch. Interactive messaging is best used in situations that need information transferred immediately.

> **Note**: If you're not familiar with the basics of the Watch Connectivity framework, make sure you work through Chapter 13 before continuing with this chapter. This chapter's starter project is a continuation of the Chapter 13 final project. You can use either your final project from that chapter, or the starter project for this chapter.

Getting started

Open the CinemaTime starter project in Xcode and then build and run the **CinemaTimeWatch** scheme. Tap on **Purchase Ticket** and explore the app.

The existing CinemaTime apps show the movie schedule for a cinema. Customers can buy movie tickets and rate movies from within either app.

Build and run the **CinemaTime** scheme and explore the iPhone app.

If you haven't already, rate a movie in either app and then view the same movie in the counterpart app. Do you see the issue?

Movie ratings in one app don't show up in the other app — the apps aren't sharing the rating data. If a user rates a movie in the iPhone app, and then later tries to view the same rating on the Watch, she might think she never rated the movie in the first place!

In the iPhone app, buy a movie ticket and view the purchased ticket, represented by a QR code, that now appears instead of the Purchase Ticket button.

Now view the same purchased movie in the Watch app. Although purchased movies from one app appear in the counterpart app, the QR code does not.

Don't worry — you're a superstar! You can solve both problems with the Watch Connectivity framework.

User info transfers

User info transfers send dictionaries of data to the counterpart app in first-in, first-out order. Once a data transfer begins, it will continue, even if the sending app is no longer running. The `WCSession` method `transferUserInfo(_:)` sends the data, and the counterpart app receives the dictionary via the `session(_:didReceiveUserInfo:)` method declared by the `WCSessionDelegate` protocol.

`transferUserInfo(_:)` returns a `WCSessionUserInfoTransfer` object that stores information about in-progress data transfers. The class provides a `transferring` property that indicates whether the transfer has completed. The `cancel()` method can be used to stop the transfer, so long as the `transferring` property is still `true`.

The `WCSessionDelegate` protocol includes the optional `session(_:didFinishUserInfoTransfer:error:)` method. When the `WCSession` object that initiated a transfer completes – or cancels – the transfer, it calls `session(_:didFinishUserInfoTransfer:error:)`. This method can be used to notify the sender that their work is complete.

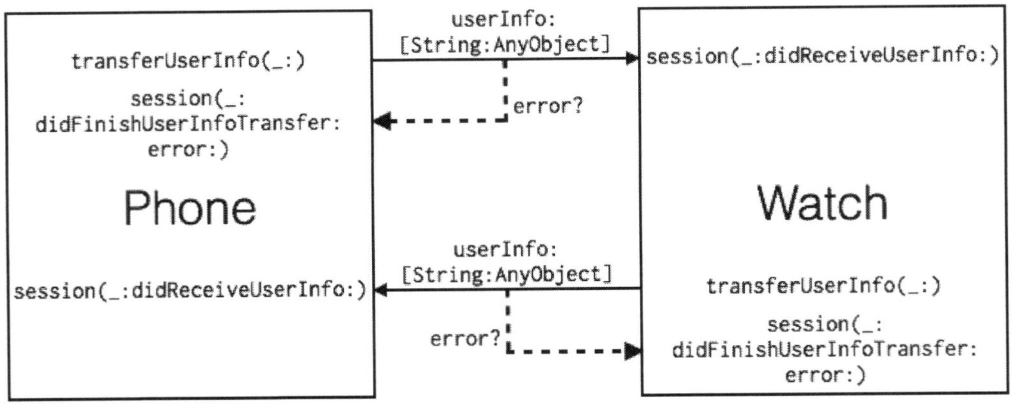

Unlike the application context transfer method discussed in Chapter 13, "Watch Connectivity", `WCSession` guarantees that all user info transfers are received in the order they are sent. Subsequent transfers do not overwrite previous ones like in an application context transfer.

A Watch game that needs to transfer the user's progress to the counterpart iPhone app would require a user info transfer. Using `transferUserInfo(_:)`, the iPhone app would receive notice of each completed level from the Watch app.

Now you'll give user info transfers a try by writing code to send movie ratings from the iPhone to the Watch. After that, you'll tackle it the other way around.

Transferring from the iPhone to the Watch

In Xcode, open **MovieDetailViewController.swift** and find `sendRatingToWatch(_:)`. The iPhone app calls this method whenever the user taps on the rating stars and then selects a rating from the action sheet.

Implement the method with the following code:

```
// 1
if WCSession.isSupported() {
  // 2
  let session = WCSession.defaultSession()
  if session.watchAppInstalled {
    // 3
    let userInfo = ["movie_id":movie.id, "rating":rating]
    session.transferUserInfo(userInfo)
  }
}
```

Let's go through this code step by step:

1. First you check if the current device supports Watch connectivity.

2. You set `session` to the default connectivity session, and check to verify installation of the Watch app. There's no need to communicate if nothing is listening!
3. Finally, you call `transferUserInfo(_:)` on the active session to transfer a dictionary that contains the `movieID` and `rating` properties.

> **Note**: Before calling any Watch Connectivity framework methods, including `transferUserInfo(_:)`, you must first set up and activate a connectivity session. The starter project for this chapter already does this for you. If you'd like a refresher, please go back to Chapter 13, "Watch Connectivity", for the details.

Now that the iPhone app is sending movie ratings, you'll set up the Watch app to receive them. `WCSessions` that receive user info transfers call the optional `WCSessionDelegate` `session(_:didReceiveUserInfo:)` protocol method when they receive data.

Open **ExtensionDelegate.swift** and add the following to the end of the class:

```
func session(session: WCSession,
  didReceiveUserInfo userInfo: [String : AnyObject]) {
  if let movieID = userInfo["movie_id"] as? String,
    let rating = userInfo["rating"] as? String {
    TicketOffice.sharedInstance.rateMovie(movieID,
      rating: rating)
  }
}
```

The `userInfo` dictionary will contain the data sent from the iPhone app. You set the `movieID` and `rating` constants from that dictionary. Then you call `rateMovie(_:rating:)`, from the `TicketOffice` singleton class, passing `movieID` and `rating`. Calling this method updates the rating for the movie in the Watch app.

Build and run the **CinemaTime** scheme to launch the iPhone app, and then rate a movie. Next, build and run the **CinemaTimeWatch** scheme and view the same movie you rated in the iPhone app. The apps will both have the rating. Nice work!

> **Note**: If you have both the iPhone and Watch apps running at the same time, this use case will still work. While interactive messaging is the most immediate way to transfer data between two running apps, background transfers work, as well.

You've just added the ability to transfer movie ratings from the iPhone to the Watch. Guess what you're going to do next?

Transferring from the Watch to the iPhone

Open **MovieRatingController.swift** and locate `sendRatingToPhone(:_)`. When the user rates a movie on the Watch, the app calls `sendRatingToPhone(_:)`. Replace the `TODO` with this code:

```
if WCSession.isSupported() {
  let userInfo = ["movie_id":movie.id, "rating":rating]
  WCSession.defaultSession().transferUserInfo(userInfo)
}
```

This code looks like what you added in the previous section, but there are some minor differences. Although, on the Watch, `WCSession.isSupported()` will always return `true`, it doesn't hurt to be careful and check. You never know if this behavior will change in future versions of watchOS. After that, you call `transferUserInfo(_:)` on the active session to transfer to the iPhone a dictionary containing information about the rating.

This code is slightly simpler than the iPhone app because there, it checked to verify the installation of the Watch app. On the Watch, you don't need to check for iPhone app installation, because the only way the Watch app can exist is if there's also an installed iPhone app.

Now that the Watch is sending movie ratings, you'll set up the iPhone to receive them.

Open **AppDelegate.swift** and add the following code to the `AppDelegate` class:

```
// 1
func session(session: WCSession,
  didReceiveUserInfo userInfo: [String : AnyObject]) {
  // 2
  if let movieID = userInfo["movie_id"] as? String,
    let rating = userInfo["rating"] as? String {
    // 3
    TicketOffice.sharedInstance.rateMovie(movieID,
      rating: rating)
  }
}
```

Here's what you're doing with this code:

1. Your code implements the `WCSessionDelegate` `session(_:didReceiveUserInfo:)` protocol method. The active connectivity session uses this method to receive a dictionary of data from the counterpart Watch app.
2. Next, you set the `movieID` and `rating` constants using the `userInfo` dictionary.
3. Finally, you call `rateMovie(_:rating:)`, from the `TicketOffice` singleton class, with the `movieID` and the `rating`. Calling this method updates the rating for the movie in the iPhone app.

Build and run both apps, but this time, rate a movie in the Watch app, and then view the same movie on the iPhone app to see the new rating.

Voila! CinemaTime customers can now rate movies from within either app and their ratings will sync across both. You're quickly becoming an A-list celebrity.

Now that you've solved the first problem, you'll work on the issue of the missing QR codes.

Interactive messaging

When both apps are active, establishing a session allows immediate communication between them via interactive messaging.

The `WCSession` methods `sendMessage(_:replyHandler:errorHandler:)` and `sendMessageData(_:replyHandler:errorHandler:)` send data, while the `WCSessionDelegate` methods `session(_:didReceiveMessage:)` and `session(_:didReceiveMessageData:)` receive sent data. Additionally, the delegate methods also each have a counterpart method that takes a `replyHandler` closure. This is used if the sender wishes to receive a reply to the message it sends.

The following diagram shows the basic flow of sending a message and receiving a reply from the watch to the phone:

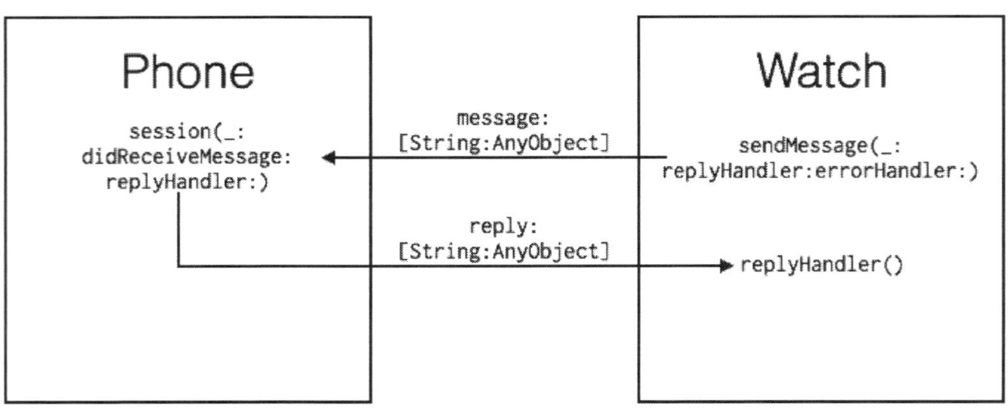

In watchOS 2, the counterpart iPhone app is considered active, or reachable, when a matching session is enabled and the iPhone is within range of communication. The iPhone app doesn't have to be in the foreground to be reachable.

In iOS, the Watch app is considered reachable when the paired Watch is in range and the Watch app is running in the foreground. If the Watch app isn't running or is in the background, then it's not reachable.

You'll make best use of interactive messaging in situations where you need information transferred immediately. For example, if your Watch app needs to trigger its companion iPhone app to do something, such as track the user's location, the interactive messaging API can communicate the request from the Watch to the iPhone.

In this section, you'll use interactive messaging to send movie ticket QR codes from the iPhone to the Watch.

> **Note**: You could also use the background file transfer method of communication to send the movie ticket QR codes to the Watch app. For CinemaTime, I've chosen to use interactive messaging because the transfer happens immediately, which means the customer sees no delay when trying to view a ticket code in the Watch app.

Messaging from the iPhone to the Watch

Right now, only the iPhone app generates a movie ticket QR code, because to do so requires the Core Image framework, which isn't available in watchOS.

The only way to show the QR code in the Watch app is to generate it in the iPhone app and then transfer the PNG version of it over to the Watch for display. When the user views the details of a purchased movie on the Watch, the app will send a message to the iPhone requesting a particular movie's QR code. The iPhone will respond with data representing a PNG of that code.

First, you'll make the request. Find `requestTicketForPurchasedMovie(:_)` in **MovieDetailInterfaceController.swift**. Replace the `TODO` with this code:

```
// 1
if WCSession.isSupported() {
  // 2
  let session = WCSession.defaultSession()
  if session.reachable {
    // 3
    let message = ["movie_id":movie.id]
    session.sendMessage(message,
      replyHandler: { (reply: [String : AnyObject]) -> Void in
      // 4
      if let movieID = reply["movie_id"] as? String,
        let movieTicket = reply["movie_ticket"] as? NSData
        where movieID == self.movie.id {
$[break]
```

```
          // 5
          self.saveMovieTicketAndUpdateDisplay(movieTicket)
        }
      }
    }, errorHandler: { (error: NSError) -> Void in
      print("ERROR: \(error.localizedDescription)")
  })
} else { // reachable
  self.showReachabilityError()
}
```

Let's go through this code step by step:

1. First, you check if the current device supports Watch connectivity.
2. Next, you get the default session and check if the iPhone app is available for communication. If the iPhone app isn't reachable, you show the user an error by calling `showReachabilityError()`.
3. You send the `message` "request" dictionary to the iPhone app by calling `sendMessage(_:replyHandler:errorHandler:)`.
4. By providing a closure for `replyHandler`, you are signaling that you want the receiver to reply with a dictionary of data as well. When the receiver does reply – by calling the closure – you set `movieID` and `movie_ticket` using the `reply` dictionary. You also verify that you received the data for the correct movie by checking if the `movie_id` key in the dictionary matches the current movie's ID.
5. Finally, the you save the movie ticket (an PNG file) and update the display by calling the private method `saveMovieTicketAndUpdateDisplay(_:)`.

> **Note**: If an app already has an existing transfer format, rather than call `sendMessage(_:replyHandler:errorHandler:)`, you can call `sendMessageData(_:replyHandler:errorHandler:)`, which takes an `NSData` object instead of a dictionary.

Now that the Watch app is sending a request for the movie ticket and reacting to replies, you'll set up the iPhone app to receive and reply to the request.

Open **AppDelegate.swift** and add the following to the end of the class:

```
// 1
func session(session: WCSession,
  didReceiveMessage message: [String : AnyObject],
  replyHandler: ([String : AnyObject]) -> Void) {
  // 2
  if let movieID = message["movie_id"] as? String {
```

```
    // 3
    if let movieTicket = QRCode(movieID) {
      // 4
      let reply = ["movie_id":movieID,
        "movie_ticket":movieTicket.PNGData]
      replyHandler(reply)
    }
  }
}
```

Here's what you're doing:

1. Your code implements the optional `WCSessionDelegate` protocol method `session(_:didReceiveMessage:replyHandler:)`. The active connectivity session uses this method to receive interactive messages from the counterpart Watch app. You are using the version that takes a `replyHandler` because you passed a closure when you called `sendMessage(_:replyHandler:errorHandler:)`.
2. Next, you get the `movie_id` value from the passed-in `message` dictionary.
3. Next, you create a `movieTicket` `QRCode` by passing `movieID` to the `QRCode` initialization method.
4. Finally, you execute `replyHandler(_:)` to transfer back to the Watch a dictionary containing the movie ID and the a PNG version of the movie ticket `QRCode`.

Build and run the **CinemaTimeWatch** scheme to launch the Watch app, and then buy and view a movie on the Watch. Scroll to the bottom of the movie details view to see the movie ticket QR code.

Congratulations movie star, you've finally made it! CinemaTime customers can now buy and view movie tickets from either app.

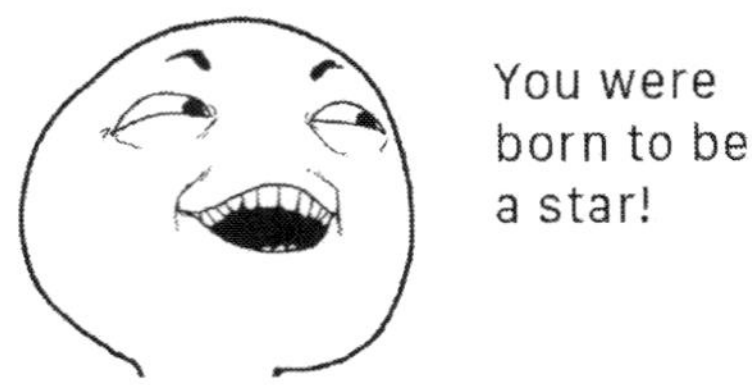

Where to go from here?

If you followed both Chapter 13 and this chapter all the way through, you've turned two independent apps that don't share data into apps that are always in sync. You'll find the final project in the folder for this chapter.

To learn more about communication methods between the Watch and iPhone, check out Apple's Watch Connectivity Framework Reference: apple.co/1JlPcnH.

Chapter 19: Advanced Complications

By Jack Wu

In Chapter 12, "Complications", you built an Apple Watch complication that displays information relevant at the current time, very much like a complication on a traditional watch. But the Apple Watch is definitely *not* a traditional watch—it offers much more.

In this chapter, you'll continue to explore the fun, innovative features of complications in WatchOS 2. Complications will become quite a bit more *complicated* in this chapter, but your reward will be implementing the coolest feature of them all: Time Travel.

No longer will the information on the Watch face be relevant only to the current time—at the user's whim, the complication will rewind to show historically relevant information, and even fast-forward to show information about the future. Want to let your users check the score of an ongoing game, and then immediately check both the score of the last game and the date and time of the next? All with a mere lift of the wrist? That's how powerful Time Travel can be.

That is an accurate picture of me when I learned about Time Travel!

You're probably now asking yourself two important questions: "How do I keep my complication data up to date?" and, "How do I keep potentially sensitive complication data private?" You need to know the answers to these questions to complete your complication—keep reading to discover them.

Getting started

This chapter will build upon the Tide Watch app from Chapter 12. Make sure you use **the new starter project** included with this chapter, as quite a few changes have been made for you.

Open **TideWatch.xcodeproj** in Xcode and take a swim through the code. There are two changes you should pay attention to:

1. The code now uses Watch Connectivity to sync the data between the iPhone and the Watch. The implementation is very similar to that of Chapter 13, "Watch Connectivity".
2. `ComplicationController` has had a slight refactor and some new methods have been added, but most of the code should look familiar.

It's time to dive in!

Traveling through time

Time Travel doesn't defy the laws of physics, but it does defy the one-dimensional conventions associated with traditional timepieces to provide a similar experience: scrolling forward or backward through time-specific information using the digital crown. And it's completely open to you as a developer to define the relevant context. You can transport your users to past or future weather conditions, stock prices, calendar events... and perhaps most excitingly, tide conditions for surfing. :]

How Time Travel works

At its core, you make Time Travel possible simply by providing a *list* of timeline entries instead of just the one. The system can then display the timeline entry that corresponds to the time the user has scrolled to using the digital crown.

> **Note**: Recall from Chapter 12, "Complications" that a timeline entry specifies the appearance of a complication via its template and when to display it.

ClockKit lets you specify whether your app will travel backward or forward in time, or both. Some apps will only need to travel in one direction. For example, you might come under the suspicions of your financial regulatory agency if your stock market app could travel forward in time.

Tide Watch already loads 48 hours of data, making it the perfect candidate for Time Travel in both directions.

Providing the data

To get started, open **ComplicationController.swift** and find `getSupportedTimeTravelDirectionsForComplication(_:withHandler:)`. In Chapter 12, you returned `.None` to the handler to disable Time Travel. You can now replace that with:

```
handler([.Forward, .Backward])
```

This tells the system that your complication can travel both forward and backward in time. You could omit either one if you only wanted to support one direction.

For each direction your complication supports, the system calls two datasource methods to retrieve the past or future data. These methods are declared in the `CLKComplicationDataSource` protocol, which your `ComplicationController` class adopts.

The first method asks for the start or end date of your timeline. Add the following method to `ComplicationController`:

```
func getTimelineStartDateForComplication(
  complication: CLKComplication,
  withHandler handler: (NSDate?) -> Void) {
  let tideConditions = TideConditions.loadConditions()
  guard let waterLevel = tideConditions.waterLevels.first else {
    // No data is cached yet
    handler(nil)
    return
  }
  handler(waterLevel.date)
}
```

Not too much is going on here. You check if you have any data and simply return the date of the earliest data point. This means that when the user travels to an earlier time, the system will dim out your complication to indicate there's no more relevant data.

You need a similar method for the end date, so implement the following in `ComplicationController`:

```
func getTimelineEndDateForComplication(
  complication: CLKComplication,
  withHandler handler: (NSDate?) -> Void) {
  let tideConditions = TideConditions.loadConditions()
  guard let waterLevel = tideConditions.waterLevels.last else {
    // No data is cached yet
    handler(nil)
    return
  }
  handler(waterLevel.date)
}
```

The only difference here is that you return the date of the last available water level to the handler, instead of the first.

Now that the system knows the bounds of your data, it calls two more delegate methods to retrieve the data. To provide data from the past, add the following method to `ComplicationController`:

```
func getTimelineEntriesForComplication(
  complication: CLKComplication, beforeDate date: NSDate,
  limit: Int, withHandler handler:
  ([CLKComplicationTimelineEntry]?) -> Void) {

  let tideConditions = TideConditions.loadConditions()

  // 1
  var waterLevels = tideConditions.waterLevels.filter {
    $0.date.compare(date) == .OrderedAscending
  }

  // 2
  if waterLevels.count > limit {
    // Remove from the front
    let numberToRemove = waterLevels.count - limit
    waterLevels.removeRange(0..<numberToRemove)
  }

  // 3
  let entries = waterLevels.flatMap { waterLevel in
    timelineEntryFor(waterLevel, family: complication.family)
  }

  handler(entries)
}
```

The method asks for the data before a certain date, up to a certain limit. This data isn't hard to gather; here's the breakdown:

1. After loading all the data, you filter out the water levels that come after `date`.
2. If the number of remaining data points exceeds the limit, you remove data from the beginning of the array. This way, you keep the most recent data.
3. For each water level, you create a `CLKComplicationTimelineEntry` using the helper method and finally, pass it to the handler.

Now for the much more exciting data, the *future* data. Implement the following, extremely similar method in `ComplicationController`:

```
func getTimelineEntriesForComplication(
  complication: CLKComplication, afterDate date: NSDate,
  limit: Int, withHandler handler:
  ([CLKComplicationTimelineEntry]?) -> Void) {

  let tideConditions = TideConditions.loadConditions()

  var waterLevels = tideConditions.waterLevels.filter {
    $0.date.compare(date) == .OrderedDescending
  }

  if waterLevels.count > limit {
    // Remove from the back
    waterLevels.removeRange(limit..<waterLevels.count)
  }

  let entries = waterLevels.flatMap { waterLevel in
    return timelineEntryFor(waterLevel,
      family: complication.family)
  }

  handler(entries)
}
```

This time, you filter out earlier dates instead of later ones. You also remove any data points that exceed the limit from the end of the array, keeping the nearest values. You finish up by passing the future entries to the handler.

That's all it takes for your app to support Time Travel. Currently, the complication still completely relies on the Watch app to download and store the data it displays, but you're going to fix that very soon.

Build and run the Watch app and let it load some data. Switch to a Utilitarian clock face and activate the Tide Watch complication. Turn the digital crown and "watch" as your complication comes to life!

> **Note**: In the simulator, you can use the scroll wheel on your mouse, or simply move your finger if you're using a Magic Mouse, to simulate the digital crown.

This is unquestionably a better way to display tide conditions for Tide Watch—it provides more information without sacrificing usability at all.

Animating through time

ClockKit provides a simple animation you can use to emphasize certain transitions when traveling through time. You can choose from among three animation behaviors:

1. **`None`** is the default value of no animation, which is your app's current behavior.
2. **`Always`** animates the change every time.
3. **`Grouped`** lets you use animation groups to specify which transitions to animate. Here, timeline entries are divided into groups, identified by a string. Animations will only occur when the displayed timeline entry changes between groups..

Tide Watch will use the most interesting of the three: grouped animations. The app already has a natural way in which the complication displays can be split into groups: each tide condition (e.g. Rising, Falling etc) will be its own group. This way, the complication will animate whenever the tide condition changes.

To get started, add the following `CLKComplicationDataSource` protocol method to `ComplicationController` to choose grouped animations:

```
func getTimelineAnimationBehaviorForComplication(
  complication: CLKComplication, withHandler handler:
  (CLKComplicationTimelineAnimationBehavior) -> Void) {
  handler(.Grouped)
}
```

This method directly returns the type of animation behavior you want to the handler.

Next, you can make use of the `timelineAnimationGroup` property of `CLKComplicationTimelineEntry` to specify the animation group for each entry. An animation will happen whenever the group changes.

Find the helper method `timelineEntryFor(_:family:)` in `ComplicationController` and locate the two calls to the initializer of `CLKComplicationTimelineEntry`. Add the optional argument `timelineAnimationGroup` and pass in `waterLevel.situation.rawValue` to each of them:

```
if family == .UtilitarianSmall {
  let smallFlat = //...
  //...
  return CLKComplicationTimelineEntry(
    date: waterLevel.date, complicationTemplate: smallFlat,
    timelineAnimationGroup: waterLevel.situation.rawValue)
} else if family == .UtilitarianLarge {
  let largeFlat = //...
  //...
  return CLKComplicationTimelineEntry(
    date: waterLevel.date, complicationTemplate: largeFlat,
    timelineAnimationGroup: waterLevel.situation.rawValue)
}
```

Recall that animation groups are specified by a string. Here you use `waterLevel.situation.rawValue` to identify the animation group so the animation group changes only when the situation changes, triggering an animation.

That's all there is to do, so build and run. Reload your complication and surf through time. The animations add a bit of sparkle to the transitions, and make it even easier for users to tell when the tide conditions change.

Keeping your data current

Your complication looks great and with its nifty animations, it feels complete. This is the perfect time to make improvements on the data-loading side.

Right now, Tide Watch's complication displays whatever it has in the cache. The system only updates the cache when the user opens the iPhone app or Watch app, which means the complication's data will be completely out of date if the user doesn't use the app for a day. Even when the user opens the app, the complication doesn't know there's new data to display—it relies solely on it's cache.

It would be nice if you could reload the complication's data whenever either of the apps (iPhone or Watch) retrieves fresh data and in certain situations, such as when the user chooses a different location to monitor.

Furthermore, Tide Watch's "future data" is a prediction, which means the data can become more accurate over time. So it would also be nice if you could update the complication's data from time to time, even if the user hasn't done anything.

ClockKit provides this functionality through a few APIs that let you extend or invalidate your data, as well as a few others that let you specify when you want to be "woken up" to fetch and supply more data to the complication. You can also update your complications through special push notifications to your app. In this section, you'll take advantage of these features to keep Tide Watch as up to date as possible.

Budgeting your time

Before you begin, notice that there's a slight conflict of interest between the system and complications. You want your complication to provide the most up-to-date data as possible, but the system also needs to worry about power consumption and giving all complications a chance to update.

The system manages this by allocating **time budgets** to each complication. Your complication can take time to update as long as it stays within its budget. Once time exceeds the budget, the system won't let the complication update its data *at all* until the system replenishes your complication's budget.

Scheduled updates

You can schedule the time of your complication's next update. This is very useful for any app that displays time-relevant information, such as weather, stocks or tide conditions.

Because the system is enforcing a time budget, you want to provide as much data as you can manage during each update, and request updates as infrequently as possible.

To begin, you first need to pass the system the time you'd next like to provide an update. Add the following method, declared by the `CLKComplicationDataSource` protocol, to `ComplicationController`:

```
func getNextRequestedUpdateDateWithHandler(
  handler: (NSDate?) -> Void) {

  let tideConditions = TideConditions.loadConditions()
  if let waterLevel = tideConditions.waterLevels.last {
    handler(waterLevel.date)
  } else {
    // Refresh Now!
    handler(NSDate())
  }
}
```

If you have data, you request that the next update happen at the time of the last known water level, ensuring the complication never runs out of data. If you don't yet have any data, you can pass in the current time to request an immediate update.

The system will call this method upon activation of your complication and again after every update, so you'll always have an update scheduled.

Next, you need a method to update the data. A scheduled update doesn't necessarily mean you'll have new data to display. When you *do* have new data, you might want to invalidate all the existing data or only add new data to the timeline. You can communicate these intentions to ClockKit with the following:

- To invalidate the existing data, call `reloadTimelineForComplication(_:)` on `CLKComplicationServer`.
- To add new data, call `extendTimelineForComplication(_:)`, also on `CLKComplicationServer`.
- If you don't have any new data, you simply don't call either of those methods. The system will still allow you to schedule the next update.

This new method will thus call `extendTimelineForComplication(_:)` to add new data to the end of the timeline in the case of a scheduled update. It also needs to handle the case where the user changes the measurement station, which requires a call to `reloadTimelineForComplication(_:)` to invalidate all the current data for the previous station.

Implement this new helper method as follows:

```
func reloadOrExtendData() {
  // 1
  let server = CLKComplicationServer.sharedInstance()
  guard let complications = server.activeComplications
    where complications.count > 0 else { return }

  // 2
  let tideConditions = TideConditions.loadConditions()
  let displayedStation = loadDisplayedStation()

  // 3
  if let id = displayedStation?.id
    where id == tideConditions.station.id {
    // 4
    // Check if there is new data
    if tideConditions.waterLevels.last?.date.compare(
      server.latestTimeTravelDate) == .OrderedDescending {
      // 5
      for complication in complications  {
        server.extendTimelineForComplication(complication)
      }
    }
  } else {
    // 6
    for complication in complications  {
      server.reloadTimelineForComplication(complication)
    }
  }
  // 7
  saveDisplayedStation(tideConditions.station)
}
```

This is quite a bit of code, so let's go through it step by step:

1. The shared instance of `CLKComplicationServer` provides you with all your active complications. You can safely return if there aren't any active ones.
2. You load the cached data as well as the currently displayed station.
3. Then, you check if the station has changed.
4. If the station hasn't changed, you check if there's any new data loaded. If there's no new data, you don't have to do anything.
5. If there is new data, you call `extendTimelineForComplication(_:)` on the complication server, once for each active complication.
6. If the station has changed or hasn't even been loaded yet, you can call `reloadTimelineForComplication(_:)` on the server, once for each active

complication.

7. Lastly, you save the station as the currently displayed station.

This method will update the complication with the current data stored within the shared instance `TideConditions`. This information might not be completely current, so you'll want to update this data before calling `reloadOrExtendData()`. Implement the following helper method:

```
func refreshData() {
  let tideConditions = TideConditions.loadConditions()
  let yesterday = NSDate(timeIntervalSinceNow: -24 * 60 * 60)
  let tomorrow = NSDate(timeIntervalSinceNow: 24 * 60 * 60)
  tideConditions.loadWaterLevels(
    from: yesterday, to: tomorrow) { success in
    if success {
      TideConditions.saveConditions(tideConditions)
      self.reloadOrExtendData()
    }
  }
}
```

This methods simply loads fresh data for the current station, saves it, and then calls the method you just created, `reloadOrExtendData()`.

When the time comes for an update, the system will call either `requestedUpdateDidBegin()` or `requestedUpdateBudgetExhausted()` on the `CLKComplicationDataSource` to let you know that the update is beginning. `requestedUpdateBudgetExhausted()` is called if you're over budget and gives you one last chance to update your data before your budget is replenished.

Implement both of these methods inside `ComplicationController`:

```
func requestedUpdateDidBegin() {
  refreshData()
}

func requestedUpdateBudgetExhausted() {
  refreshData()
}
```

These methods call the same helper method you just created, `refreshData()`, in a fashion very similar to how the Watch app or iPhone app loads new data.

It's a bit tricky to see this functionality in action. You can modify `getNextRequestedUpdateDateWithHandler(_:)` to specify an update date in the very near future. Remember, though, that the system has total control and can't guarantee the exact time of your update. If you schedule the update for a few seconds into the future, keep a breakpoint around and go make some tea—with any luck, your update will have begun by the time you get back. :]

Updating from the Watch app

Whenever a user opens the Tide Watch app and loads new data, you can directly inform the system to refresh the complication using the same `CLKComplicationServer` methods. This will let you reduce the time in your complication's budget taken up by network requests.

In Tide Watch, you should update the complication's timeline whenever new Tidal data is retrieved. Open **ExtensionDelegate.swift** and implement the following helper method at the bottom of `ExtensionDelegate`:

```
func updateComplicationData() {
  let complicationsController = ComplicationController()
  complicationsController.reloadOrExtendData()
}
```

This method simply calls `reloadOrExtendData()` on `ComplicationController`, which you just implemented to update the timeline.

Conveniently, Tide Watch calls `conditionsUpdated(_:)` in `ExtensionDelegate` each time new data arrives in order to send the new data to the iPhone. You can take advantage of this and refresh the complication at the same time. Add the call to `updateComplicationData()` near the end of `conditionsUpdated(_:)`, inside the `dispatch_async()` closure:

```
func conditionsUpdated(tideConditions:TideConditions) {
  TideConditions.saveConditions(tideConditions)
  dispatch_async(dispatch_get_main_queue()) {
    let notificationCenter =
      NSNotificationCenter.defaultCenter()
    notificationCenter.postNotificationName(
      PhoneUpdatedDataNotification, object: tideConditions)
    self.updateComplicationData()
  }
}
```

The Watch app will now refresh the complication whenever it retrieves new data.

Updating from the iPhone app

You'll also want to refresh the complication whenever the user changes the measurement station on the iPhone app.

As you saw in Chapter 13, in watchOS 2, Watch Connectivity handles all the communication between the iPhone and the Watch.

Watch Connectivity includes a special method precisely for when a complication needs updating: `transferCurrentComplicationUserInfo(_:)`.

To implement this functionality, you can again hook into the existing Watch Connectivity code. Open **AppDelegate.swift** (in the **TideWatch** group) and find the private method `sendUpdatedDataToWatch(_:)`. Replace the inner `if` statement with the following snippet:

```
if session.watchAppInstalled,
  let conditions = notification.userInfo?["conditions"]
  as? TideConditions, let isNewStation =
  notification.userInfo?["newStation"]?.boolValue {
  do {
    let data =
      NSKeyedArchiver.archivedDataWithRootObject(conditions)
    let dictionary = ["data": data]
    // Transfer complications info
    if isNewStation {
      session.transferCurrentComplicationUserInfo(dictionary)
    } else {
      try session.updateApplicationContext(dictionary)
    }
  } catch {
    print("ERROR: \(error)")
  }
}
```

There's only a small change here at the comment: If the user switches stations, you call `transferCurrentComplicationUserInfo(_:)` to directly refresh the complication instead of updating the application context. By refreshing the complication, you're still updating the Watch app.

The Watch extension's `ExtensionDelegate` now requires a new method to receive this data. Open **ExtensionDelegate.swift** and implement the following method:

```
func session(session: WCSession,
  didReceiveUserInfo userInfo: [String : AnyObject]) {
  if let data = userInfo["data"] as? NSData {
    if let tideConditions =
      NSKeyedUnarchiver.unarchiveObjectWithData(data) as?
      TideConditions {
      conditionsUpdated(tideConditions)
    }
  }
}
```

After retrieving the data, you call the helper method `conditionsUpdated(_:)`, which in turn updates the Watch app as well as the complication.

Updating from a server

The last way you can send updates to a complication is via push notifications directly from your server. There's a new type of push notification in iOS 9, made especially for complications, that is only delivered if your complication is active.

It's the iPhone that receives the push notification, so Watch Connectivity is required to send the payload to the Watch. Time spent processing the information from the push notification *on the iPhone* also counts towards your complication's budget.

Since you don't own the Tide Watch server, you won't need to implement this type of update in Tide Watch. However, this is an important way to refresh your complications, so here are the steps you would take:

1. First, create a delegate class that conforms to `PKPushRegistryDelegate`;
2. Next, create a `PKPushRegistry` and set its delegate to the delegate class;
3. Set `desiredPushTypes` of the push registry to `PKPushTypeComplication`;
4. The system will call `pushRegistry(_:didUpdatePushCredentials:forType:)` on the delegate to provide you with a push token;
5. Upload the push token to your server just like a regular push notification;
6. When the iPhone receives a push notification, the system will call `pushRegistry(_:didReceiveIncomingPushWithPayload:forType:)`;
7. You can then parse the payload and send it to the Watch using `transferCurrentComplicationUserInfo(_:)`.

The advantage of this special push notification over regular push notifications is that it doesn't require permission from the user. However, with this extra freedom comes extra responsibility, and the system will stop delivering your notifications if you pass a daily limit that

Now you know all the ways to keep your complications up to date!

Privacy in complications

The finish line is coming right up! There's one last method in `CLKComplicationDataSource` that `ComplicationController` doesn't implement.

Complications can sometimes display extremely private information. Tide Watch is not one of these cases, but many complications, such as calendars and fitness apps, may display information that the user wouldn't want others to see.

ClockKit provides a way to indicate that the information your complication displays is private. The result is that the system will hide your complication's data if the Watch is locked.

Open **ComplicationController.swift** and implement the following method:

```
func getPrivacyBehaviorForComplication(
  complication: CLKComplication, withHandler handler:
  (CLKComplicationPrivacyBehavior) -> Void) {
  handler(.ShowOnLockScreen)
}
```

There are two self-explanatory options here, `.ShowOnLockScreen` and `.HideOnLockScreen`. To see the effect, change the value to `.HideOnLockScreen` and then build and run. Reload the complication and go to the lock screen. The Watch will no longer display the data, similar to the activity rings:

> **Note**: The simulator doesn't display the lock screen, so you'll need a device to see this effect.

Taking your users' privacy seriously is exactly the behavior they expect, and with a device as personal as the Apple Watch, it has never been more important.

Where to go from here?

Congratulations—you've implemented every single method in `CLKComplicationDataSource`!

With all of this new knowledge, you may have developed your own ideas for complications. The next step is to turn them into reality.

Complications are truly one of the most exciting features to come to any computing device in recent years. I can't wait to see all the exciting ways you find to make use of them. :]

Chapter 20: Handoff

By Soheil Azarpour

In iOS 8 Apple introduced a magical continuity feature named Handoff, a way to facilitate the seamless transfer of tasks between two devices. Handoff lets you immediately continue an activity you start on one device on another, hassle-free. For example, Handoff allows you to start writing an email on your iPhone and then continue writing from exactly the same spot on your Mac. Since its introduction, Handoff has been broadly accepted. Whether it's a news app, weather app or a music app, you can see that big name apps in the App Store use Handoff to deep-link to their app.

When it comes to the Apple Watch, you are limited to a subset of content or functionality from your main app. There is no better way than Handoff to let the user see your full content or the functionality without interruption. Imagine you have a news app that shows the headline and the summary of a news article on the Watch. It's not convenient to read a 5-page long article on that small screen. Instead of manually finding your app in a clutter of apps on the iPhone, your user can navigate directly to your app, and to the news article with a single swipe on the iPhone lock screen.

In this chapter, you'll use Handoff to create continuity between the Apple Watch and a paired iPhone for a raywenderlich.com newsfeed app. When you finish, you'll have a firm grasp of the basics of this feature and how to make it work in your Watch apps.

It's time to make some magic!

Note: At the time of writing, Handoff does not work on the iOS simulator. Therefore, to follow along with this chapter, you'll need an Apple Watch that's paired with an iPhone.

Getting started

The starter project you'll use in this chapter is called **RWDigest**. Open the starter project, **RWDigest.xcodeproj** in Xcode and make sure the **RWDigest** scheme for the iPhone is selected. Build and run using the iPhone simulator, and you'll see the following screens:

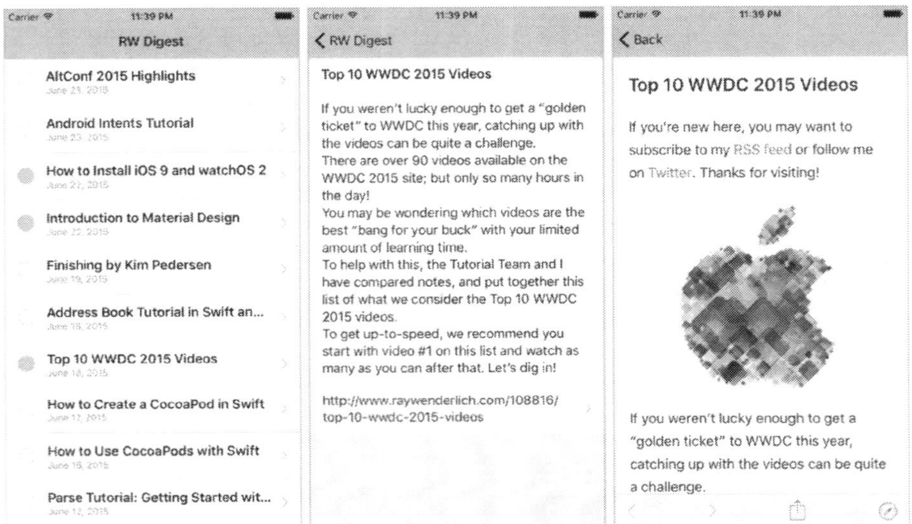

With RWDigest, you can check out the latest news on the go with just a twist of your wrist! The app displays a list of the most recent articles and tutorials from raywenderlich.com. If you tap on an item, you're presented with a brief introduction and a link that loads the entire article in an instance of `SFSafariViewController`.

Now stop the app and change the scheme to **RWDigest-Watch**. Build and run using the Apple Watch simulator. This time, you'll see the following screens:

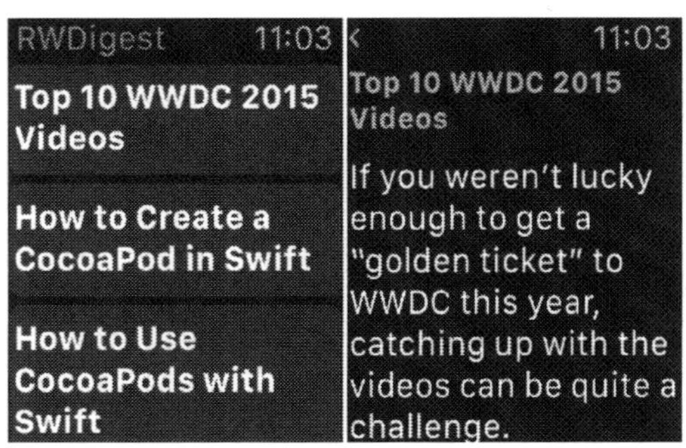

The Watch app has a flow that mirrors its companion iPhone app. However, notice that the brief is shorter and there's no link to the full article. That's by design—the Watch app is a bird's eye view of the iPhone app, so users can't read the full articles on the Watch. Your task is to add Handoff support so that users can seamlessly continue reading the same article that they are reading on the Apple Watch on the paired iPhone.

Handoff functionality depends on few things:

1. **An iCloud account**: you must be logged in to the same iCloud account on each device you wish to use Handoff.
2. **Bluetooth LE 4.0**: Handoff broadcasts activities via Bluetooth LE signals, so both the broadcasting and receiving devices must have Bluetooth LE 4.0 support.
3. **iCloud paired**: devices should have been already paired through iCloud.

In the context of the Apple Watch, both the Watch and the iPhone that supports Apple Watch have Bluetooth LE 4.0, and they are paired. So you're good to go!

Setting your team

In Handoff you always have two apps: a sending app and a receiving app. For Handoff to work, both the sending and receiving apps must be signed by the same Team ID. From your app's standpoint, unless streaming, Handoff is a one-time data exchange event during which the sending device delivers a package of data to the receiving device.

Select the **RWDigest** target from your project settings, and in the **General** tab, switch the **Team** to your team:

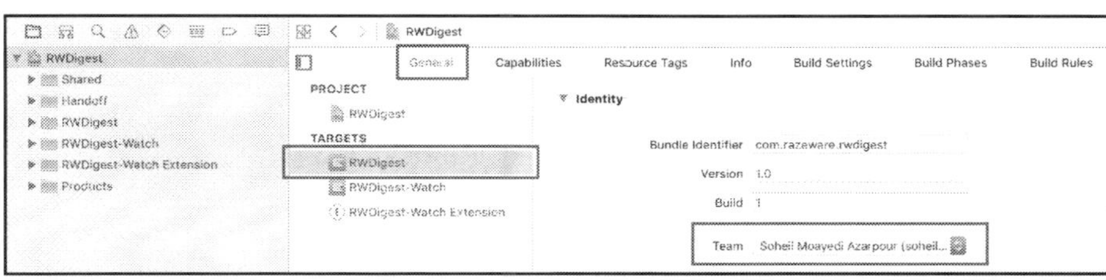

Similarly, update the **Team** for the **RWDigest-Watch** and **RWDigest-Watch Extension** targets.

Build and run the app on your iOS device as well as on the Watch to make sure it runs without problems.

Configuring activity types

Handoff is based on the concept of a user activity. You'll learn more about user activity in a bit. When you create a user activity, you must specify an activity type for it. An activity type is simply a unique string, usually in reverse DNS notation, like `com.razeware.rwdigest.view`. The activity type won't be shown to the user but as a best practice make sure you choose a meaningful activity type that clearly indicates its intention.

Each app that's capable of receiving a user activity must declare the activity types it will accept. This is much like declaring the URL schemes your app supports.

The next step is to configure the activity types. Expand the **RWDigest** group in the project navigator and find and open **Info.plist**. Click the **+** button that appears next to **Information Property List** to add a new item to its dictionary, like so:

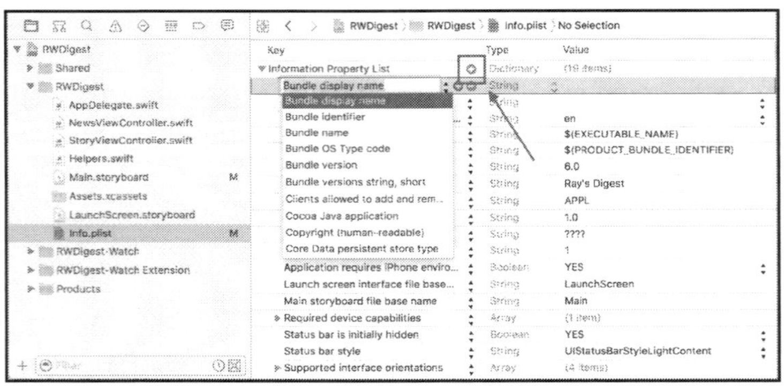

Enter `NSUserActivityTypes` for the key name and make it an `Array` type. Add two items under `NSUserActivityTypes`—`Item 0` and `Item 1`—and set their types to `String`. Enter `com.razeware.rwdigest.news` for `Item 0`, and `com.razeware.rwdigest.story` for `Item 1`.

When you're done, your new entry will look like this:

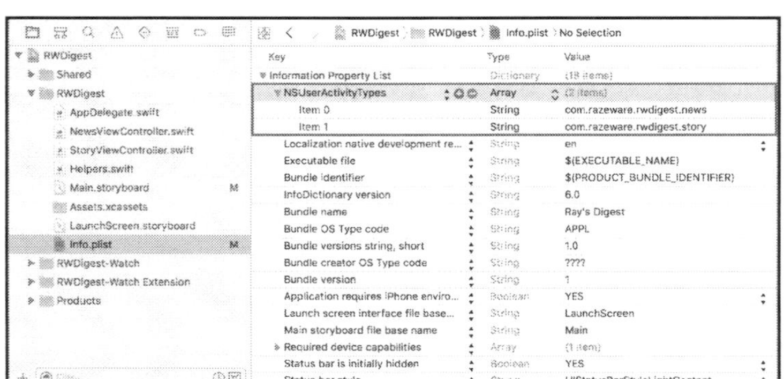

Here you add two different activity types because you're going to implement two distinct behaviors, and each should have its own unique identifier:

- Hand off the top level screen where all news stories are displayed.
- Hand off a specific story where you'll drill down to that specific story.

These are arbitrary activity types unique to your app. Since you'll refer to them in code from multiple places in the app, it's good practice to add them as constants in a separate file. So, right-click on the **RWDigest** project in the project navigator, select **New Group** and name it **Handoff**.

Then right-click on the **Handoff** group and from the menu, select **New File\iOS\Source \Swift File**. Name it **HandoffHelper.swift** and ensure your new file is added to both the **RWDigest** and **RWDigest-Watch Extension** targets.

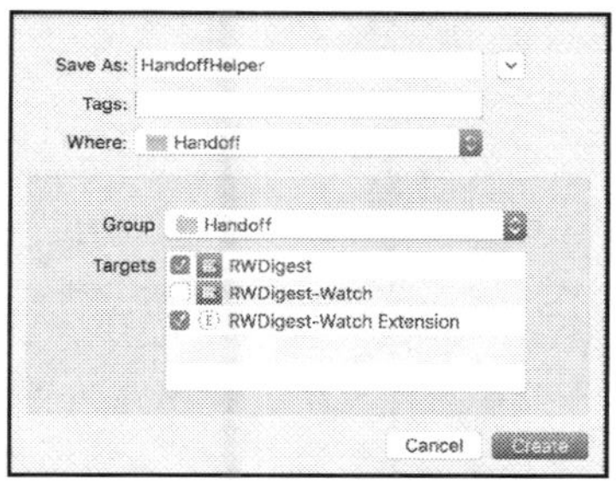

Open **HandoffHelper.swift** and update it by adding the following to the end of the file:

```
// 1
struct Handoff {
  // 2
  enum ActivityType: String {
    case ViewNews   = "com.razeware.rwdigest.news"
    case ReadStory  = "com.razeware.rwdigest.story"
  }
  // 3
  let activityValueKey = "activityValue"
}
```

Here's what you're doing with the above code:

1. You'll use some constants with Handoff and refer to them from multiple places in the app. It's good practice to modularize those constants in a well-defined structure.
2. You add an `enum` that represents the registered user activity types from the app's Info.plist. For each registered user activity type, you add a distinct `enum` value.
3. Some activity types may have an associated value. For example, if a user is reading an article, you also want to specify which article it is. Soon you'll use `activityValueKey` to store such values in the payload of a user activity so that they can be passed to the receiving app.

Before moving on to performing a simple Handoff, let's take a look at the essential user activity dictionary.

User activities

Handoff is based on the concept of **user activities**: stand-alone units of information that you can hand off without any dependencies on other information. Consider the task of writing an email. To continue the email on another device, the activity must include the recipient, subject, message body, any attachments and possibly even the insertion point of the cursor at the time the email is handed off.

In iOS, Handoff uses `NSUserActivity` objects to package information to transfer. The user activity that you pass from the Watch app contains a `userInfo` dictionary where you store information about the current state of the app. If the user continues a Watch activity on the iPhone, that contextual information is passed to the app delegate of the iPhone app, which you can then use to configure the receiving app appropriately.

Keys and values in the dictionary may only be classes compatible with the plist format: `NSArray`, `NSData`, `NSDate`, `NSDictionary`, `NSNull`, `NSNumber`, `NSSet`, `NSString` or `NSURL`. Under the hood, Handoff uses the plist format to exchange data with different devices.

When passing `NSURL`s don't pass local file URLs, as the receiver won't be able to translate and map the URL properly. Instead send a relative path and re-construct the URL manually on the receiving side. Likewise, do not use platform-specific values like the content offset of a scroll view. Instead, send a landmark that makes sense in the context of your data model–like an index to an array.

Next, you'll implement a simple Handoff to take user from the news screen of the Watch app to the news screen of the iPhone app. The user activity you create here will allow the user to view the list of stories.

A quick end-to-end Handoff

It's time to implement a simple end-to-end Handoff. Open **InterfaceController.swift** and add the following to the end of `willActivate()`:

```
// Handoff.
let handoff = Handoff()
let userInfo: [NSObject: AnyObject] =
  [handoff.activityValueKey: ""]
updateUserActivity(Handoff.ActivityType.ViewNews.rawValue,
```

```
    userInfo: userInfo,
    webpageURL: nil)
```

Here's what's going on:

`WKInterfaceController` has a method, `updateUserActivity(_:userInfo:webpageURL:)`, that updates and begins to broadcast a `NSUserActivity` can be handed off. You can call this method at any time during the execution of the interface controller's code. The system stores the `userInfo` dictionary and will transfer it to the target device when appropriate.

However, if the device suspends execution of your code, you need to start broadcasting again, so you need to put your Handoff code somewhere it will get executed when the app returns to the foreground. This typically makes `willActivate()` a good place to start broadcasting Handoff.

You wrap the state of the app in the `userInfo` dictionary. When the user is viewing the top-level news stories, you broadcast a user activity with the `Handoff.ActivityType.ViewNews` type. Since there's no specific associate value, you pass an empty string for `activityValueKey` in the `userInfo` dictionary.

> **Note**: Although `userInfo` dictionary is optional and you can pass `nil`, as a best practice you usually want to pass something meaningful instead. At the end of the chapter, you'll add an important versioning value to the dictionary.

You pass in `nil` for `webpageURL`, as this handoff won't be navigating data in your app that could also be shown in Safari. The system would use the URL to load the webpage in a browser when the user continues the activity on a Mac or iOS device that does not have your app installed. You can learn more about native app-to-web browser handoff and vice versa in Apple's **Handoff Programming Guide**: apple.co/1uIWL00

At this point, you have the minimum you need to start broadcasting, so let's move on to receiving.

On the receiving side, when user swipes up on your app icon on the lock screen, the operating system launches your app and then it starts downloading the Handoff payload in the background. As transfer of data happens, you'll get call backs in your iPhone app delegate, which you'll see next.

Open **AppDelegate.swift** and add the following code:

```
// 1
let handoff = Handoff()

// 2
```

```
func application(application: UIApplication,
  continueUserActivity userActivity: NSUserActivity,
  restorationHandler: ([AnyObject]?) -> Void) -> Bool {
  // 3
  guard let userInfo = userActivity.userInfo
    else { return true }
  print(userInfo)
  // 4
  guard let controller = (window?.rootViewController
    as? UINavigationController)?.viewControllers.first
    as? NewsViewController
    else { return true }
  controller.restoreUserActivityState(userActivity)
  // 5
  return true
}
```

Here is what's going on line by line:

1. For convenience, you create a `handoff` property from the `Handoff` structure, because you'll be using it in multiple places within your app delegate.
2. You implement `application(_:continueUserActivity:restorationHandler:)`. This method in `UIApplicationDelegate` is called when everything goes well and a user activity is successfully transferred.
3. You unwrap the `userInfo` dictionary of the passed-in activity and log a message.
4. You safely access the root view controller of the app and pass along the `userActivity` object you received. `restoreUserActivityState(_:)` is the designated method for Handoff state restoration. It's declared at the `UIResponder` level, so many common UIKit classes like `UIViewController` inherit it. You'll learn more about state restoration later in this chapter.
5. You return `true` to indicate you handled the user activity. If you return `false`, you leave it to the OS to handle Handoff, which usually does nothing except launching your app! :]

That's it for a quick, simple, end-to-end Handoff–let's try it out! There's a little coordination required to get this working on two devices, so follow along carefully:

1. Install and run the app on your iPhone.
2. Make sure the app gets installed on the paired Apple Watch. You may need to open the Watch app on the iPhone and manually flick the switch.
3. Make sure you're debugging the app in Xcode so you can see your `print()` output.
4. Put the iPhone to sleep by pressing the power button.

5. On the Watch, launch the app and press the Home button on the iPhone to light up the screen. In a couple of seconds, you'll see the RWDigest app icon appear in the bottom-left corner of the screen. From there, you'll be able to launch the app and see the log message in Xcode's console:

```
[activityValue: ]
```

> **Note**: If you don't see the app icon on the lock screen, make sure the Watch screen stays on for a while. You may also put the palm of your hand on the Watch screen to put it to sleep, then tap on the Watch screen again to wake it up. This triggers `willActivate()` and forces the OS to restart broadcasting. Also, check the device console to see if there are any error messages from Handoff.

Alerting the user and handling errors

Even though the app seems to work well, there are a few things you need to implement to ensure everything is handled properly.

When the user indicates that she wants to continue a user activity on the receiving device–by swiping up on the app icon–the OS launches the corresponding app, then calls `application(_:willContinueUserActivityWithType:)`. This is where you can get prepared for an incoming Handoff. Open **AppDelegate.swift** and add the following method:

```
func application(application: UIApplication,
  willContinueUserActivityWithType
  userActivityType: String) -> Bool {
    return true
}
```

At this point, your app hasn't yet downloaded the `NSUserActivity` instance and its `userInfo` payload, but the OS tells you in advance what type of activity is coming your way. If you want to alert your user that the activity is on its way and you need to do some preparations, this is the place to do it. For example, you can pop to the root view controller of your navigation controller or dismiss a modally presented view controller.

Now the OS has started transferring data from one device to another. You've already covered the happy path along which everything goes well. But it's conceivable that the Handoff activity will fail at some point.

Add the following method to **AppDelegate.swift** to handle this case:

```
func application(application: UIApplication,
  didFailToContinueUserActivityWithType
```

```
    userActivityType: String, error: NSError) {
    if error.code != NSUserCancelledError {
      let message = "The connection to your other device may have
        been interrupted. Please try again.
        \(error.localizedDescription)"
      let controller = AlertHelper.
        dismissOnlyAlertControllerWithTitle("Handoff Error",
        message: message)
      window?.rootViewController?.presentViewController(
        controller, animated: true, completion: nil)
    }
  }
```

If you receive anything except `NSUserCancelledError`, then something went wrong along the way, and you won't be able to restore the activity. In this case, you display an appropriate message to the user. However, if the user explicitly canceled the Handoff action, then there's nothing else for you to do here but abort the operation.

Build and run to ensure that the handoff still works are expected. You can hand off from the Watch app's main interface to the iPhone app as before; but now, if an error happens, you appropriately display an error message.

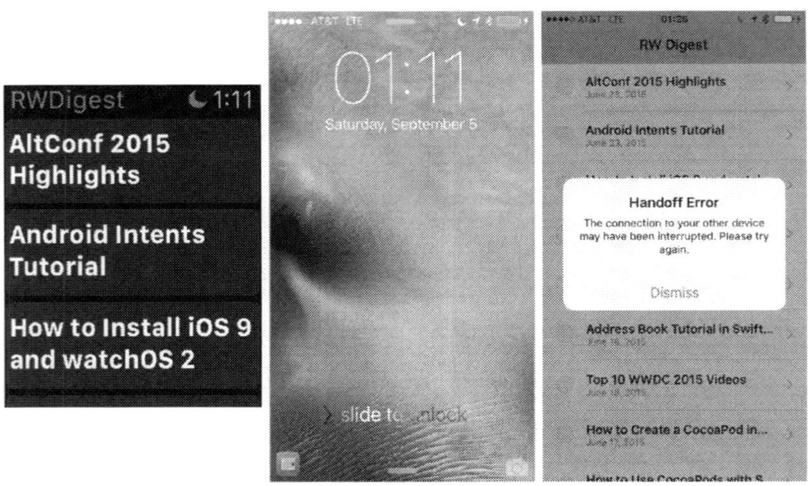

Handoff state restoration

Now that you've successfully implemented a simple handoff, it's time to code a more complicated one that requires you to do some state restoration.

You probably agree that while broadcasting from the main interface controller is handy, it's not very useful to the user. One very important place to broadcast a handoff is from `StoryInterfaceController`, where the user reads an article.

Open **StoryInterfaceController.swift** and find `willActivate()`. Add the following to the end of the method:

```
// Handoff.
let handoff = Handoff()
guard let story = story else { return }
let userInfo: [NSObject: AnyObject] = [
  handoff.activityValueKey: story.identifier
]
updateUserActivity(Handoff.ActivityType.ReadStory.rawValue,
  userInfo: userInfo,
  webpageURL: nil)
```

Much like the main interface controller, when the user selects a story in the Watch app, `willActivate()` is called. You then create and broadcast a `ReadStory` activity that contains the story identifier.

Build and run. Verify that everything works as expected by navigating to an article in the Watch app and handing it off to the iPhone app. You'll see the story identifier of the article logged in the console:

```
[activityValue: RWNL2015062306]
```

Now it's time for state restoration. Remember how in the `AppDelegate`, you passed the `userActivity` object to `NewsViewController` by calling `restoreUserActivityState(_:)`? The default implementation of `restoreUserActivityState(_:)` doesn't do much for you. You need to override it and perform your own state restoration as it suits you.

Open **NewsViewController.swift** and override `restoreUserActivityState(_:)`:

```
override func restoreUserActivityState(activity: NSUserActivity)
{
  // 1
  super.restoreUserActivityState(activity)

  // 2
  navigationController?.popToViewController(self,
    animated: true)

  // 3
  guard let userInfo = activity.userInfo else { return }

  let handoff = Handoff()
  switch activity.activityType {
  // 4
    case Handoff.ActivityType.ReadStory.rawValue:
      guard let storyID = userInfo[handoff.activityValueKey]
        as? String else {
        presentStoryNotFoundAlertController()
```

```
        return
      }
      guard let story = news?.storyWithIdentifier(storyID)
        else {
        presentStoryNotFoundAlertController()
        return
      }
      let controller = presentStoryViewControllerWithStory(
        story, animated: false)
      controller.restoreUserActivityState(activity)
    // 5
    case Handoff.ActivityType.ViewNews.rawValue: fallthrough
    default: break
  }
}
```

The code block may seem lengthy, but it's quite easy. Here is a detailed explanation:

1. You call `super` so that it gets a chance to do anything it has to do for state restoration.
2. You always want to know the current state of your app before doing any state restoration. The simplest way here is to make sure you're at the root of your navigation controller.
3. You safely unwrap the `userInfo` dictionary and evaluate the activity type of the handoff.
4. If it's a `ReadStory` activity type, you do some fail-safe checking and generic error handling before passing the activity on to the `StoryViewController`. You pass along the `userActivity` to `StoryViewController` in the same way, by calling `restoreUserActivityState(_:)` on it.
5. For a `ViewNews` activity type, you don't have to do anything, since the user is already in `NewsViewController`. This is also your default behavior for any unknown activity types.

Build and run. Navigate again to an article on the Watch app and hand it off to the iPhone app. This time, you'll be magically taken to the same story on your iPhone!

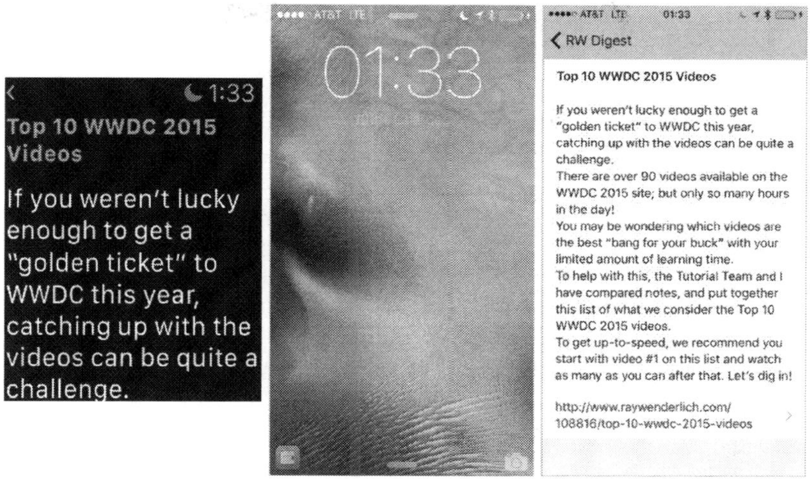

Jumping right to the browser

You did a good job adding Handoff support to the RWDigest app, but there's still room for one improvement.

When the user hands off reading an article from the Watch to the iPhone, there's little value in merely showing `StoryViewController`, because the user still has to tap on the link and load the full article. You can improve the user experience by taking one more tap away and immediately loading the full article for a `ReadStory` activity type.

Open **StoryViewController.swift** and add the following to the end of the `class` definition:

```
override func restoreUserActivityState(
  activity: NSUserActivity) {
  super.restoreUserActivityState(activity)
  guard let story = story else { return }
  let controller = SFSafariViewController(URL: story.link,
    entersReaderIfAvailable: true)
  navigationController?.pushViewController(controller,
    animated: true)
}
```

Here, you safely check for a valid story. Since the parent view controller, `NewsViewController`, has done the heavy lifting of error handling, you can silently fail and follow the happy path. If there's a valid story, you load the full article.

Build and run, and give it a try. You'll see an immediate improvement in the user experience.

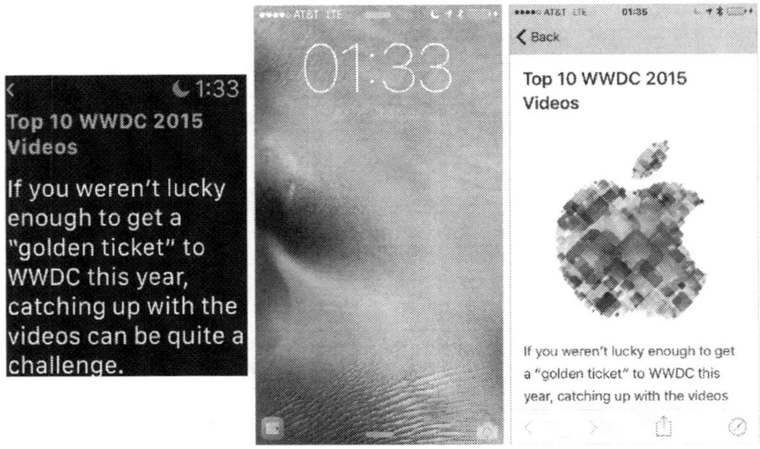

Stopping the broadcast

There are times that you want to stop broadcasting for Handoff because the context has changed or user has started a new activity. Note that you can broadcast only one activity at a time. If you don't do it yourself, you leave it to the OS to decide when to stop broadcasting.

In the context of the Apple Watch the recommended way is to leave it to the OS to stop broadcasting on the Watch. Unlike iOS, you'll manually invalidate Handoff on the Watch only when you need to do so. This is because the OS does some optimizations to ensure that Handoff broadcast lasts a bit longer–even after the Watch screen turns off–for the convenience of the user. You usually don't want to interrupt that.

`WKInterfaceController` has a convenient method, `invalidateUserActivity()`, that you can use to stop the broadcast. You can call `invalidateUserActivity()` at any time during the execution of your code.

Versioning support

Versioning is an important best practice when working with Handoff. You might add new data formats or remove values entirely from your `userInfo` dictionary in future versions of the app. You want to make sure older versions of your app don't break if they receive a newer version of Handoff, or vice versa.

One strategy to deal with this is to add a version number to each handoff you send, and only accept handoffs from your current version number, and potentially earlier. Let's try this.

Open **HandoffHelper.swift** and update it as follows:

```
struct Version {
  let key: String
  let number: Int
}

struct Handoff {
  // ... existing code ...
  let version = Version(key: "version", number: 1)
}
```

Here, you declare a `Version` struct to hold your versioning data. Then in the `Handoff` structure, you add a new property that holds the current versioning info. This gives you a basic versioning system. You can extend this in the future for your own purposes.

Open **InterfaceController.swift** and find `willActivate()`. Update the `userInfo` dictionary by adding versioning:

```
let userInfo: [NSObject: AnyObject] = [
  handoff.version.key: handoff.version.number,
  handoff.activityValueKey: ""
]
```

Similarly, update the `userInfo` dictionary in **StoryInterfaceController.swift**:

```
let userInfo: [NSObject: AnyObject] = [
  handoff.version.key: handoff.version.number,
  handoff.activityValueKey: story.identifier
]
```

Now update `AppDelegate` so that it knows how to deal with versioning. Open **AppDelegate.swift** and update the implementation of `application(_:continueUserActivity:restorationHandler:)` as follows:

```
func application(application: UIApplication,
  continueUserActivity userActivity: NSUserActivity,
  restorationHandler: ([AnyObject]?) -> Void) -> Bool {

  guard let userInfo = userActivity.userInfo
    else { return true }
  guard let version = userInfo[handoff.version.key] as? Int
    else { return true }

  if version == handoff.version.number {
    guard let controller = (window?.rootViewController
      as? UINavigationController)?.viewControllers.first
      as? NewsViewController
      else { return true }
    controller.restoreUserActivityState(userActivity)
```

```
    }

    return true
  }
```

Here, you improve the implementation by explicitly checking for the version number that's passed in with the user activity payload. If it's a version that you know about, you perform the state restoration. Otherwise, you simply return `true` indicating that you handled it.

Where to go from here?

Handoff makes it easier than ever to provide users with a seamless experience of your apps across multiple devices. I hope you leave this chapter comfortable with the basics of Handoff and confident that you can make use of this exciting Continuity feature in your own apps.

If you're curious to learn more about Handoff, be sure to check out these sources:

- Adopting Handoff on iOS and OS X: apple.co/1CJglQv
- Handoff Programming Guide: apple.co/1uIWL00
- `NSUserActivity` Class Reference: apple.co/1e8jHAB

Chapter 21: Core Motion

By Audrey Tam

Are you keeping your Apple Watch happy by standing and walking more often? Seeing your stats in the Activity app is great motivation to rack up those last few minutes of exercise and reach today's calorie-burn target.

But the Activity app only displays your daily stats and totals for the current week. Don't you wish you could watch your distance *adding up*? Then you could set imaginary goals, like walking the distance of a marathon or three, then moving on to walk the length or breadth of your continent.

In this chapter, you'll use watchOS 2's new **Core Motion** framework to build an app that tracks your progress towards your dream walk. Do some stretches and let's get moving!

> **Note**: You need an Apple Watch paired with an iPhone in order to test Core Motion in watchOS 2.

Getting started

iOS 4 delivered the Core Motion framework, enabling developers to access an iOS device's accelerometer and gyroscope data. Later iOS versions added compass, altimeter and pedometer data, as well as detection of the user's probable activity—stationary, walking, running or automotive.

watchOS 2 brings Core Motion to Apple Watch! *Well, some of it...*

This chapter looks at what is and isn't in Core Motion on watchOS 2, and uses `CMPedometer` distance data in a Watch app that calculates your progress along walks of different lengths. Ever wanted to know how many steps it would take to walk the Tour du Mont Blanc or hike the entire Pacific Coast trail? If you haven't, this app might inspire you!

What is Core Motion?

The Core Motion framework contains levels of abstraction ranging from raw sensor data to processed sensor data, interpreted to identify the user's current activity.

Sensors

Let's take a look at the different levels of abstraction in Core Motion.

> **Note**: Psst! At the time of writing, the Watch has only the accelerometer and some of the processed data, so if you're only interested in Core Motion on the Watch, you can skip most of this section.

At the most fine-grained level, devices return the following data:

- **Accelerometer**: the device's acceleration, in Gs, along x, y and z axes. A **G** is the standard unit of gravity. Accelerometer values include the influence of gravity, which **device motion**, below, separates from acceleration imparted by the user.
- **Altimeter**: *changes* in the device's altitude. It works by sensing air pressure, so if your app takes readings over several days, a weather change could register an increase of 15 meters! If an iPhone is in a rigid waterproof case, the altimeter might not work as expected.
- **Gyroscope**: the device's rotation around x, y, and z axes. These should be zero when the device isn't moving, but all sensors have some bias, often due to temperature changes. Device motion, below, corrects this bias.
- **Magnetometer**: the Earth's magnetic field plus bias from the device and its

surroundings. Device motion, below, removes the device's bias.

Device motion abstracts raw sensor data by encapsulating gyroscope, magnetometer and accelerometer data to provide the device's altitude and rotation rate. It uses gyroscope data to separate raw acceleration data into `gravity` and `userAcceleration` properties. Its `rotationRate` and `magneticField` properties remove the bias from the raw gyroscope and magnetometer data.

Processed data

Algorithms that interpret sensor data to count steps, measure distance or detect motion type rely on analyzing a lot of sample data to identify patterns and criteria. Apple encourages Watch wearers to take their iPhones along on workouts, to use its GPS to fine-tune the accuracy of the steps-to-distance calculation.

- **Pedometer**: lets you access step counts, current pace in seconds per meter, current cadence in steps per second and estimated distance in meters. Devices with an altimeter can count the number of floors that the user *walks or runs* up or down, which means you can cheat a little by walking up escalators. :]
- **Activity**: assesses the user's current motion type—stationary, walking, running, cycling or automotive—with low, medium or high confidence.

Checking availability

You should always check whether sensors and processed data are available on your app's target device before attempting to use them.

- To check the availability of accelerometer, gyroscope, magnetometer and device motion, create a `CMMotionManager` object and call its `<sensor>Available` properties:

```
let motionManager = CMMotionManager()
if motionManager.accelerometerAvailable {
  print("accelerometer available")
}
```

- Use `CMAltimeter.isRelativeAltitudeAvailable()` to check for an altimeter.
- Check pedometer data availability with `CMPedometer` class methods; for example, `CMPedometer.isPaceAvailable()`.
- Use `CMMotionActivityManager.isActivityAvailable()` to check whether the device can assess motion type.

What's in Core Motion on Apple Watch?

Compared with iPhone 6, there isn't much available on the Watch.

- **Sensors**: Only the accelerometer is available.
- **Processed data**: The pedometer provides step counting, current pace, current cadence and distance, *but not floor-counting*. **Activity** detects stationary, walking, running and cycling, *but not automotive motion type*. This might explain why my Watch thinks I'm exercising hard when I'm sitting on the train!

The good news is, the watchOS 2 documentation includes currently missing sensors and processed data, so check availability in every Xcode update.

The starter project

Do you need motivation to walk more? Imagine you're on a long distance trek in an exotic location—the more you walk, the closer you get to your goal! **DreamWalker** tracks your progress towards ten dream walks, ranging from a 10-kilometer fun run to the 2663-mile Pacific Crest Trail.

Open the **DreamWalker** starter project. This project uses sample pedometer data, so you can run it in the simulator. Select the **DreamWalker WatchKit App**, then build and run it. Once the Watch app runs, open the iPhone app in the simulator. It shows progress towards each goal using the total distance recorded in the sample data. All sample data can be displayed by tapping the **History** button.

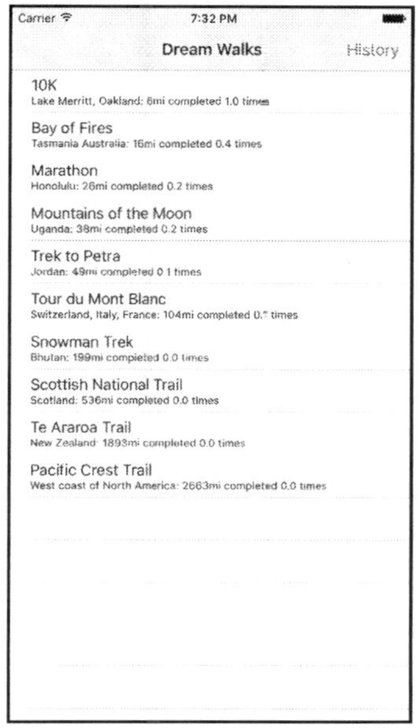

Select a walk to view an image of its location, a progress bar, information about the walk and a **map** button, which opens **Maps** in hybrid mode to show the terrain of the walk.

The Watch app displays a list of the ten walks, each with a progress bar indicating how much of the walk you have completed. The bars are color-coded in 25% increments. A star indicates the user has finished that walk at least once.

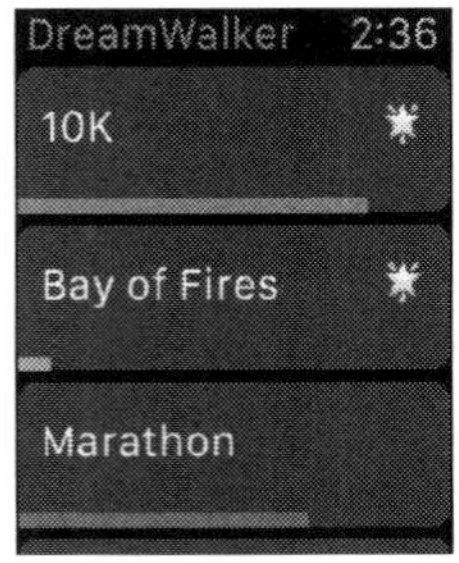

When the user selects a walk, the app displays information about it. The detail view shows the walk's distance and the user's progress against a background image. It also shows the number of times she's finished the walk, her total distance and total steps.

In this chapter, you'll replace the sample data with real updates from the Watch's pedometer.

Using Watch pedometer data

Open **PedometerData.swift** and add the following statement to import the Core Motion framework:

```
import CoreMotion
```

Then add the following property at the top of the `PedometerData` class, just above the **sample pedometer data** properties:

```
let pedometer = CMPedometer()
```

While you're here, initialize these **sample pedometer data** properties to zero, as shown below:

```
// sample pedometer data: set these two properties to zero
var totalSteps = 0
var totalDistance: CGFloat = 0.0
```

`CMPedometer` provides two methods to access pedometer data:

- **`startPedometerUpdatesFromDate(_:withHandler:)`** provides continual *live updates* of pedometer data from a start date to the *current time*. Upon calling this method, the pedometer object will start calling your handler regularly with data. When the user stops looking at the app, the app is suspended, and the delivery of updates stops temporarily. When the user looks at the app again, the pedometer object resumes updates.
- **`queryPedometerDataFromDate(_:toDate:withHandler:)`** accesses *historical data* between the specified dates; the start date may be up to seven days in the past. In the DreamWalker Watch app, you'll call this method to get the data for a complete day.

Both methods pass a `CMPedometerData` or `NSError` object to your `CMPedometerHandler`. The `CMPedometerData` object includes motion data like start and end dates, steps and distance values, and current pace and cadence.

Supplying the app's information needs

DreamWalker displays the total steps and distance since the app's start date, as well as steps and distance for the current day. How can you get the necessary information from `CMPedometer` using its live update and historical query methods?

The live update method provides cumulative data from a start date (the green vertical line in the diagram below) up to the current time (the purple dot)—you can't set its end date. The following method call would provide the *total* steps and distance since the app's start date:

```
startPedometerUpdatesFromDate(appStartDate)
```

The historical query lets you set both start and end dates, but you can only access data for the past seven days. The following method call would provide the *current day's* steps and distance:

```
queryPedometerDataFromDate(startOfDay, toDate: now)
```

The diagram below shows a historical query getting the data for a full day, which would be useful after the next day begins:

```
queryPedometerDataFromDate(startOfDay, toDate: endOfDay)
```

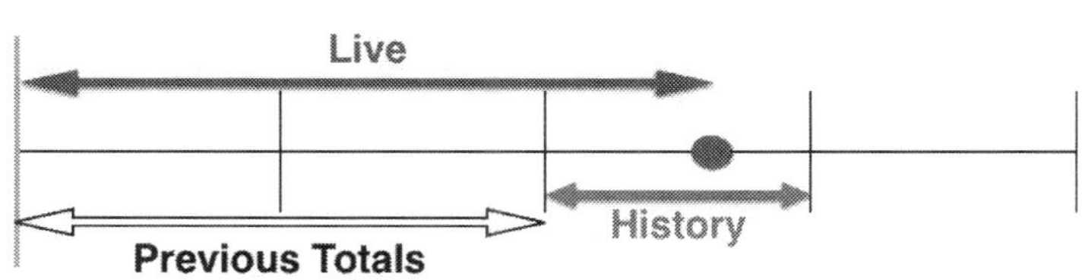

Here are three options for using these methods to get both cumulative and the current day's data:

1. Get the total steps and distance from a live update, and the current day's steps and distance from a historical query: This requires two method calls to update the screen info.
2. Keep track of the total steps and distance, up to the end of the *previous* day (the **Previous Totals** arrow in the diagram above), and *subtract* these values from a live update's cumulative data, to get the current day's data.
3. Keep track of the previous total steps and distance, and *add* these values to a historical query's current-day data, to get the current cumulative data.

Either of the last two options would work. However, one more consideration is: how do you trigger the method call when the user activates the app? The live update method has the advantage of resuming automatically when the user activates the app, so DreamWalker uses option 2. It gets cumulative data from a live update, then calculates the current day's data.

Choosing the app's start date

To allow the queries to work correctly, you'll need to set and track an `appStartDate` variable. But, how should you pick this date from the past?

The live update method can retrieve all the pedometer data recorded since the day you tore open the box, strapped on your Watch, and paired it with your iPhone. But DreamWalker stores daily data, and the historical query method can only get daily data for the past seven days.

However, this would require firing off seven queries when the app first starts and sending their data to the iPhone app—a complicated and asynchronous process. There's no guarantee that processing of the seven queries would happen in the same order that you created them. And anyway, you can get daily data much more efficiently using HealthKit's `HKStatisticsCollectionQuery`—see the next chapter, "HealthKit".

> **Note**: Why not go straight to HealthKit? Why use Core Motion on its own? Well, Core Motion is much simpler to use, and you don't have to worry about capabilities or privacy issues. DreamWalker works quite well, and doesn't need the complexity of HealthKit.

If you don't care about keeping track of daily data before the day you install the app, you could set `appStartDate` to the first day you wore your Watch, and just feel good about the huge values on day 1. But you won't have the current day's data, so you won't be able to check that the app is recording the same number of steps as the Activity app.

TL;DR: Set appStartDate to be the start of the day that you first run the app on the Watch; this is already initialized in the starter app as startOfDay. You can check DreamWalker's values with the Activity app—the app's steps and distance values should be the same as Activity's. The app's values might be higher if Activity isn't up to date.

When the app first launches, the previous total steps and distance values are 0, so the first day's total values will be the same as its daily values. But you'll update these previous total values *when a new day begins.* Cue high-adrenalin music. :]

Handling pedometer data

The live update and historical query methods have handlers whose main job is to update the total and daily steps and distance values. Open **PedometerData.swift** and add the following enum and helper method to the // MARK: Pedometer Data section:

```
enum PedometerDataType {
  case Live
  case History
}

func updatePropertiesFrom(data: CMPedometerData,
  ofType type: PedometerDataType) {
  switch type {
    case .Live:  // 1
      totalSteps = data.numberOfSteps.integerValue
      steps = totalSteps - prevTotalSteps
      if let rawDistance = data.distance?.integerValue
        where rawDistance > 0 {
        totalDistance = CGFloat(rawDistance) / 1000.0
        distance = totalDistance - prevTotalDistance
      }
    case .History:  // 2
      steps = data.numberOfSteps.integerValue
      totalSteps = steps + prevTotalSteps
      if let rawDistance = data.distance?.integerValue
        where rawDistance > 0 {
        distance = CGFloat(rawDistance) / 1000.0
        totalDistance = distance + prevTotalDistance
      }
  }
}
```

This method implements the calculations described in options 2 and 3 above.

1. You store the live update's cumulative numberOfSteps and distance data in totalSteps and totalDistance, with distance converted from meters to kilometers. Then you subtract the previous total values to get the current day's steps and distance values.

2. You store the historical query's data in the current day's `steps` and `distance`, and *add* the previous total values to get the cumulative `totalSteps` and `totalDistance` values.

Now find `startLiveUpdates()` in the `// MARK: Pedometer Data` section and replace its `TODO` comment with the following lines:

```
guard CMPedometer.isStepCountingAvailable() else { return }
pedometer.startPedometerUpdatesFromDate(appStartDate) { data,
  error in
  if let data = data {
    self.updatePropertiesFrom(data, ofType: .Live)
    self.sendData()
  }
}
```

This method checks availability of step-counting, and calls the live updates method. The handler passes the pedometer data to `updatePropertiesFrom(_:ofType:)` and then sends the data to the iPhone app.

Similarly, implement `queryHistoryFrom(_:toDate:)` with the following:

```
guard CMPedometer.isStepCountingAvailable() else { return }
pedometer.queryPedometerDataFromDate(startDate, toDate:
  toDate) { data, error in
  if let data = data {
    self.updatePropertiesFrom(data, ofType: .History)
    self.sendData()
  }
}
```

Make sure that you pass `.History` as the `ofType` value.

Replacing the starter simulation code

Before you test the app, clean up the starter project's code to replace the sample pedometer data in the iPhone app. Open **WalksTableViewController.swift** and, in `viewDidLoad()`, replace the call to `loadDayData()` with the following line, then delete `loadDayData()` all together:

```
history.insert(DayData(), atIndex: 0)
```

The iPhone app stores each day's pedometer data in its `history` array of `DayData` items—the first item is the current day's data. `loadDayData()` created a sample history array, which you don't need anymore. Instead, you create the first `history` item.

Running the apps on your devices

Connect your iPhone, then select the **DreamWalker WatchKit App\iPhone + Apple Watch** devices scheme. Build and run the Watch app. If you've already walked around today while wearing your Watch, the Watch app will update with non-zero values.

The iPhone app has also updated with non-zero values for today.

This is all you need to get live updates on the total distance the wearer has walked ... on the first day.

Starting a new day

By now, you might be feeling spooked by all this talk of *current day* and *previous totals*, because you haven't done anything to change these values. So far, the app works fine, because the first time the app launches, `appStartDate` is the same as `startOfDay`, and the previous total steps and distance values are `0`. But what should happen at midnight?

- `startOfDay` should be reset to be the start of the new current day.
- The previous total steps and distance values should be set to the old current day's total steps and distance values.

How do you detect when a new day begins, where should you check for this, and where do you store the daily data?

Flagging dayEnded to the iPhone app

To answer the storage question, remember that the iPhone app has a `history` array where it stores each day's pedometer data. Open **WalksTableViewController.swift** and find `session(_:didReceiveUserInfo:)`. It contains the following lines:

```
if userInfo["dayEnded"] as! Bool {
  history.insert(DayData(), atIndex: 0)
  history[0].totalSteps = history[1].totalSteps
  history[0].totalDistance = history[1].totalDistance
}
```

Aha! The iPhone app expects the Watch app to set a `dayEnded` flag when it sends the last set of data for `history`'s current day. The iPhone app then inserts a new `DayData` item at the start of the `history` array and initializes its `total` properties. The `DayData` initializer has already set the new item's `date` to today and initialized today's properties to `0`. The new `history` item is now ready to receive today's live update, so start by adding some code to `PedometerData` to set and send this `dayEnded` flag.

Open **PedometerData.swift** and find `sendData()`. Add a `dayEnded` argument:

```
func sendData(dayEnded: Bool) {
```

And add the corresponding item to `applicationDict`:

```
let applicationDict = [
  "dayEnded":dayEnded,
  "steps":steps,
  "distance":distance,
  "totalSteps":totalSteps,
  "totalDistance":totalDistance
]
```

Xcode will immediately show you the two calls to `sendData(_:)` in **PedometerData.swift** that you need to fix by adding a `Bool` argument. There's one in `startLiveUpdates()`, in the `startPedometerUpdatesFromDate(_:)` handler—this is the "business as usual" not-end-of-day case, so pass `false` as the argument:

```
self.sendData(false)
```

The other `sendData(_:)` call is in `queryHistoryFrom(_:toDate:)`, in the `queryPedometerDataFromDate(_:toDate:)` handler—this *is* the end-of-day case, so pass `true` as the argument:

```
self.sendData(true)
```

Detecting when a new day begins

Now return to the question: how and where do you detect when a new day begins? Well, live updates are "business as usual", except for the first time a live update's end date is after the end of the current day. So a good place to check is in `startLiveUpdates()`, in the `startPedometerUpdatesFromDate(_:)` handler.

Find `startLiveUpdates()` in **PedometerData.swift**. Immediately after you check for data via `if let data = data`, add the following lines:

```
// 1
if self.calendar.isDate(data.endDate,
  afterDate: self.endOfDay) {
  // 2
  self.pedometer.stopPedometerUpdates()
  // 3
  self.queryHistoryFrom(self.startOfDay, toDate: self.endOfDay)
  return
}
```

Here's what you're doing:

1. `data.endDate` is the current live update's end date. The `endOfDay` property of `PedometerData` is the start of the next day. The `calendar` object's helper method returns `true` if `data.endDate` is after `endOfDay`.
2. You stop the live updates to prevent the new day's live update data from sneaking into the iPhone app's `history` before the iPhone app has created a new item for it.
3. You get yesterday's data. `queryHistoryFrom(_:toDate:)` also sends the data to the iPhone app, with `dayEnded` set to `true`.

The `queryPedometerDataFromDate(_:toDate:)` handler must also update and save the day-dependant properties and restart live updates. So find the handler in `queryHistoryFrom(_:toDate:)` and add the following lines below `self.sendData(true)`:

```
// update and save day-dependent properties
self.setStartAndEndOfDay()
self.prevTotalSteps = self.totalSteps
self.prevTotalDistance = self.totalDistance
self.saveData()
```

Now build and run the Watch app, walk around while wearing your Watch and take a screenshot of today's values before midnight. Check the app after midnight—the total values will be higher than your screenshot, but the Today values will be close to zero.

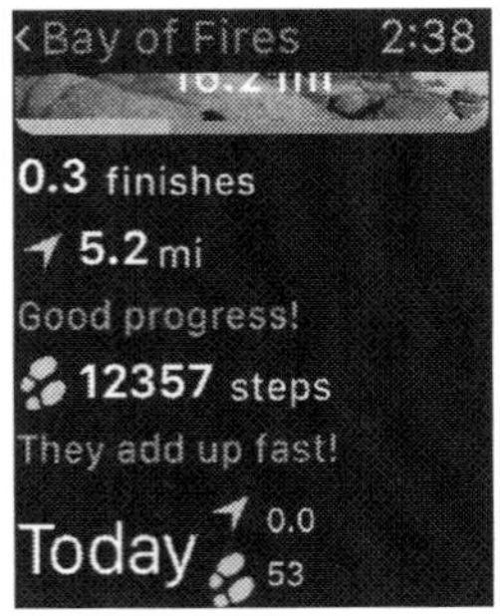

In the iPhone app, the history table's first item will show a new near-zero item for today.

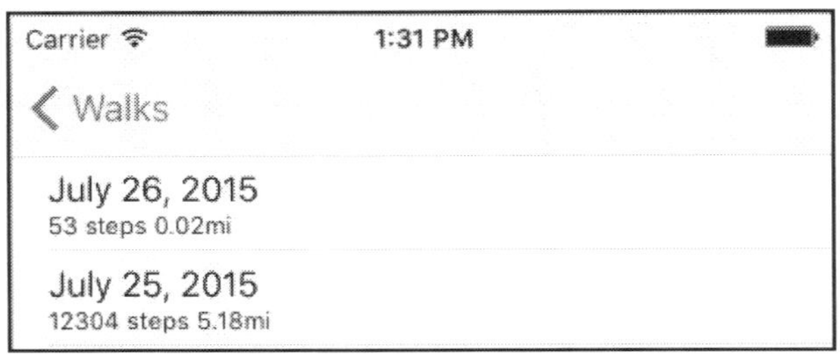

Your iPhone Activity app's history will confirm yesterday's data.

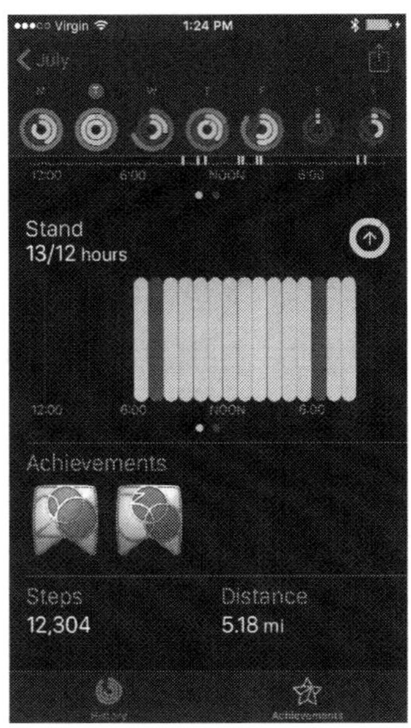

You've done it! Now get out there and *walk!*

Using the historical accelerometer

This chapter's app doesn't use the Watch's accelerometer directly, but some people are doing cool things with it, and watchOS 2 introduces a new `CMSensorRecorder` API. This section provides a brief overview of how it works, according to the *Historical Accelerometer* segment of the WWDC 2015 "What's New in Core Motion" video #705, available here: apple.co/1KrIv4X.

> **Note**: Using accelerometer data in an app usually requires analyzing many data samples to identify significant patterns and criteria to implement as algorithms—for example, to detect the wearer falling (1.usa.gov/1JEjo9A), or to count laps in a swimming pool (bit.ly/1KpJ2Sa).

`CMSensorRecorder` provides access to historical sensor data—specifically, historical *accelerometer* data. Your app can access data for up to three days, and this data is collected even when your app isn't running. When your app *is* running, it can perform custom algorithms on long streams of accelerometer data.

To begin, your app checks availability of accelerometer recordings with `CMSensorRecorder.isAccelerometerRecordingAvailable()`. If this method returns `true`, your app creates a `CMSensorRecorder` object, which calls `recordAccelerometerDataFor(duration:)` to initiate the sensor recorder.

The Watch might go to sleep and your app might be suspended, but when your app is active again, it can call `accelerometerDataFrom(_:to:)` to query for sensor data. This query returns a `CMSensorDataList`, which lets you enumerate over its sequence of `CMRecordedAccelerometerData` objects. Each data object has `startDate`, `identifier` and `acceleration` properties.

Historical accelerometer best practices

Your app might not have enough time to process large strings of sensor data, so Apple advises the following best practices:

1. Query data for the minimum duration your app needs.
2. Data is available at 50 Hz, but unless your algorithm requires a high sensor rate, sample the data at a lower frequency.

Managing limited processing time

Even using the minimum amount of data, a Watch app that processes sensor data needs to be able to cope with the limited processing time allowed by the very short activation periods that are typical for Watch apps.

1. If your app uses `CMAccelerometer` or `CMSensorRecorder` data, design it to expect data only when the app is onscreen.
2. Prepare for your task being suspended by processing the data in the block of `performExpiringActivityWithReason(_:usingBlock:)`.

Where to go from here?

In this chapter, you've seen how to access Apple Watch's pedometer data directly on the Watch. Getting cumulative data is pretty straightforward, but daily data requires some effort. It gets messy if you need more than a day's data when the app restarts.

Fortunately, there's another way to access historical pedometer data, and the next chapter tells you all about it! HealthKit provides access to huge amounts of data from multiple devices, and you can create a `HKStatisticsCollectionQuery` to get daily data for several days—all at once, with much less date-wrangling!

This chapter's app doesn't use the pedometer's `cadence` and `pace` properties because these are more relevant in a workout timeframe:

- **Running at a high cadence** is more efficient and can prevent injuries; the article at bit.ly/1CW4jDm recommends checking cadence frequently during a workout.
- **A brisk walking pace** has fitness benefits—the article at http://abt.cm/1eniFAK tries to answer "How Fast is Brisk Walking?".

You could create a Watch app that shows the wearer's current `cadence` and `pace`, or add these two properties to a workout app like the one in the next chapter.

> **Note**: The pedometer measures *current pace* in seconds per meter. The Workout app shows your *average pace* in minutes per kilometer or mile.

Chapter 22: HealthKit

By Scott Atkinson

If you're like me, you love the watchOS 2 Workout app. It tracks your calories burned, heart rate and custom attributes for a large number of different workout types. It stays in the foreground for the duration of your workout. A simple flick of the wrist quickly displays your stats. When you've completed your workout, the app saves all of the new data in the HealthKit database, where you can view it later via Apple's Activity app or let other HealthKit-enabled apps consume it.

But, Workout is a bit simplistic. Wouldn't it be nice to create a more advanced app for the specialized exercises you do? Maybe you want track HIIT bit.ly/1oVlhrP workouts, or process custom Core Motion data for very specific movement analysis. Well, watchOS 2 makes it possible to build HealthKit-supported apps like Workout. In this chapter, you'll add HealthKit features to a Workout-style app for interval training!

The features of HealthKit are quite impressive. In this chapter, you'll focus on the fitness aspects of it. But, Apple has designed a framework that allows developers to track and access nearly all facets of personal health. As you work through this chapter, keep an open mind to other interesting health-related data that a user might want to track on their Watch.

> **Note:** Since you'll be jumping right into HealthKit on watchOS 2, if you don't already have some working knowledge of HealthKit, we recommend you check out the following tutorials first:
>
> HealthKit Tutorial with Swift, Part 1: bit.ly/1LPOmQu
>
> HealthKit Tutorial with Swift, Part 2: bit.ly/1OyW8gE.
>
> Once you've worked through this tutorial and have a good understanding of HealthKit, you'll be ready to get to it.

Getting started

Released with iOS 8, HealthKit provides a rich system for storing and retrieving health data on a device. Its features include:

- A defined schema for categorizing health-related data, like workouts, body measurements and nutrition;
- A logical set of units and measurement types that allow for easy conversions and formatting;
- A secure, shared database for storing health information;
- Access control features that allow users to grant various levels of access to apps;
- A programming interface for querying, writing and deleting health data;
- The Health app, which allows users to review all of the health data on their devices.

iOS 9 went further to add even more data types and ways to track them, as well as introduced support for the Apple Watch. HealthKit's watchOS 2 functionality includes:

- The ability to create a **workout session** that places the Watch in a special mode where the app can receive sensor data and continue running in the foreground;
- Access to the same programming interface as in iOS;
- Seamless data synchronization between the Watch and a paired iOS device;
- The ability to contribute data to the iOS Activity app.

That was a bit of a sprint through the new HealthKit features. I hope you're not too out of breath to learn more!

Introducing Groundhog

Let's begin by checking out the **Groundhog** starter project. It's a lot like the Apple Workout app, but it allows the user to set up an interval training workout, or one that records a repeating set of "Active" and "Rest" intervals within one session. Read more about interval training here: bit.ly/1I82m3t

Open **Groundhog.xcodeproj** and have a look around. The app contains a working version of a watch interval timer as well as a simple iOS app that allows you to see your recorded workouts. You won't see any data yet in the iOS app, as you've not yet recorded any data to HealthKit.

Choose the **Groundhog WatchKit App** scheme, and build and run. It will look like this:

Select a workout type, adjust your intervals by selecting time periods with the digital crown and tap Go. You'll see the timer repeat your increments over and over and over and over. Just like in the movie *Groundhog Day* it doesn't seem to end. Fear not... to stop the workout timer, force press and choose the Stop menu item! Finish by attempting to save the workout—it won't yet save to the HealthKit datastore. That's where you come in!

Provisioning for HealthKit

When using HealthKit, you must provision your app targets with the HealthKit entitlement.

> **Note**: To provision your app correctly and use HealthKit, you must have a valid Apple Developer account. If you don't have a valid account, the HealthKit permission requests you write in the next section will fail.

Select the **Groundhog** project from the project navigator and then select the

Groundhog project in the editor. Select the **Build Settings** tab and scroll to the very bottom. You'll see a user-defined variable named **`W2T_BUNDLE_PREFIX`**. Select the existing value and enter your own. Any string will do, but generally, it's best to use your domain in reverse order.

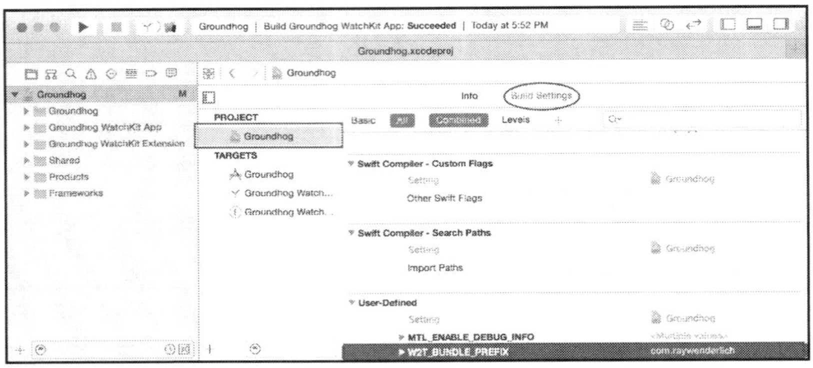

This will change the bundle identifiers for each target in the project so that they use your own prefix, making them unique. Now you need to enable the HealthKit entitlement in each target. Still in the project editor, select the **Groundhog** target, then select the **General** tab and click **Fix Issue**. This will force Xcode to generate a new App ID and provisioning profile.

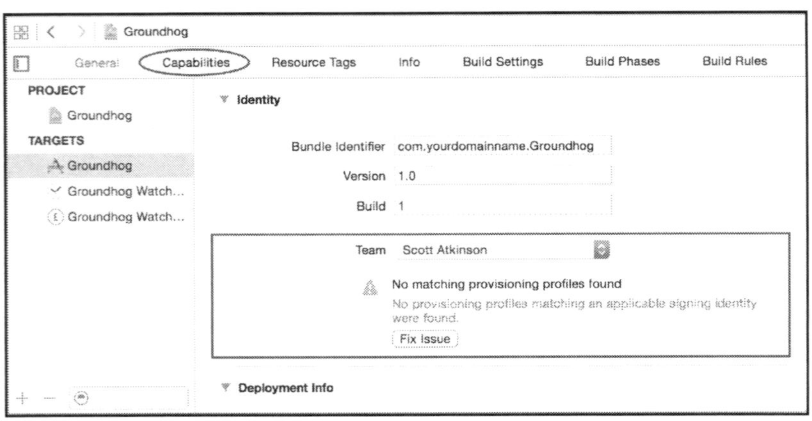

Finally, switch to the **Capabilities** tab, scroll down to HealthKit and turn **on** the capability.

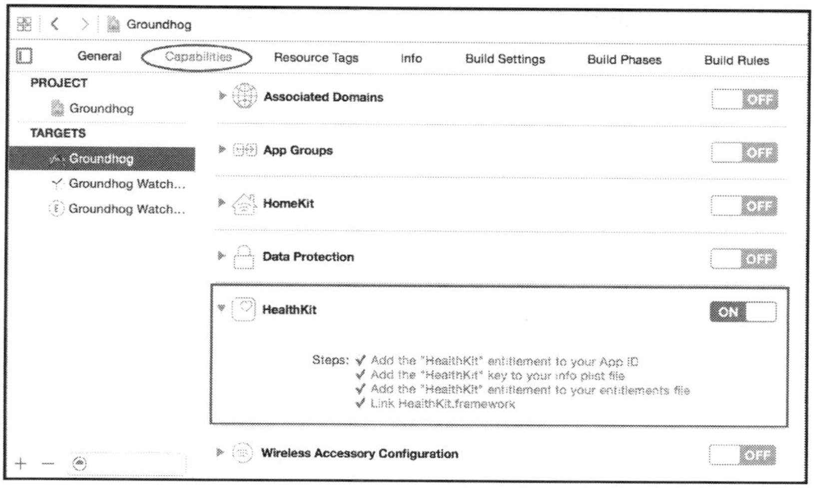

Repeat the same steps for the **Groundhog WatchKit Extension** target. Finally, switch to the **Groundhog WatchKit App** target and click **Fix Issue** there.

Clean (**Shift-Command-K**) and build (**Command-B**) your targets. Your app is now properly provisioned and ready to run on your devices.

Asking for permission

Your users' health data is among the most private they may share with you. As a result, Apple has created a very fine-grained permissions system. Unlike the binary options for Location Services or access to Contacts, you need to ask your users for access to specific types of data.

In Xcode, in the **Shared\HealthKit\Services** folder, open **HealthDataService.swift**. The `HealthDataService` class provides a number of methods that your app will use to access a device's HealthKit data. Notice there are a number of `HKObjectType` constants at the top of the file; you'll use these throughout the app. Also, an internal `HKHealthStore` object has been declared. This is the main object you'll use to interact with HealthKit.

Immediately below `init()`, add the following:

```
func authorizeHealthKitAccess(completion:
  ((success: Bool, error: NSError!) -> Void)!) {
  let typesToShare = Set(
    [HKObjectType.workoutType(),
    energyType,
    cyclingDistanceType,
    runningDistanceType,
```

```
      hrType
      ])
    let typesToSave = Set([
      energyType,
      cyclingDistanceType,
      runningDistanceType,
      hrType
      ])

    healthKitStore.requestAuthorizationToShareTypes(typesToShare,
      readTypes: typesToSave) { success, error in
      completion(success: success, error: error)
    }
  }
```

Here you create two sets of `HKObjectTypes`: a set of types that you wish to read from the database, and a set of types that you want to write back to HealthKit. In this case, you want to read and write the same types of data. Once the sets are created, you simply call `requestAuthorizationToShareTypes(_:readTypes:completion:)`.

Now you need to call this new method. Open **WorkoutTypesInterfaceController.swift** d. This is the interface controller that you'll first present to the user. Locate `willActivate()` and add the following after the call to `super`:

```
let healthService:HealthDataService = HealthDataService()
healthService.authorizeHealthKitAccess { success, error in
  if success {
    print("HealthKit authorization received.")
  } else {
    print("HealthKit authorization denied!")
    if error != nil {
      print("\(error)")
    }
  }
}
```

When the interface controller activates, you simply create an instance of your `HealthDataService` and make a call to its `authorizeHealthKitAccess()` method.

There's one more thing to do before you test this. In reality, it's not the Watch that requests HealthKit permissions; instead, the host iPhone app presents an interface. So you'll need to present and handle the results of the user's interactions with that UI.

Open **AppDelegate.swift** and import HealthKit:

```
import HealthKit
```

Then add the following method before the closing brace:

```
let healthStore = HKHealthStore()
```

```
func applicationShouldRequestHealthAuthorization(application:
  UIApplication) {
  healthStore.handleAuthorizationForExtensionWithCompletion {
    success, error in

  }
}
```

You'll call this method when the watchOS 2 extension calls `requestAuthorizationToShareTypes()`. Here you simply ask the iPhone app to handle the authorization. When the user completes the request, the completion block is fired. In your case, there's nothing to do, so you simply leave the block empty.

You're ready to go, so build and run the WatchKit app. A couple of things will happen: The Watch will show an alert telling you to open the app on your phone, and at the same time, the phone will show a similar alert.

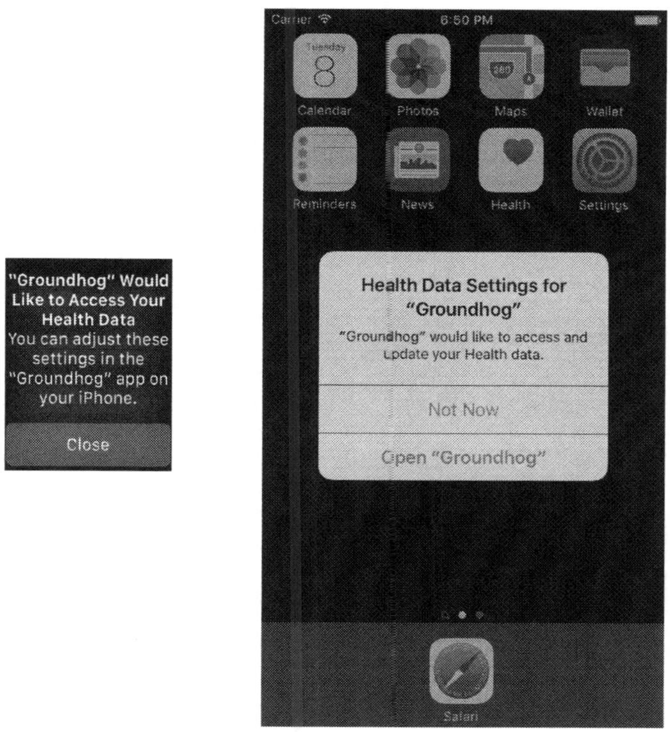

Tap **Open** on the iOS device. Groundhog will launch and present you with the "Health Access Screen". Tap **All Categories On** and then **Allow**.

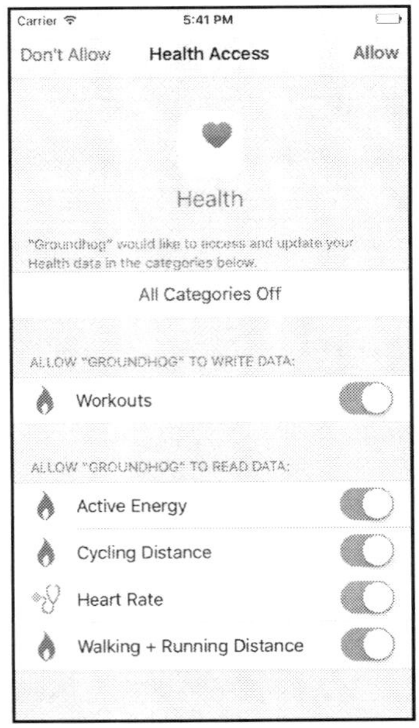

It's possible, in fact likely, that your users will open the iOS app before launching Groundhog from their Watches, so you should probably make sure you request HealthKit access there, too. In Xcode, open **WorkoutListViewController.swift** and insert the following code at the end of `viewDidLoad()`.

```
let healthService:HealthDataService = HealthDataService()
healthService.authorizeHealthKitAccess { accessGranted, error in
  dispatch_async(dispatch_get_main_queue(), { () -> Void in
    if accessGranted {
      self.refresh(nil)
    } else {
      print("HealthKit authorization denied! \n\(error)")
    }
  })
}
```

This code is pretty much the same as the code you placed in the `AppDelegate`, but in this case, you refresh the controller's `tableView` if the user grants access. Also, note that you dispatch to the main thread: `HKHealthStore` doesn't make any guarantees that it will call completion blocks on the queue that a method was called upon, so you'll need to dispatch UIKit methods to the main thread, as usual.

Now you have access to HealthKit for reading and writing. Let's create some data!

Creating workout sessions

The class that really brings a watchOS 2 fitness app to life is `HKWorkoutSession`. When HealthKit starts a session with an instance of this class, it places the Watch in workout mode. In this state, your app will stay in the foreground until the user clicks the digital crown or stops the session; at the same time, you'll be able to query for additional sensor data that the Watch generates, like distance and heart rate.

`HKWorkoutSession` is a relatively simple object that's created with a `workoutType` and a `locationType` of either indoor or outdoor. A delegate protocol provides information about the current state of a workout session.

To implement this protocol, open **WorkoutSessionService.swift** from the **Groundhog Watchkit Extension** group and give it a quick review. This class provides all of the functionality for managing a workout session, querying sensor data and returning that information to a delegate. Much of it has been implemented already, but there are important details left for you to finish.

First, locate the beginning of the class implementation. After the declaration of the `configuration` constant, declare an `HKWorkoutSession` object:

```
let session: HKWorkoutSession
```

Now, find `init(configuration:)` and add the following code after `self.configuration` is set:

```
session = HKWorkoutSession(activityType:
  configuration.exerciseType.workoutType,
  locationType: configuration.exerciseType.location)
```

This creates a new `HKWorkoutSession` object from the `configuration` object that is passed in. The `WorkoutConfiguration` class provides a place to store an exercise type as well as the parameters for how long the workout's active and rest times will be.

Now you'll set a delegate. This is going to create a small compile error which you'll fix in just a moment. At the bottom of the same `init(configuration:)` method, add the following:

```
session.delegate = self
```

The `WorkoutSessionService` object will act as the delegate for the `HKWorkoutSession` you just created.

You need to implement `startSession()` and `stopSession()` so that the user can start the session from the Watch's interface.

First locate the `startSession()` stub method and add the following:

```
healthService.healthKitStore.startWorkoutSession(session)
```

Locate `stopSession()` and replace the current implementation with the following:

```
healthService.healthKitStore.endWorkoutSession(session)
```

These two methods simply start and stop the `HKWorkoutSession`, respectively. Note that you're doing this via methods on an instance of `HKHealthStore`.

At this point, you've probably seen a pesky little error around where you assign the session's `delegate` to `self`. That's because you haven't implemented the `HKWorkoutSessionDelegate` protocol yet. So, add a new class extension to the bottom of **WorkoutSessionService.swift**:

```
extension WorkoutSessionService: HKWorkoutSessionDelegate {

}
```

Add two helper methods to the class extension to do the work of reacting to the session's changing state:

```
private func sessionStarted(date: NSDate) {
  startDate = date
  // Let the delegate know
  delegate?.workoutSessionService(self,
    didStartWorkoutAtDate: date)
}

private func sessionEnded(date: NSDate) {
  endDate = date
  // Let the delegate know
  self.delegate?.workoutSessionService(self,
    didStopWorkoutAtDate: date)
}
```

So far, these are simple methods; they record the start and end dates of the workout and then let the `WorkoutSessionService`'s delegate know that the session's state changed. Now implement the `HKWorkoutSessionDelegate` protocol's two methods:

```
func workoutSession(workoutSession: HKWorkoutSession,
  didChangeToState toState: HKWorkoutSessionState,
  fromState: HKWorkoutSessionState, date: NSDate) {

    dispatch_async(dispatch_get_main_queue()) { () -> Void in
      switch toState {
        case .Running:
          self.sessionStarted(date)
```

```
        case .Ended:
          self.sessionEnded(date)
        default:
          print("Something weird happened. Not a valid state")
      }
    }
  }

  func workoutSession(workoutSession: HKWorkoutSession,
    didFailWithError error: NSError) {
    sessionEnded(NSDate())
  }
```

When the workout session's state changes, you simply call the appropriate helper method you just created. In the event of an error, you treat it as if the session has ended by calling `sessionEnded()`.

That's all you need to do to create an `HKWorkoutSession`! Open **ActiveWorkoutInterfaceController.swift** and check out `awakeWithContext(_:)`. Notice that the `NSTimer` is set to call `start()` after a short countdown, and if you scroll down to the implementation of that method, you'll see where a `WorkoutSessionService` instance is created and started.

Build and run the Watch app to see what happens. Once the app starts, choose a workout type, adjust your time intervals and get sweating!

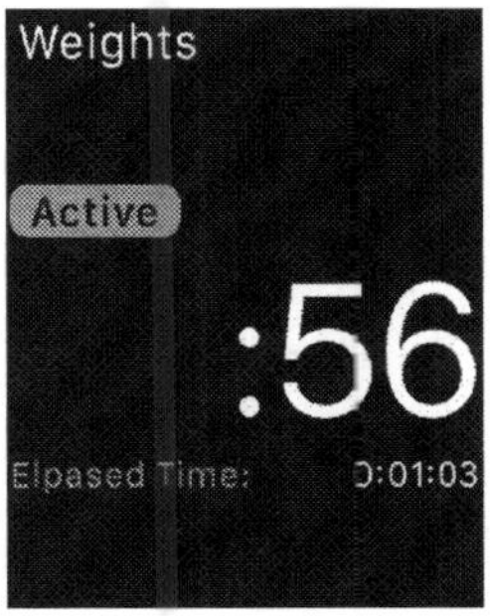

Notice that now, the app doesn't go to the background. When you look at your Watch, Groundhog appears! **Force press** to stop and save the workout. Maybe some wind sprints?

Wait... did you implement a way to save the workout? Nope, not yet. But now you will.

Saving a workout

Open **HealthDataService_Watch.swift** from the **Groundhog Watchkit Extension** group and have a look around. The first thing you'll notice is that this is an extension of the `HealthDataService` class.

If you look at the file inspector, you'll see that the file is a member of just the "Groundhog Watchkit Extension" target. Since `HKWorkoutSession` is a member of HealthKit in watchOS 2 but not in iOS, you'll add functionality to save it only on the Watch side.

Add the following code inside the extension:

```
func saveWorkout(workoutService: WorkoutSessionService,
  completion: (Bool, NSError!) -> Void) {

  // 1
  guard let start = workoutService.startDate, end =
    workoutService.endDate else {return}

  // 2
  var metadata = workoutService.configuration.
    dictionaryRepresentation()
  metadata[HKMetadataKeyIndoorWorkout] = workoutService.
    configuration.exerciseType.location == .Indoor

  // 3
  let workout = HKWorkout(activityType:
    workoutService.configuration.exerciseType.workoutType,
    startDate: start,
    endDate: end,
    duration: end.timeIntervalSinceDate(start),
    totalEnergyBurned: workoutService.energyBurned,
    totalDistance: workoutService.distance,
    device: HKDevice.localDevice(),
    metadata: metadata)

    // 4
  healthKitStore.saveObject(workout) { success, error in
          completion(success, error)
  }
}
```

That looks like a lot! But it's actually pretty straightforward.

1. First, you check to make sure that the app has recorded both a start and end date. If not, you bail out, as `saveWorkout()` was called prematurely.
2. Next, you create a small dictionary of metadata that you'll store in the HealthKit database. This data records the interval time configuration so you can reconstitute

the intervals later.

3. You create an `HKWorkout` object with data from the `WorkoutSessionService` and its `configuration`.
4. You use the `HKHealthStore` object to save the workout.
5. Finally, if all goes well, you call the method's completion handler.

Before you can save a workout, make sure you call `saveWorkout(_:completion:)`. Open **WorkoutSessionService.swift** and locate `saveSession()`. Add the following implementation to the method:

```
healthService.saveWorkout(self) { success, error in
  if success {
    self.delegate?.workoutSessionServiceDidSave(self)
  }
}
```

You call this method, which simply saves the workout, when the user taps "Save" after stopping a workout. If everything goes well, then the `WorkoutSessionService`'s delegate gets notified that the workout was saved.

Build and run the Watch extension. Run through a workout and then stop and save it. At this point, through the magic of HealthKit, your data will be saved both to a small, local data store on the Watch and also to the main data store on the paired iOS device.

Open **Groundhog** on the iOS device. Pull down to refresh the main workout list; your saved workout should appear. Cool, right? Now open the **Health** app on the iOS device. Select the **Health Data** tab and navigate to **Fitness\Workouts\Show All Data**. Select one of the workouts to view detailed data about it.

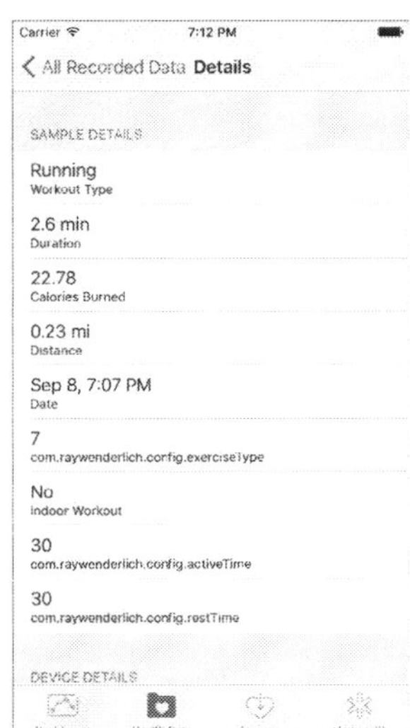

Note: Apple doesn't indicate in its documentation when exactly HealthKit data is synchronized from the Watch to the iOS device. In my experience, data can take a couple of minutes to appear, so if you experience a delay, keep trying: eventually it will show up.

Displaying data while working out

Now that you're saving basic workout data, it's time to get something a bit more interesting from the Watch: heart rate information. In this section, you'll create an "anchored query" that runs through the duration of the workout session and returns heart rate data as it's discovered.

An anchored object query

To receive continually updating data during an `HKWorkoutSession`, you must create an `HKAnchoredObjectQuery`. An anchored query is similar to a standard `HKQuery`, with a couple of notable exceptions:

- An anchored query returns a cursor, or anchor, to the last data returned by the query. You use that anchor to get only new data created since the last anchor.
- An anchored query provides an `updateHandler` block that indicates the query should continue to run until it's explicitly stopped.

These two features are exactly what you need to get a continuous stream of heart rate data. Open **WorkoutSessionService_Queries.swift** from the **Groundhog Watchkit Extension** group. This is a class extension of `WorkoutSessionService`. You'll see a couple of methods already written that you'll use in a bit—but first, you'll create a new query to get heart rate data.

First, implement `newHRSamples(samples:)` to record the samples returned by the query:

```
private func newHRSamples(samples: [HKSample]?) {
  // Abort if the data isn't right
  guard let samples = samples as? [HKQuantitySample] where
    samples.count > 0 else { return }

  dispatch_async(dispatch_get_main_queue()) {
    self.hrData += samples
    if let hr = samples.last?.quantity {
      self.heartRate = hr
      self.delegate?.workoutSessionService(self,
```

```
        didUpdateHeartrate: hr.doubleValueForUnit(hrUnit))
    }
  }
}
```

This method first checks to see if the samples are the right type and that there's at least one of them. Then, it updates the workout session's heart rate with the latest value, adds all the samples to an internal array and finally, informs the delegate that there's new heart rate data.

Add the following code at the top of the extension:

```
internal func heartRateQuery(withStartDate start: NSDate)
  -> HKQuery {
  // 1
  // Query all samples from the beginning of the workout session
  let predicate = HKQuery.predicateForSamplesWithStartDate(
    start, endDate: nil, options: .None)

  // 2
  let query:HKAnchoredObjectQuery = HKAnchoredObjectQuery(
    type: hrType,
    predicate: predicate,
    anchor: hrAnchorValue,
    limit: Int(HKObjectQueryNoLimit)) {
      (query, sampleObjects, deletedObjects, newAnchor, error)
      -> Void in

        // 3
      self.hrAnchorValue = newAnchor
      self.newHRSamples(sampleObjects)
  }

  // 4
  query.updateHandler = {(query, samples, deleteObjects,
    newAnchor, error) -> Void in
    self.hrAnchorValue = newAnchor
    self.newHRSamples(samples)
  }

  // 5
  return query
}
```

Did that elevate your heart rate a bit? It's easy, though. Here's the breakdown:

1. Using one of the `HKQuery` helper methods, you create a predicate to get all data since the workout session began.
2. Next, you create an `HKAnchoredObjectQuery` instance indicating you'd like to get heart rate samples using the predicate you just created, anchored to the anchor point

you're tracking.

3. Upon the initial response from the query, you record a new anchor value and add the new heart rate samples to the data set. More on that in a moment.
4. Also, you create an `updateHandler` to indicate you want the query to run until you tell it to stop. The handler will treat the new samples just like in the initial response.
5. You return the query object to the caller.

Now that you can create a query, you'll put it to use. Open **WorkoutSessionService.swift** from the **Groundhog Watchkit Extension** group and locate `sessionStarted(date:)`. At the top of the method, create three new queries and append them to an array of queries:

```
// Create and Start Queries
queries.append(distanceQuery(withStartDate: date))
queries.append(heartRateQuery(withStartDate: date))
queries.append(energyQuery(withStartDate: date))
```

Loop through the array to start each one in turn:

```
for query in queries {
  healthService.healthKitStore.executeQuery(query)
}
```

Don't worry, you didn't miss creating `distanceQuery` and `energyQuery`. These methods are very similar to `heartRateQuery`, which you created above, so they were provided for you in the sample code. They're structurally very similar but they query for different pieces of data: energy and distance.

Build and run the Watch app. Start a new workout and get to work. After a few seconds, you'll see your heart rate appear on the Watch!

Saving the sample data

If you saved that last workout and checked it out in the Health app, you may have noticed that you haven't yet saved any detailed data. Previously, when you implemented `saveWorkout(workoutService:)`, you simply saved the workout, which didn't include any detailed data. You have to save that data explicitly, so open **HealthDataService_Watch.swift** from the **Groundhog Watchkit Extension** and locate `saveWorkout(workoutService:)`.

After you create your workout object, add the following code:

```
// Collect the sampled data
var samples: [HKQuantitySample] = [HKQuantitySample]()
samples += workoutService.hrData
samples += workoutService.distanceData
samples += workoutService.energyData
```

Do you recall in your implementation of `newHRSamples(samples:)` that you appended those samples to the `hrData` array? Here's why! In the code above, you concatenate all of the heart rate, distance and energy samples into one array. All of the samples are of the same type, `HKQuantitySample`, so you can do this in a type-safe way with Swift.

Finally, replace the completion handler for the call to `healthKitStore.saveObject()` with the following:

```
if (!success || samples.count == 0) {
  completion(success, error)
  return
}

self.healthKitStore.addSamples(samples, toWorkout: workout,
  completion: { success, error  in
  completion(success, error)
})
```

If there are no samples, or the initial save wasn't successful, you simply call the passed-in completion handler. However, if there are samples to be saved, you can add them to the current workout by calling `addSamples(_:toWorkout:completion:)` on the `HKHealthStore`. It will immediately save the data and call a completion handler when it's done.

Build and run the Watch app one last time, do another workout and save it.

You must really be exhausted by now! Open Groundhog on your iOS device and check out all the interval data you just saved. How well did you do?

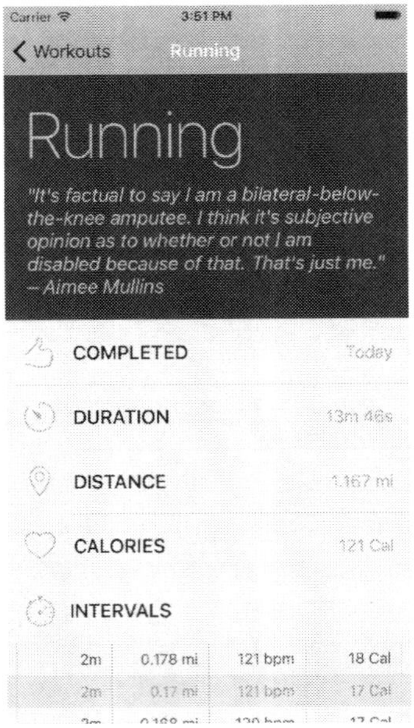

Where to go from here?

Congrats! You've just made a watchOS 2 workout app! In this chapter, you've encountered a number of exciting techniques for using the Health functions of the Apple Watch. You've learned:

- How to ask for permissions to save and access HealthKit data from the Watch;
- How to create a workout session and get sensor and other health data while the session is running;
- How to save a workout to the HealthKit data store and add your own metadata to it.

Take some time to explore the rest of Groundhog—the project contains a lot more HealthKit functionality. Pay particular attention to the various `NSFormatter` instances in **Constants.swift**. You'll see a couple of health-related formatters that will definitely make your life easier. You can see them in action in **IntervalCell.swift**.

You may also want to play around with Core Motion information in your own health-related app. Maybe you'd like to add a jumping jack counter or measure the speed of a tennis swing? Be sure to check out, if you haven't already, Chapter 21, "Core Motion" for details about how to integrate step counts and other motion-related data.

Chapter 23: Core Location

By Soheil Azarpour

One of watchOS 2's new features is direct access to Core Location, a framework that lets you determine the current position of the device. Whereas before, Core Location would only work from the iPhone, you can now query the user's location even when the iPhone isn't in the vicinity of the Watch. Along with other new features in watchOS 2, this is a huge improvement.

In this chapter, you'll learn how to make best use of location services on the Watch, both as a standalone device and in coordination with a paired iPhone.

The starter project you'll use in this chapter is called **Meetup Finder**. With Meetup Finder for Apple Watch, users can find iOS-related meetups in their areas with just a twist of the wrist, along with details such as the meetup location and the next upcoming event. It couldn't be easier than that!

But the app isn't quite there yet: It doesn't know about the user's current location. You're going to add Core Location to the Watch app, and by the end of this chapter, the app will look like this:

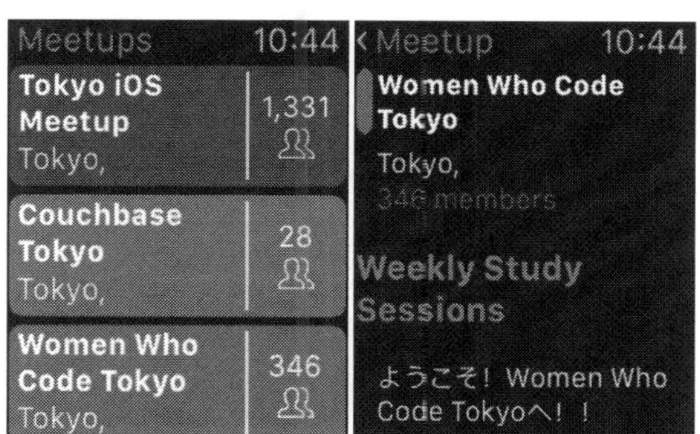

Without further delay, let's get started!

Getting started with Meetup.com

Meetup Finder uses the popular Meetup.com API to find meetups near you. Most of the work of interacting with the API has been done for you. But, you'll need to set a few things up to get going.

Signing up

Before you dive into the code, you need to sign up with Meetup.com as a developer so you can get your own private token to access its API.

If you're already a member of Meetup.com, you can skip to "Getting your API key".

The signup process is easy. Open your favorite browser and go to meetup.com. Click on **Sign up** and you'll be presented with the registration page:

Enter your name, email address and password and then click **Sign up**. Make sure you enter a valid email address, because you'll need to verify your registration:

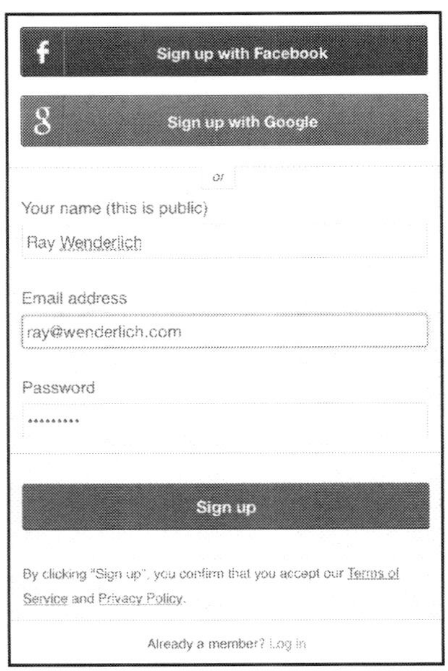

You'll be presented with optional questions about your age, location and so on, which you can skip for now by clicking **Next**. You can always go back to your profile to update this information later.

Once you get the confirmation, go to your email and follow the instructions to verify and enable your Meetup account. Once you're verified, go to meetup.com again and log in:

Getting your API key

After you're logged in, go to secure.meetup.com/meetup_api/key in your browser, where you can find your private API key:

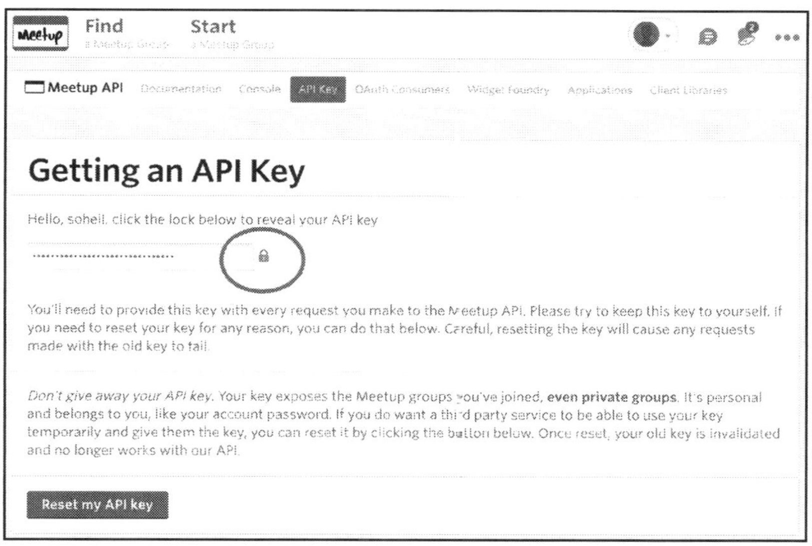

Click the **Lock** icon to reveal the key, and copy it to the clipboard.

To verify that you've done everything right and your token works, load bit.ly/1Mcmb04 in your browser. If something goes wrong, you'll get a response that says, `You are not authorized to make that request.`

Now you need to add the token to the requests you send from the iPhone and Watch apps. Open the **Meetup Finder** starter project in Xcode and open **MeetupRequestFactory.swift**. Replace **`YOUR_API_TOKEN`** with your new token:

```
private let APIKey = "YOUR_API_TOKEN"
```

Core Location on the Watch

I'm sure you're eager to add location services to get Meetup Finder working, but first it's important to address some limitations of Core Location in watchOS 2, as compared with its iOS counterpart. Knowing these limitations in advance will help you make best use of the framework as you implement it throughout the rest of this chapter.

The limits of Core Location in watchOS 2

As in iOS, you need to ask for user authorization to access a user's location in the Watch app. You can ask for two types of authorization:

- **When in use**, where the location is only accessible while the app is in the foreground.
- **Always**, where the location is accessible at any time, as long as the device is running.

While your Watch app may request authorization, the user will need to accept the authorization on the paired iPhone. So, you must construct your app so that it can operate without access to location information.

If you're familiar with Core Location on iOS, you know it's possible to subscribe to ongoing location updates from Core Location. In watchOS 2, you can only ask for a one-time location update via a new API called `requestLocation()`; you cannot subscribe to continuous change notifications. While this new method limits your tracking flexibility, it does simplify the process of getting the Watch's current location. You'll see this API in action later in the chapter.

Finally, there are no continuous, background or deferred location updates in watchOS 2, nor is there region monitoring, because all of these require background update capability. If your Watch app requires any of these location updates, you'll have to leverage the Watch Connectivity framework and coordinate with your iPhone app to communicate these updates. You'll see this type of coordination in action later in this chapter.

Getting locations

With your Meetup-ready app and a better sense of what's coming, you're fully prepared to get some locations! Go back to your Xcode project, open **InterfaceController.swift** and add the following import statement:

```
import CoreLocation
```

You've linked against the `CoreLocation` framework, so you can start to use it. Add the following variable to `InterfaceController`:

```
private let locationManager = CLLocationManager()
```

`CLLocationManager` is the main class responsible for location delivery.

Requesting user authorization

Recall that there are two types of location authorizations: `AuthorizedAlways` and `AuthorizedWhenInUse`. In iOS, you must ask for either type and check the current authorization status before requesting location updates.

This concept now carries over to watchOS. In Meetup Finder, you want to request the location every time the app launches. Add the following to the end of `willActivate()`:

```
let authorizationStatus =
  CLLocationManager.authorizationStatus()
handleLocationServicesAuthorizationStatus(authorizationStatus)
```

Here, you check the location services authorization status of your app via `authorizationStatus()`, a class method on `CLLocationManager`, and then pass its value to `handleLocationServicesAuthorizationStatus(_:)`, a helper method you'll implement next.

Implement `handleLocationServicesAuthorizationStatus(_:)` in `InterfaceController` as follows:

```
func handleLocationServicesAuthorizationStatus(
  status: CLAuthorizationStatus) {
  switch status {
    case .NotDetermined:
      handleLocationServicesStateNotDetermined()
    case .Restricted, .Denied:
      handleLocationServicesStateUnavailable()
    case .AuthorizedAlways, .AuthorizedWhenInUse:
      handleLocationServicesStateAvailable()
  }
}
```

You evaluate all possible values of the authorization status and call appropriate helpers for each case:

- **`.NotDetermined`**: You get this state when the user hasn't yet made a choice with regard to your app. This is usually the case when the user first installs the app and hasn't run it yet. You'll handle this case in `handleLocationServicesStateNotDetermined()`.
- **`.Restricted`** and **`.Denied`**: You get either of these states when the user has explicitly denied location access to your app, or location services are unavailable due to other circumstances. Either way, you'll treat this case in a generic way in `handleLocationServicesStateUnavailable()`.
- **`.AuthorizedAlways`** or **`.AuthorizedWhenInUse`**: Both of these cases mean the user

has granted your app access to location services. Since `.AuthorizedAlways` and `.AuthorizedWhenInUse` are mutually exclusive, and you can only have one type of authorization at a time, you consider each case a happy path and handle it in `handleLocationServicesStateAvailable()`.

It's time to define these helper methods. First, for the "not determined" case, add the following code to `InterfaceController`:

```
func handleLocationServicesStateNotDetermined() {
  updateVisibilityOfInterfaceGroups()
  messageLabel.setText(pendingAccessMessage)
  locationManager.requestWhenInUseAuthorization()
}
```

In `handleLocationServicesStateNotDetermined()`, you update the visibility of some interface elements, and then you display an appropriate message to the user and instruct her to make a decision. At the end, you ask the `CLLocationManager` instance to request authorization for `AuthorizedWhenInUse` status by calling `requestWhenInUseAuthorization()`.

An iOS app must provide a good reason why it requires access to the user's location by setting `NSLocationWhenInUseUsageDescription`, `NSLocationAlwaysUsageDescription` or both in the app's Info.plist. Meetup Finder already has both keys set in the Info.plist of the iPhone app.

Depending on what type of authorization the app asks for by calling either `requestWhenInUseAuthorization()` or `requestAlwaysAuthorization()`, the system displays the request, along with an appropriate reason for access, in a system prompt to the user.

The system prompt in iOS is an alert view, but on the Watch, the system presents a modal dialog to the user and informs her that she can grant or deny access on her iPhone, instead. Since the user can dismiss the modal view without making any decision, you need to design and update the interface so that it appears properly.

To see this in action, select the **Meetup Finder Watch** scheme and then build and run. You'll be presented with the following:

The iPhone presents the system alert view while the Watch displays the modal view. Dismiss the modal view on the Watch. The Watch screen now shows an appropriate message.

Next, you'll handle unauthorized access. From within Xcode, stop running the app. In the iPhone simulator, deny location access to the app by tapping **Don't Allow**.

Still in **InterfaceController.swift**, define `handleLocationServicesStateUnavailable()` as follows:

```
func handleLocationServicesStateUnavailable() {
  interfaceModel.state = MainInterfaceState.NotAuthorized
  updateVisibilityOfInterfaceGroups()
  messageLabel.setText(locationAccessUnauthorizedMessage)
}
```

Here, you update the state of your interface model by setting it to `MainInterfaceState.NotAuthorized`, update the visibility of the UI, and display a message telling the user that location services aren't available.

Build and run. You'll see the following:

Since a user can authorize location services at any time, you need to make sure you get notified about changes in authorization status. The `CLLocationManager` will notify its delegate about these changes, so you'll need to comply with the `CLLocationManagerDelegate` protocol and implement `locationManager(_:didChangeAuthorizationStatus:)`.

Open **InterfaceController.swift** and add the following line to the end of `awakeWithContext(_:)`:

```
locationManager.delegate = self
```

Xcode gives you an error. Now that you've indicated you want to be the delegate of `CLLocationManager`, you need to comply with the `CLLocationManagerDelegate` protocol. Add the following extension to the end of **InterfaceController.swift**:

```
extension InterfaceController: CLLocationManagerDelegate {
  func locationManager(manager: CLLocationManager,
    didChangeAuthorizationStatus
    status: CLAuthorizationStatus) {
      handleLocationServicesAuthorizationStatus(status)
  }

  func locationManager(manager: CLLocationManager,
    didUpdateLocations locations: [CLLocation]) {
      // More to come ...
  }

  func locationManager(manager: CLLocationManager,
    didFailWithError error: NSError) {
      // More to come ...
  }
}
```

Here you implement `locationManager(_:didChangeAuthorizationStatus:)` and call into the helper method you've already implemented to handle any changes in the authorization status while your app is running. To prevent a runtime exception, you also add placeholders for `locationManager(_:didUpdateLocations:)` and `locationManager(_:didFailWithError:)`.

Using the location

OK! You've handled the error conditions, so now it's time to work with the user's location once she grants the app access. Still in **InterfaceController.swift**, implement the following method:

```
func handleLocationServicesStateAvailable() {
  updateVisibilityOfInterfaceGroups()
  showLoadingMessageIfApplicable()
  locationManager.requestLocation()
}
```

Once again, you update the visibility of some UI elements, display a loading message and request a one-time location update from the `CLLocationManager` instance.

Now build and run the Meetup Finder Watch scheme. First the app will present you with a message that location services are disabled. In the iPhone simulator, open the **Settings** app, go to **Privacy\Location Services\Meetup Finder** and change the authorization to **While Using the App**. Once you make that change, you'll see the Watch screen update:

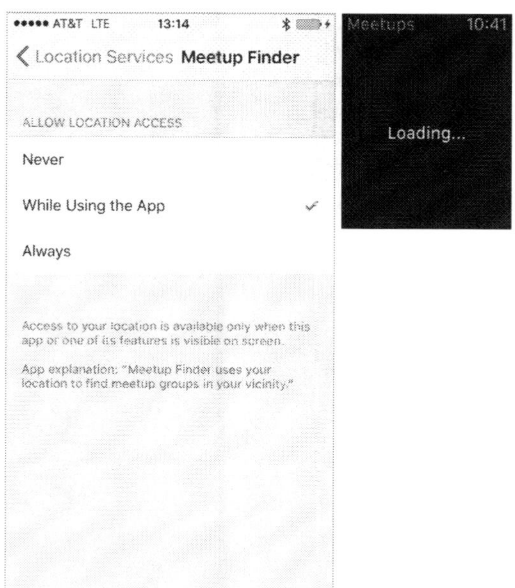

That's excellent, but where are the locations? Stop the simulator and go back to Xcode.

In **InterfaceController.swift**, find the implementation of `locationManager(_:didUpdateLocations:)` and update its implementation as follows:

```
func locationManager(manager: CLLocationManager,
  didUpdateLocations locations: [CLLocation]) {
  print("Did update locations: \(locations)")
  guard let mostRecentLocation = locations.last else { return }
  queryMeetupsForLocation(mostRecentLocation)
}
```

`CLLocationManager` calls this delegate method when Core Location generates location events. Since you called `requestLocation()` earlier, you'll get only one callback here. The array of `locations` always contains at least one `CLLocation` object. The objects in the array are organized by the order in which they occurred. So if you get more than one `CLLocation` at a time, the most recent location update is at the end of the array.

Once you get the most recent location, you pass it to a helper method, `queryMeetupsForLocation(_:)`, to query the backend for meetups. Afterward, the UI will update automatically.

Build and run. This time, depending on the speed of your Internet connection, you'll briefly see the loading message, and then the interface will update to show meetup groups:

> **Note**: If the Watch simulator continues to show "Loading..." and doesn't get a location fix, stop the simulator. Select the **Meetup Finder** scheme, and build and run in the iPhone simulator once. Then, build and run the Meetup Finder Watch scheme in the Watch simulator again.

Handling location errors

Before you move on to the next section, there's another delegate method in `CLLocationManagerDelegate` that you should implement to cover all possible cases: `locationManager(_:didFailWithError:)`.

Update its placeholder implementation as follows:

```
func locationManager(manager: CLLocationManager,
  didFailWithError error: NSError) {
  print("CL failed: \(error)")
  interfaceModel.state = .Error
  updateVisibilityOfInterfaceGroups()
  messageLabel.setText("Failed to get a valid location.")
}
```

Here you log the error to the console, update the state of the interface model and display an error message to the user. There isn't a great way for you to force an error to see this code in action, but you can feel good knowing you built in decent error handling for your users. :]

Limiting location queries

Just like any other backend service, Meetup API has safety measures to prevent excessive requests. If you exceed your allotted number of requests, Meetup will temporarily deny your requests. That won't be a good experience for your users. To avoid such a problem, you'll update the app so it only queries the backend when a user's location has changed enough to grant a new update.

Open **InterfaceController.swift** and find the implementation of `isLocationChangedSignificantly(_:)`. This helper method takes a `CLLocation` input and returns a Boolean to indicate whether it's a significant change. Update its implementation as follows:

```
func isLocationChangedSignificantly(updatedLocation: CLLocation)
  -> Bool {
  guard let lastQueriedLocation = lastQueriedLocation
    else { return true }
  let distance =
    lastQueriedLocation.distanceFromLocation(updatedLocation)
  return distance >
    CLLocationDistance(MeetupSignificantDistanceChange)
}
```

Here, you use a convenience method on `CLLocation` to get the distance from the input `CLLocation` and the last queried location you have stored in a property on `InterfaceController`. The distance is in meters. If the distance is more than `MeetupSignificantDistanceChange`, you flag it as a significant change by returning `true`.

`MeetupSignificantDistanceChange` is calculated based on the app's business logic. Since the app queries the backend for meetups within a radius of 50 miles from the current location, if the new location is less than 20 miles away from the previous location, the results of the previous query are still valid. `MeetupSignificantDistanceChange` is the result of converting 20 miles to meters; that's 20 * 1609.34.

Next, add the following `if` statement to the end of `willActivate()` in **InterfaceController.swift**:

```
if let lastQueriedLocation = lastQueriedLocation {
  queryMeetupsForLocation(lastQueriedLocation)
}
```

If you have a valid location from the last time you queried the API, you dispatch a request to load content for that location. You query the Meetup API at the same time as you try to get a location fix from `CLLocationManager`.

When `locationManager(_:didUpdateLocations:)` returns the result of the location update, you dispatch another request if the new location is significantly different from the previous one. This way, you won't have to wait for `CLLocationManager` to complete before loading the content. You'll have already loaded the content using the last location you had.

> **Note**: If the iPhone isn't reachable and the Watch has to get a location fix on its own, the best accuracy level you can get from `CLLocationManager` is `kCLLocationAccuracyHundredMeters`.

Build and run in the Watch simulator. First, the app will present you with meetup groups near the current location. Now from the Watch simulator menu, select **Hardware\Lock** to lock the Watch screen and then select **Debug\Location\Apple**. Again, from the menu select **Hardware\Lock** to unlock the Watch. This triggers `willActivate()`. Verify that the app has updated the meetups based on the new location.

Your app is now finding local meetups. This would be a great time to take a break and contemplate new networking options!

Coordination

The app works reasonably well, but there's still room for improvement. There are certain things in Core Location that aren't available to a WatchKit extension, such as continuous updates. Getting a location update may also take a few seconds and in some cases, the location manager may even fail to get a location fix.

Even though the Watch app can now query location updates and display appropriate content, it's still functioning in conjunction with its iPhone app. So it's a good idea to leverage this partnership and make the Watch app faster, more efficient and more responsive to location changes.

The app already leverages the Watch Connectivity framework to communicate the last location update from the iPhone app to the Watch app. Location updates come via a `session(_:didReceiveApplicationContext:)` callback of `WCSessionDelegate`. When the Watch app isn't running, Watch Connectivity caches any updates and will deliver the most recent one on the next launch.

> **Note**: Watch Connectivity is covered in depth in Chapter 13 and Chapter 18.

Next, you'll update the Watch app so that it uses the cached location. Open **InterfaceController.swift** and find and update the implementation of `session(_:didReceiveApplicationContext:)`, as follows:

```
func session(session: WCSession,
  didReceiveApplicationContext
  applicationContext: [String:AnyObject]) {

  guard let data = applicationContext["lastQueriedLocation"] as?
    NSData else { return }

  guard let location =
    NSKeyedUnarchiver.unarchiveObjectWithData(data) as?
    CLLocation else { return }

  queryMeetupsForLocation(location)
}
```

Here, you try to get location data from the context dictionary, turn it into a `CLLocation` and query meetups for that location by calling `queryMeetupsForLocation(_:)`.

It's time to see the coordination in action. The iPhone is designed in such a way that if you change location access authorization to Always, it will turn on continuous updates.

In the iPhone simulator, open the **Settings** app, go to **Privacy\Location Services**

Meetup Finder and change the authorization to **Always**.

There's a little coordination required to get this working on two simulators, so follow along carefully:

1. Select the **Meetup Finder** scheme for the iPhone, and build and run the iPhone app in the iPhone simulator. To verify that everything is working as expected, check out the console log for the iPhone app. You'll see that the app is logging locations at approximately 1-second intervals. You'll also see a message in the console that says `"New query to meetups ignored because current location hasn't changed significantly."`
2. Still running the iPhone app in the simulator, open the Watch app in the Watch simulator. Verify that you see similar results in the Watch app.

3. While both apps are running, from the iPhone simulator menu, select **Debug > Location > Apple**. In a few seconds, both the iPhone and the Watch app will update their contents for the new location.

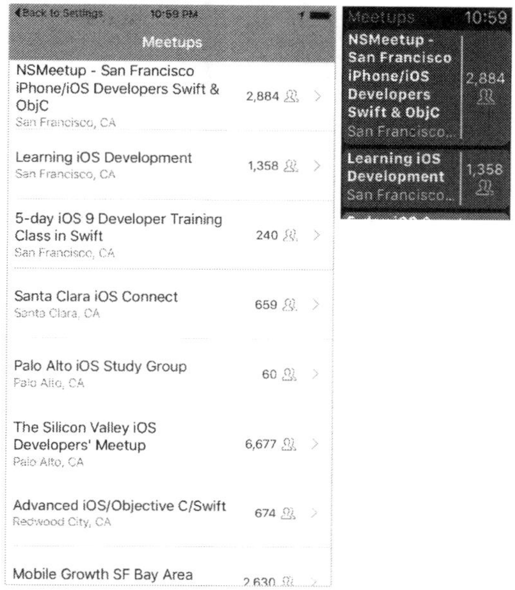

Background location updates

Since continuous location updates aren't available in watchOS 2, it's not surprising that background location updates aren't available, either. This is another area where you can benefit from the coordination between the iPhone app and the Watch app.

In previous versions of iOS, you simply had to turn on Background Modes for your iPhone app target and select the entry for location updates:

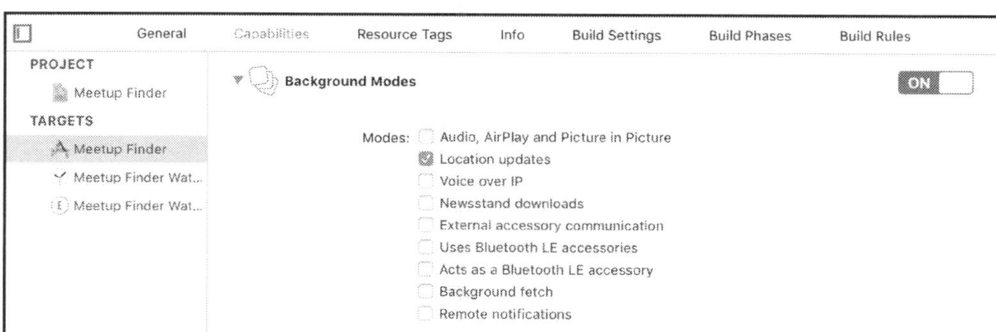

New in iOS 9, you also have to set the value of the `allowsBackgroundLocationUpdates` property on your `CLLocationManager` instance to `true`. You must set this property for each `CLLocationManager` instance.

To make sure Meetup Finder continues receiving location updates in the background, open **MeetupsViewController.swift**, find the implementation of `viewDidLoad()` and add the following line after you set the delegate of `locationManager`:

```
locationManager.allowsBackgroundLocationUpdates = true
```

Build and run to give it a try. Again, there's a little coordination required to get this working on two simulators:

1. Select the **Meetup Finder** scheme for the iPhone and build and run the iPhone app in an iPhone simulator.
2. Still running the iPhone app in the simulator, open the Watch app in the Watch simulator. Verify the Watch app loads its content successfully and that it matches the content of the iPhone app.
3. From the iPhone simulator menu, select **Hardware\Home** to put the iPhone app in the background. You can verify that the iPhone has entered the background by checking the console log for an `Application entered background.` message.
4. Simulate a location change by selecting **Debug\Location\Custom Location** from the iPhone simulator menu. Enter **51.50998000** for **Latitude** and **-0.13370000** for **Longitude**. Verify that after a few seconds, the Watch app updates with new meetups for the new location.

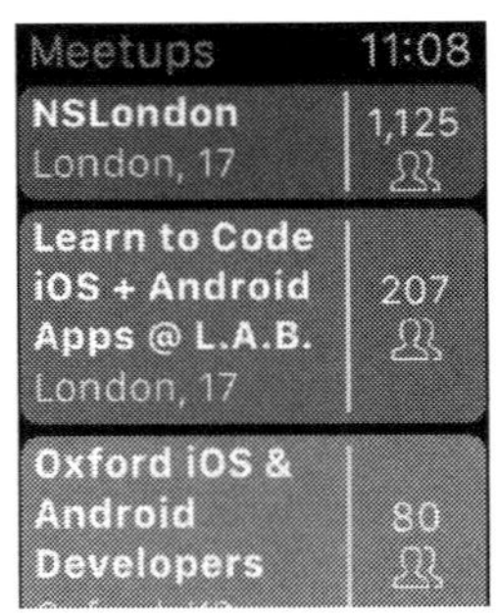

Optimizations

The app is in great shape, but there's a small problem: It continues to receive a significant number of background updates. The chance that the user has moved to a new location that's significantly different is very low. The way the app queries location updates drains the user's battery quickly.

To optimize the app for better power management, open **MeetupsViewController.swift**, find the implementation of `queryMeetupsForLocation(_:)` and add the following to the end of the function:

```
locationManager.allowDeferredLocationUpdatesUntilTraveled(
  MeetupSignificantDistanceChange,
  timeout: MeetupSignificantDistanceChangeTimeout)
```

Here you update the private helper method that queries Meetup based on a given `CLLocation`. This method runs the query only if the new location is significantly different from the previous location, so it makes sense to tell `locationManager` that you're happy with the current location fix until the user's location significantly changes.

`allowDeferredLocationUpdatesUntilTraveled(_:timeout:)` is an old API that's been around for a long time, but it probably hasn't gotten as much attention as it deserves.

In the era of the Apple Watch and its limited resources, you want to optimize your code as much as you can to deliver a good user experience. Via this API, you tell the GPS hardware to store new locations internally until the specified distance or timeout conditions are met.

When either of the criteria is met, the location manager calls `locationManager(_:didFinishDeferredUpdatesWithError:)` to end deferred locations and delivers the cached locations via `locationManager(_:didUpdateLocations:)`. If your app is in the foreground, the location manager doesn't defer the delivery of events.

There are a number of things you'll want to keep in mind about `allowDeferredLocationUpdatesUntilTraveled(_:timeout:)`:

1. The location manager allows deferred updates only when GPS hardware is available on the device and when the desired accuracy is set to `kCLLocationAccuracyBest` or `kCLLocationAccuracyBestForNavigation`. Otherwise, you'll get a `kCLErrorDeferredFailed` error. If you set the accuracy to an unsupported value, you'll get a `kCLErrorDeferredAccuracyTooLow` error.
2. You must set the `distanceFilter` property of the location manager to `kCLDistanceFilterNone` or you'll get a `kCLErrorDeferredDistanceFiltered` error.
3. Call `allowDeferredLocationUpdatesUntilTraveled(_:timeout:)` after you've got your first batch of location updates. You call this once you're happy with your current updates and want to defer future updates until the distance or time criteria are met.
4. Don't call `allowDeferredLocationUpdatesUntilTraveled(_:timeout:)` more often than you need to, because each time you call it, it cancels the previous deferral. You should keep track of whether updates are currently deferred and call it again only when you want to change the deferral criteria.

5. The system delivers deferred updates only when it enters a low-power state. Deferred updates don't occur during debugging, because Xcode prevents your app from sleeping and so prevents the system from entering that low-power state.

Now that you've created a fantastic Meetup Finder app, get out there and meet up with your fellow iOS devs!

Where to go from here?

Core Location is a powerful technology that has many practical and far-reaching applications. In this chapter, you learned about the framework and its limitations in WatchKit Extensions and watchOS 2. You implemented authorization handling, requested locations and leveraged the Watch Connectivity framework to coordinate your iPhone and Watch apps to communicate continuous and background updates.

If you're still curious about what's new in Core Location, make sure you check out WWDC15 Session 714, available here: apple.co/1EcdPD7. And if you're thinking of improving the user experience by expanding coordination between the iPhone and Watch apps, head over to Chapter 13, "Watch Connectivity", to learn all about it.

Chapter 24: Networking

By Scott Atkinson

In the bad old days of watchOS 1, developers had to do crazy things to make their Watch apps *appear* to get data from the Internet. Common mechanisms included:

- Having your Watch extension call `openParentApplication(_:reply:)` and making the `UIApplicationDelegate` get data from the extension and return results to the extension;
- Having the parent application get data and share it in a common file location;
- Passing small bits of data around using "Darwin Notifications" and having the main app perform requests upon receipt.

Needless to say, the process was cumbersome, and it resulted in a lot of confusing and often duplicated code.

With watchOS 2, you can now use `NSURLSession` to make network calls directly from your Watch extension. Most of the time, these calls will still be executed by the iPhone. But it will, at least, be transparent to you as a developer. Even better, if your Watch doesn't happen to be connected to your iPhone but you're in range of a known Wi-Fi network, the Watch will make the network request itself!

In this chapter, you'll add network requests to a watchOS 2 app that provides personalized access to human population data. Along the way, you'll experiment with some of watchOS 2's new networking features.

> **Note**: This chapter will briefly review `NSURLSession`. For more in-depth coverage of networking, study some of the networking tutorials on our site:
>
> **NSURLSession Tutorial**: bit.ly/1h4DRxG
>
> **Cookbook: Using NSURLSession**: bit.ly/1gC3hln

Getting started

Short of some very simple utility apps like calculators, and maybe a few games, you'd be hard-pressed to find many apps that don't require networking of some sort. Whether it's downloading images, files or other assets, or making web service requests, it's inevitable that you'll need to deal with networking at some point in your iOS career. Since the Apple Watch currently seems to be much more of a consumption device than a creation device, it's even more likely that the watchOS apps you build will require getting data from somewhere else.

A brief overview of NSURLSession

As you've probably experienced, networking can be challenging. A large range of complicated sounding protocols, layers, devices and stacks conspire to hinder you in your quest to get data from remote servers.

Luckily for you, many have created iOS and watchOS libraries to help simplify your interactions with the network. Two excellent and popular tools are **AFNetworking** (afnetworking.com) and its "Swiftified" sibling, **Alamofire** (github.com/Alamofire/Alamofire). These are great tools, and for very large projects are probably the way to go.

Apple also provides a set of straightforward APIs in `NSURLSession`. For simple projects, it's probably sufficient for all of your networking needs. You won't plumb the depths of `NSURLSession` in this chapter; for that, check out Apple's *URL Loading System Programming Guide* (apple.co/1JeMx0I) and in particular, the "Using NSURLSession" section (apple.co/1DPOcHE). But let's walk through some of the basics.

The `NSURLSession` class provides functionality for asynchronously getting or sending data from a remote server using the `HTTP` or `HTTPS` protocols. It supports authentication, exchanging cookies and various other configuration options.

You can configure a session to run in the foreground or the background of an app. Generally, you'll create a session once and reuse it for multiple data requests, called "tasks". There are a number of class methods that make it easy to create a pre-configured `NSURLSessionConfiguration` instance, but once it's configured, it cannot be changed.

After you've created and configured your `NSURLSession` object, you'll need to create one of three types of tasks on that session—**data**, **download** or **upload**—using an `NSURLRequest` object. This object wraps a URL and lets you customize things, like timeout values, for the particular task you're about to execute.

Curiously, you call `resume()` on a task to actually kick it off.

Finally, for most tasks, the data is returned in a completion handler associated with the task. However, sometimes you'll need more advanced control—for example, if you need to react to authentication challenges or execute a task in the background. If you do need more control, then you'll need to implement one or more of the `NSURLSession`-related delegate protocols, like `NSURLSessionDelegate` or `NSURLSessionTaskDelegate`.

Well, that was a whirlwind! Let's check out an app and add some code already!

Introducing Populace

The nice folks over at The World Population Project, population.io, have provided a really nice API to access their human population data. You'll be working with a cool little app called **Populace** that collects simple information from the user and then displays interesting data derived from the World Population Project, like the individual's life expectancy and rank by age in the selected country.

Open **Populace.xcodeproj** and have a look around. You'll see there's both an iOS and a WatchKit app. You'll get to the code in a moment, but first select the **Populace** scheme and build and run. It will look like this:

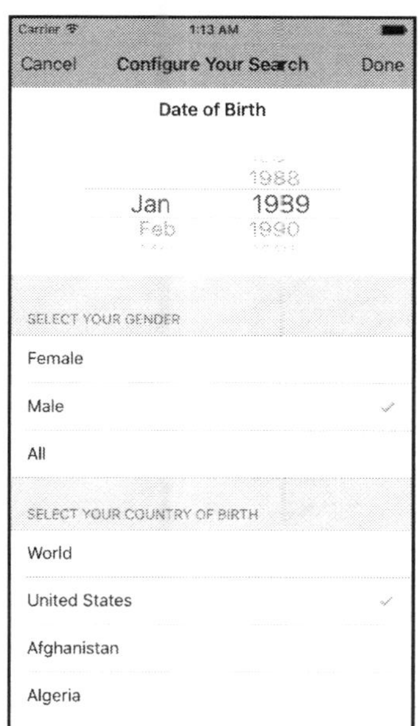

The app presents you with a configuration screen where you can enter your birthdate, gender and country of birth. Of course, you can enter this information for any real or hypothetical person to see the corresponding age-related data. Enter the details of your choice and tap **Done** to make your first network request. This time, you'll see the following:

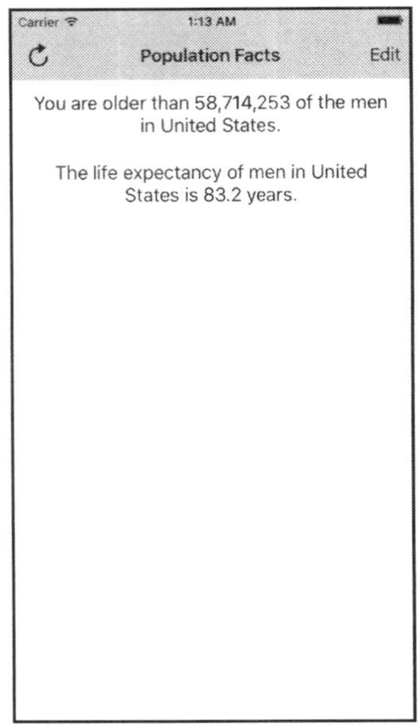

That's pretty thought-provoking... or it might be more than you want to know! Back in Xcode, select the **Populace WatchKit App** scheme and build and run. The app will present you with a welcome screen. Tap **Configure** and check out the configuration screen:

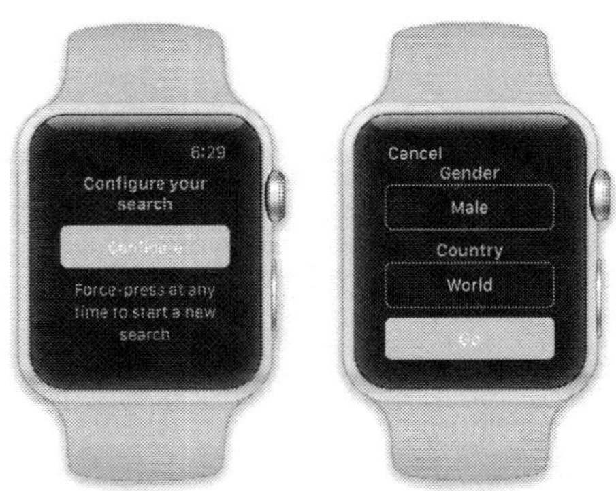

Pick your options and tap **Go**. Just like before, you'll get some fascinating data!

Hold on a minute. What just happened? Well, you haven't implemented the networking features for the Watch extension. So... no data.

In Xcode, open **WebService.swift** from the **Shared** group and take a couple of minutes to look through the network-based code in the project. In short, this class provides basic networking for calls to a generic web service.

Find `init(rootURL:)`. You'll see it creates an `NSURLSession` with a default configuration, one that makes `HTTP` requests in the foreground of the app. This class also provides two generic methods, `executeDictionaryRequest(_:completion:)` and `executeArrayRequest(_:completion:)`, for making web service requests that are expected to return JSON dictionary or array results, respectively.

Next, review `checkResponseForErrors(_:)`. Every `NSURLSessionTask` returns an `NSURLResponse` object when it completes. This method is responsible for looking through the response for errors.

Finally, you'll see two utility methods that take `NSData` JSON objects and return `NSDictionary` or `NSArray` objects, if possible. `executeDictionaryRequest(_:completion:)` and `executeArrayRequest(_:completion:)` use these to parse data that's returned to them.

This generic class forms the basis of all the network requests you'll make in Populace. You'll update or implement concrete subclasses of `WebService` to talk to specific web services like population.io. In the next section, you'll use an existing `WebService` subclass to make your first calls directly from the watchOS extension.

Calling the web service

As you saw when you ran the iPhone version of the app, the project has limited ability to make calls to population.io's web services. You'll add more web service functionality in a bit, but for now, you'll simply call the existing methods from the Watch extension.

Open **PopulationController.swift** from the **Populace WatchKit Extension** group and give it a quick review. This class is responsible for displaying results from web service calls in a table on the Watch.

First, you need to create a `WorldPopulationService` object. Find the "Models" `MARK` near the top of the file and add the following line:

```
let populationService = WorldPopulationService()
```

Population controller will use the `populationService` object throughout the lifecycle of the controller to make web service requests to get population data.

Now, scroll to `refresh(_:)`. This method is called whenever the table needs to be updated with new data from the Internet. You'll need to be sure that the user has properly configured his information, so immediately after the end of the first `if`-statement in `refresh(_:)`, add the following code:

```
// If there is no configuration, get one first
guard let configuration = configuration else {
  changeConfiguration(sender)
  return
}
```

This `guard` statement simply checks to make sure the optional `configuration` object has been set. If it hasn't, the method ends early and the app presents the `ConfigurationController` screen instead.

Once the user has properly entered his information, you'll call a series of web services. Immediately after the `self.interfaceStatus = .Loading` line, add the following:

```
// Get Rank Data
populationService.getRankInCountry(configuration) {
  rank, error in
  // 1
  print("Rank: \(rank)\nError: \(error?.localizedDescription)")

  // 2
  // Hide the Loading Indicator
  dispatch_async(dispatch_get_main_queue()) {
    self.interfaceStatus = .Results
  }

  // 3
  guard let rank = rank else {
    return
  }
```

```
    // 4
    dispatch_async(dispatch_get_main_queue()) {
      self.addFactToTable(rank)
    }
  }
```

This code block uses the `populationService` object to make a call to `getRankInCountry(_:completion:)`. Don't worry too much about the implementation of this method; later, you'll build a very similar method yourself. For now, all you need to know is that it will get the rank within a country based on the passed-in configuration. Once the rank data web service returns, the service object calls the `completion` closure. Here's what this method does:

1. It prints the results of the web service call to the console for debugging.
2. It hides the loading indicator.
3. It makes a check to ensure that the web service returned a valid `PopulationRank` object.
4. It adds the rank data as a new cell to the `WKInterfaceTable`.

That's all you need to make your first Watch-based web service call. Select the **Populace WatchKit App** scheme and build and run. Configure your information and tap **Go**.

Now what's happened? You should see a configuration screen after the API call completes. Read on to find out what went wrong.

Configuring App Transport Security

It's a good thing you added that `print()` command above. In Xcode, open the debugging console by pressing **Shift-Command-Y**. You'll see logging information that looks something like this:

```
2015-08-13 19:13:22.579 Populace WatchKit
Extension[42052:1752327] App Transport Security has blocked a
cleartext HTTP (http://) resource load since it is insecure.
Temporary exceptions can be configured via your apps Info.plist
file.
```

This warning is followed by the error message you printed:

```
Rank: nil
Error: Optional("The resource could not be loaded because the
App Transport Security policy requires the use of a secure
connection.")
```

To better protect user information, Apple has increased the default level of security in iOS 9 and watchOS 2 apps. By default, iOS 9 will no longer allow any `NSURLSession` tasks using HTTP. Apple expects developers to use only HTTPS (TLS). Open **WorldPopulationService.swift** from the **Shared** group and find this line:

```
private let baseURL = NSURL(string: "http://api.population.io")!
```

Notice that `baseURL` uses just HTTP. Luckily, Apple has provided a mechanism to opt-out of the HTTPS requirement by adding some keys to **Info.plist**. In the project navigator, expand the **Populace WatchKit Extension** group and right-click the **Info.plist** file in that group. Select **Open As/Source Code** from the menu.

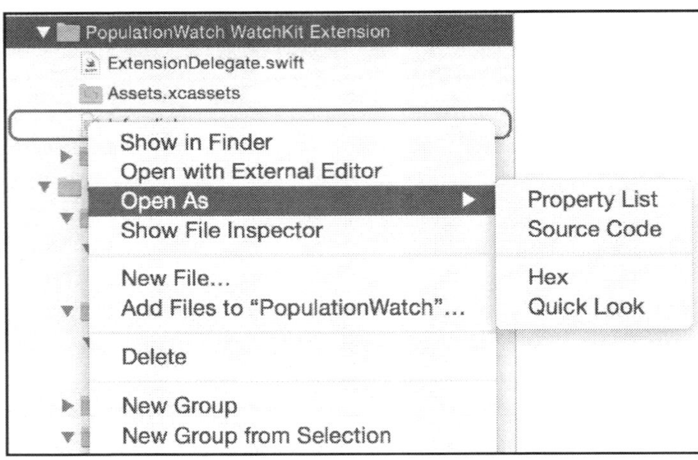

Immediately above the very last <\dict> line, insert the following XML:

```
<key>NSAppTransportSecurity</key>
<dict>
    <key>NSAllowsArbitraryLoads</key>
    <true/>
</dict>
```

This key instructs the WatchKit app extension to allow the loading of non-HTTPS URLs. Build and run again, and "Watch" what happens.

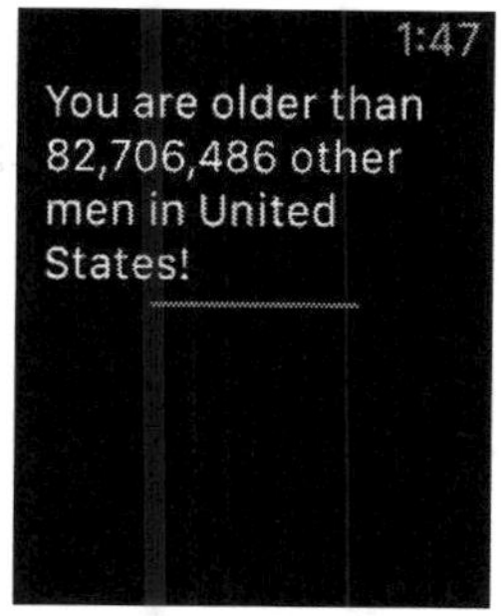

Congratulations: You've just completed your first network request from the Apple Watch!

> **Note**: The key you've entered is the simplest of all the App Transport Security functionalities. If you'd like to learn more about what it can do, be sure to check out WWDC 2015 Session #711 on `NSURLSession`: apple.co/1hBa4g8.

Making another call

Now that you know you can get data from the Internet on a WatchOS app, you'll add one more method. This method will use the population service to get life expectancy values from the web service. In Xcode, open **PopulationController.swift**. Again, add the following in `refresh(_:)`, immediately after the call to `getRankInCountry(_:completion:)`:

```
// Get Life Expectancy Data
populationService.getLifeExpectancy(configuration) {
  expectancy, error in
  print("Expectancy: \(expectancy)\nError:
    \(error?.localizedDescription)")

  // Hide the Loading Indicator
  dispatch_async(dispatch_get_main_queue()) {
    self.interfaceStatus = .Results
  }
  guard let expectancy = expectancy else {
    return
  }
  dispatch_async(dispatch_get_main_queue()) {
    self.addFactToTable(expectancy)
  }
}
```

This code looks familiar! You simply call `getLifeExpectancy(_:completion:)`, which returns a `LifeExpectancy` object to the `completion` closure. Like before, you check to make sure you received good data, and if so, you add the new data to the table. Notice that in this second call, you've reused the `populationService` object. This, in turn, reuses the same `NSURLSession` object.

Build and run again to see how it looks. Make sure you select a gender so you can get a life expectancy:

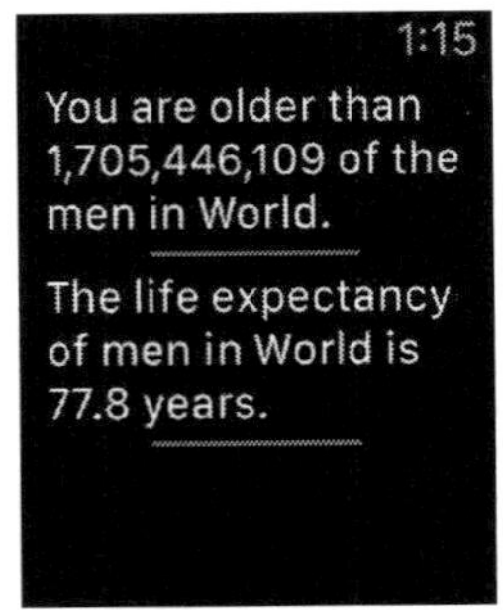

Looking good! In the next section, you'll explore `NSURLSession` a bit more by creating your own data task.

Getting a table of data

With all of this interesting information about ages and life expectancies around the world, wouldn't it be smart and cool to get a table of data, instead of just a single datapoint? Luckily for you, population.io provides a couple of APIs that will return multiple data points.

Before you write your networking code, first have a look at how it will eventually be used. Open **WorldPopulationService.swift** in the **Shared** group in Xcode and locate `getPopulationTable(_:country:completion:)`. Here's the code for reference:

```
func getPopulationTable(year: Int, country: String,
  completion: (table:PopulationTable?, error: NSError!)
  -> Void) {

  // 1
  let path = "/1.0/population/\(year)/\(country)"

  // 2
  let encodedPath = path.
    stringByAddingPercentEncodingWithAllowedCharacters
    (NSCharacterSet.URLPathAllowedCharacterSet())

  // 3
  executeArrayRequest(encodedPath!) {
    (array, error) -> Void in
```

```
    // 4
    // Make sure you get an array back
    guard let array = array else {
      completion(table: nil, error: error)
      return
    }

    // 5
    completion(table: PopulationTable(withJson: array),
      error: error)
  }
}
```

1. First, you create a `path` string that represents the RESTful web request to get population data. In this case, you call the "population" method and pass it the birth year and country that the user entered.
2. Because some of the data inserted into `path` may contain invalid characters, like spaces, the string is URL-encoded.
3. Next, you call `executeArrayRequest(_:completion:)`, passing in the encoded string.
4. Once the request is complete, you check to make sure it returned an array. If it didn't, you call the completion handler passed to `getPopulationTable(_:country:completion:)` without a returned table.
5. If you do have an array, you convert it into a `PopulationTable` object, which you return in the completion closure.

> **Note**: If you'd like more information about how a simple array is converted into a `PopulationTable` object, check out **PopulationTable.swift**. `init(withJson:)` maps each element in the array onto a `PopulationData` object. It then performs a number of calculations to add summary data to the `PopulationTable` instance it returns.

The above functionality seems solid. I mentioned that you'd be building some `NSURLSession` code in this section. So where is it, you ask? **Command-Click** on **executeArrayRequest** to navigate to it's implementation in **WebService.swift**. You'll see that it's currently not implemented. Add the following code to the body of `executeArrayRequest`:

```
print("Executing Request With Path: \(requestPath)")
if let request = requestWithURLString(requestPath) {
  // TODO
} else {
```

```
    // It was a bad URL, so just fire an error
    let error = NSError(domain:NSURLErrorDomain,
      code:NSURLErrorBadURL,
      userInfo:[ NSLocalizedDescriptionKey : "There was a problem
        creating the request URL:\n\(requestPath)"] )
    completion(array: nil, error: error)
  }
```

This code creates an NSURLRequest using the path passed to the method. Recall that NSURLRequest wraps an NSURL and can optionally add request-level options like a unique timeout value. In this case, you're not adding any additional options, so the request simply embodies the requestPath appended to the root URL. In the case of WorldPopulationService, the URL would end up looking like this:

```
http://api.population.io/1.0/population/1973/United%20States
```

In the event that requestWithURLString(_:) couldn't create a URL with the requestPath, executeArrayRequest(_:completion:) will create a NSURLErrorBadURL NSError object and return it to the caller.

Now that you have a valid request, you'll create a data task related to that request. Inside the if-statement you just added, insert the following code:

```
// Create the task
let task = session.dataTaskWithRequest(request) {
  data, response, error in
  // TODO
}
task.resume()
```

Using the session, you create an NSURLSessionDataTask with the request you created above. An NSURLSessionDataTask represents a task that will execute an HTTP GET request. Since you don't need to do anything fancy like answer authentication requests, you use a variant of dataTaskWithRequest(_:) that takes a completion closure. Finally, you kick off the request by calling resume().

At this point, you *could* run that app and it would go get data from the web service. However, not much would happen with the results. You still need to write the code to take the data returned and do something with it. Let's write code to do the initial error-checking and parsing of the response.

Populating the table

If don't already have it open, then open **WebService.swfit** in the in the **Shared** group. In executeArrayRequest(_:completion:), add the following to the body of the `completionHandler` closure of `dataTaskWithRequest(_:completionHandler:)`:

```
// 1
if error != nil {
  completion(array: nil, error: error)
  return
}

// 2 - Check to see if there was an HTTP Error
let cleanResponse = self.checkResponseForErrors(response)

// 3
if let errorCode = cleanResponse.errorCode {
  print("An error occured: \(errorCode)")
  completion(array: nil, error: error)
  return
}

// 4 - Make sure you got an array back after parsing
guard let dataArray = self.jsonArray(withData: data!) else {
  print("Parsing Issues")
  completion(array: nil, error: error)
  return
}

// 5
// Things went well, call the completion handler
completion(array: dataArray, error: error)
```

If you've built any apps that use networking, you know that much of your development and testing time is spent dealing with the myriad ways that a network request can fail. The code above is a small sample of the checks that you need to make with a network response. Let's walk through them:

1. If the data task returns a generic error, simply call the passed-in `completion` closure and exit the method.
2. Assuming there are no generic errors, take the `NSURLResponse response` object and attempt to further inspect it for errors. `checkResponseForErrors(_:)` takes the response and runs a few checks on it.

   First, it makes sure there is an actual response. Then, it converts the response to an `NSHTTPURLResponse`. You can do this because you know that you're making HTTP calls in this scenario, so the cast will work.

   Next, it checks to see if the response contained an HTTP response code of something other than 200, meaning success. Finally, it returns the findings as a tuple containing a `NSHTTPURLResponse` and an error code.
3. With that `cleanResponse` tuple, you check for an error code. If you find one, you again call the `completion` closure and exit.

4. If you've gotten this far, the web service successfully returned you *something*. Since this method is designed to get an array of data, you use `jsonArray(withData:)` to extract an `NSArray` from the `NSData` that the data task returned. The `guard` statement also checks to be sure there's at least one element in the array. If there's no array, you call the `completion` closure with no results.
5. Finally, it seems that you have an array with elements and no errors! So return it to the caller.

You're not quite at the point where you can see anything happen in the app. But you can, at least, make the web service call and log the results. Open **PopulationController.swift** in the **Populace WatchKit Extension** group and add the following to the bottom of `refresh(_:)`:

```
populationService.getPopulationTable(configuration.dobYear,
  country: configuration.country) { table, error in
    print("Table: \(table)\nError:
    \(error?.localizedDescription)")
}
```

Build and run the Watch extension. As before, enter your information and tap **Go**. Open the debugging console, and you'll see a couple of lines in the log that look like this:

```
Table: Optional(Populace.PopulationTable)
Error: nil
```

The fact that *something* is listed on the "Table:" line shows that the web service returned data and the population service created a `PopulationTable` object. Now you'll write code to do something impressive with it!

Fetching a chart

Right now, your apps look a bit bland. Why don't you spruce them up with a nice bar graph? It's a good thing you just figured out how to download a table of data from the web service!

You'll be using the Google Charts API to request a stacked bar graph image. The graph will show the male and female population by age, in 10 year increments, for the country you select. In Xcode, open **GoogleChartService.swift** in the **Shared** group. This `WebService` subclass contains one public method: `getStackedBarChart(_:bottomSeries:bottomColor:topSeries:topColor:completion:)`. You're going to implement that method.

As you can see from the method signature, it takes a number of parameters:

- The size of the image to get

- An array of integer values for the bottom stack
- The fill color for the bottom data series
- An array of integer values for the top stack (Optional)
- The fill color for the top data series (Optional)
- A completion closure that returns the image or an error (Optional)

Much like the population.io web services, the Google Chart APIs use data encoding in a `GET` request URL to return the proper graph image. So first, construct a path by adding the following to the beginning of `getStackedBarChart(_:bottomSeries:bottomColor:topSeries:topColor:completion:)`:

```
var path = "/chart?cht=bvs&chbh=a"
path += "&\(seriesMaxValueString(bottomSeries,
  series2: topSeries))"
path += "&\(sizeParameterString(size))"
path += "&\(seriesColorParameterString(bottomColor,
  color2: topColor))"
path += "&\(seriesParameterString(bottomSeries, series2:
  topSeries))"
let encodedPath =
  path.stringByAddingPercentEncodingWithAllowedCharacters(
    NSCharacterSet.URLQueryAllowedCharacterSet())
```

You are constructing the `path` string by using a number of utility methods that encode the size and scale of the image, the data in the chart and the colors for the chart. Once constructed, the `path` is URL-encoded so that all characters can be properly represented.

> **Note**: In this case, you are passing `stringByAddingPercentEncodingWithAllowedCharacters(_:)` the `URLQueryAllowedCharacterSet()`. Google Charts uses query strings to encode data, so the path must be encoded with the allowed query string parameters. In `WorldPopulationService`, the methods use `URLPathAllowedCharacterSet()`, as the data is encoded in the URL's path instead.

If all goes well, the `encodedPath` will look something like this:

```
/chart?cht=bvs&chbh=a&chds=0,41817223&chs=375x375&chco=0000ff,
ff0000&chd=t:18337423,21311304,17483109,12454256,12041058,
10904231,7795215,4032779,1410069,151169,2010%7C17515219,
20505919,17480411,12387222,12190604,11598529,9269157,5838332,
2505656,327302,5815
```

Now that you've encoded the population data into a query string, you need to create the request and the task. Add the following to the method:

```
if let request = requestWithURLString(encodedPath!) {
  // Create the download task
  let downloadTask = session.downloadTaskWithRequest(request) {
    url, response, error in
    // TODO
  }
  downloadTask.resume()
}
```

Like before, you create an `NSURLRequest` object that represents the path you just created. Then, instead of creating a data task, you create a `NSURLSessionDownloadTask`. Unlike data tasks, download tasks are designed to download large files or objects. These tasks are generally used for background downloads, although here you're using one in the foreground.

Notice that the parameters for the `completionHandler` closure include a `url`. Download tasks don't return their results to the `completionHandler`—they might be huge! Instead, the `NSURLSession` returns a local file URL that tells the closure where it can find the downloaded results on disk. And as before, you'll initiate the network request by calling `resume()` on the `downloadTask`.

Once the request finishes, you need to process the results. Implement the body of the `completionHandler` with the following code:

```
// 1 - There was an error
if (error != nil) {
  completion(image: nil, error: error)
  return
}

// 2 - Check to see if there was an HTTP Error
let cleanResponse = self.checkResponseForErrors(response)
if let errorCode = cleanResponse.errorCode {
  print("An error occured: \(errorCode)")
  completion(image: nil, error: error)
  return
}

// 3 - Check to see if a URL was returned
guard let url = url else {
  print("No Results URL")
  completion(image: nil, error: error)
  return
}

// 4 - Get the image from the local URL
guard let data = NSData(contentsOfURL: url),
```

```
  let image = UIImage(data: data) else {
    print("No Image")
    completion(image: nil, error: error)
    return
}

// 5 - Everything worked out, send back the image
completion(image: image, error: error)
```

Much of this code looks similar to the `executeArrayRequest(_:completion:)` method you implemented above. Here's the breakdown:

1. First, you check for generic errors and return early if there are any.
2. Then, exactly like before, you look at the `response` object to see if there are any errors there.
3. If there are no errors, you check to make sure the URL you were given is valid. If it isn't, you return early.
4. At this point, you use the URL to get an `NSData` object from the contents of the local file. If the data exists, you attempt to convert it into a `UIImage` object. If either of these steps fail, you stop processing the data.
5. All the tests have passed! You have a valid image that you can return to the caller via the `completion` closure.

This is getting exciting, isn't it? You now have an image in memory, so all you have to do is show it!

Displaying the chart

Open **PopulationController.swift** in the **Populace WatchKit Extension** group and declare a `GoogleChartService` constant below the `populationService` declaration:

```
let chartService = GoogleChartService()
```

Scroll down to `refresh(_:)` and add the following to the bottom of the `completion` closure for your call to `getPopulationTable(_:country:completion:)`:

```
// 1
guard let table = table else {
  // Hide the Loading Indicator
  dispatch_async(dispatch_get_main_queue()) {
    self.interfaceStatus = .Results
  }
  return
```

```
}

// 2 Get the Bar Chart for the population data
self.chartService.getStackedBarChart(
  CGSize(width: 300, height: 300),
  bottomSeries: table.malePopulationByDecade,
  bottomColor: maleColor,
  topSeries: table.femalePopulationByDecade,
  topColor: femaleColor,
  completion: { image, error in
  // 3
  dispatch_async(dispatch_get_main_queue()) {
    self.interfaceStatus = .Results
    self.table.insertRowsAtIndexes(
      NSIndexSet(index: self.facts!.count),
        withRowType: "ChartRowController")
    let row = self.table.
      rowControllerAtIndex(self.facts!.count) as!
        ChartRowController
    row.image = image
  }
})
```

By adding this code inside the completion closure of the call to get the data table, you are "daisy-chaining" the calls together: Once you get your population table, you use that data to create a graph of it. Let's walk through the specifics:

1. First, you check to make sure that you actually did get back a `PopulationTable` object. If you didn't, you simply hide the loading indicator.
2. You now make the call to the method you just created. The `PopulationTable` object does much of the work of organizing the data into arrays of decades instead of single years. So you simply pass the decade data for both men and women, along with some color choices and the size of the image you wish to receive.
3. Assuming everything goes well and the `GoogleChartService` returns a valid image, you now hide the loading indicator and insert a new cell into the `WKInterfaceTable`.

Build and run the Watch extension and then run a new query. If all went well, you'll see the graph appear at the bottom of the table:

Nicely done! Now you can see both how old you're getting *and* just how many young people there are in the world!

The last thing you need to do is update your iPhone app to show the graph. Open **PopulationViewController.swift** in the **Population** group and add a `GoogleChartService` instance right below the `populationService` declaration:

```
let chartService = GoogleChartService()
```

Just like in the Watch app, `refresh(_:)` makes a call to `getPopulationTable(_:country:)`. In the `completion` closure, add the following:

```
guard let table = table else {
  return
}
let width = self.table.frame.size.width
self.chartService.getStackedBarChart(
  CGSize(width: width, height: width),
  bottomSeries: table.malePopulationByDecade,
  bottomColor: maleColor,
  topSeries: table.femalePopulationByDecade,
  topColor: femaleColor,
  completion: { (image, error) -> Void in
  dispatch_async(dispatch_get_main_queue(), { () -> Void in
    self.graphImage = image
    self.table.reloadSections(
      NSIndexSet(index: self.kGraphSection),
      withRowAnimation: .Automatic)
  })
})
```

This will look very familiar. With the exception of how rows are added to the `UITableView` of the `PopulationViewController`, this code is identical to the code in the Watch extension.

That's it! Switch to the **Populace scheme**, and build and run one last time. Enter your information and tap **Done**.

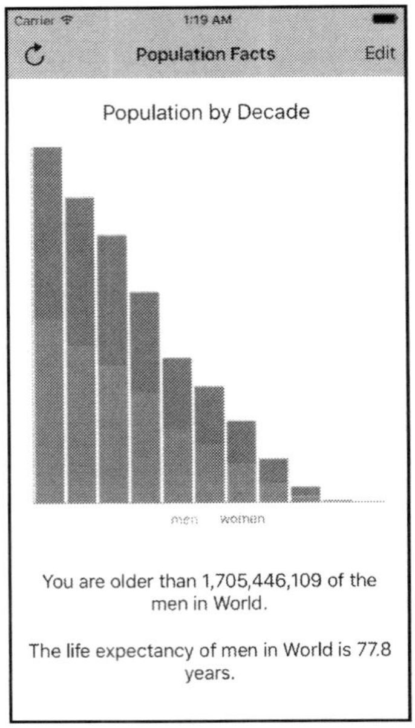

Where to go from here?

You can feel proud: Your Apple Watch can now make network calls all by itself! In this chapter, you explored a number of interesting things about `NSURLSession`:

- Designing reusable web service classes
- How to create, configure and execute an `NSURLSessionTask`
- The differences between an `NSURLSessionDataTask` and a `NSURLSessionDownloadTask`
- A couple of cool—and free!—web services
- App Transport Security

Take some time to explore the rest of the project. In particular, have a look at the `init(withJson:)` methods of the `PopulationRank`, `LifeExpectancy` and `PopulationData` classes to see how you can use Swift to easily verify and parse JSON dictionaries.

Also, play around with your Watch to see how it behaves when it's not connected to your iPhone. If you're near a known Wi-Fi network, Populace will still work!

Chapter 25: Haptic Feedback

By Audrey Tam

Do you love it when your Watch taps your wrist? Even though you're *already standing!* Maybe you've used Maps on your Watch to go from A to B. According to **The Apple Watch User Guide**: apple.co/1L5C46Y, *"A steady series of 12 taps means turn right at the intersection you're approaching; three pairs of two taps means turn left."*

These endearing taps are **haptic feedback**: tactile alerts to convey important information from apps on your Watch. Produced by the Watch's **Taptic Engine** and augmented by complementary audio tones, they draw your attention to significant events when you might not be looking at your Watch.

The exciting news is: as of watchOS 2, you can now play haptics from your own apps, and it's super easy to do! And because it's so easy, I'm going to cut to the chase and give you this chapter's *real* takeaway messages:

1. **Exercise restraint**. As Apple's Mike Stern says in WWDC 2015 video #802, "Designing for Apple Watch": *"Use [haptics] sparingly [for] truly important events in your app. Their effectiveness will diminish greatly if everything a person does in their app causes their Watch to vibrate and make sounds."*
2. **Use haptics the right way**. Mike's words again, from video #802: *"Please use these haptic tones and patterns as they were intended to be used. If haptic and auditory feedback isn't used consistently across all of the apps that we make, they are going to lose their meaning."*

This chapter begins with a list of the nine haptics you can use in your apps, with brief descriptions of when to use each. Then you'll put a few of these haptics to use in a real app.

Naturally, the app you'll build in this chapter will be a good haptics citizen. It will present a foreign language vocabulary quiz that provides haptic feedback for the user's answers. This is an ideal haptic opportunity: Haptic feedback will happen only while the user is engaged with the app, and most people love to get positive feedback from a quiz.

Here's a teaser of what the app will look like when you've finished:

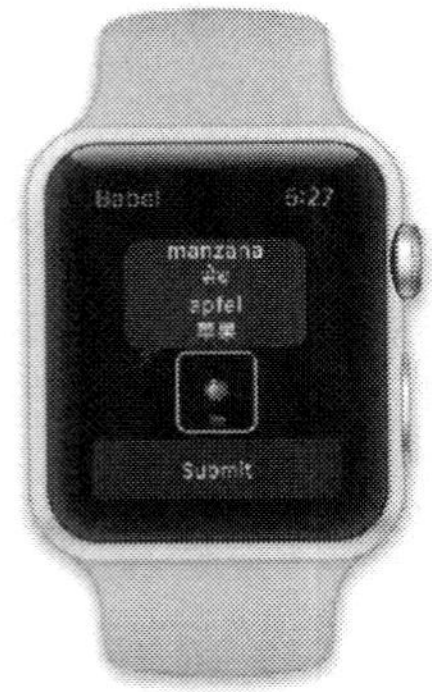

What is the Taptic Engine?

The Taptic Engine is an electromagnetic linear actuator—an electric motor that controls a magnetic field, to move a system in a straight line. The Taptic Engine's system is a tiny, heavy weight mounted on springs. Step 6 of ifixit.com's *Apple Watch X-ray Teardown* bit.ly/1WbW4t1 shows an X-ray and teardown photos of the Taptic Engine—pretty scary!

The nine haptics you can play

To use a haptic in your app, you simply insert the following line of code, replacing `WKHapticType` with one of its values, such as `.Success`.

```
WKInterfaceDevice.currentDevice().playHaptic(WKHapticType)
```

> **Note**: Apple's `WKInterfaceDevice` documentation warns, *"Do not use this method while gathering heart rate data using Health Kit. If you use this method to create haptic feedback, WatchKit delays the gathering of heart rate data until after the haptic engine has finished."* apple.co/1JZiaGD

Mike Stern said during WWDC 2015 video #802 that he'd *"had all of [the] chairs rigged with 14 super high-powered Taptic Engines"* so the audience would be able to feel the haptics.

Mike was just kidding, of course, but this chapter *does* have a bonus **TapTap** app that you can install on your Watch right now, so you can play each haptic as you study the following list.

1. `.Notification`: High tone with a tap followed quickly by a buzzy tap. This is the normal local notification haptic. Use it to alert the user when something significant has happened that needs attention.
2. `.DirectionUp`: Two quick rising tones played in time with mid-Watch-to-upper-Watch taps. Use this to alert the user when a significant value has crossed *above* a threshold.
3. `.DirectionDown`: Two quick falling tones played in time with mid-Watch-to-lower-Watch taps. Use this to alert the user when a significant value has crossed *below* a threshold.
4. `.Success`: Three quick rising tones with a single tap; it's designed to sound very positive. Use this to give users positive feedback when they do something like correctly answer a quiz or complete a level in a game.
5. `.Failure`: Quick high-high-low tones with a buzzy tap; it's designed to sound negative and discouraging. Use this to alert the user when an action fails and there's no way to recover.
6. `.Retry`: Mid-tone repeated three times quickly with a buzzy tap; it's designed to sound encouraging and inviting. Use this to alert users when an action fails, but your app will let them try again.
7. `.Start`: High tone with a tap. Use this to indicate the start of an activity, such as a timer or the companion iOS app recording audio or video.
8. `.Stop`: Two high tones played in time with two well-spaced taps. Use this to indicate when an activity stops.
9. `.Click`: *Very* quiet click with a subtle tap. Use this to give the sensation of a dial clicking at tick marks.

Note: The Taptic Engine won't play simultaneous or overlapping haptics. It plays the ones that it can, and drops the others.

According to Apple's `WKInterfaceDevice` documentation: *"If the haptic engine is already engaged when you call this method, the system stops the current feedback and imposes a minimum delay of 100 milliseconds before engaging the engine to generate the new feedback."*

> This can be a problem if, for example, your app plays clicks as the user rotates the digital crown—if the user turns it too quickly, only some of the clicks will play, and this could confuse the user. This might also explain why a haptic metronome app doesn't work well at faster tempos—too many clicks getting in each other's way!

This chapter's language quiz app will use the `.Success` and `.Retry` haptics.

Getting started

Open the **Babel** starter project and build and run it. It's an iPhone app that quizzes the user on numbers, colors and objects in four languages: Spanish, Hindi, German and Simplified Chinese. This gives the user the opportunity to learn unfamiliar words—assuming he doesn't already read all four of these languages, of course!

The possible answers come in the form of visual cues: either a digit, color circle or emoji, which might be more likely to imprint a memory and trigger recall than the English word—and it's more fun! The haptic and auditory feedback you're going to implement will also reinforce the correct answer in the user's mind.

The user taps one of the possible answers, and the app checks her answer and then presents an alert. If her answer is correct, she'll get a new question; otherwise, he can try again.

The Watch app will use the same question and answer lists, but the user will select her answer from a picker. For better control while developing and testing the app, you'll use a button to submit answers.

At the end of this chapter, you'll implement the `WKInterfaceController` `pickerDidSettle(_:)` method that makes Watch pickers behave like iPhone pickers— the interface controller calls this method after the user stops scrolling and the picker value remains steady for a reasonable period of time. Then you can remove the button.

Similar to the iPhone app, alerts will provide written feedback, but the real difference will be the accompanying haptic feedback: `.Success` when the the user gets the right answer, and `.Retry` when he needs to, well, try again.

Creating the Babel Watch app

OK, you know the drill by now. You'll be installing this app on your Watch, so you'll need to customize the bundle identifier to match that of your own provisioning account.

1. Customize the Babel target's **bundle identifier**. This should be in the reverse domain name format, `com.razeware.Babel`.
2. Create a new **watchOS\Application\WatchKit App** target.
3. Name it **Babel Watch**, customize the **Organization Name** and *don't* include the notification scene.
4. Activate the scheme, if prompted.

I know you're eager to get to the haptics, so these instructions will move along briskly.

Creating the Watch interface

Open **BabelWatch\Assets.xcassets**. Create a **New Image Set**, name it **bubble**, and in Attributes Inspector, set its **Devices** to **watchOS\Apple Watch**. Uncheck **Devices\All \Universal**. Drag the 38mm and 42mm bubble images from this chapter's **Starter** folder into the corresponding slots.

It should look like this:

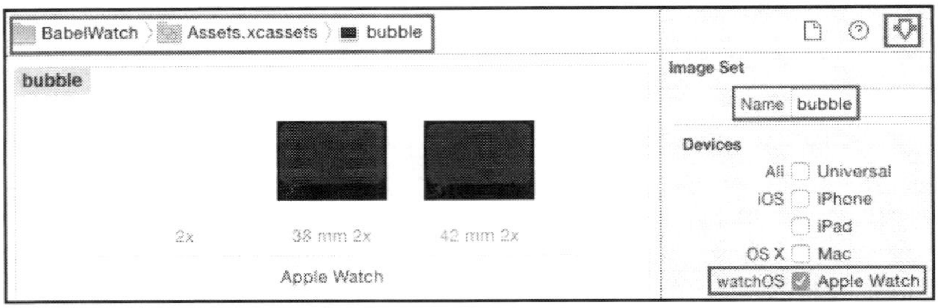

Open **Interface.storyboard**. Drag a **group** onto the scene and give it the following settings:

- **Group\Layout**: Vertical
- **Background**: bubble
- **Mode**: Top
- **Alignment\Horizontal**: Center
- **Alignment\Vertical**: Center

> **Note**: The bubble image's appearance in the storyboard is a little strange, but don't worry, it'll look just fine when you run the app.

Drag a **label** into the group and give it the following settings:

- **Label\Text**: Question
- **Label\Font**: System 14.0
- **Label\Alignment**: centered
- **Label\Lines**: 4
- **Alignment\Horizontal**: Center

Drag a **picker** into the group, below the Question label, and give it the following settings:

- **Picker\Focus Style**: Outline
- **Alignment\Horizontal**: Center
- **Size\Width**: Fixed\50
- **Size\Height**: Fixed\50

Drag a **button** onto the scene, *outside of the group*, and give it the following settings:

- **Button\Title**: Submit

- **Button\Font**: Footnote
- **Alignment\Horizontal**: Center
- **Alignment\Vertical**: Bottom

Your **Interface Controller Scene** will now look like this:

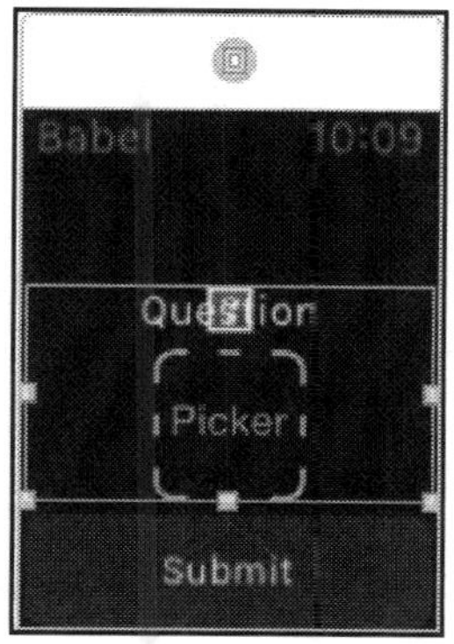

Connecting the interface objects

Open the assistant editor and **InterfaceController.swift** will appear.

Create the following **outlets** for the **label** and **picker**:

```
@IBOutlet var questionLabel: WKInterfaceLabel!
@IBOutlet var answerPicker: WKInterfacePicker!
```

Create the following **actions** for the **picker** and **button**:

```
@IBAction func pickerValueChanged(value: Int) {
}

@IBAction func checkAnswer() {
}
```

Delete `willActivate()` and `didDeactivate()`.

Sharing BabelData

BabelData.swift in the **Babel** group contains data arrays for the iPhone app's questions and answers. The Watch app needs most of these, so you're going to set up BabelData.swift as a shared project file.

Right-click on **BabelData.swift** in the project navigator and select **New Group from Selection**. Name this group **Shared** and *move it out of the Babel folder*, so it sits between the Babel and Babel Watch folders.

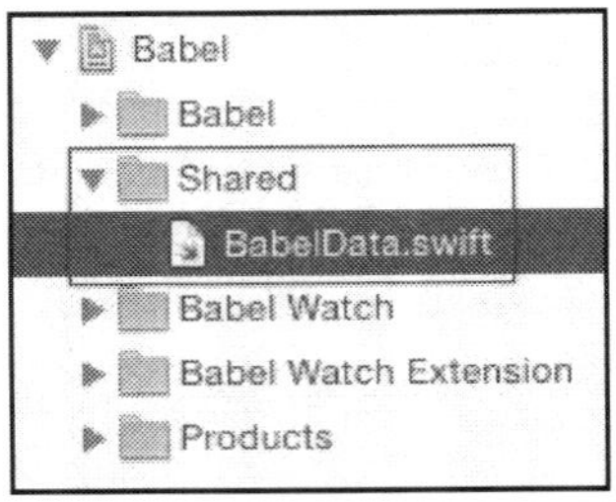

Open the **Shared** folder, select **BabelData.swift** and show the **File Inspector**. In the **Target Membership** section, check **Babel Watch Extension**.

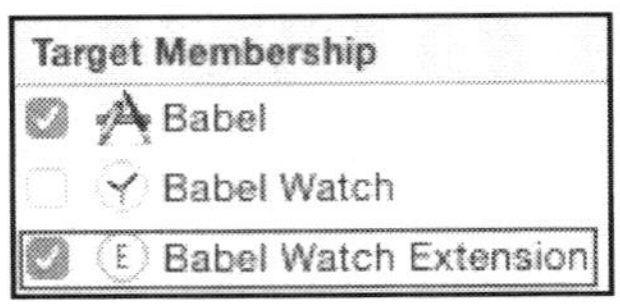

Showing the question

Open **InterfaceController.swift** in the **Babel Watch Extension** group and add the following properties below your outlet declarations:

```
let data = BabelData()
var questionNumber = 0
```

This code creates a `BabelData` object, providing access to the arrays of questions and answers, as well as to the enumeration `QuestionType`. The app will set `questionNumber` when it picks a question, and then it will check the user's answer against this value.

Add the following two methods to **`InterfaceController`**:

```
func pickQuestion(questions: [String]) {
  questionNumber = questions.count.random()
  questionLabel.setText(questions[questionNumber])
}

func showQuestion() {
  if let questionType = QuestionType(rawValue:
    QuestionType.count.random()) {
    switch questionType {
    case .Number: pickQuestion(data.numberQuestions)
    case .Color: pickQuestion(data.colorQuestions)
    case .Emoji: pickQuestion(data.emojiQuestions)
    }
  }
}
```

This code is almost identical to the iPhone app's code: `showQuestion()` picks a `QuestionType` at random, then calls `pickQuestion(_:)` to pick a number, color or emoji question at random and set the text of the `questionLabel` to this question.

To test and make sure everything's working as expected, you'll need to call your newly created methods. Add a call to **`showQuestion()`** in `awakeWithContext(_:)`. This will automatically set up the first question when the Watch app launches.

For the sake of testing, add another call to **`showQuestion()`** in `checkAnswer()` so that you can change the question with the touch of a button. Build and run in the simulator. Tap the button to show more questions.

Tweaking the label's font size

On a 42mm Watch face, the question text fits reasonably well in the bubble background image, but it could be 1 point larger. However, on a 38mm screen, the current 14-point text *doesn't* fit into the bubble. What to do? You'd like to set different font sizes for the two screen sizes...

Easy as pie! Open **Interface.storyboard** from the **Babel Watch** group. Select the **Question** label and then hop over to the Attributes Inspector. See the + sign next to **Label\Font**?

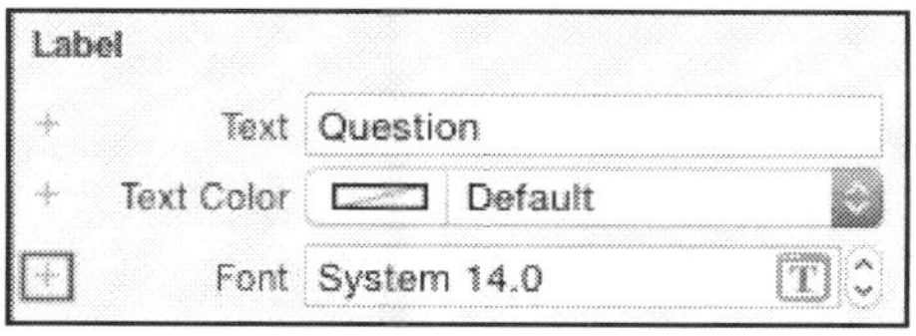

Click the + sign and select **Apple Watch 42mm** from the pop-up menu:

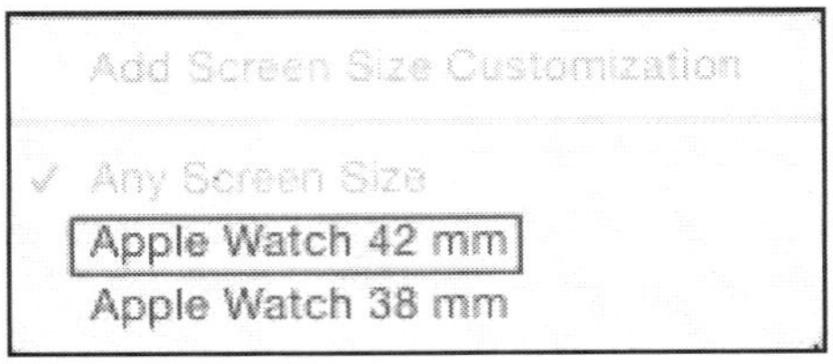

Increase the 42mm font size to **System 15.0**. Then add an **Apple Watch 38mm** font item, and decrease its size to **System 13.0**:

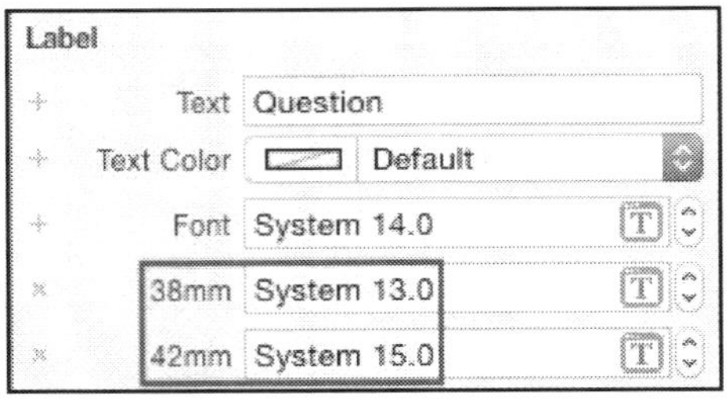

Build and run using both Watch sizes, and tweak further, if necessary.

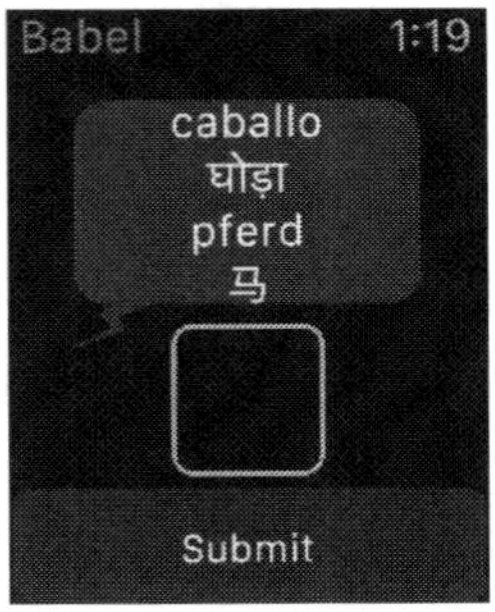

Setting the picker items

For each `QuestionType`, the Watch picker will display a list of possible answers. A Watch picker doesn't need a data source and delegate, but you do need to set up the arrays of picker items, one for each `QuestionType`.

Open **InterfaceController.swift** in the **Babel Watch Extension** group and add the following helper method, which will convert an array of titles into an array of `WKPickerItems`:

```
private func pickerItemsFromTitles(titles: [String])
  -> [WKPickerItem] {
  let items = titles.map {(title: String) -> WKPickerItem in
    let pickerItem = WKPickerItem()
    pickerItem.title = title
```

```
      return pickerItem
    }
    return items
  }
```

This one's simple enough. All it does is iterate over each title passed into the method and create a new `WKPickerItem` using that title.

This takes care of the `.Number` and `.Emoji` cases, but `.Color` won't be represented as a string; rather, it will be a visual representation of the color. Unfortunately, `WKPickerItem` doesn't have a background color property, but it does have a `contentImage` property. And the **`colorImages`** folder of this chapter contains some suitable images. Add them to **Assets.xcassets** of **Babel Watch**, as you see below.

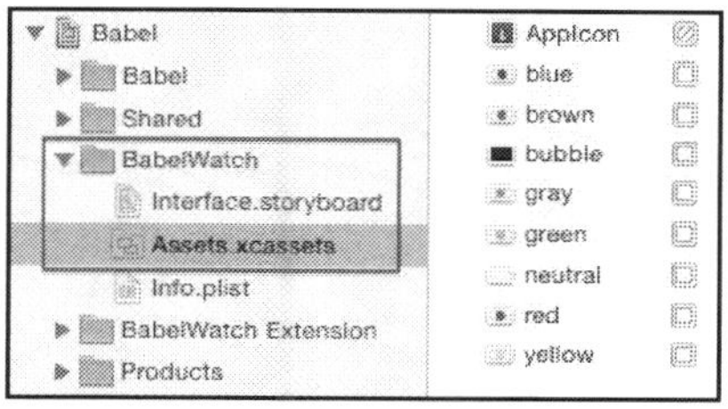

You're going to use the `imageName` initializer of `WKImage` to set the picker item's `contentImage` property. Add the following helper method to **InterfaceController.swift** in the **Babel Watch Extension** group to create a list of `WKPickerItem` objects from an array of image names:

```
  private func pickerItemsFromImageNames(imageNames: [String])
    -> [WKPickerItem] {
    let items = imageNames.map {(name: String) -> WKPickerItem in
      let pickerItem = WKPickerItem()
      pickerItem.contentImage = WKImage(imageName: name)
      return pickerItem
    }
    return items
  }
```

This looks almost identical to the previous method you added, except this time, you set the `contentImage` property of `WKPickerItem`.

Now that you have the methods to create each picker item, add the following method to create the correct list of items based on the `QuestionType`:

```
  func pickerItemsWithQuestionType(questionType: QuestionType)
    -> [WKPickerItem] {
    switch questionType {
      case .Number:
        return pickerItemsFromTitles(data.numberAnswers)
      case .Emoji:
```

```
      return pickerItemsFromTitles(data.emojiAnswers)
    case .Color:
      return pickerItemsFromImageNames(data.colorAnswers)
    }
  }
```

Lastly, use this helper method to lazy-load each of the arrays based on the `QuestionType` of each:

```
lazy var numberItems: [WKPickerItem] =
  self.pickerItemsWithQuestionType(.Number)
lazy var emojiItems: [WKPickerItem] =
  self.pickerItemsWithQuestionType(.Emoji)
lazy var colorItems: [WKPickerItem] =
  self.pickerItemsWithQuestionType(.Color)
```

Now, in each `case` in `showQuestion()`, call `answerPicker.setItems(_:)` with the appropriate array of picker items and set the picker to its first item. `showQuestion()` should now look like this:

```
func showQuestion() {
  if let questionType = QuestionType(rawValue:
    QuestionType.count.random()) {
    switch questionType {
      case .Number:
        pickQuestion(data.numberQuestions)
        answerPicker.setItems(numberItems)
      case .Color:
        pickQuestion(data.colorQuestions)
        answerPicker.setItems(colorItems)
      case .Emoji:
        pickQuestion(data.emojiQuestions)
        answerPicker.setItems(emojiItems)
    }
  }
}
```

One last thing: to ensure the picker starts at item 0, override the following `WKInterfaceController` method in **InterfaceController.swift**:

```
override func didAppear() {
  answerPicker.setSelectedItemIndex(0)
}
```

Build and run the Watch app in the simulator. Use your trackpad or mouse scroll button to select an answer, and then tap the button to show another question. The picker will always start at item 0, not at the last position you scrolled to.

Selecting an answer and tapping the button will only show another set of question and answer lists, so the next step is to implement the answer-checking code.

Checking the answer

First, add the following property to store the picker's value:

```
var answerValue = 0
```

Set this property's value in `pickerValueChanged(_:)` by adding the following line:

```
answerValue = value
```

Finally, the fun part! You're going to check the answer, and if the answer is correct, you'll pop up an alert and play a `.Success` haptic. If the answer isn't correct, you'll play a `.Retry` haptic.

Hold on a second ... an alert? In a Watch app? Yes, indeed! watchOS 2's new features include alerts and action sheets. They come in three styles: `Alert`, `SideBySideButtonsAlert` and `ActionSheet`, as shown in this illustration:

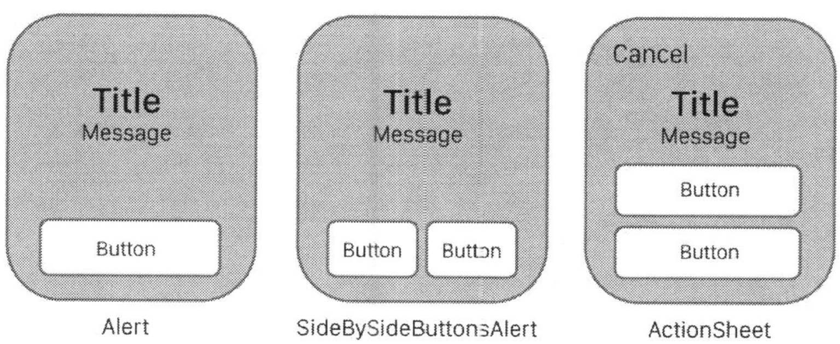

watchOS alerts are more streamlined than their iOS cousins: Instead of creating an alert controller, adding actions one by one and finally presenting the controller, you simply create an array of actions and call the following method:

```
presentAlertControllerWithTitle(_:message:preferredStyle:
  actions:)
```

You can find the details of this method at apple.co/1GgP8Re.

The actions array must contain at least one action; for `SideBySideButtonsAlert`, the array must contain *exactly two actions*. Action styles are the same as for iOS: `Default`, `Cancel` and `Destructive`. An action sheet supplies a default `Cancel` button in the upper-left corner if your array doesn't contain a `Cancel` action.

In this chapter's app, you'll just use an `Alert` with a single `Default` action. To see this *in action* (pun intended!), find `checkAnswer()`, and replace `showQuestion()` with the following lines:

```
// 1
let okAction = WKAlertAction(title: "OK", style: .Default)
  { _ in }
// 2
if answerValue == questionNumber + 1 {
  // 3
  WKInterfaceDevice.currentDevice().playHaptic(.Success)
  presentAlertControllerWithTitle("Correct!",
    message: "New question...", preferredStyle: .Alert,
    actions: [okAction])
  showQuestion()
} else {
  // 4
  WKInterfaceDevice.currentDevice().playHaptic(.Retry)
  presentAlertControllerWithTitle("Sorry!",
    message: "Try again", preferredStyle: .Alert,
    actions: [okAction])
}
```

This is what you're doing in `checkAnswer()`:

1. First, you define a standard OK action to use with both alerts.
2. The correct `answerValue` is `questionNumber + 1` because the first answer item is a question mark or neutral color—that is, it's not a valid answer.
3. If the answer is correct, you show another question.
4. If the answer is not correct, you set the picker back to the first item.

Build and run the app on your Watch, and have fun learning some new words, with all the positive haptic and auditory feedback!

Uber Bonus: Enhancing the behavior

Eliminate the need to tap the button, by overriding the following `WKInterfaceController` method to **InterfaceController.swift**:

```
override func pickerDidSettle(picker: WKInterfacePicker) {
  checkAnswer()
}
```

Build and run the app. Select an answer but don't tap the button: the appropriate alert will appear! Your app is now supercharged!

But there's a problem: when a new question appears, the picker sets itself to select the first item. The interface controller thinks the picker has settled, and immediately pops up the "Try again!" alert. Fix the problem by adding this guard statement at the beginning of `pickerDidSettle(_:)`:

```
guard answerValue > 0 else { return }
```

You can delete or hide the button now. :]

Note: In the Watch simulator, the picker becomes active when a new question appears—the picker outline turns green. If this doesn't happen when you run the app on your Watch, add `answerPicker.focus()` to `didAppear()`.

Being a good citizen with haptics

It's time to repeat the real takeaway messages:

1. **Exercise restraint**: *"Use [haptics] sparingly [for] truly important events in your app."*
2. **Use haptics the right way**: *"Please use these haptic tones and patterns as they were intended to be used."*

Here are some suggestions to help you find your way:

- Watch Mike Stern's WWDC 2015 video #802, "Designing for Apple Watch": apple.co/1MhukyH. The discussion of haptic feedback starts at the 22-minute mark.
- Internalize the **Apple Watch Human Interface Guidelines** so they become second nature: apple.co/1J0BUfY. These include two recommendations to make your haptic feedback more effective: 1) *"Provide visual cues to correspond with haptics...[This] creates a deeper connection between the user's action and the result."* 2) *"Initiate the playback of haptics at the appropriate time... as the first step in performing the corresponding task, rather than as the last step."*
- Be aware of your own feelings about other apps' haptic feedback, and ask your friends and colleagues how they feel about it.
- Remember that users can adjust Watch settings for notifications, sounds and haptics: Advice for saving Watch battery life, in articles like bit.ly/1IBsRRd, includes turning off notifications and reducing the strength of haptics or the volume of alert sounds.

Where to go from here?

Yes, go crazy and haptic all the things, just to get it out of your system. :] Then examine each haptic in your app and make it convince you that it's really adding value and delighting the user. If it doesn't fit the guidelines, throw it out!

Chapter 26: Localization

By Ben Morrow

With the painless global distribution provided by the App Store, you can release your app in over 150 countries with only a single click. You never know where it might take off and how that might change the fortunes of your company.

Here's a story I love:

When the Evernote app launched in 2008, it unexpectedly became very popular in Japan. Since the app was built in English, the company's leaders decided they could expand sales even faster if they optimized the interface for Japanese. The team scrambled, and with a bit of local help, they were able to offer Evernote in the new language.

Interestingly, as time went on, this move began to affect the company in larger ways. The team started traveling in Japan and noticed that some local partner companies were over 100 years old. That's when CEO Phil Libin rallied the team, saying:

"Let's build a company that has the long-term planning and thinking of some of these great Japanese companies, combined with the best of the Silicon Valley startup mentality. We don't just want to build a 100-year company, we want to build a 100-year startup."

Before you can run like Evernote, you first have to learn to walk. To grow your reach internationally, you'll have to make sure you've optimized the language, number formatting and layout of your app for many different regions and cultures.

In this chapter, you're going to learn how to localize your app so you can reach that larger audience, as well as learn what techniques and tools are available to aid that process.

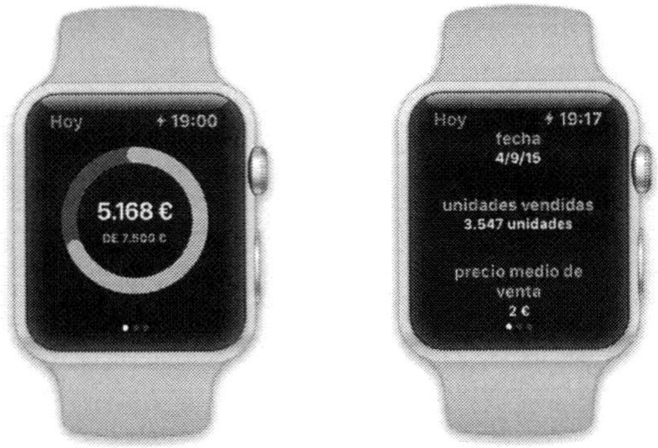

> **Note**: As of the time of writing, there is a bug in the watch simulator that prevents changing language and locale. In order to complete the chapter, you'll need a physical Apple Watch device (Radar #22027500). Hopefully, Apple will fix this bug in a future release.

Getting started

Launch Xcode and open the **Progress** project from the starter directory for this chapter.

You'll be making localization changes to an enterprise app for an international company with operations ranging from food production to military hardware. It has recently been involved in the political scene, but most of the time, the company flies under the radar.

One of the important aspects of the company's culture is to always watch the numbers. Management says this will help them shake off a few slaps on the wrist the company received last year for financial shenanigans.

This app lets an employee see how close the company is to meeting its sales goals. It shows units sold and total revenue for the day, week and month. The company wants to deploy the app across divisions located in different countries.

To meet your client's expectations, you'll need to adapt the app to linguistic, regional and cultural differences.

If you're ready for the challenge, there are tools in Xcode that allow the text in the app to change like magic to match the user's preferences.

Internationalizing your app

Internationalization? Globalization? Localization? Translation? There are many different ways to describe the myriad of work associated with preparing your app for a more diverse group of people. In truth, there's a lot of inconsistency in how people in the industry use these different words. For the purposes of this tutorial, however, let's establish a distinction between internationalization and localization.

Internationalization is the process of making strings from storyboard or code externally editable. It also involves using formatting classes for things like dates and numbers. It's up to you, the app developer, to perform internationalization.

By contrast, **localization** is the process of translating those externalized strings into a given language. You'll usually hire a localization company to do this work.

Together, internationalization and localization ensure your app looks as good in Chinese or Arabic as it does in English.

Language-specific thoughts

Because languages have different average word lengths, it's crucial to set up your interface to accommodate these differences. By default, the layout engine in WatchKit lets content reflow quite easily as long as you're not setting fixed sizes. Here are some language-specific considerations to remember while you're designing an app.

The layout engine supports languages that read right-to-left, like Hebrew and Arabic. If the user selects one of these languages, the engine will automatically flip the entire interface horizontally.

As of 2015, 41% of iOS users are from either China or Japan. Neither Chinese nor Japanese uses an alphabetic script, so there are no spaces to separate words. This means your layout may look a lot terser and more compact in these languages. Consider if the interface would look too bare with vast whitespace.

On the other end of the spectrum is German. Since it's a lengthy language compared with English, you'll always want to make sure you allow enough space in your interface to accommodate longer text. This can be especially tricky with elements like buttons, where the label can wrap to multiple lines.

Adding a language

Adding the capability for a certain language is a snap. In the project navigator, select your app's name, **Progress**. Then select the **Project** in the sidebar, and in the **Info** tab, you'll see a section for **Localizations**. Click the **+** button and choose **Spanish (es)**:

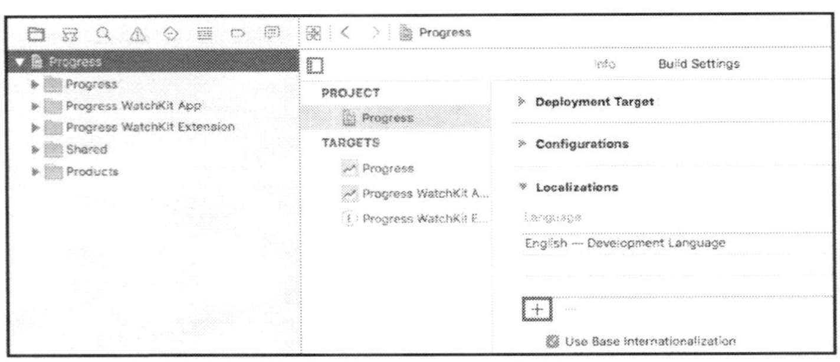

The next screen asks you which files you want to localize, showing only your storyboards and .xib files. Keep them all selected and click **Finish**.

At this point, Xcode has set up directories behind the scenes that contain separate storyboards for each language you selected. To see this for yourself, expand **Interface.storyboard** in the **Progress WatchKit App** group in the project navigator by clicking the disclosure triangle:

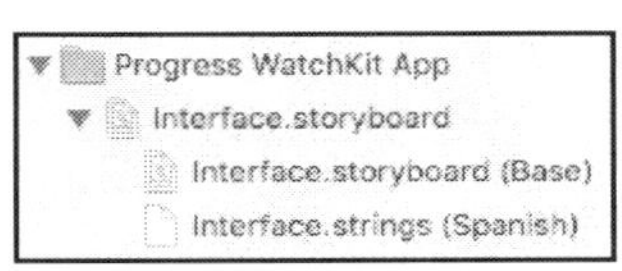

About the .strings file

Open **Interface.strings (Spanish)**. Your shiny new .strings file follows a strict but fairly simple format. First, notice the comment above each line:

```
/* Comment */
```

These comments provide a little context about where the translated text will go in the app.

Then, you'll see a key/content pair:

```
"KEY" = "CONTENT";
```

These pairs work like the key and value in a dictionary. This will be where your Spanish translations eventually reside. The Interface Builder file uses its generated names, but your .strings file later in the chapter will use more human-readable components.

> **Note**: Even though you've been writing Swift code for the entire book, don't be deceived—the strings file is not in Swift! The semicolon is required at the end of every line.

Separating text from code

There is other text that's not in your storyboard. You have literal strings in code that you insert into your UI at runtime.

As an astute observer, you may have noticed a helpful convention used in this storyboard. Any text that starts and ends with square brackets will be replaced by code at runtime:

Notice how "start date", "units sold" and " average selling price" don't have square brackets. They will *not* be replaced at runtime. Everything else with brackets will be replaced based on calculations made by the app.

For the text that will be replaced, you'll use a global function to translate literal strings in your code:

```
func NSLocalizedString(
  // 1
  key: String,
  //    2
  tableName: String,
  // 3
  bundle: NSBundle,
  // 4
  value: String,
  // 5
  comment: String
) -> String
```

Here's what each parameter does:

1. This is a unique key distinguishing this string from all other strings in your code.
2. For larger, complex apps, you define a `tableName` to put different localized strings in different `.strings` files. For the purposes of this tutorial, you won't need this feature and can simply leave this parameter null.
3. The bundle parameter allows you to define a language or locale for which you want to pull a string. 99% of the time, you'll want to use the default of `NSBundle.MainBundle()`, which determines the bundle based on the user's operating system settings.
4. The `value` is the default string, which will show up for any languages that aren't translated.
5. The `comment` parameter contains instructions for the person translating this string; for example, “This is the title of an alert that comes up when the user did this bad thing”. This is super important because the translator can’t see the context where the app uses the string.

Because you'll typically only care about the key, value and comment fields, most of your string code will look like this:

```
let localString = NSLocalizedString("FOO_KEY", value: "Foo",
  comment: “This string is shown when …”)
```

> **Note**: It's very tempting to use the default value as your key. This is a big mistake that will come back to bite you as you get deeper into localization. Consider that the same word in your language might suffice in two places—in other words, it might have two completely different meanings—but you may need two separate words for those meanings in another language.
>
> For example, in English, the word "watch" has many meanings, including "to observe" and "wristwatch" (like an Apple Watch!). However, in Spanish you would use "observar" for observe and "reloj" for wristwatch. If you tried to use the English "watch" as the key in `NSLocalizedString`, your keys would not be unique and you'd tear your hair out trying to find a bug. DON'T DO IT!

Formatting values

In addition to translating text, you'll also need to correctly format numbers and dates. There are a whole range of formatters available to you. Here are some examples of their output:

- **`NSNumberFormatter`**: Decimal: "3.145", Currency: "$3.14", Ordinal: "3rd", Percent: "314%"
- **`NSDateFormatter`**: Short: "11/23/37", Medium: "Nov 23, 1937", Long: "November 23, 1937", Full: "Tuesday, April 12, 1952 AD"
- **`NSDateComponentsFormatter`**: Positional: "1:10", Abbreviated: "1h 10m", Short: "1hr 10min", Full: "1 hour, 10 minutes", SpellOut: "One hour, ten minutes"
- **`NSByteCountFormatter`**: "342 KB"
- **`NSLengthFormatter`**: "621 mi"
- **`NSEnergyFormatter`**: "239 cal"
- **`NSMassFormatter`**: "2,205 lb"

> **Note**: These output examples are a small introduction to the functionality of each formatter. The full capabilities of each formatter is too lengthy to list here. Check out Apple's documentation for each formatter for all the juicy details.

These formatters automatically transform your numbers to use the correct punctuation for the region and the correct label for the language. Here are the differences you would see between an app running on a device in Spain versus one running in the United

States.

- **NSNumberFormatter**: "3,145" versus "3.145" and "€3,14" versus "$3.56"
- **NSDateFormatter**: "21/12/12" versus "12/21/12"
- **NSLengthFormatter**: "1,000 km" versus "621 mi"
- **NSEnergyFormatter**: "1,000 J" versus "239 cal"
- **NSMassFormatter**: "1,000 kg" versus "2,205 lb"

There are a couple of caveats to watch out for when you use these formatters for your own apps:

1. For currency, you need to account for the exchange rate before formatting.
2. Store length, energy and mass as SI units: meters, joules and kilograms. Those formatters provide convenient methods to convert from the raw SI value into the correct locale formatting.

Formatting values in the Progress app

Open **ProgressInterfaceController.swift** in the **Progress WatchKit Extension** group by selecting it in the project navigator. In `awakeWithContext(_:)`, you can see that there are three formatters: `dateFormatter`, `currencyFormatter`, and `numberFormatter`. These have properties to set their style so that they'll be ready for use in the methods that follow. I'll explain their output when you walk though code in the next section.

With the formatters in place, you're ready to internationalize the literal strings in your code.

Preparing literal strings for localization

There are several places where you can see strings baked into the code. You now know that you'll somehow have to extract those strings so that a translator can see them.

The first bit of code that has string literals is the `switch` statement in `awakeWithContext()`. Replace it with the following:

```
switch context {
  case "week":
    dayCount = 7
    self.setTitle(NSLocalizedString("oneWeekTitle",
      value: "7-day", comment: "label at the top of the report
      for the past 7 days"))
  case "month":
    dayCount = 30
    self.setTitle(NSLocalizedString("oneMonthTitle",
      value: "30-day", comment: "label at the top of the report
```

```
        for the past 30 days"))
    default:
      self.setTitle(NSLocalizedString("oneDayTitle",
        value: "Today", comment: "label at the top of the report
        for just today"))
  }
```

The changes here are small. You use `NSLocalizedString()` in place of a normal `String`. Notice the descriptive comments for each piece of text. As I mentioned earlier, comments are important so the translator can understand where this text is in the app.

The next string literal is inside `updateDateLabel()`. This method prepares a date with the correct regional formatting and fills in the corresponding label in the interface. Replace the contents of that method with this code:

```
// 1
let formattedStartDate = dateFormatter.
  stringFromDate(summary.startDate)
// 2
let preamble = String(
  format: NSLocalizedString("dateStartLabelFormat",
  value: "beginning %@",
  comment: "announcing start of a date range:
  beginning 7/11/11"),
  formattedStartDate)
// 3
let title = dayCount > 1 ? preamble : formattedStartDate
dateLabel.setText(title)
```

Here's what's going on:

1. You use the date formatter to put the month or day first, depending on the regional preference. The `.ShortStyle` date format will give output in the format "12/31/2021".
2. You're using `NSLocalizedString` as you did before, but instead of a string literal, you have a formatted string. You arrange the text this way because in some languages, the word to explain the beginning of a date range might go after the date, such as the equivalent of "31/12/2021 started". So anytime you have text labeling a number, you want to use this string initializer with a format so the translator has the option to swap the terms if it's appropriate for the language. In case you're unfamiliar with the format syntax, `%@` simply means "the representation of a string will go here". You can see all the string format specifiers at apple.co/1PTDz8t. The `%@` works well with the .strings file and allows the translator to choose where the date will go in the translation string.
3. The ternary operator is an inline `if`-statement. If there's more than one day, use the preamble text; otherwise, just the date is fine.

The next method, `updateRevenueLabels()`, will fill in the current status and revenue goal labels inside the progress ring. This method has some text that needs localizing. Update its contents with the following code:

```
// 1
let totalRevenue =
  currencyFormatter.stringFromNumber(summary.totalRevenue)
statusLabel.setText(totalRevenue)
// 2
guard let totalGoal =
  currencyFormatter.stringFromNumber(summary.totalGoal) else {
    return
}
// 3
let totalGoalText = String(
  format: NSLocalizedString("totalGoalLabel",
  value: "of %@",
  comment: "before the total amount, like: of $500"),
  totalGoal).uppercaseString
goalLabel.setText(totalGoalText)
```

Here 's the breakdown, step by step:

1. The number formatter for currency will use the correct currency symbol and punctuation according to the regional preference, like "€5,07". In this case, you've set the `maximumFractionDigits` to zero so there won't be any more precision than a whole integer.
2. The `totalGoal` uses the currency formatter as well. This time, you're ensuring you get a string with `guard let` before proceeding. The number formatter can return `nil` if it can't parse the value. The `String(format:)` initializer expects a non-`nil` value, so you have to make sure the `totalGoal` is unwrapped.
3. You use `NSLocalizedString` as before, with one addition. The `uppercaseString` computed property will ensure the text is delivered in all caps, like the design in the storyboard.

The last string literal in the file it in `updateUnitLabels()`, which calculates the average selling price per unit. Replace its implementation with this code:

```
guard let formattedTotalUnits =
  numberFormatter.stringFromNumber(summary.totalUnits) else {
    return
}
let totalUnitsText = String(
  format: NSLocalizedString("totalUnitsLabelFormat",
  value: "%@ units",
  comment: "describing the total number of units sold"),
  formattedTotalUnits)
unitsLabel.setText(totalUnitsText)
```

```
let avgSellingPrice =
  summary.totalRevenue / Double(summary.totalUnits)
let formattedAvgPrice =
  currencyFormatter.stringFromNumber(avgSellingPrice)
averageSellingPriceLabel.setText(formattedAvgPrice)
```

This code doesn't introduce any new concepts; you simply use the best practice with number and string formatters. The number formatter will deliver the number as a string with the correct thousands separator, depending on the region.

Congratulations—you've internationalized your app! You can't test the language in the simulator because the strings haven't been translated yet. That will come next. You can, however, test that the number formatters are working correctly. To do that, you need to perform a bit of setup to run a different language and locale in the simulator.

Running a language scheme

The fastest way to test language and locale in the simulator isn't what you might expect. You could, of course, go into the simulator's Settings app and change the language of the iPhone and the Watch, but thankfully, there's a less cumbersome way.

You need to create a run scheme, just like you did in Chapter 10, "Glances". Open the **Scheme** menu and click **Manage Schemes**:

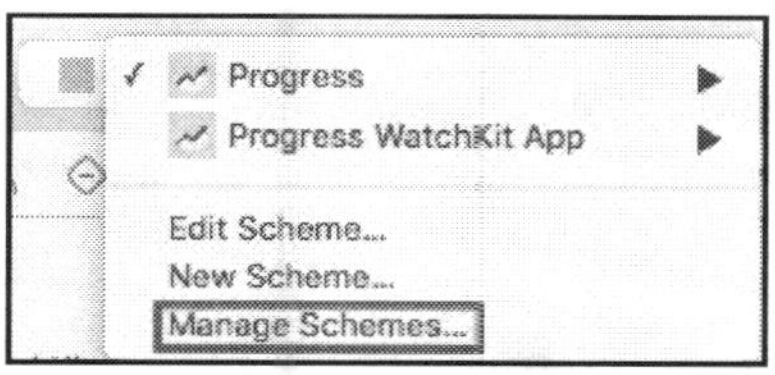

Select **Progress WatchKit App**, and using the **Gear** menu, choose **Duplicate**:

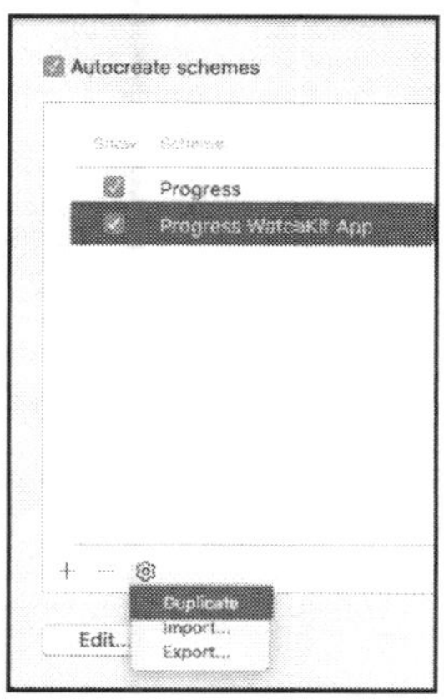

Name the scheme **watchOS Spanish**. Select the **Run** tab from the sidebar and select the **Options** tab along the top. Change the **Application Language** to **Spanish** and the **Application Region** to **Europe\Spain**:

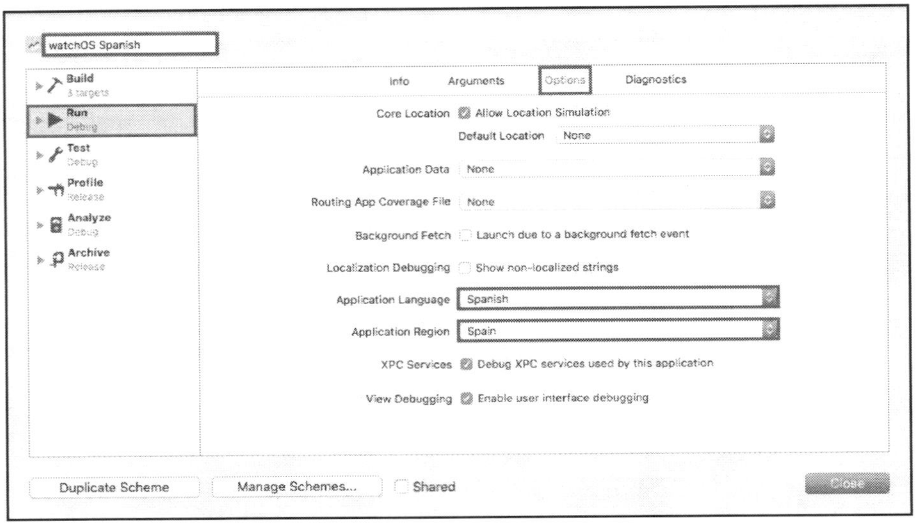

Click **Close**, and **Close** again to exit the scheme editor. You're ready to see if all of this work has been worth it! Run the new **watchOS Spanish** scheme.

> **Note**: It's a known issue for Xcode 7 that the language scheme for watchOS doesn't work in the simulator. As a workaround, install the app on a physical device.
>
> You can change the language settings in the Apple Watch app for iPhone: My Watch\General\Language & Region. Change the **Language** to **Spanish** and the **Region Format** to **Spain**. Once you're got this, hop back into Xcode and run the **Progress for watchOS** scheme on your [iPhone + Apple Watch] device.

Localizing the app

The time has come to translate the text in the app. This is a simple out-and-back-in process. You'll generate a **.xliff** (**XML Localization Interchange File Format**) file for each language.

With **Progress** selected in the project navigator, click **Editor\Export For Localization**:

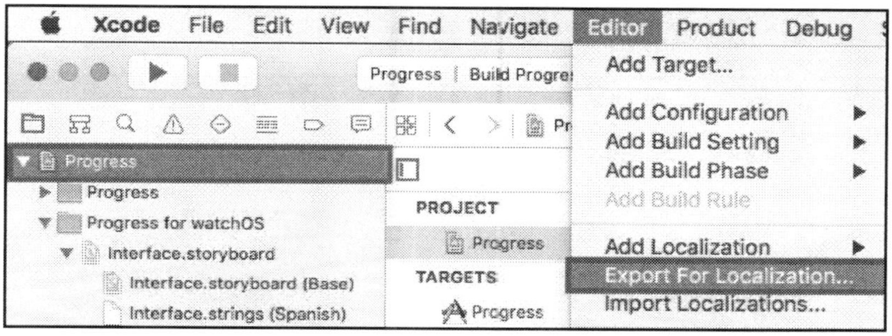

Change the name to **ToTranslator** and the location to your **Downloads** folder. Ensure that **Spanish** is selected, and click **Save**:

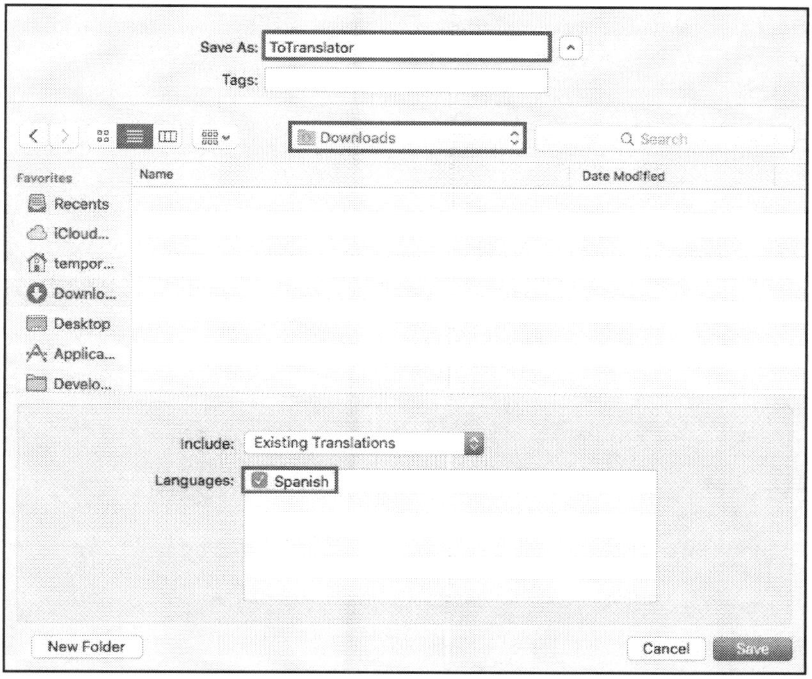

To edit this file, you're going to use an online tool. A real translation shop would have a more robust tool that parses the XML into a user interface to make the file easier to work with.

Open your favorite browser on your Mac and navigate to bit.ly/1PySGTR. Click **Choose File** and browse the **es.xliff** file you just generated. Click **Start Translating**:

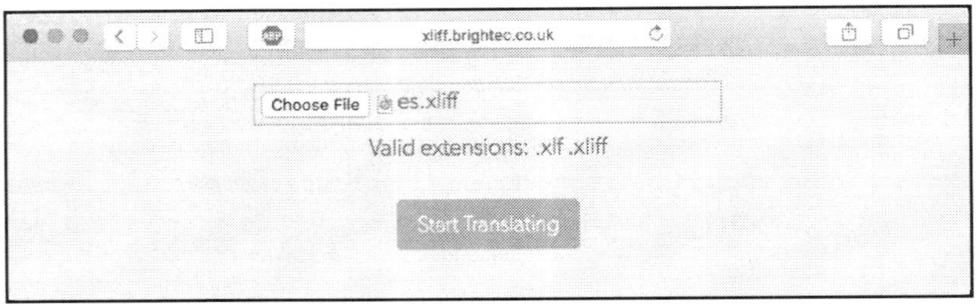

You can see a list of all the files that need localized strings. Within each file, the strings show the `source` text as a header and have a text box for the `target` text:

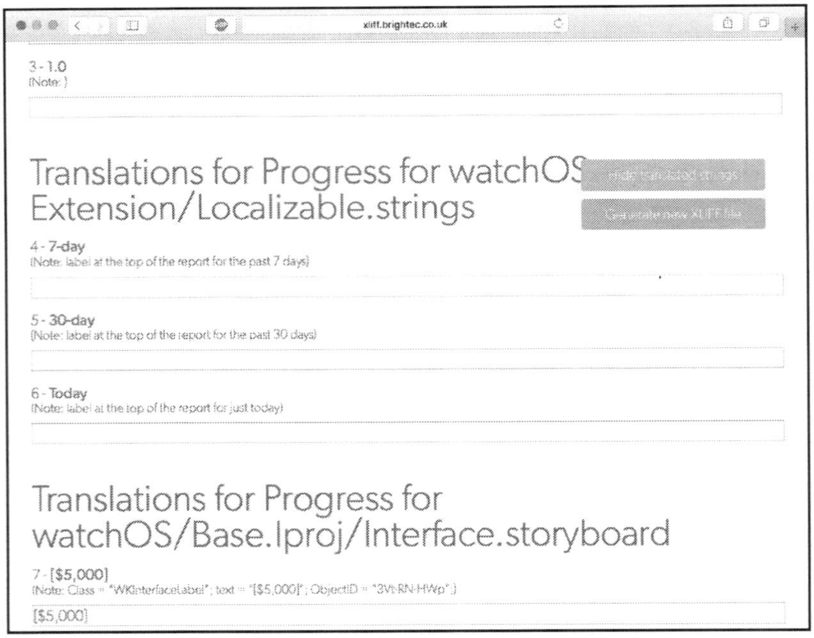

If you're curious and want to view the XML file as plaintext, it looks like this:

```
<source>7-day</source>
<target>7 días</target>
<note>label at the top of the report for the past 7 days</note>
```

It's much nicer to have a user interface to edit the values. Fill in the `target` text boxes on the web tool with these important translations:

> **Note**: This section is limited to the translations you need, so not all the fields on the form are listed here. These translations use the format: `[source] | [target]`

Translations for Progress for watchOS Extension/Localizable.strings

- beginning `%@` | a partir `%@`
- Today | Hoy
- 30-day | 30 días
- 7-day | 7 días
- of `%@` | de `%@`
- `%@` units | `%@` unidades

Translations for Progress for watchOS/Base.lproj/Interface.storyboard

- date | fecha
- average selling price | precio medio de venta
- units sold | unidades vendidas

You can leave the rest of the fields alone. There is, however, one caveat: every field needs to have a value; you can't leave any blank. If you do, when you import the file into Xcode, the import wizard will crash.

So for the fields that currently have an empty text box, copy the `source` text header and paste it in the `target` text box:

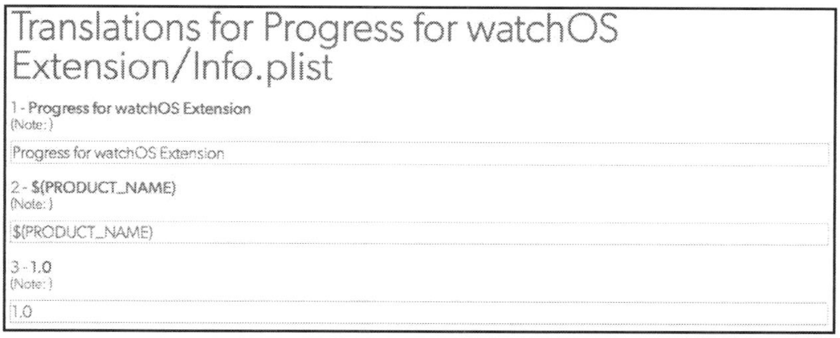
Translations for Progress for watchOS Extension/Info.plist

1 - Progress for watchOS Extension
(Note:)
Progress for watchOS Extension

2 - $(PRODUCT_NAME)
(Note:)
$(PRODUCT_NAME)

3 - 1.0
(Note:)
1.0

These include:

Translations for Progress for watchOS Extension/Info.plist

- Progress for watchOS Extension
- `$(PRODUCT_NAME)`

- 1.0

Translations for Progress for watchOS/Info.plist

- Progress
- `$(PRODUCT_NAME)`
- 1.0

Translations for Progress/Info.plist

- `$(PRODUCT_NAME)`
- 1.0

That was a lot of work, but it will pay off in the end! Once you're done editing the text boxes, click **Generate new XLIFF file** in the upper-right part of the screen.

Your computer will download the generated file. Hop back into Xcode. With **Progress** selected in the project navigator, click **Editor\Import Localizations**:

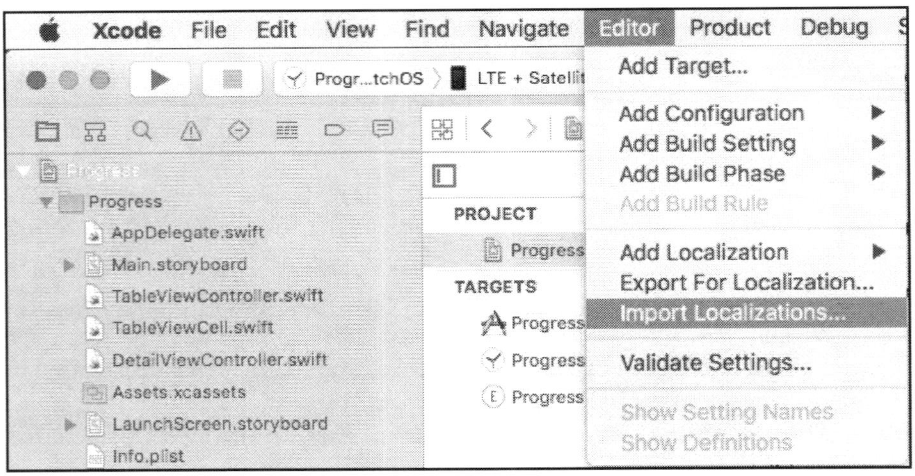

Browse to the generated file, **new.xliff**, in your **Downloads** folder. Select it and click **Open**. Xcode will run through the process of importing the localizations. If you added all the fields, you won't run into any errors.

Previewing the localization

The time has come to collect the rewards of all your hard work. There are a couple of different ways to see the translated text in your app; the quickest is to view it in the storyboard directly.

Open **Interface.storyboard** in the **Progress WatchKit App** group by selecting it in the project navigator, and then open the **assistant editor** and choose the **Preview** pane. In the lower-right, there's a language tool; choose **Spanish**:

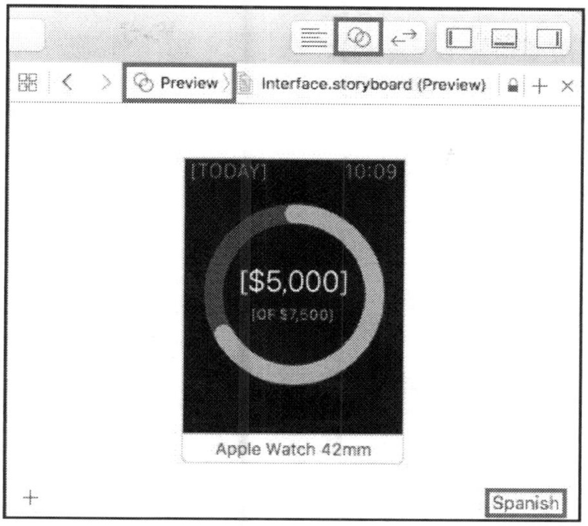

Xcode is drawing your attention to untranslated strings by transforming that text into all caps, as in "UNITS". Since the preview only shows the visible screen area for the Watch, you don't see the rest of the interface "below the fold" that a user would reach by scrolling. You'll learn how to see this text and test the translations from the code soon enough.

But first, try a different technique. Remembering how languages like German can be long, select **Double-Length Pseudolanguage** from the language tool at the lower-right:

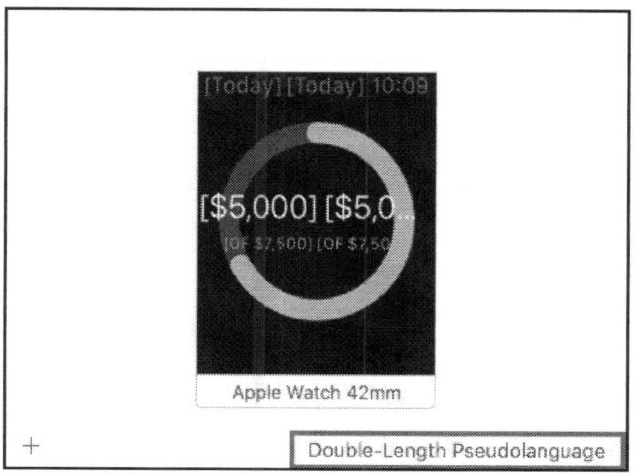

The preview duplicates the content inside each user interface text element, offering a quick check to see what happens when there's a lot more text. The double-length pseudolanguage is also a great way to test how your app would handle very large numbers.

In this case, some of the labels cover parts of images and others flow off the side of the screen. You'd have your work cut out for you if you wanted to prep the interface for German, but for now, let's stay focused on Spanish.

Run the app using the **watchOS Spanish** scheme.

> **Note**: If the Spanish translations don't show up in the Simulator due to the bug mentioned earlier in the chapter, you may alternatively run the app on the device with its language settings changed.

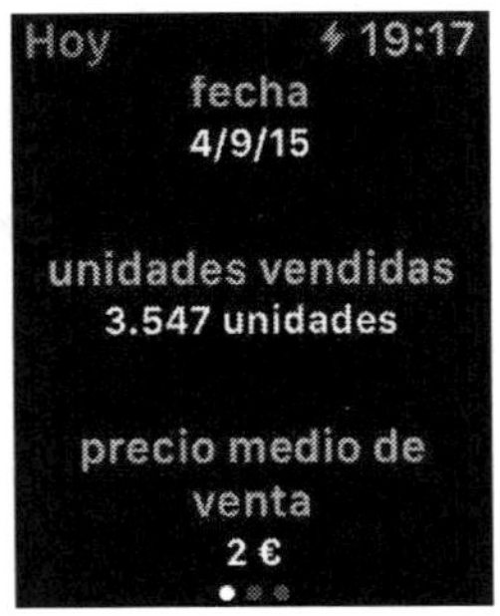

Jolly good show–or rather, alegre buen espectáculo!

- You've translated text from literal strings in the code;
- You've translated text from the storyboard;
- Numbers use a period as the thousands separator;
- Date components are in the correct order;
- Currency uses the euro symbol!

> **Note**: As of the time of writing, there is a bug in Xcode. Importing translations with XLIFF fails to generate base language strings for WatchKit apps. Curiously, the XLIFF import *does* work correctly for iPhone apps. Any time you use `NSLocalizedString(_:value:comment:)` in a WatchKit app, you will always see the translated string even if you run the app in English (Radar #22501637).
>
> In this app for example, the page title will always be in Spanish, for example, "Hoy". The fix is to add a Base language translation of the .strings file manually. By following the screenshot below, you can get English strings back into the app. Hopefully, Apple will fix this bug in a future release.

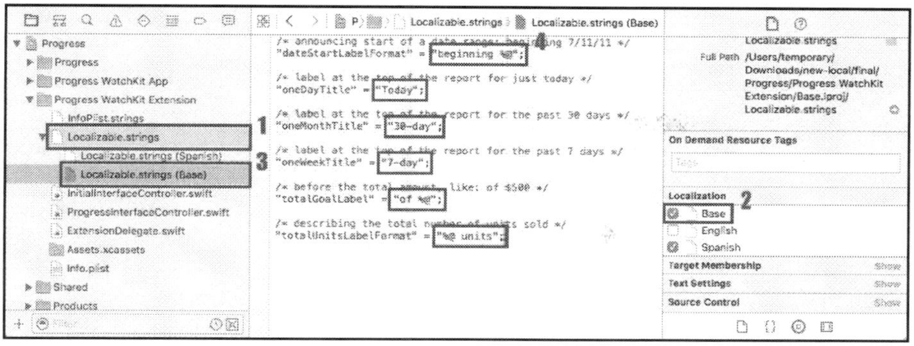

Where to go from here?

You've now got a firm understanding of how to work with languages and locale formatting. At WWDC 2015, Apple announced that 69% of revenue—more than two thirds—comes from outside of the United States. That goes to show why it can be lucrative to make your app speak your customer's language.

This is a vast topic, though, so if you want to dive deeper, the **Apple Watch Programming Guide** covers some of the steps you need to take for localization: apple.co/1LBzUNV.

For localizing the words themselves, you may be able to get away with using Google's free translation service at google.com/translate, but the results are very hit or miss. If you can spare a few bucks, there are several third-party vendors listed at the bottom of Apple's Internationalization and Localization page. Pricing varies from vendor to vendor, but is typically less than 10 cents per word: apple.co/1WT0BB3.

If you're looking to be at the top of your game, here's a bonus tip:
You can use the Localizable.strings file for image names, too. See if you can display a different image for Spanish speakers by using `setImageNamed(_:)` with `NSLocalizedString(_:comment:)` in your app.

Now that your app is ready for use across the world, may your WatchKit skills take you far and wide! :]

Chapter 27: Accessibility

By Ben Morrow

Your apps will have many types of users. In this chapter, you'll learn about a certain subset of these users: those with visual or hearing impairments. These users present us developers with a special opportunity: We can empower them to do things they might not otherwise be able to do.

After all, you've already decided to create apps to allow people to do amazing things. So let's build apps everyone can use, regardless of who they are or how they interact with the world.

Over the years, iOS has amassed an impressive array of accessibility features. If you've never seen these features in action, you might be surprised to learn about the many alternative ways of interacting with a mobile device. Assistive technologies include VoiceOver, Switch Control, Assistive Touch, Zoom and Guided Access. The Apple Watch is no different; it boasts many of these same features.

In this chapter, you'll discover the accessibility features available in watchOS and learn about the classes and methods available in WatchKit. Then, you'll implement many of those SDK features in a stock tracker app, making the interface more accessible to users with visual impairments.

Assistive technology overview

To introduce all of the accessibility features available on the Apple Watch, a user named Ava will walk you through her day. Ava has a serious visual impairment, but that doesn't stop her from being an avid user of her Watch.

Settings on the Watch

There are several accessibility features available in the **Settings** Watch app. Open the app using a real device and navigate to **General\Accessibility** to try out these features.

VoiceOver

VoiceOver is an alternate interface for users with visual impairments. The idea behind it is simple: VoiceOver dictates whatever is under the user's finger.

For example, when Ava taps on the Clock app icon on the Home screen, VoiceOver highlights the icon with a white rectangle and reads aloud the app's name, "Clock".

Ava can use VoiceOver on the clock face, on the Home screen or inside any app. In addition to tapping, Ava can drag her finger across the screen slowly to hear interface objects read aloud, or she can swipe left and right quickly to hear items read aloud sequentially. Since a single tap on an interface item triggers the VoiceOver dictation, Ava double-taps when she wants to activate an item such as a button.

Zoom

Zoom magnifies the interface so that it's easier to see. With Zoom turned on, only part of the screen is visible, so Ava uses the digital crown to scroll the viewable area horizontally. When the viewfinder reaches the end of the screen area, it hops down to the beginning of the next line like a carriage return.

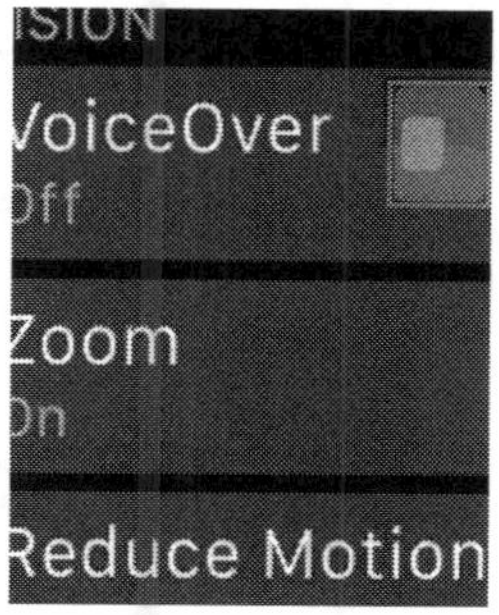

To activate Zoom, Ava uses a two-finger double-tap onscreen. To adjust the zoom level, she uses a two-finger double-tap and scrolls her fingers up and down.

Extra-large Watch face

To access the extra-large Watch face, Ava force-touches on the clock face and selects the **X-LARGE** face. Since the font is so large, it's a good fit for her blurry vision.

Settings on the Watch app for iPhone

A few more small visual tweaks are available on the **iPhone**.

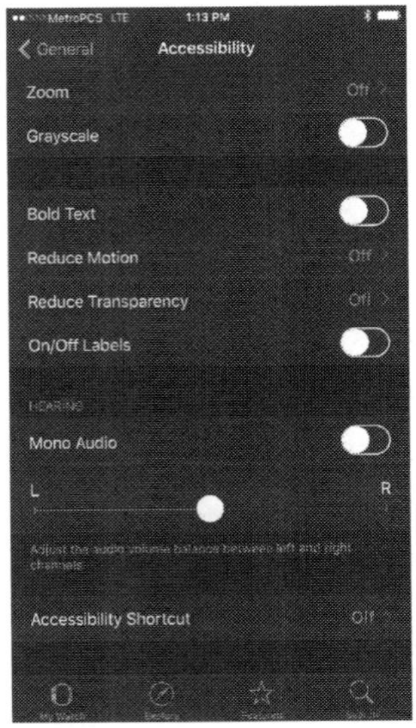

Open the **Watch app** and navigate to **General\Accessibility**.

a b c

Here are some of the settings you can adjust:

- **Bold text** makes text in apps have a larger font weight (a). For Ava, this makes the text appear less blurry and more discernable.
- **Grayscale** removes all colors (b). For a person with color blindness, it is much easier to distinguish between colors when they are represented by different shades of grey, so this feature can make it easier to read menus and view images.
- **Reduce transparency** removes blur effects (c). This helps Ava see text clearly due to the increased contrast of a simple color background.
- **Reduce motion** removes the zoom-in animation from the clock face and Home screen, which can be nauseating to Ava.

A couple of audio settings are also useful in conjunction with a Bluetooth headset. These features benefit users with hearing impairments:

- **Mono audio** makes left and right audio channels the same. If a user has one ear that's more capable than the other, this setting ensures the user doesn't miss any sound on the opposite channel.
- Similarly, a user can adjust the **left/right balance** with a slider if one ear needs higher volume than the other.

Finally, the Accessibility Shortcut setting allows Ava to triple-click the digital crown to activate her choice of VoiceOver or Zoom. This is much easier than having to drill down into the settings each time she wants to turn the feature on and off.

Turn on the **Accessibility Shortcut** for **VoiceOver**. You'll use it later in the chapter, once you make the app accessible.

WatchKit Accessibility API overview

For your app to work with these accessibility features, you'll have to set a few properties on the interface items in your app. Let's go over these properties.

Each interface item is a subclass of `WKInterfaceObject`. Descendants of this class have access to a number of methods that let you annotate your accessibility information and make the items accessible. Let's begin with this method:

```
setIsAccessibilityElement(_:)
```

VoiceOver needs to know what is and what isn't an element. Accessibility elements are what the user swipes through and double-taps when VoiceOver is enabled. By default, the framework gives a lot of this to you: buttons, labels and switches are all accessibility elements. But sometimes you need to get away from the default—for example, if you want to expose an image.

Another reason you might stray from the defaults is when you want to group together a few elements to make it easy for the user to navigate the screen quickly. An example for this would be a conversation group that contains three labels for the sender, message and date. You can do this by calling `setIsAccessibilityElement(true)` on an interface item—in this case, a group.

Ava learns what's onscreen by hearing a short description spoken aloud. It's called an accessibility label:

```
setAccessibilityLabel(_:)
```

VoiceOver automatically infers that the accessibility label is the text contained in standard user interface objects. Most of the time, this works well, but sometimes the inferred description may be misleading or nonexistent. Ava encountered an example of this earlier with the Clock icon on the Home screen. The app icons aren't associated with text, so in situations like this, you have to set the accessibility label yourself.

The Watch reads out the accessibility value after reading aloud the accessibility label:

```
setAccessibilityValue(_:)
```

The accessibility value is useful when the value changes on an interactive interface item. A good example of an interface object with a changing value is the picker used for the minute hand of a timer.

Sometimes, you need more of a description than just the accessibility label, so you can set an accessibility hint:

```
setAccessibilityHint(_:)
```

This is the case with the current location button in Maps on the iPhone. Tapping the button once moves the map to your current location. Tapping and holding—also known as long pressing—activates the compass. A hint for the current location button might be, "tap and hold to activate compass".

If an image has multiple parts, you can annotate image regions with descriptions:

```
setAccessibilityImageRegions(_:)
```

It's a common pattern on the Watch to put an assortment of information into an image that you then present to the user. The Weather app is a good example:

By carving up the image into different regions, you can associate particular information with each region.

Below is a global function you can use to find out when VoiceOver is running, allowing you to adjust your app for your users:

```
WKAccessibilityIsVoiceOverRunning()
```

For example, when VoiceOver is on, you might need to enlarge the tap targets for your labels. Since VoiceOver relies on the user being able to tap on the different parts of a screen, your labels might need to have greater height and width to make room for a finger tap.

If you're building a custom interface component for your app, you might consider setting the combination of accessibility traits that best characterize the component:

```
setAccessibilityTraits(_:)
```

VoiceOver will treat a button differently than a label. Accessibility traits tell an assistive application how an accessibility element behaves or should be treated.

You might use the `UpdatesFrequently` trait to characterize the readout of a stopwatch. You could use the `StartsMediaSession` trait to silence VoiceOver during audio playback from your app, or during a recording session. The full list of accessibility traits follows; use them to make sure your app provides the best possible user experience:

- **`None`**
- **`Button`**
- **`Link`**
- **`SearchField`**
- **`Image`**
- **`Selected`**
- **`PlaysSound`**
- **`KeyboardKey`**

- `StaticText`
- `SummaryElement`
- `NotEnabled`
- `UpdatesFrequently`
- `StartsMediaSession`
- `Adjustable`
- `AllowsDirectInteraction`
- `CausesPageTurn`
- `Header`

You don't need to add an accessibility trait for a regular old label or button, but it's good to know the full breadth of accessibility elements you have at your disposal.

Congratulations on your grit and dedication—you've made it through the book-learning! The time has come to get your hands dirty with a real app.

Playing with VoiceOver

BigMovers is an app that shows the stocks with the biggest gains or losses for the day. Using sample stock data for some tech companies, the starter project draws each stock's graph in real time and renders it as an image. It sorts the list of stocks by those that had the highest percentage change, positive or negative. During the rest of this chapter, you'll make the app accessible for users with visual impairments by changing the interface to work with VoiceOver.

Open **BigMovers** in Xcode from the starter directory for this chapter.

Instead of using the simulator, you'll want to test the app on a real Watch. Make sure your iPhone is connected with the USB cable. Select the **BigMovers for watchOS** scheme and choose your iPhone and Watch as the run devices:

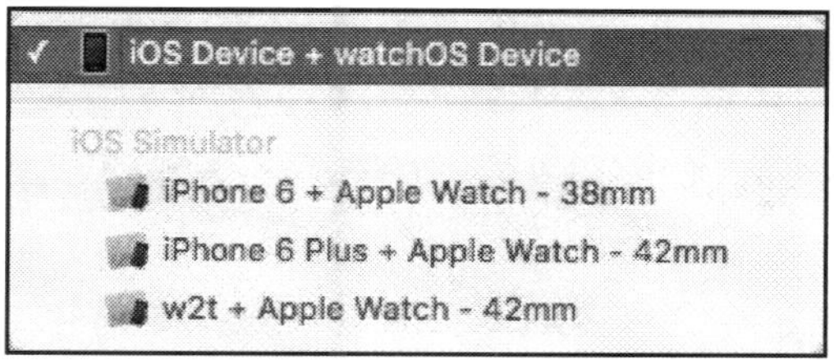

Build and run the app, and you'll see a page-based layout showing you the five-day earnings graph for different companies. Triple-click the digital crown to turn on VoiceOver.

Note: In case you didn't set up the accessibility shortcut earlier, you can turn on VoiceOver in the Settings app. However, your life will be simpler if you turn on the shortcut in the Apple Watch app for iPhone.

Try tapping on different elements, and Siri will read the accessibility label for each. Notice:

1. You have to tap on each label in the bottom section individually. You can swipe left and right to focus on the next interface item, but the experience still isn't good enough. Ideally, you'd want the voice to read all the labels in that group together.
2. The labels in the bottom group are hard to tap because their tap target overlaps with the graph and the page indicator dots.
3. To scroll between pages, you tap on the page indicator dots, and then outside of the tap target, swipe up and down.

To make the app work better with VoiceOver, you'll need to group together the adjacent labels, expand tap targets and break out the graph data points.

Adding accessibility to your app

In the project navigator, select **PageInterfaceController.swift** and add the following code to `updateForAccessibility()`:

```
if WKAccessibilityIsVoiceOverRunning() {
  makeLayoutAccessible()
  makeGraphAccessible()
  makeGroupAccessible()
}
```

This method is called from `willActivate()`, and will run each time you show an interface to the user. If VoiceOver is turned on, you'll make several changes to the interface, represented by the three methods above. You'll write the implementation for each of those methods next.

Making the layout accessible

Remember how hard it was to tap on the stock details at the bottom of the screen? You'd like to make the graph smaller so that the labels can be a bit taller. Right now the groups have a height set in Interface Builder to be "Relative to container":

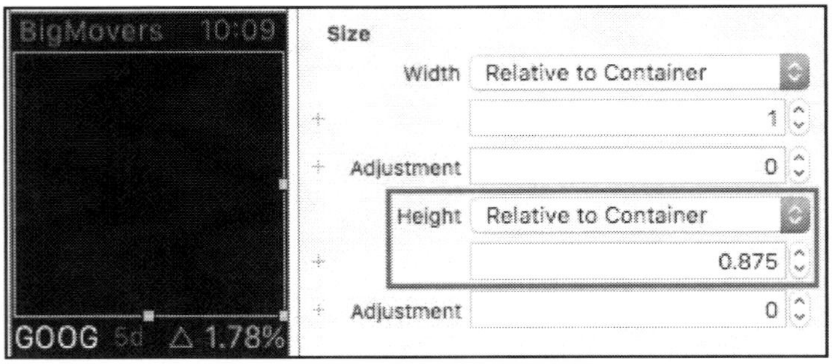

Add this implementation to `makeLayoutAccessible()`:

```
graphHeightRatio = 0.6
detailsHeightRatio = 0.4

graphImage.setHeight(graphHeightRatio * screenSize.height)
detailsGroup.setHeight(detailsHeightRatio * screenSize.height)
```

By moving from a 87.5%:12.5% ratio to a 60%:40% ratio, you make the bottom details section much larger.

Build and run on the device to confirm it works. If you've got VoiceOver turned on, you'll see the tap area for the details is a lot larger:

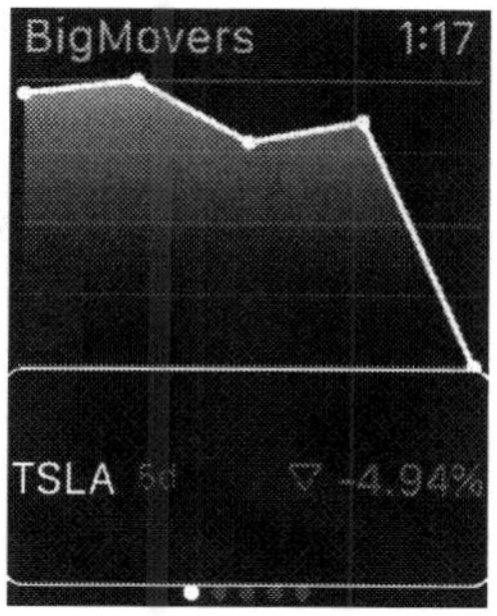

Excellent work! Now that the details group has a bit of breathing room, turn your attention to the graph.

Making the graph accessible

The graph is a wonderful visual, but for visually impaired users, there's no way to make sense of the data depicted, because it's a single image. Imagine if your app could read aloud the data. With image regions, it can!

Add the following code to `makeGraphAccessible()`:

```
// 1
var imageRegions = [WKAccessibilityImageRegion]()
// 2
for index in 0..<stock.last5days.count {
  // 3
  if index == 0 { continue } // skip the first day
  // 4
  let imageRegion = WKAccessibilityImageRegion()
  // 5
  imageRegion.frame = imageRegionFrameForTrailingIndex(index)
  // 6
  imageRegion.label = summaryForTrailingIndex(index)
  // 7
  imageRegions.append(imageRegion)
}
// 8
graphImage.setAccessibilityImageRegions(imageRegions)
```

There are quite a few things happening here. Let's go over it step by step:

1. First, you create an empty array of image regions so you have a spot to store them as you create each one.
2. You iterate through each day for the stock to find the daily change.
3. You skip the first item in the array, because you're looking at the change from the previous day, and the first day doesn't have a previous day before it. The `continue` keyword immediately exits this iteration of the loop and starts the next one.

4. You create a new blank image region that you'll add attributes to next. When you're finished with this iteration of the loop, you'll add it to the array you created at the beginning.
5. You'll implement the method that calculates the size of the image in a bit.
6. Soon after that, you'll implement the method that provides the phrase for Siri to speak aloud.
7. You construct each image region out of a label, a size and a position. Once you've set those, the image region is ready to be added to the array.
8. When the `for`-loop finishes, you can add the image region array to an image, and the VoiceOver feature will work as expected.

With the code in place to iterate through each day's data, you need to calculate the size of each image region.

Calculating the dimensions of an image region

Replace the implementation of `imageRegionFrameForTrailingIndex(_:)` with this code:

```
let height = screenSize.height * graphHeightRatio
let width =
  screenSize.width / CGFloat(stock.last5days.count - 1)
let x = width * (CGFloat(trailingIndex) - 1)
return CGRect(x: x, y: 0, width: width, height: height)
```

There's one fewer image region than the number of data points. This is like the space between your fingers—you've got five fingers but only four spaces between them. This code calculates the dimensions and position for the image region between two data points.

Preparing a spoken description

The next nut to crack is providing the words that VoiceOver will speak aloud. Replace the code in `summaryForTrailingIndex(_:)` with this implementation:

```
// 1
let percentageDescription = changePercentageForVoiceOver(
  stock.last5days[trailingIndex - 1],
  current: stock.last5days[trailingIndex])
// 2
var timeDescription = String()
switch trailingIndex {
  case 1:
    timeDescription = "3 days ago"
  case 2:
    timeDescription = "day before yesterday"
  case 3:
    timeDescription = "yesterday"
  case 4:
    timeDescription = "today"
  default:
    break
}
// 3
return "\(percentageDescription) \(timeDescription)"
```

Here's what's happening in this method:

1. The change needs to make sense when spoken; it isn't enough to say "negative 5%". The conversational way to say that is "down 5%". You'll implement the method for this next.
2. Since VoiceOver will speak this summary aloud, it will also be nice to have conversational time values to go along with each data point.
3. You construct the `label` for the accessibility item from the percentage change from one day to the next and its "time ago" phrase.

To get the change percentage to sound conversational when spoken aloud, you need a bit of logic. Replace the code in `changePercentageForVoiceOver(_:current:)` with this implementation:

```
// 1
let numberFormatter = NSNumberFormatter()
numberFormatter.numberStyle = .PercentStyle
numberFormatter.minimumFractionDigits = 2
numberFormatter.maximumFractionDigits = 2
// 2
let change = (current - previous) / previous
// 3
let direction = change > 0 ? "up" : "down"
```

```
// 4
let percent = numberFormatter.stringFromNumber(abs(change))!
// 5
return "\(direction) \(percent)"
```

Let's go through this step by step:

1. You instantiate a number formatter that will output a percentage with two decimal places.
2. You calculate the percentage change. It can be positive or negative, depending on the way the stock moved.
3. If the change is positive, you set the label text to "up", and if the change was negative, you set the label text to "down".
4. Now that you've got the "down" phrase if the change is negative, you can remove the negative sign by using the absolute value function. The number formatter will return the percentage with the settings from step 1.
5. The change phrase is composed of "up" or "down" and the percentage change.

You've made it all the way through the image region code!

It takes quite a bit of code to provide a good user experience for image regions, but your users will appreciate being able to tap on the individual parts of the graph and have them read aloud.

Build and run the app on the device. With VoiceOver enabled, you can tap on the lines between data points on the graph to hear nice summaries of the daily change:

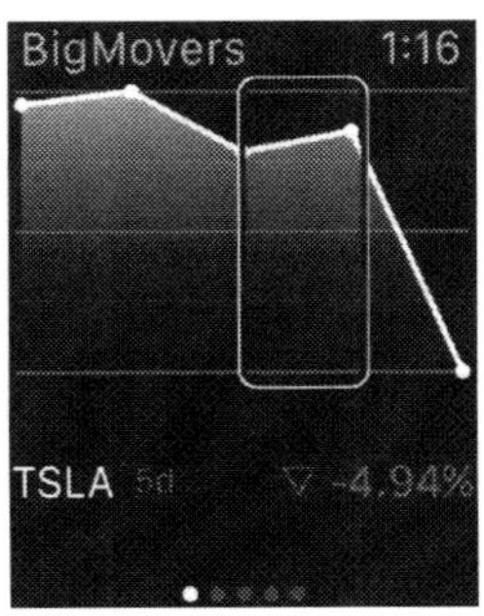

Making a group accessible

When you first ran the app, it took a long time to use VoiceOver to get a grip on all the content onscreen. One big problem was that you had to tap on each stock detail label independently, like the ticker symbol in this screenshot:

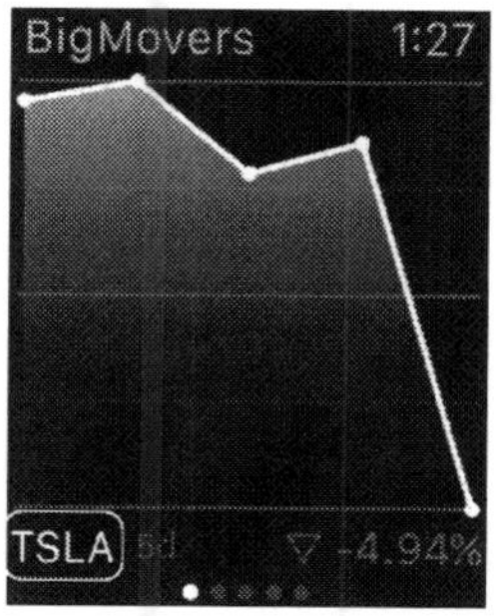

What if you could tap on the group and have the app read a summary of everything inside? With one tap, the voice could announce, "Tesla, past five days, down 4.94 percent." That's just what you'll implement in this section.

In `makeGroupAccessible()`, add the following code:

```
// 1
detailsGroup.setIsAccessibilityElement(true)
// 2
let percentage = changePercentageForVoiceOver(
  stock.last5days.first!, current: stock.last5days.last!)
// 3
let label =
  "\(stock.companyName), past five days, \(percentage)"
// 4
detailsGroup.setAccessibilityLabel(label)
// 5
detailsGroup.setAccessibilityTraits(
  UIAccessibilityTraitSummaryElement)
```

Here's what's happening in this snippet:

1. First, you tell the compiler that the details group has accessibility attributes. This will override all the default accessibility attributes of the sub-items of the group, so now the labels won't have VoiceOver interactivity themselves.
2. Just as you did with the graph, you use a function to give a nice string representation of the percentage change.
3. You construct the accessibility label with the three pieces of data from each of the labels in this group.
4. You add the accessibility label to the group itself.

5. Finally, you mark the group as a `SummaryElement` by setting the accessibility trait, which lets VoiceOver know that the element provides summary information when the app starts. This is perfect for labels with current conditions, settings or state, such as the current temperature in the Weather app.

The time has come to see the finished app on your Watch! Build and run. With VoiceOver enabled, you can tap on the details at the bottom to hear the full summary for the stock during the five-day week.

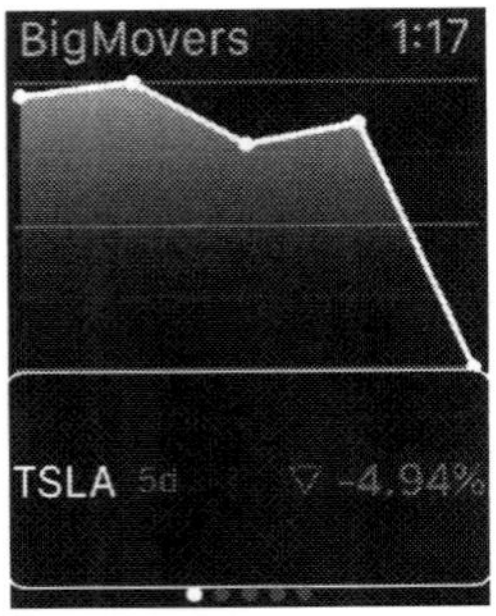

Try out the trick you learned at the beginning of the chapter: navigate with VoceOver by swiping left and right. Accessibility elements are highlighted in sequence and you'll hear their description read aloud.

Where to go from here?

You've learned how to make your app accessible for users with visual impairments. In the process, you got acquainted with the accessibility settings and features in watchOS and WatchKit.

As a bonus, you also learned some handy tricks. Consider how the additions you made for VoiceOver might benefit the standard user experience. For example, you could make tapping on the graph show a stock's daily change even without VoiceOver enabled. Instead of using accessibility image regions on the graph, you could overlay a transparent button above each daily change and update the label appropriately when a user taps on the button.

Since you've made it this far in the book, not only are you capable of building wonderful experiences for your users—you can empower them. Pervasive GPS has made it possible for all of us to journey from place to place in the world without getting lost. You have the power to give a similar freedom to your customers with visual impairments, who might otherwise be shut out from what you and the Apple Watch have to offer. Imagine a Watch that speaks to you when you simply tap parts of its face! It all sounds very futuristic, but it's here now.

Remember, the service you're providing with assistive technology is rare and valuable. These users might just become your biggest fans!

Conclusion

We hope you had a ton of fun working through this book. If you cherry-picked chapters according to your own interests and projects, then fair enough—you surely learned a lot and got your watchOS 2 projects started off on the right foot. And if you read this entire book from cover to cover, then take a bow my friend—you're officially a watchOS ninja!

You now have a wealth of experience with watchOS 2 and know what it takes to build rich, engaging and performant apps for the Apple Watch, using a host of exciting concepts and techniques that are unique to the platform. If you're like us, learning about all these cutting-edge technologies and concepts has you overflowing with ideas. We can't wait to see what you build!

If you have any questions or comments, please do stop by our forums at raywenderlich.com/forums.

Thank you again for purchasing this book. Your continued support is what makes the tutorials, books and other things we do at raywenderlich.com possible—we all truly appreciate it!

Best of luck with your Apple Watch adventures,

- Ryan, Jack, Scott, Soheil, Matt, Ben, Audrey, Eric, Mike, B.C., Sam, Brian, Mic, William, Ray and Vicki

47870120R10255

Made in the USA
Charleston, SC
17 October 2015